ST PAUL
Sunday Missal

2023 – Cycle A

ST PAUL
Sunday Missal

2023 – Cycle A

Texts approved for use in
Ireland, England & Wales and Scotland

ST PAULS

Imprimatur:
✠ Most Reverend Dermot Farrell, D.D.
Archbishop of Dublin

Concordat cum originali:
Rev. Damian McNeice

1 June 2022

ST PAULS
Moyglare Road, Maynooth, Co. Kildare, W23 NX34, Ireland.
187 Battersea Bridge Road, London SW11 3AS, UK.

ISBN: 978-1-911178-54-5

© ST PAULS, 2022

Typeset by MIDDLEDOT Ltd.

Printed by Walsh Colour Print.

ST PAULS is an activity of the Priests and the Brothers of the Society of St Paul who proclaim the Gospel through the media of social communication.

CONTENTS

THE ORDER OF MASS

THE INTRODUCTORY RITES

Entrance Antiphon – see Mass of the day

Greeting

In the name of the Father, and of the Son, and of the Holy Spirit.
Amen.

The grace of our Lord Jesus Christ,
and the love of God,
and the communion of the Holy Spirit
be with you all.

Or:

Grace to you and peace from God our Father
and the Lord Jesus Christ.

Or:

The Lord be with you.

And with your spirit.

The Priest may briefly introduce the faithful to the Mass of the day.

Penitential Act*

Brethren (brothers and sisters), let us acknowledge our sins,
and so prepare ourselves to celebrate the sacred mysteries.

A brief pause for silence follows. Then all recite together the formula
of general confession:

I confess to almighty God
and to you, my brothers and sisters,
that I have greatly sinned,
in my thoughts and in my words,
in what I have done and in what I have failed to do,

and, striking their breast, they say:

through my fault, through my fault,
through my most grievous fault;

---

* From time to time on Sundays, especially in Easter Time, instead of the
customary Penitential Act, the blessing and sprinkling of water may take place
as a reminder of Baptism (see page 9).

Then they continue:

therefore I ask blessed Mary ever-Virgin,
all the Angels and Saints,
and you, my brothers and sisters,
to pray for me to the Lord our God.

May almighty God have mercy on us,
forgive us our sins,
and bring us to everlasting life.
Amen.

Or:

Have mercy on us, O Lord.
For we have sinned against you.

Show us, O Lord, your mercy.
And grant us your salvation.

May almighty God have mercy on us,
forgive us our sins,
and bring us to everlasting life.
Amen.

Or:

Brethren (brothers and sisters), let us acknowledge our sins,
and so prepare ourselves to celebrate the sacred mysteries.

A brief pause for silence follows. The Priest then says:

Lord, have mercy.	**Lord, have mercy.**
Christ, have mercy.	**Christ, have mercy.**
Lord, have mercy.	**Lord, have mercy.**

Or:

Kyrie, eleison.	**Kyrie, eleison.**
Christe, eleison.	**Christe, eleison.**
Kyrie, eleison.	**Kyrie, eleison.**

Or:

Brethren (brothers and sisters), let us acknowledge our sins,
and so prepare ourselves to celebrate the sacred mysteries.

A brief pause for silence follows.

The Priest, or a Deacon or another minister, then says the following
or other invocations with Kyrie, eleison (Lord, have mercy):

You were sent to heal the contrite of heart:
| Lord, have mercy. | Or: Kyrie, eleison. |
| **Lord, have mercy.** | Or: **Kyrie, eleison.** |

You came to call sinners:
Christ, have mercy. Or: Christe, eleison.
Christ, have mercy. Or: **Christe, eleison.**

You are seated at the right hand of the Father to intercede for us:
Lord, have mercy. Or: Kyrie, eleison.
Lord, have mercy. Or: **Kyrie, eleison.**

May almighty God have mercy on us,
forgive us our sins,
and bring us to everlasting life.
Amen.

The Kyrie

A plea for mercy is not said here if it has already been incorporated in the penitential rite.

Rite for the Blessing and Sprinkling of Water

On Sundays, especially in Easter Time, the blessing and sprinkling of water as a memorial of Baptism may take place.

The Priest greets the people. A vessel containing the water to be blessed is placed before him.

He calls upon the people to pray in these or similar words:

Dear brethren (brothers and sisters),
let us humbly beseech the Lord our God
to bless this water he has created,
which will be sprinkled on us
as a memorial of our Baptism.
May he help us by his grace
to remain faithful to the Spirit we have received.

And after a brief pause for silence, he continues with hands joined:

Almighty ever-living God,
who willed that through water,
the fountain of life and the source of purification,
even souls should be cleansed
and receive the gift of eternal life;
be pleased, we pray, to ✠ bless this water,
by which we seek protection on this your day, O Lord.
Renew the living spring of your grace within us
and grant that by this water we may be defended
from all ills of spirit and body,
and so approach you with hearts made clean
and worthily receive your salvation.

Through Christ our Lord.
Amen.

Or:

Almighty Lord and God,
who are the source and origin of all life,
whether of body or soul,
we ask you to ✠ bless this water,
which we use in confidence
to implore forgiveness for our sins
and to obtain the protection of your grace
against all illness and every snare of the enemy.
Grant, O Lord, in your mercy,
that living waters may always spring up for our salvation,
and so may we approach you with a pure heart
and avoid all danger to body and soul.
Through Christ our Lord.
Amen.

Or, during Easter Time:

Lord our God,
in your mercy be present to your people's prayers,
and, for us who recall the wondrous work of our creation
and the still greater work of our redemption,
graciously ✠ bless this water.
For you created water to make the fields fruitful
and to refresh and cleanse our bodies.
You also made water the instrument of your mercy:
for through water you freed your people from slavery
and quenched their thirst in the desert;
through water the Prophets proclaimed the new covenant
you were to enter upon with the human race;
and last of all,
through water, which Christ made holy in the Jordan,
you have renewed our corrupted nature
in the bath of regeneration.
Therefore, may this water be for us
a memorial of the Baptism we have received,
and grant that we may share
in the gladness of our brothers and sisters
who at Easter have received their Baptism.
Through Christ our Lord.
Amen.

Where the circumstances of the place or the custom of the people suggest that the mixing of salt be preserved in the blessing of water, the Priest may bless salt, saying:

We humbly ask you, almighty God:
be pleased in your faithful love to bless ✠ this salt
you have created,
for it was you who commanded the prophet Elisha
to cast salt into water,
that impure water might be purified.
Grant, O Lord, we pray,
that, wherever this mixture of salt and water is sprinkled,
every attack of the enemy may be repulsed
and your Holy Spirit may be present
to keep us safe at all times.
Through Christ our Lord.
Amen.

The Priest pours the salt into the water, without saying anything. Afterwards, the Priest sprinkles himself and the ministers and people.

Meanwhile, one of the following chants, or another appropriate chant is sung.

Outside Easter Time

Antiphon 1   Ps 50:9

Sprinkle me with hyssop, O Lord, and I shall be cleansed;
wash me and I shall be whiter than snow.

Antiphon 2   Ezk 36:25-26

I will pour clean water upon you,
and you will be made clean of all your impurities,
and I shall give you a new spirit, says the Lord.

Hymn   Cf. 1 Pt 1:3-5

Blessed be the God and Father of our Lord Jesus Christ,
who in his great mercy has given us new birth into a living hope
through the Resurrection of Jesus Christ from the dead,
into an inheritance that will not perish,
preserved for us in heaven
for the salvation to be revealed in the last time!

During Easter Time

Antiphon 1   Cf. Ezk 47:1-2.9

I saw water flowing from the Temple,
from its right-hand side, alleluia:
and all to whom this water came
were saved and shall say: Alleluia, alleluia.

Antiphon 2   Cf. Ws 3:8; Ezk 36:25

On the day of my resurrection, says the Lord, alleluia,
I will gather the nations and assemble the kingdoms
and I will pour clean water upon you, alleluia.

Antiphon 3   Cf. Dn 3:7.79

You springs and all that moves in the waters,
sing a hymn to God, alleluia.

Antiphon 4   1 Pt 2:9

O chosen race, royal priesthood, holy nation,
proclaim the mighty works of him
who called you out of darkness into his wonderful light, alleluia.

Antiphon 5

From your side, O Christ,
bursts forth a spring of water,
by which the squalor of the world is washed away
and life is made new again, alleluia.

When he returns to his chair and the singing is over, the Priest
stands facing the people and, with hands joined, says:

May almighty God cleanse us of our sins,
and through the celebration of this Eucharist
make us worthy to share at the table of his Kingdom.
Amen.

Gloria

**Glory to God in the highest,
and on earth peace to people of good will.**

**We praise you,
we bless you,
we adore you,
we glorify you,
we give you thanks for your great glory,
Lord God, heavenly King,**

O God, almighty Father.

Lord Jesus Christ, Only Begotten Son,
Lord God, Lamb of God, Son of the Father,
you take away the sins of the world,
    have mercy on us;
you take away the sins of the world,
    receive our prayer;
you are seated at the right hand of the Father,
    have mercy on us.

For you alone are the Holy One,
you alone are the Lord,
you alone are the Most High,
Jesus Christ,
with the Holy Spirit,
in the glory of God the Father.
Amen.

Collect

Turn to the Mass of the day.

The Liturgy of the Word

Readings, Responsorial Psalm, Gospel Acclamation

Turn to the Mass of the day.

Profession of Faith (Nicene Creed)

I believe in one God,
the Father almighty,
maker of heaven and earth,
of all things visible and invisible.

I believe in one Lord Jesus Christ,
the Only Begotten Son of God,
born of the Father before all ages.
God from God, Light from Light,
true God from true God,
begotten, not made, consubstantial with the Father;
through him all things were made.
For us men and for our salvation
he came down from heaven,

> At the words that follow, up to and including *and became man*, all bow.

and by the Holy Spirit was incarnate of the Virgin Mary,
and became man.

For our sake he was crucified under Pontius Pilate,
he suffered death and was buried,
and rose again on the third day
in accordance with the Scriptures.
He ascended into heaven
and is seated at the right hand of the Father.
He will come again in glory
to judge the living and the dead
and his kingdom will have no end.

I believe in the Holy Spirit, the Lord, the giver of life,
who proceeds from the Father and the Son,
who with the Father and the Son is adored and glorified,
who has spoken through the prophets.

I believe in one, holy, catholic and apostolic Church.
I confess one Baptism for the forgiveness of sins
and I look forward to the resurrection of the dead
and the life of the world to come. Amen.

Profession of Faith (Apostles' Creed)

I believe in God,
the Father almighty,
Creator of heaven and earth,
and in Jesus Christ, his only Son, our Lord,

> At the words that follow, up to and including the Virgin Mary,
> all bow.

who was conceived by the Holy Spirit,
born of the Virgin Mary,
suffered under Pontius Pilate,
was crucified, died and was buried;
he descended into hell;
on the third day he rose again from the dead;
he ascended into heaven,
and is seated at the right hand of God the Father almighty;
from there he will come to judge the living and the dead.

I believe in the Holy Spirit,
the holy catholic Church,
the communion of saints,
the forgiveness of sins,
the resurrection of the body,
and life everlasting. Amen.

The Prayer of the Faithful follows.

THE LITURGY OF THE EUCHARIST

Preparation of the Gifts

Blessed are you, Lord God of all creation,
for through your goodness we have received
the bread we offer you:
fruit of the earth and work of human hands,
it will become for us the bread of life.
Blessed be God for ever.

By the mystery of this water and wine
may we come to share in the divinity of Christ
who humbled himself to share in our humanity.

Blessed are you, Lord God of all creation,
for through your goodness we have received
the wine we offer you:
fruit of the vine and work of human hands,
it will become our spiritual drink.
Blessed be God for ever.

With humble spirit and contrite heart
may we be accepted by you, O Lord,
and may our sacrifice in your sight this day
be pleasing to you, Lord God.

Wash me, O Lord, from my iniquity
and cleanse me from my sin.

Pray, brethren (brothers and sisters),
that my sacrifice and yours
may be acceptable to God,
the almighty Father.

May the Lord accept the sacrifice at your hands
for the praise and glory of his name,
for our good
and the good of all his holy Church.

Prayer over the Offerings

Turn to the Mass of the day.

The Eucharistic Prayer

The Lord be with you.
And with your spirit.

Lift up your hearts.
We lift them up to the Lord.

Let us give thanks to the Lord our God.
It is right and just.

At the end of the Preface people sing or say aloud:

Holy, Holy, Holy Lord God of hosts.
Heaven and earth are full of your glory.
Hosanna in the highest.
Blessed is he who comes in the name of the Lord.
Hosanna in the highest.

Prefaces

Preface I of Advent

From the First Sunday of Advent to 16 December.

It is truly right and just, our duty and our salvation,
always and everywhere to give you thanks,
Lord, holy Father, almighty and eternal God,
through Christ our Lord.

For he assumed at his first coming
the lowliness of human flesh,
and so fulfilled the design you formed long ago,
and opened for us the way to eternal salvation,
that, when he comes again in glory and majesty
and all is at last made manifest,
we who watch for that day
may inherit the great promise
in which now we dare to hope.

And so, with Angels and Archangels,
with Thrones and Dominions,
and with all the hosts and Powers of heaven,
we sing the hymn of your glory,
as without end we acclaim:

Holy, Holy, Holy Lord God of hosts …

Preface II of Advent

From 17 to 24 December.

It is truly right and just, our duty and our salvation,
always and everywhere to give you thanks,
Lord, holy Father, almighty and eternal God,
through Christ our Lord.

For all the oracles of the prophets foretold him,
the Virgin Mother longed for him
with love beyond all telling,
John the Baptist sang of his coming
and proclaimed his presence when he came.

It is by his gift that already we rejoice
at the mystery of his Nativity,
so that he may find us watchful in prayer
and exultant in his praise.

And so, with Angels and Archangels,
with Thrones and Dominions,
and with all the hosts and Powers of heaven,
we sing the hymn of your glory,
as without end we acclaim:

Holy, Holy, Holy Lord God of hosts …

Preface I of the Nativity of the Lord

Nativity of the Lord and of its Octave Day.

It is truly right and just, our duty and our salvation,
always and everywhere to give you thanks,
Lord, holy Father, almighty and eternal God.

For in the mystery of the Word made flesh
a new light of your glory has shone upon the eyes of our mind,
so that, as we recognize in him God made visible,
we may be caught up through him in love of things invisible.

And so, with Angels and Archangels,
with Thrones and Dominions,
and with all the hosts and Powers of heaven,
we sing the hymn of your glory,
as without end we acclaim:

Holy, Holy, Holy Lord God of hosts …

Preface II of the Nativity of the Lord
From the Nativity of the Lord and of its Octave Day.

It is truly right and just, our duty and our salvation,
always and everywhere to give you thanks,
Lord, holy Father, almighty and eternal God,
through Christ our Lord.

For on the feast of this awe-filled mystery,
though invisible in his own divine nature,
he has appeared visibly in ours;
and begotten before all ages,
he has begun to exist in time;
so that, raising up in himself all that was cast down,
he might restore unity to all creation
and call straying humanity back to the heavenly Kingdom.

And so, with all the Angels, we praise you,
as in joyful celebration we acclaim:

Holy, Holy, Holy Lord God of hosts …

Preface III of the Nativity of the Lord
From the Nativity of the Lord and of its Octave Day.

It is truly right and just, our duty and our salvation,
always and everywhere to give you thanks,
Lord, holy Father, almighty and eternal God,
through Christ our Lord.

For through him the holy exchange that restores our life
has shone forth today in splendour:
when our frailty is assumed by your Word
not only does human mortality receive unending honour
but by this wondrous union we, too, are made eternal.

And so, in company with the choirs of Angels,
we praise you, and with joy we proclaim:

Holy, Holy, Holy Lord God of hosts …

Preface I of Lent

It is truly right and just, our duty and our salvation,
always and everywhere to give you thanks,
Lord, holy Father, almighty and eternal God,
through Christ our Lord.

For by your gracious gift each year
your faithful await the sacred paschal feasts

with the joy of minds made pure,
so that, more eagerly intent on prayer
and on the works of charity,
and participating in the mysteries
by which they have been reborn,
they may be led to the fullness of grace
that you bestow on your sons and daughters.

And so, with Angels and Archangels,
with Thrones and Dominions,
and with all the hosts and Powers of heaven,
we sing the hymn of your glory,
as without end we acclaim:

Holy, Holy, Holy Lord God of hosts …

Preface II of Lent

It is truly right and just, our duty and our salvation,
always and everywhere to give you thanks,
Lord, holy Father, almighty and eternal God.

For you have given your children a sacred time
for the renewing and purifying of their hearts,
that, freed from disordered affections,
they may so deal with the things of this passing world
as to hold rather to the things that eternally endure.

And so, with all the Angels and Saints,
we praise you, as without end we acclaim:

Holy, Holy, Holy Lord God of hosts …

Preface III of Lent

It is truly right and just, our duty and our salvation,
always and everywhere to give you thanks,
Lord, holy Father, almighty and eternal God.

For you will that our self-denial should give you thanks,
humble our sinful pride,
contribute to the feeding of the poor,
and so help us imitate you in your kindness.

And so we glorify you with countless Angels,
as with one voice of praise we acclaim:

Holy, Holy, Holy Lord God of hosts …

Preface IV of Lent

It is truly right and just, our duty and our salvation,
always and everywhere to give you thanks,
Lord, holy Father, almighty and eternal God.

For through bodily fasting you restrain our faults,
raise up our minds,
and bestow both virtue and its rewards,
through Christ our Lord.

Through him the Angels praise your majesty,
Dominions adore and Powers tremble before you.
Heaven and the Virtues of heaven and the blessed Seraphim
worship together with exultation.
May our voices, we pray, join with theirs
in humble praise, as we acclaim:

Holy, Holy, Holy Lord God of hosts …

Preface II of Easter

It is truly right and just, our duty and our salvation,
at all times to acclaim you, O Lord,
but in this time above all to laud you yet more gloriously,
when Christ our Passover has been sacrificed.

Through him the children of light rise to eternal life
and the halls of the heavenly Kingdom
are thrown open to the faithful;
for his Death is our ransom from death,
and in his rising the life of all has risen.

Therefore, overcome with paschal joy,
every land, every people exults in your praise
and even the heavenly Powers, with the angelic hosts,
sing together the unending hymn of your glory,
as they acclaim:

Holy, Holy, Holy Lord God of hosts …

Preface III of Easter

It is truly right and just, our duty and our salvation,
at all times to acclaim you, O Lord,
but in this time above all to laud you yet more gloriously,
when Christ our Passover has been sacrificed.

He never ceases to offer himself for us
but defends us and ever pleads our cause before you:

he is the sacrificial Victim who dies no more,
the Lamb, once slain, who lives for ever.

Therefore, overcome with paschal joy,
every land, every people exults in your praise
and even the heavenly Powers, with the angelic hosts,
sing together the unending hymn of your glory,
as they acclaim:

Holy, Holy, Holy Lord God of hosts …

Preface IV of Easter

It is truly right and just, our duty and our salvation,
at all times to acclaim you, O Lord,
but in this time above all to laud you yet more gloriously,
when Christ our Passover has been sacrificed.

For, with the old order destroyed,
a universe cast down is renewed,
and integrity of life is restored to us in Christ.

Therefore, overcome with paschal joy,
every land, every people exults in your praise
and even the heavenly Powers, with the angelic hosts,
sing together the unending hymn of your glory,
as they acclaim:

Holy, Holy, Holy Lord God of hosts …

Preface V of Easter

It is truly right and just, our duty and our salvation,
at all times to acclaim you, O Lord,
but in this time above all to laud you yet more gloriously,
when Christ our Passover has been sacrificed.

By the oblation of his Body,
he brought the sacrifices of old to fulfilment
in the reality of the Cross
and, by commending himself to you for our salvation,
showed himself the Priest, the Altar, and the Lamb of sacrifice.

Therefore, overcome with paschal joy,
every land, every people exults in your praise
and even the heavenly Powers, with the angelic hosts,
sing together the unending hymn of your glory,
as they acclaim:

Holy, Holy, Holy Lord God of hosts …

Preface I of the Sundays in Ordinary Time

It is truly right and just, our duty and our salvation,
always and everywhere to give you thanks,
Lord, holy Father, almighty and eternal God,
through Christ our Lord.

For through his Paschal Mystery,
he accomplished the marvellous deed,
by which he has freed us from the yoke of sin and death,
summoning us to the glory of being now called
a chosen race, a royal priesthood,
a holy nation, a people for your own possession,
to proclaim everywhere your mighty works,
for you have called us out of darkness
into your own wonderful light.

And so, with Angels and Archangels,
with Thrones and Dominions,
and with all the hosts and Powers of heaven,
we sing the hymn of your glory,
as without end we acclaim:

Holy, Holy, Holy Lord God of hosts …

Preface II of the Sundays in Ordinary Time

It is truly right and just, our duty and our salvation,
always and everywhere to give you thanks,
Lord, holy Father, almighty and eternal God,
through Christ our Lord.

For out of compassion for the waywardness that is ours,
he humbled himself and was born of the Virgin;
by the passion of the Cross he freed us from unending death,
and by rising from the dead he gave us life eternal.

And so, with Angels and Archangels,
with Thrones and Dominions,
and with all the hosts and Powers of heaven,
we sing the hymn of your glory,
as without end we acclaim:

Holy, Holy, Holy Lord God of hosts …

Preface III of the Sundays in Ordinary Time

It is truly right and just, our duty and our salvation,
always and everywhere to give you thanks,
Lord, holy Father, almighty and eternal God.

For we know it belongs to your boundless glory,
that you came to the aid of mortal beings with your divinity
and even fashioned for us a remedy out of mortality itself,
that the cause of our downfall
might become the means of our salvation,
through Christ our Lord.

Through him the host of Angels adores your majesty
and rejoices in your presence for ever.
May our voices, we pray, join with theirs
in one chorus of exultant praise, as we acclaim:

Holy, Holy, Holy Lord God of hosts …

Preface IV of the Sundays in Ordinary Time

It is truly right and just, our duty and our salvation,
always and everywhere to give you thanks,
Lord, holy Father, almighty and eternal God,
through Christ our Lord.

For by his birth he brought renewal
to humanity's fallen state,
and by his suffering, cancelled out our sins;
by his rising from the dead
he has opened the way to eternal life,
and by ascending to you, O Father,
he has unlocked the gates of heaven.

And so, with the company of Angels and Saints,
we sing the hymn of your praise,
as without end we acclaim:

Holy, Holy, Holy Lord God of hosts …

Preface V of the Sundays in Ordinary Time

It is truly right and just, our duty and our salvation,
always and everywhere to give you thanks,
Lord, holy Father, almighty and eternal God.

For you laid the foundations of the world
and have arranged the changing of times and seasons;
you formed man in your own image

and set humanity over the whole world in all its wonder,
to rule in your name over all you have made
and for ever praise you in your mighty works,
through Christ our Lord.

And so, with all the Angels, we praise you,
as in joyful celebration we acclaim:

Holy, Holy, Holy Lord God of hosts …

Preface VI of the Sundays in Ordinary Time

It is truly right and just, our duty and our salvation,
always and everywhere to give you thanks,
Lord, holy Father, almighty and eternal God.

For in you we live and move and have our being,
and while in this body
we not only experience the daily effects of your care,
but even now possess the pledge of life eternal.

For, having received the first fruits of the Spirit,
through whom you raised up Jesus from the dead,
we hope for an everlasting share in the Paschal Mystery.

And so, with all the Angels, we praise you,
as in joyful celebration we acclaim:

Holy, Holy, Holy Lord God of hosts …

Preface VII of the Sundays in Ordinary Time

It is truly right and just, our duty and our salvation,
always and everywhere to give you thanks,
Lord, holy Father, almighty and eternal God.

For you so loved the world
that in your mercy you sent us the Redeemer,
to live like us in all things but sin,
so that you might love in us what you loved in your Son,
by whose obedience we have been restored to those
    gifts of yours
that, by sinning, we had lost in disobedience.

And so, Lord, with all the Angels and Saints,
we, too, give you thanks, as in exultation we acclaim:

Holy, Holy, Holy Lord God of hosts …

Preface VIII of the Sundays in Ordinary Time

It is truly right and just, our duty and our salvation,
always and everywhere to give you thanks,
Lord, holy Father, almighty and eternal God.

For, when your children were scattered afar by sin,
through the Blood of your Son and the power of the Spirit,
you gathered them again to yourself,
that a people, formed as one by the unity of the Trinity,
made the body of Christ and the temple of the Holy Spirit,
might, to the praise of your manifold wisdom,
be manifest as the Church.

And so, in company with the choirs of Angels,
we praise you, and with joy we proclaim:

Holy, Holy, Holy Lord God of hosts …

THE EUCHARISTIC PRAYERS

Eucharistic Prayer I
(The Roman Canon)

The Lord be with you.
And with your spirit.

Lift up your hearts.
We lift them up to the Lord.

Let us give thanks to the Lord our God.
It is right and just.

Then follows the Preface, which concludes:

Holy, Holy, Holy Lord God of hosts.
Heaven and earth are full of your glory.
Hosanna in the highest.
Blessed is he who comes in the name of the Lord.
Hosanna in the highest.

To you, therefore, most merciful Father,
we make humble prayer and petition
through Jesus Christ, your Son, our Lord:
that you accept
and bless ✠ these gifts, these offerings,
these holy and unblemished sacrifices,
which we offer you firstly
for your holy catholic Church.
Be pleased to grant her peace,
to guard, unite and govern her
throughout the whole world,
together with your servant N. our Pope
and N. our Bishop,
and all those who, holding to the truth,
hand on the catholic and apostolic faith.

Remember, Lord, your servants N. and N.
and all gathered here,
whose faith and devotion are known to you.
For them, we offer you this sacrifice of praise
or they offer it for themselves
and all who are dear to them:

for the redemption of their souls,
in hope of health and well-being,
and paying their homage to you,
the eternal God, living and true.

In communion with those whose memory we venerate,
especially the glorious ever-Virgin Mary,
Mother of our God and Lord, Jesus Christ,
† and blessed Joseph, her Spouse,
your blessed Apostles and Martyrs,
Peter and Paul, Andrew,
(James, John,
Thomas, James, Philip,
Bartholomew, Matthew,
Simon and Jude;
Linus, Cletus, Clement, Sixtus,
Cornelius, Cyprian,
Lawrence, Chrysogonus,
John and Paul,
Cosmas and Damian)
and all your Saints;
we ask that through their merits and prayers,
in all things we may be defended
by your protecting help.
(Through Christ our Lord. Amen.)

Proper Forms of the *Communicantes*

On the Nativity of the Lord and throughout the Octave
Celebrating the most sacred night (day)
on which blessed Mary the immaculate Virgin
brought forth the Saviour for this world,
and in communion with those whose memory we venerate,
especially the glorious ever-Virgin Mary,
Mother of our God and Lord, Jesus Christ, †

On the Epiphany of the Lord
Celebrating the most sacred day
on which your Only Begotten Son,
eternal with you in your glory,
appeared in a human body, truly sharing our flesh,
and in communion with those whose memory we venerate,
especially the glorious ever-Virgin Mary,
Mother of our God and Lord, Jesus Christ, †

From the Mass of the Easter Vigil until the Second Sunday of Easter

Celebrating the most sacred night (day)
of the Resurrection of our Lord Jesus Christ in the flesh,
and in communion with those whose memory we venerate,
especially the glorious ever-Virgin Mary,
Mother of our God and Lord, Jesus Christ,†

On the Ascension of the Lord

Celebrating the most sacred day
on which your Only Begotten Son, our Lord,
placed at the right hand of your glory
our weak human nature,
which he had united to himself,
and in communion with those whose memory we venerate,
especially the glorious ever-Virgin Mary,
Mother of our God and Lord, Jesus Christ, †

On Pentecost Sunday

Celebrating the most sacred day of Pentecost,
on which the Holy Spirit
appeared to the Apostles in tongues of fire,
and in communion with those whose memory we venerate,
especially the glorious ever-Virgin Mary,
Mother of our God and Lord, Jesus Christ, †

Therefore, Lord, we pray:
graciously accept this oblation of our service,
that of your whole family;
order our days in your peace,
and command that we be delivered from eternal damnation
and counted among the flock of those you have chosen.
(Through Christ our Lord. Amen.)

From the Mass of the Easter Vigil until the Second Sunday of Easter

Therefore, Lord, we pray:
graciously accept this oblation of our service,
that of your whole family,
which we make to you
also for those to whom you have been pleased to give
the new birth of water and the Holy Spirit,
granting them forgiveness of all their sins;
order our days in your peace,
and command that we be delivered from eternal damnation

and counted among the flock of those you have chosen.
(Through Christ our Lord. Amen.)

Be pleased, O God, we pray,
to bless, acknowledge,
and approve this offering in every respect;
make it spiritual and acceptable,
so that it may become for us
the Body and Blood of your most beloved Son,
our Lord Jesus Christ.

On the day before he was to suffer,
he took bread in his holy and venerable hands,
and with eyes raised to heaven
to you, O God, his almighty Father,
giving you thanks, he said the blessing,
broke the bread
and gave it to his disciples, saying:

TAKE THIS, ALL OF YOU, AND EAT OF IT,
FOR THIS IS MY BODY,
WHICH WILL BE GIVEN UP FOR YOU.

In a similar way, when supper was ended,
he took this precious chalice
in his holy and venerable hands,
and once more giving you thanks, he said the blessing
and gave the chalice to his disciples, saying:

TAKE THIS, ALL OF YOU, AND DRINK FROM IT,
FOR THIS IS THE CHALICE OF MY BLOOD,
THE BLOOD OF THE NEW AND ETERNAL COVENANT,
WHICH WILL BE POURED OUT FOR YOU AND FOR MANY
FOR THE FORGIVENESS OF SINS.

DO THIS IN MEMORY OF ME.

The mystery of faith.

**We proclaim your Death, O Lord,
and profess your Resurrection
until you come again.**

　　Or:

**When we eat this Bread and drink this Cup,
we proclaim your Death, O Lord,
until you come again.**

Or:

**Save us, Saviour of the world,
for by your Cross and Resurrection
you have set us free.**

Or, for Ireland only:

My Lord and my God.

Therefore, O Lord,
as we celebrate the memorial of the blessed Passion,
the Resurrection from the dead,
and the glorious Ascension into heaven
of Christ, your Son, our Lord,
we, your servants and your holy people,
offer to your glorious majesty
from the gifts that you have given us,
this pure victim,
this holy victim,
this spotless victim,
the holy Bread of eternal life
and the Chalice of everlasting salvation.

Be pleased to look upon these offerings
with a serene and kindly countenance,
and to accept them,
as once you were pleased to accept
the gifts of your servant Abel the just,
the sacrifice of Abraham, our father in faith,
and the offering of your high priest Melchizedek,
a holy sacrifice, a spotless victim.

In humble prayer we ask you, almighty God:
command that these gifts be borne
by the hands of your holy Angel
to your altar on high
in the sight of your divine majesty,
so that all of us, who through this participation at the altar
receive the most holy Body and Blood of your Son,
may be filled with every grace and heavenly blessing.
(Through Christ our Lord. Amen.)

Remember also, Lord, your servants N. and N.,
who have gone before us with the sign of faith
and rest in the sleep of peace.
Grant them, O Lord, we pray,

and all who sleep in Christ,
a place of refreshment, light and peace.
(Through Christ our Lord. Amen.)

To us, also, your servants, who, though sinners,
hope in your abundant mercies,
graciously grant some share
and fellowship with your holy Apostles and Martyrs:
with John the Baptist, Stephen,
Matthias, Barnabas,
(Ignatius, Alexander,
Marcellinus, Peter,
Felicity, Perpetua,
Agatha, Lucy,
Agnes, Cecilia, Anastasia)
and all your Saints;
admit us, we beseech you,
into their company,
not weighing our merits,
but granting us your pardon,
through Christ our Lord.

Through whom
you continue to make all these good things, O Lord;
you sanctify them, fill them with life,
bless them, and bestow them upon us.

Through him, and with him, and in him,
O God, almighty Father,
in the unity of the Holy Spirit,
all glory and honour is yours,
for ever and ever.
Amen.

Turn to page 53.

Eucharistic Prayer II

Preface (may be substituted with another)

The Lord be with you.
And with your spirit.

Lift up your hearts
We lift them up to the Lord.

Let us give thanks to the Lord our God.
It is right and just.

It is truly right and just, our duty and our salvation,
always and everywhere to give you thanks, Father most holy,
through your beloved Son, Jesus Christ,
your Word through whom you made all things,
whom you sent as our Saviour and Redeemer,
incarnate by the Holy Spirit and born of the Virgin.

Fulfilling your will and gaining for you a holy people,
he stretched out his hands as he endured his Passion,
so as to break the bonds of death and manifest the resurrection.

And so, with the Angels and all the Saints
we declare your glory,
as with one voice we acclaim:

Holy, Holy, Holy Lord God of hosts.
Heaven and earth are full of your glory.
Hosanna in the highest.
Blessed is he who comes in the name of the Lord.
Hosanna in the highest.

You are indeed Holy, O Lord,
the fount of all holiness.

Make holy, therefore, these gifts, we pray,
by sending down your Spirit upon them like the dewfall,
so that they may become for us
the Body and ✠ Blood of our Lord Jesus Christ.

At the time he was betrayed
and entered willingly into his Passion,
he took bread and, giving thanks, broke it,
and gave it to his disciples, saying:

TAKE THIS, ALL OF YOU, AND EAT OF IT,
FOR THIS IS MY BODY,
WHICH WILL BE GIVEN UP FOR YOU.

In a similar way, when supper was ended,
he took the chalice
and, once more giving thanks,
he gave it to his disciples, saying:

Take this, all of you, and drink from it,
for this is the chalice of my Blood,
the Blood of the new and eternal covenant,
which will be poured out for you and for many
for the forgiveness of sins.

Do this in memory of me.

The mystery of faith.

**We proclaim your Death, O Lord,
and profess your Resurrection
until you come again.**

Or:

**When we eat this Bread and drink this Cup,
we proclaim your Death, O Lord,
until you come again.**

Or:

**Save us, Saviour of the world,
for by your Cross and Resurrection
you have set us free.**

Or, for Ireland only:

My Lord and my God.

Therefore, as we celebrate
the memorial of his Death and Resurrection,
we offer you, Lord,
the Bread of life and the Chalice of salvation,
giving thanks that you have held us worthy
to be in your presence and minister to you.

Humbly we pray
that, partaking of the Body and Blood of Christ,
we may be gathered into one by the Holy Spirit.

Remember, Lord, your Church,
spread throughout the world,
and bring her to the fullness of charity,
together with N. our Pope and N. our Bishop
and all the clergy.

In Masses for the Dead, the following may be added.

Remember your servant N.,
whom you have called (today)
from this world to yourself.
Grant that he (she) who was united with your Son in a death
  like his,
may also be one with him in his Resurrection.

Remember also our brothers and sisters
who have fallen asleep in the hope of the resurrection,
and all who have died in your mercy:
welcome them into the light of your face.
Have mercy on us all, we pray,
that with the Blessed Virgin Mary, Mother of God,
with blessed Joseph, her Spouse,
with the blessed Apostles,
and all the Saints who have pleased you throughout the ages,
we may merit to be coheirs to eternal life,
and may praise and glorify you
through your Son, Jesus Christ.

Through him, and with him, and in him,
O God, almighty Father,
in the unity of the Holy Spirit,
all glory and honour is yours,
for ever and ever.
Amen.

Turn to page 53.

Eucharistic Prayer III

The Lord be with you.
And with your spirit.

Lift up your hearts.
We lift them up to the Lord.

Let us give thanks to the Lord our God.
It is right and just.

Then follows the Preface, which concludes:

Holy, Holy, Holy Lord God of hosts.
Heaven and earth are full of your glory.
Hosanna in the highest.
Blessed is he who comes in the name of the Lord.
Hosanna in the highest.

You are indeed Holy, O Lord,
and all you have created
rightly gives you praise,
for through your Son our Lord Jesus Christ,
by the power and working of the Holy Spirit,
you give life to all things and make them holy,
and you never cease to gather a people to yourself,
so that from the rising of the sun to its setting
a pure sacrifice may be offered to your name.

Therefore, O Lord, we humbly implore you:
by the same Spirit graciously make holy
these gifts we have brought to you for consecration,
that they may become the Body and ✠ Blood
of your Son our Lord Jesus Christ,
at whose command we celebrate these mysteries.

For on the night he was betrayed
he himself took bread,
and, giving you thanks, he said the blessing,
broke the bread and gave it to his disciples, saying:

Take this, all of you, and eat of it,
for this is my Body,
which will be given up for you.

In a similar way, when supper was ended,
he took the chalice,
and, giving you thanks, he said the blessing,
and gave the chalice to his disciples, saying:

TAKE THIS, ALL OF YOU, AND DRINK FROM IT,
FOR THIS IS THE CHALICE OF MY BLOOD,
THE BLOOD OF THE NEW AND ETERNAL COVENANT,
WHICH WILL BE POURED OUT FOR YOU AND FOR MANY
FOR THE FORGIVENESS OF SINS.
DO THIS IN MEMORY OF ME.

The mystery of faith.

**We proclaim your Death, O Lord,
and profess your Resurrection
until you come again.**

Or:

**When we eat this Bread and drink this Cup,
we proclaim your Death, O Lord,
until you come again.**

Or:

**Save us, Saviour of the world,
for by your Cross and Resurrection
you have set us free.**

Or, for Ireland only:

My Lord and my God.

Therefore, O Lord, as we celebrate the memorial
of the saving Passion of your Son,
his wondrous Resurrection
and Ascension into heaven,
and as we look forward to his second coming,
we offer you in thanksgiving
this holy and living sacrifice.

Look, we pray, upon the oblation of your Church
and, recognizing the sacrificial Victim by whose death
you willed to reconcile us to yourself,
grant that we, who are nourished
by the Body and Blood of your Son
and filled with his Holy Spirit,
may become one body, one spirit in Christ.

May he make of us
an eternal offering to you,
so that we may obtain an inheritance with your elect,
especially with the most Blessed Virgin Mary, Mother of God,

with blessed Joseph, her Spouse,
with your blessed Apostles and glorious Martyrs
(with Saint N.: the Saint of the day or Patron Saint)
and with all the Saints,
on whose constant intercession in your presence
we rely for unfailing help.

May this Sacrifice of our reconciliation,
we pray, O Lord,
advance the peace and salvation of all the world.
Be pleased to confirm in faith and charity
your pilgrim Church on earth,
with your servant N. our Pope and N. our Bishop,
the Order of Bishops, all the clergy,
and the entire people you have gained for your own.

Listen graciously to the prayers of this family,
whom you have summoned before you:
in your compassion, O merciful Father,
gather to yourself all your children
scattered throughout the world.
† To our departed brothers and sisters
and to all who were pleasing to you
at their passing from this life,
give kind admittance to your kingdom.
There we hope to enjoy for ever the fullness of your glory
through Christ our Lord,
through whom you bestow on the world all that is good.

In Masses for the Dead, the following may be said:

† Remember your servant N.
whom you have called (today)
from this world to yourself.
Grant that he (she) who was united with your Son in a death
    like his,
may also be one with him in his Resurrection,
when from the earth
he will raise up in the flesh those who have died,
and transform our lowly body
after the pattern of his own glorious body.
To our departed brothers and sisters, too,
and to all who were pleasing to you
at their passing from this life,
give kind admittance to your kingdom.

There we hope to enjoy for ever the fullness of your glory,
when you will wipe away every tear from our eyes.
For seeing you, our God, as you are,
we shall be like you for all the ages
and praise you without end,
through Christ our Lord,
through whom you bestow on the world all that is good.

Through him, and with him, and in him,
O God, almighty Father,
in the unity of the Holy Spirit,
all glory and honour is yours,
for ever and ever.
Amen.

Turn to page 53.

Eucharistic Prayer IV

The Lord be with you.
And with your spirit.

Lift up your hearts.
We lift them up to the Lord.

Let us give thanks to the Lord our God.
It is right and just.

It is truly right to give you thanks,
truly just to give you glory, Father most holy,
for you are the one God living and true,
existing before all ages and abiding for all eternity,
dwelling in unapproachable light;
yet you, who alone are good, the source of life,
have made all that is,
so that you might fill your creatures with blessings
and bring joy to many of them by the glory of your light.

And so, in your presence are countless hosts of Angels,
who serve you day and night
and, gazing upon the glory of your face,
glorify you without ceasing.

With them we, too, confess your name in exultation,
giving voice to every creature under heaven,
as we acclaim:

Holy, Holy, Holy Lord God of hosts.
Heaven and earth are full of your glory.
Hosanna in the highest.
Blessed is he who comes in the name of the Lord.
Hosanna in the highest.

We give you praise, Father most holy,
for you are great
and you have fashioned all your works
in wisdom and in love.
You formed man in your own image
and entrusted the whole world to his care,
so that in serving you alone, the Creator,
he might have dominion over all creatures.
And when through disobedience he had lost your friendship,
you did not abandon him to the domain of death.
For you came in mercy to the aid of all,
so that those who seek might find you.
Time and again you offered them covenants
and through the prophets
taught them to look forward to salvation.

And you so loved the world, Father most holy,
that in the fullness of time
you sent your Only Begotten Son to be our Saviour.
Made incarnate by the Holy Spirit
and born of the Virgin Mary,
he shared our human nature
in all things but sin.
To the poor he proclaimed the good news of salvation,
to prisoners, freedom,
and to the sorrowful of heart, joy.
To accomplish your plan,
he gave himself up to death,
and, rising from the dead,
he destroyed death and restored life.

And that we might live no longer for ourselves
but for him who died and rose again for us,
he sent the Holy Spirit from you, Father,
as the first fruits for those who believe,
so that, bringing to perfection his work in the world,
he might sanctify creation to the full.

Therefore, O Lord, we pray:
may this same Holy Spirit
graciously sanctify these offerings,
that they may become
the Body and ✠ Blood of our Lord Jesus Christ
for the celebration of this great mystery,
which he himself left us
as an eternal covenant.

For when the hour had come
for him to be glorified by you, Father most holy,
having loved his own who were in the world,
he loved them to the end:
and while they were at supper,
he took bread, blessed and broke it,
and gave it to his disciples, saying:

TAKE THIS, ALL OF YOU, AND EAT OF IT,
FOR THIS IS MY BODY,
WHICH WILL BE GIVEN UP FOR YOU.

In a similar way,
taking the chalice filled with the fruit of the vine,
he gave thanks,
and gave the chalice to his disciples, saying:

TAKE THIS, ALL OF YOU, AND DRINK FROM IT,
FOR THIS IS THE CHALICE OF MY BLOOD,
THE BLOOD OF THE NEW AND ETERNAL COVENANT,
WHICH WILL BE POURED OUT FOR YOU AND FOR MANY
FOR THE FORGIVENESS OF SINS.

DO THIS IN MEMORY OF ME.

The mystery of faith.

**We proclaim your Death, O Lord,
and profess your Resurrection
until you come again.**

Or:

**When we eat this Bread and drink this Cup,
we proclaim your Death, O Lord,
until you come again.**

Or:

**Save us, Saviour of the world,
for by your Cross and Resurrection
you have set us free.**

Or, for Ireland only:

My Lord and my God.

Therefore, O Lord,
as we now celebrate the memorial of our redemption,
we remember Christ's Death
and his descent to the realm of the dead,
we proclaim his Resurrection
and his Ascension to your right hand,
and, as we await his coming in glory,
we offer you his Body and Blood,
the sacrifice acceptable to you
which brings salvation to the whole world.

Look, O Lord, upon the Sacrifice
which you yourself have provided for your Church,
and grant in your loving kindness
to all who partake of this one Bread and one Chalice
that, gathered into one body by the Holy Spirit,
they may truly become a living sacrifice in Christ
to the praise of your glory.

Therefore, Lord, remember now
all for whom we offer this sacrifice:
especially your servant N. our Pope,
N. our Bishop, and the whole Order of Bishops,
all the clergy,
those who take part in this offering,
those gathered here before you,
your entire people,
and all who seek you with a sincere heart.

Remember also
those who have died in the peace of your Christ
and all the dead,
whose faith you alone have known.

To all of us, your children,
grant, O merciful Father,
that we may enter into a heavenly inheritance
with the Blessed Virgin Mary, Mother of God,
with blessed Joseph, her Spouse,
and with your Apostles and Saints in your kingdom.
There, with the whole of creation,
freed from the corruption of sin and death,

may we glorify you through Christ our Lord,
through whom you bestow on the world all that is good.

Through him, and with him, and in him,
O God, almighty Father,
in the unity of the Holy Spirit,
all glory and honour is yours,
for ever and ever.
Amen.

Turn to page 53.

Eucharistic Prayer for Use in Masses
for Various Needs IV

The Lord be with you.
And with your spirit.

Lift up your hearts.
We lift them up to the Lord.

Let us give thanks to the Lord our God.
It is right and just.

It is truly right and just, our duty and our salvation,
always and everywhere to give you thanks,
Father of mercies and faithful God.

For you have given us Jesus Christ, your Son,
as our Lord and Redeemer.

He always showed compassion
for children and for the poor,
for the sick and for sinners,
and he became a neighbour
to the oppressed and the afflicted.

By word and deed he announced to the world
that you are our Father
and that you care for all your sons and daughters.

And so, with all the Angels and Saints,
we exalt and bless your name
and sing the hymn of your glory,
as without end we acclaim:

Holy, Holy, Holy Lord God of hosts.
Heaven and earth are full of your glory.

Hosanna in the highest.
Blessed is he who comes in the name of the Lord.
Hosanna in the highest.

You are indeed Holy and to be glorified, O God,
who love the human race
and who always walk with us on the journey of life.
Blessed indeed is your Son,
present in our midst
when we are gathered by his love
and when, as once for the disciples, so now for us,
he opens the Scriptures and breaks the bread.

Therefore, Father most merciful,
we ask that you send forth your Holy Spirit
to sanctify these gifts of bread and wine,
that they may become for us
the Body and ✠ Blood
of our Lord Jesus Christ.

On the day before he was to suffer,
on the night of the Last Supper,
he took bread and said the blessing,
broke the bread and gave it to his disciples, saying:

Take this, all of you, and eat of it,
for this is my Body,
which will be given up for you.

In a similar way, when supper was ended,
he took the chalice, gave you thanks
and gave the chalice to his disciples, saying:

Take this, all of you, and drink from it,
for this is the chalice of my Blood,
the Blood of the new and eternal covenant,
which will be poured out for you and for many
for the forgiveness of sins.

Do this in memory of me.

The mystery of faith.

We proclaim your Death, O Lord,
and profess your Resurrection
until you come again.

    Or:

When we eat this Bread and drink this Cup,

we proclaim your Death, O Lord,
until you come again.

Or:

Save us, Saviour of the world,
for by your Cross and Resurrection
you have set us free.

Or, for Ireland only:

My Lord and my God.

Therefore, holy Father,
as we celebrate the memorial of Christ your Son, our Saviour,
whom you led through his Passion and Death on the Cross
to the glory of the Resurrection,
and whom you have seated at your right hand,
we proclaim the work of your love until he comes again
and we offer you the Bread of life
and the Chalice of blessing.

Look with favour on the oblation of your Church,
in which we show forth
the paschal Sacrifice of Christ that has been handed on to us,
and grant that, by the power of the Spirit of your love,
we may be counted now and until the day of eternity
among the members of your Son,
in whose Body and Blood we have communion.

Bring your Church, O Lord,
to perfect faith and charity,
together with N. our Pope and N. our Bishop,*
with all Bishops, Priests and Deacons,
and the entire people you have made your own.

Open our eyes
to the needs of our brothers and sisters;
inspire in us words and actions
to comfort those who labour and are burdened.
Make us serve them truly,
after the example of Christ and at his command.
And may your Church stand as a living witness
to truth and freedom,
to peace and justice,
that all people may be raised up to a new hope.

Remember our brothers and sisters (N. and N.),
who have fallen asleep in the peace of your Christ,

and all the dead, whose faith you alone have known.
Admit them to rejoice in the light of your face,
and in the resurrection give them the fullness of life.

Grant also to us,
when our earthly pilgrimage is done,
that we may come to an eternal dwelling place
and live with you for ever;
there, in communion with the Blessed Virgin Mary,
    Mother of God,
with the Apostles and Martyrs,
(with Saint N.: the Saint of the day or Patron)
and with all the Saints,
we shall praise and exalt you
through Jesus Christ, your Son.

Through him, and with him, and in him,
O God, almighty Father,
in the unity of the Holy Spirit,
all glory and honour is yours,
for ever and ever.
Amen.

Turn to page 54.

Eucharistic Prayer for Reconciliation I

The Lord be with you.
And with your spirit.

Lift up your hearts.
We lift them up to the Lord.

Let us give thanks to the Lord our God.
It is right and just.

It is truly right and just
that we should always give you thanks,
Lord, holy Father, almighty and eternal God.

For you do not cease to spur us on
to possess a more abundant life
and, being rich in mercy,
you constantly offer pardon
and call on sinners
to trust in your forgiveness alone.

Never did you turn away from us,
and, though time and again we have broken your covenant,
you have bound the human family to yourself
through Jesus your Son, our Redeemer,
with a new bond of love so tight
that it can never be undone.

Even now you set before your people
a time of grace and reconciliation,
and, as they turn back to you in spirit,
you grant them hope in Christ Jesus
and a desire to be of service to all,
while they entrust themselves
more fully to the Holy Spirit.

And so, filled with wonder,
we extol the power of your love,
and, proclaiming our joy
at the salvation that comes from you,
we join in the heavenly hymn of countless hosts,
as without end we acclaim:

Holy, Holy, Holy Lord God of hosts.
Heaven and earth are full of your glory.
Hosanna in the highest.
Blessed is he who comes in the name of the Lord.
Hosanna in the highest.

You are indeed Holy, O Lord,
and from the world's beginning
are ceaselessly at work,
so that the human race may become holy,
just as you yourself are holy.

Look, we pray, upon your people's offerings
and pour out on them the power of your Spirit,
that they may become the Body and ✠ Blood
of your beloved Son, Jesus Christ,
in whom we, too, are your sons and daughters.
Indeed, though we once were lost
and could not approach you,
you loved us with the greatest love:
for your Son, who alone is just,
handed himself over to death,
and did not disdain to be nailed for our sake
to the wood of the Cross.

But before his arms were outstretched between heaven
      and earth,
to become the lasting sign of your covenant,
he desired to celebrate the Passover with his disciples.

As he ate with them,
he took bread
and, giving you thanks, he said the blessing,
broke the bread and gave it to them, saying:

TAKE THIS, ALL OF YOU, AND EAT OF IT,
FOR THIS IS MY BODY,
WHICH WILL BE GIVEN UP FOR YOU.

In a similar way, when supper was ended,
knowing that he was about to reconcile all things in himself
through his Blood to be shed on the Cross,
he took the chalice, filled with the fruit of the vine,
and once more giving you thanks,
handed the chalice to his disciples, saying:

TAKE THIS, ALL OF YOU, AND DRINK FROM IT,
FOR THIS IS THE CHALICE OF MY BLOOD,
THE BLOOD OF THE NEW AND ETERNAL COVENANT,
WHICH WILL BE POURED OUT FOR YOU AND FOR MANY
FOR THE FORGIVENESS OF SINS.

DO THIS IN MEMORY OF ME.

The mystery of faith.

**We proclaim your Death, O Lord,
and profess your Resurrection
until you come again.**

> Or:

**When we eat this Bread and drink this Cup,
we proclaim your Death, O Lord,
until you come again.**

> Or:

**Save us, Saviour of the world,
for by your Cross and Resurrection
you have set us free.**

> Or, for Ireland only:

My Lord and my God.

Therefore, as we celebrate
the memorial of your Son Jesus Christ,
who is our Passover and our surest peace,
we celebrate his Death and Resurrection from the dead,
and looking forward to his blessed Coming,
we offer you, who are our faithful and merciful God,
this sacrificial Victim
who reconciles to you the human race.

Look kindly, most compassionate Father,
on those you unite to yourself
by the Sacrifice of your Son,
and grant that, by the power of the Holy Spirit,
as they partake of this one Bread and one Chalice,
they may be gathered into one Body in Christ,
who heals every division.

Be pleased to keep us always
in communion of mind and heart,
together with N. our Pope and N. our Bishop.
Help us to work together
for the coming of your Kingdom,
until the hour when we stand before you,
Saints among the Saints in the halls of heaven,
with the Blessed Virgin Mary, Mother of God,
the blessed Apostles and all the Saints,
and with our deceased brothers and sisters,
whom we humbly commend to your mercy.

Then, freed at last from the wound of corruption
and made fully into a new creation,
we shall sing to you with gladness
the thanksgiving of Christ,
who lives for all eternity.

Through him, and with him, and in him,
O God, almighty Father,
in the unity of the Holy Spirit,
all glory and honour is yours,
for ever and ever.
Amen.

Turn to page 53.

Eucharistic Prayer for Reconciliation II

The Lord be with you.
And with your spirit.

Lift up your hearts.
We lift them up to the Lord.

Let us give thanks to the Lord our God.
It is right and just.

It is truly right and just
that we should give you thanks and praise,
O God, almighty Father,
for all you do in this world,
through our Lord Jesus Christ.

For though the human race
is divided by dissension and discord,
yet we know that by testing us
you change our hearts
to prepare them for reconciliation.

Even more, by your Spirit you move human hearts
that enemies may speak to each other again,
adversaries join hands,
and peoples seek to meet together.

By the working of your power
it comes about, O Lord,
that hatred is overcome by love,
revenge gives way to forgiveness,
and discord is changed to mutual respect.

Therefore, as we give you ceaseless thanks
with the choirs of heaven,
we cry out to your majesty on earth,
and without end we acclaim:

Holy, Holy, Holy Lord God of hosts.
Heaven and earth are full of your glory.
Hosanna in the highest.
Blessed is he who comes in the name of the Lord.
Hosanna in the highest.

You, therefore, almighty Father,
we bless through Jesus Christ your Son,
who comes in your name.
He himself is the Word that brings salvation,

the hand you extend to sinners,
the way by which your peace is offered to us.
When we ourselves had turned away from you
on account of our sins,
you brought us back to be reconciled, O Lord,
so that, converted at last to you,
we might love one another
through your Son,
whom for our sake you handed over to death.

And now, celebrating the reconciliation
Christ has brought us,
we entreat you:
sanctify these gifts by the outpouring of your Spirit,
that they may become the Body and ✠ Blood of your Son,
whose command we fulfil
when we celebrate these mysteries.

For when about to give his life to set us free,
as he reclined at supper,
he himself took bread into his hands,
and, giving you thanks, he said the blessing,
broke the bread and gave it to his disciples, saying:

TAKE THIS, ALL OF YOU, AND EAT OF IT,
FOR THIS IS MY BODY,
WHICH WILL BE GIVEN UP FOR YOU.

In a similar way, on that same evening,
he took the chalice of blessing in his hands,
confessing your mercy,
and gave the chalice to his disciples, saying:

TAKE THIS, ALL OF YOU, AND DRINK FROM IT,
FOR THIS IS THE CHALICE OF MY BLOOD,
THE BLOOD OF THE NEW AND ETERNAL COVENANT,
WHICH WILL BE POURED OUT FOR YOU AND FOR MANY
FOR THE FORGIVENESS OF SINS.

DO THIS IN MEMORY OF ME.

The mystery of faith.

**We proclaim your Death, O Lord,
and profess your Resurrection
until you come again.**

Or:

**When we eat this Bread and drink this Cup,
we proclaim your Death, O Lord,
until you come again.**

Or:

**Save us, Saviour of the world,
for by your Cross and Resurrection
you have set us free.**

Or, for Ireland only:

My Lord and my God.

Celebrating, therefore, the memorial
of the Death and Resurrection of your Son,
who left us this pledge of his love,
we offer you what you have bestowed on us,
the Sacrifice of perfect reconciliation.

Holy Father, we humbly beseech you
to accept us also, together with your Son,
and in this saving banquet
graciously to endow us with his very Spirit,
who takes away everything
that estranges us from one another.

May he make your Church a sign of unity
and an instrument of your peace among all people
and may he keep us in communion
with N. our Pope and N. our Bishop
and all the Bishops
and your entire people.

Just as you have gathered us now at the table of your Son,
so also bring us together,
with the glorious Virgin Mary, Mother of God,
with your blessed Apostles and all the Saints,
with our brothers and sisters
and those of every race and tongue
who have died in your friendship.
Bring us to share with them the unending banquet of unity
in a new heaven and a new earth,
where the fullness of your peace will shine forth
in Christ Jesus our Lord.

Through him, and with him, and in him,
O God, almighty Father,
in the unity of the Holy Spirit,

all glory and honour is yours,
for ever and ever.
Amen.

Then follows the Communion Rite.

THE COMMUNION RITE

At the Saviour's command
and formed by divine teaching,
we dare to say:

The Priest together with the people, continues:

**Our Father, who art in heaven,
hallowed be thy name;
thy kingdom come,
thy will be done
on earth as it is in heaven.
Give us this day our daily bread,
and forgive us our trespasses,
as we forgive those who trespass against us;
and lead us not into temptation,
but deliver us from evil.**

Deliver us, Lord, we pray, from every evil,
graciously grant peace in our days,
that, by the help of your mercy,
we may be always free from sin
and safe from all distress,
as we await the blessed hope
and the coming of our Saviour, Jesus Christ.

**For the kingdom,
the power and the glory are yours
now and for ever.**

Lord Jesus Christ,
who said to your Apostles:
Peace I leave you, my peace I give you,
look not on our sins,
but on the faith of your Church,
and graciously grant her peace and unity
in accordance with your will.
Who live and reign for ever and ever.
Amen.

The peace of the Lord be with you always.
And with your spirit.

Then, if appropriate, the Priest adds:

Let us offer each other the sign of peace.

And all offer one another a sign, in keeping with local customs, that expresses peace, communion, and charity.

May this mingling of the Body and Blood
of our Lord Jesus Christ
bring eternal life to us who receive it.

Meanwhile the following is sung or said:

**Lamb of God, you take away the sins of the world,
    have mercy on us.
Lamb of God, you take away the sins of the world,
    have mercy on us.
Lamb of God, you take away the sins of the world,
    grant us peace.**

Lord Jesus Christ, Son of the living God,
who, by the will of the Father
and the work of the Holy Spirit,
through your Death gave life to the world,
free me by this, your most holy Body and Blood,
from all my sins and from every evil;
keep me always faithful to your commandments,
and never let me be parted from you.

    Or:

May the receiving of your Body and Blood,
Lord Jesus Christ,
not bring me to judgement and condemnation,
but through your loving mercy
be for me protection in mind and body
and a healing remedy.

The Priest while facing the people, says aloud:

Behold the Lamb of God,
behold him who takes away the sins of the world.
Blessed are those called to the supper of the Lamb.

**Lord, I am not worthy
that you should enter under my roof,
but only say the word
and my soul shall be healed.**

May the Body of Christ
keep me safe for eternal life.

May the Blood of Christ
keep me safe for eternal life.

The Priest raises a host slightly and shows it to each of the
communicants, saying:

The Body of Christ.
Amen.

When Communion is ministered under both kinds, the minister of
the chalice offers it to each of the communicants, saying:

The Blood of Christ.
Amen.

While the Priest carries out the purification he says quietly:

What has passed our lips as food, O Lord,
may we possess in purity of heart,
that what has been given to us in time
may be our healing for eternity.

If appropriate, a sacred silence may be observed for a while, or a
psalm or other canticle of praise or a hymn may be sung. Then, the
Priest says:

Prayer after Communion

Turn to the Mass of the day.

Let us pray.

All pray in silence with the Priest for a while, unless silence has just
been observed. Then the Priest says the **Prayer after Communion**, at
the end of which the people acclaim:

Amen.

THE CONCLUDING RITES

The Lord be with you.
And with your spirit.

May almighty God bless you,
the Father, and the Son, ✠ and the Holy Spirit.
Amen.

Go forth, the Mass is ended.

 Or:

Go and announce the Gospel of the Lord.

 Or:

Go in peace, glorifying the Lord by your life.

 Or:

Go in peace.
Thanks be to God.

Solemn Blessings

Advent

May the almighty and merciful God,
by whose grace you have placed your faith
in the First Coming of his Only Begotten Son
and yearn for his coming again,
sanctify you by the radiance of Christ's Advent
and enrich you with his blessing.
Amen.

As you run the race of this present life,
may he make you firm in faith,
joyful in hope and active in charity.
Amen.

So that, rejoicing now with devotion
at the Redeemer's coming in the flesh,
you may be endowed with the rich reward of eternal life
when he comes again in majesty.
Amen.

And may the blessing of almighty God,
the Father, and the Son, ✠ and the Holy Spirit,
come down on you and remain with you for ever.
Amen.

Easter Time

May God, who by the Resurrection of his Only Begotten Son
was pleased to confer on you
the gift of redemption and of adoption,
give you gladness by his blessing.
Amen.

May he, by whose redeeming work
you have received the gift of everlasting freedom,
make you heirs to an eternal inheritance.
Amen.

And may you, who have already risen with Christ
in Baptism through faith,
by living in a right manner on this earth,
be united with him in the homeland of heaven.
Amen.

And may the blessing of almighty God,
the Father, and the Son, ✠ and the Holy Spirit,
come down on you and remain with you for ever.
Amen.

Ordinary Time I

May the Lord bless you and keep you.
Amen.

May he let his face shine upon you
and show you his mercy.
Amen.

May he turn his countenance towards you
and give you his peace.
Amen.

And may the blessing of almighty God,
the Father, and the Son, ✠ and the Holy Spirit,
come down on you and remain with you for ever.
Amen.

Ordinary Time II

May the peace of God,
which surpasses all understanding,
keep your hearts and minds
in the knowledge and love of God,
and of his Son, our Lord Jesus Christ.
Amen.

And may the blessing of almighty God,
the Father, and the Son, ✠ and the Holy Spirit,
come down on you and remain with you for ever.
Amen.

Ordinary Time III

May almighty God bless you in his kindness
and pour out saving wisdom upon you.
Amen.

May he nourish you always with the teachings of the faith
and make you persevere in holy deeds.
Amen.

May he turn your steps towards himself
and show you the path of charity and peace.
Amen.

And may the blessing of almighty God,
the Father, and the Son, ✠ and the Holy Spirit,
come down on you and remain with you for ever.
Amen.

Ordinary Time IV

May the God of all consolation order your days in his peace
and grant you the gifts of his blessing.
Amen.

May he free you always from every distress
and confirm your hearts in his love.
Amen.

So that on this life's journey
you may be effective in good works,
rich in the gifts of hope, faith and charity,
and may come happily to eternal life.
Amen.

And may the blessing of almighty God,
the Father, and the Son, ✠ and the Holy Spirit,
come down on you and remain with you for ever.
Amen.

Ordinary Time V

May almighty God always keep every adversity far from you
and in his kindness pour out upon you the gifts of his blessing.
Amen.

May God keep your hearts attentive to his words,
that they may be filled with everlasting gladness.
Amen.

And so, may you always understand what is good and right,
and be found ever hastening along
in the path of God's commands,
made coheirs with the citizens of heaven.
Amen.

And may the blessing of almighty God,
the Father, and the Son, ✠ and the Holy Spirit,
come down on you and remain with you for ever.
Amen.

Ordinary Time VI

May God bless you with every heavenly blessing,
make you always holy and pure in his sight,
pour out in abundance upon you the riches of his glory,
and teach you with the words of truth;
may he instruct you in the Gospel of salvation,
and ever endow you with fraternal charity.
Through Christ our Lord.
Amen.

And may the blessing of almighty God,
the Father, and the Son, ✠ and the Holy Spirit,
come down on you and remain with you for ever.
Amen.

THE ORDER OF MASS IN LATIN

People's Parts

The Introductory Rites

In nómine Patris, et Fílii, et Spíritus Sancti.
Amen.

   Or:

Dóminus vobíscum.

   Or another greeting:

Et cum spíritu tuo.

Confiteor

Confíteor Deo omnipoténti et vobis, fratres,
quia peccávi nimis
cogitatióne, verbo, ópere et omissióne:
(All strike their breast)
mea culpa, mea culpa, mea máxima culpa.
Ideo precor beátam Maríam semper Vírginem,
omnes Angelos et Sanctos,
et vos, fratres, oráre pro me
ad Dóminum Deum nostrum.

Kyrie

Kyrie, eléison.	**Kyrie, eléison.**
Christe, eléison.	**Christe, eléison.**
Kyrie, eléison.	**Kyrie, eléison.**

Gloria

Glória in excélsis Deo
et in terra pax homínibus bonæ voluntátis.
Laudámus te,
benedícimus te,
adorámus te,
lorificámus te,
grátias ágimus tibi propter magnam glóriam tuam,
Dómine Deus, Rex cæléstis,
Deus Pater omnípotens.

Dómine Fili unigénite, Iesu Christe,
Dómine Deus, Agnus Dei, Fílius Patris,
qui tollis peccáta mundi, miserére nobis;

qui tollis peccáta mundi, súscipe deprecatiónem nostram.
Qui sedes ad déxteram Patris, miserére nobis.

Quóniam tu solus Sanctus, tu solus Dóminus,
    tu solus Altíssimus,
Iesu Christe, cum Sancto Spíritu:
in glória Dei Patris. Amen.

After the first and second readings

Deo grátias.

Before the Gospel

Dóminus vobíscum.
Et cum spíritu tuo.

Léctio sancti Evangélii secúndum N.
Glória tibi, Dómine.

At the end of the Gospel

Verbum Dómini.
Laus tibi, Christe.

Credo

Credo in unum Deum,
Patrem omnipoténtem, factórem cæli et terræ,
visibílium ómnium et invisibílium.
Et in unum Dóminum Iesum Christum,
Fílium Dei unigénitum,
et ex Patre natum ante ómnia sæcula.
Deum de Deo, lumen de lúmine, Deum verum de Deo vero,
génitum, non factum, consubstantiálem Patri:
per quem ómnia facta sunt.
Qui propter nos hómines et propter nostram salútem
descéndit de cælis.

All bow during the next two lines

Et incarnátus est de Spíritu Sancto
ex María Vírgine, et homo factus est.
Crucifíxus étiam pro nobis sub Póntio Piláto;
passus et sepúltus est,
et resurréxit tértia die, secúndum Scriptúras,
et ascéndit in cælum, sedet ad déxteram Patris.
Et íterum ventúrus est cum glória, iudicáre vivos et mórtuos,
cuius regni non erit finis.
Et in Spíritum Sanctum, Dóminum et vivificántem:
qui ex Patre Filióque procédit.

Qui cum Patre et Fílio simul adorátur et conglorificátur:
qui locútus est per prophétas.
Et unam, sanctam, cathólicam et apostólicam Ecclésiam.
Confíteor unum baptísma in remissiónem peccatórum.
Et exspécto resurrectiónem mortuórum,
et vítam ventúri sǽculi. Amen.

Response to offertory prayers
Benedíctus Deus in sǽcula.

Response to the Orate Fratres
Suscípiat Dóminus sacrifícium de mánibus tuis
ad laudem et glóriam nóminis sui,
ad utilitátem quoque nostram
totiúsque Ecclésiæ suæ sanctæ.

Dialogue before the Preface
Dóminus vobíscum.
Et cum spíritu tuo.

Sursum corda.
Habémus ad Dóminum.

Grátias agámus Dómino Deo nostro.
Dignum et iustum est.

Sanctus
Sanctus, Sanctus, Sanctus Dóminus Deus Sábaoth.
Pleni sunt cæli et terra glória tua.
    Hosánna in excélsis.
Benedíctus qui venit in nómine Dómini.
    Hosánna in excélsis.

After the Consecration
Mystérium fidei.

1. **Mortem tuam annuntiámus, Dómine,**
   et tuam resurrectiónem confitémur, donec vénias.

2. **Quotiescúmque manducámus panem hunc**
   et cálicem bíbimus,
   mortem tuam annuntiámus, Dómine, donec vénias.

3. **Salvátor mundi, salva nos,**
   qui per crucem et resurrectiónem tuam liberásti nos.

Pater Noster

Præcéptis salutáribus móniti,
et divína institutióne formáti,
audémus dicere:

**Pater noster, qui es in cælis:
sanctificétur nomen tuum;
advéniat regnum tuum;
fiat volúntas tua, sicut in cælo, et in terra.
Panem nostrum cotidiánum da nobis hódie;
et dimítte nobis débita nostra,
sicut et nos dimíttimus debitóribus nostris;
et ne nos indúcas in tentatiónem;
sed líbera nos a malo.**

Acclamation after the Líbera nos

**Quia tuum est regnum,
et potéstas, et glória in sæcula.**

At the Pax

Pax Dómini sit semper vobíscum.
Et cum spíritu tuo.

Agnus Dei

**Agnus Dei, qui tollis peccáta mundi:
miserére nobis.
Agnus Dei, qui tollis peccáta mundi:
miserére nobis.
Agnus Dei, qui tollis peccáta mundi:
dona nobis pacem.**

Lord, I am not worthy

**Domine, non sum dignus ut intres sub tectum meum:
sed tantum dic verbo, et sanabitur ánima mea.**

Conclusion

Dóminus vobíscum.
Et cum spíritu tuo.

Benedícat vos omnípotens Deus,
Pater, et Fílius, ✠ et Spíritus Sanctus.
Amen.

Ite, missa est.
Deo grátias.

PROPER OF TIME

1 JANUARY
SOLEMNITY OF MARY,
THE HOLY MOTHER OF GOD

The title 'Mother of God' is the equivalent in the Western or Latin branch of Christianity of the earlier Eastern or Greek title of Theotokos which literally means 'God-bearer'. This word was used of Mary from at least the time of the theologian Origen (died c. 254). It was the cause of some controversy on the basis that its meaning failed to reflect the humanity of Jesus over against his divinity, but it was upheld by the great Councils of Ephesus (431) and Chalcedon (451).

Entrance Antiphon

**Hail, Holy Mother, who gave birth to the King
who rules heaven and earth for ever.**

    Or: Cf. Is 9:1.5; Lk 1:33

**Today a light will shine upon us, for the Lord is born for us;
and he will be called Wondrous God,
Prince of peace, Father of future ages:
and his reign will be without end.**

Greeting, Penitential Rite, Gloria – pages 7-13.

Collect

O God, who through the fruitful virginity of Blessed Mary
bestowed on the human race
the grace of eternal salvation,
grant, we pray,
that we may experience the intercession of her,
through whom we were found worthy
to receive the author of life,
our Lord Jesus Christ, your Son.
Who lives and reigns with you in the unity of the Holy Spirit,
one God, for ever and ever.

FIRST READING Nb 6:22-27

A reading from the book of Numbers.

They are to call down my name on the sons of Israel, and I will bless them.

The Lord spoke to Moses and said, 'Say this to Aaron and his sons: "This is how you are to bless the sons of Israel. You shall say to them:

May the Lord bless you and keep you.
May the Lord let his face shine on you and be gracious
    to you.
May the Lord uncover his face to you and bring you peace."

This is how they are to call down my name on the sons of Israel, and I will bless them.'

The word of the Lord.

RESPONSORIAL PSALM Ps 66:2-3.5.6.8

℟ **O God, be gracious and bless us.**

1. God, be gracious and bless us
   and let your face shed its light upon us.
   So will your ways be known upon earth
   and all nations learn your saving help. ℟

2. Let the nations be glad and exult
   for you rule the world with justice.
   With fairness you rule the peoples,
   you guide the nations on earth. ℟

3. Let the peoples praise you, O God;
   let all the peoples praise you.
   May God still give us his blessing
   till the ends of the earth revere him. ℟

SECOND READING Gal 4:4-7

A reading from the letter of St Paul to the Galatians.

God sent his Son, born of a woman.

When the appointed time came, God sent his Son, born of a woman, born a subject of the Law, to redeem the subjects of the Law and to enable us to be adopted as sons. The proof that you are sons is that God has sent the Spirit of his Son into our hearts: the Spirit that cries, 'Abba, Father', and it is this that makes you a son, you are not a slave any more; and if God has made you son, then he has made you heir.

The word of the Lord.

GOSPEL ACCLAMATION   Heb 1:1-2

Alleluia, alleluia!
At various times in the past
and in various different ways,
God spoke to our ancestors through the prophets;
but in our own time, the last days,
he has spoken to us through his Son.
Alleluia!

GOSPEL   Lk 2:16-21

A reading from the holy Gospel according to Luke.

They found Mary and Joseph and the baby… When the eighth day came, they gave him the name Jesus.

The shepherds hurried away to Bethlehem and found Mary and Joseph, and the baby lying in the manger. When they saw the child they repeated what they had been told about him, and everyone who heard it was astonished at what the shepherds had to say. As for Mary, she treasured all these things and pondered them in her heart. And the shepherds went back glorifying and praising God for all they had heard and seen; it was exactly as they had been told.

When the eighth day came and the child was to be circumcised, they gave him the name Jesus, the name the angel had given him before his conception.

The Gospel of the Lord.

Profession of Faith – pages 14-15.

Prayer over the Offerings

O God, who in your kindness begin all good things
and bring them to fulfilment,
grant to us, who find joy in the Solemnity of the holy
    Mother of God,
that, just as we glory in the beginnings of your grace,
so one day we may rejoice in its completion.
Through Christ our Lord.

Preface I: The Motherhood of the Blessed Virgin Mary

The Lord be with you.
And with your spirit.

Lift up your hearts.
We lift them up to the Lord.

Let us give thanks to the Lord our God.
It is right and just.

It is truly right and just, our duty and our salvation,
always and everywhere to give you thanks,
Lord, holy Father, almighty and eternal God,
and to praise, bless, and glorify your name
on the Solemnity of the Motherhood
of the Blessed ever-Virgin Mary.

For by the overshadowing of the Holy Spirit
she conceived your Only Begotten Son,
and without losing the glory of virginity,
brought forth into the world the eternal Light,
Jesus Christ our Lord.

Through him the Angels praise your majesty,
Dominions adore and Powers tremble before you.
Heaven and the Virtues of heaven and the blessed Seraphim
worship together with exultation.
May our voices, we pray, join with theirs
in humble praise, as we acclaim:

Holy, Holy, Holy Lord God of hosts …

Communion Antiphon   Heb 13:8
Jesus Christ is the same yesterday, today, and for ever.

Prayer after Communion
We have received this heavenly Sacrament with joy, O Lord:
grant, we pray,
that it may lead us to eternal life,
for we rejoice to proclaim the blessed ever-Virgin Mary
Mother of your Son and Mother of the Church.
Through Christ our Lord.

Solemn Blessing
The Priest invites people to bow down for the blessing.
May God, who through the childbearing of the Blessed
    Virgin Mary
willed in his great kindness to redeem the human race,
be pleased to enrich you with his blessing.
Amen.

May you know always and everywhere the protection of her,
through whom you have been found worthy to receive the
    author of life.
Amen.

May you, who have devoutly gathered on this day,
carry away with you the gifts of spiritual joys and heavenly
    rewards.
Amen.

And may the blessing of almighty God,
the Father, and the Son, ✠ and the Holy Spirit,
come down on you and remain with you for ever.
Amen.

—————— 6 JANUARY ——————

THE EPIPHANY OF THE LORD

(Celebrated today in Ireland, England and Wales
and in Scotland on 8 January)

*In our deepest selves, each of us is a mystery: Where do I come from?
Where am I going? Why am I here? How should I live? The risk in
our present culture is to sleepwalk through life, to be satisfied with a
merely material existence. But the human "project" is much greater.
Each of us is really on a pilgrimage, a quest to become my true self,
in image and likeness of God. My truest self is found by being open
to God, in whom we live and move and have our being. By following
Jesus, by listening to our conscience and our inner selves, we come
home to God.*

Entrance Antiphon   Cf. Mal 3:1; 1 Chr 29:12
**Behold, the Lord, the Mighty One, has come;
and kingship is in his grasp, and power and dominion.**

Greeting, Penitential Rite, Gloria – pages 7-13.

Collect
O God, who on this day
revealed your Only Begotten Son to the nations
by the guidance of a star,
grant in your mercy

that we, who know you already by faith,
may be brought to behold the beauty of your sublime glory.
Through our Lord Jesus Christ, your Son,
who lives and reigns with you in the unity of the Holy Spirit,
one God, for ever and ever.

FIRST READING   Is 60:1-6
A reading from the prophet Isaiah.
Above you the glory of the Lord appears.

Arise, shine out Jerusalem, for your light has come,
the glory of the Lord is rising on you,
though night still covers the earth
and darkness the peoples.

Above you the Lord now rises
and above you his glory appears.
The nations come to your light
and kings to your dawning brightness.

Lift up your eyes and look round:
all are assembling and coming towards you,
your sons from far away
and daughters being tenderly carried.

At this sight you will grow radiant,
your heart throbbing and full;
since the riches of the sea will flow to you;
the wealth of the nations come to you;

camels in throngs will cover you,
and dromedaries of Midian and Ephah;
everyone in Sheba will come,
bringing gold and incense
and singing the praise of the Lord.

 The word of the Lord.

RESPONSORIAL PSALM   Ps 71:1-2.7-8.10-13

℟ **All nations shall fall prostrate before you, O Lord.**

1. O God, give your judgement to the king,
   to a king's son your justice,
   that he may judge your people in justice
   and your poor in right judgement. ℟

2. In his days justice shall flourish
   and peace till the moon fails.

He shall rule from sea to sea,
from the Great River to earth's bounds. ℟

3. The kings of Tarshish and the sea coasts
shall pay him tribute.
The kings of Sheba and Seba
shall bring him gifts.
Before him all kings shall fall prostrate,
all nations shall serve him. ℟

4. For he shall save the poor when they cry
and the needy who are helpless.
He will have pity on the weak
and save the lives of the poor. ℟

SECOND READING   Ep 3:2-3.5-6
A reading from the letter of St Paul to the Ephesians.
It has now been revealed that pagans share the same inheritance.

You have probably heard how I have been entrusted by God
with the grace he meant for you, and that it was by a revelation
that I was given the knowledge of the mystery. This mystery that
has now been revealed through the Spirit to his holy apostles
and prophets was unknown to any men in past generations; it
means that pagans now share the same inheritance, that they
are parts of the same body, and that the same promise has been
made to them, in Christ Jesus, through the gospel.

The word of the Lord.

GOSPEL ACCLAMATION   Mt 2:2
Alleluia, alleluia!
We saw his star as it rose
and have come to do the Lord homage.
Alleluia!

GOSPEL   Mt 2:1-12
A reading from the holy Gospel according to Matthew.
We saw his star and have come to do the king homage.

After Jesus had been born at Bethlehem in Judaea during the
reign of King Herod, some wise men came to Jerusalem from
the east. 'Where is the infant king of the Jews?' they asked. 'We
saw his star as it rose and have come to do him homage.' When
King Herod heard this he was perturbed, and so was the whole

of Jerusalem. He called together all the chief priests and the scribes of the people, and enquired of them where the Christ was to be born. 'At Bethlehem in Judaea', they told him 'for this is what the prophet wrote:

> And you, Bethlehem, in the land of Judah,
> you are by no means least among the leaders of Judah,
> for out of you will come a leader
> who will shepherd my people Israel.'

Then Herod summoned the wise men to see him privately. He asked them the exact date on which the star had appeared, and sent them on to Bethlehem. 'Go and find out all about the child', he said 'and when you have found him, let me know, so that I too may go and do him homage.' Having listened to what the king had to say, they set out. And there in front of them was the star they had seen rising; it went forward and halted over the place where the child was. The sight of the star filled them with delight, and going into the house they saw the child with his mother Mary, and falling to their knees they did him homage. Then, opening their treasures, they offered him gifts of gold and frankincense and myrrh. But they were warned in a dream not to go back to Herod, and returned to their own country by a different way.

The Gospel of the Lord.

Profession of Faith – pages 14-15.

Prayer over the Offerings

Look with favour, Lord, we pray,
on these gifts of your Church,
in which are offered now not gold or frankincense or myrrh,
but he who by them is proclaimed,
sacrificed and received, Jesus Christ.
Who lives and reigns for ever and ever.

Preface of the Epiphany of the Lord

The Lord be with you.
And with your spirit.

Lift up your hearts.
We lift them up to the Lord.

Let us give thanks to the Lord our God.
It is right and just.

It is truly right and just, our duty and our salvation,
always and everywhere to give you thanks,
Lord, holy Father, almighty and eternal God.

For today you have revealed the mystery
of our salvation in Christ
as a light for the nations,
and, when he appeared in our mortal nature,
you made us new by the glory of his immortal nature.

And so, with Angels and Archangels,
with Thrones and Dominions,
and with all the hosts and Powers of heaven,
we sing the hymn of your glory,
as without end we acclaim:

Holy, Holy, Holy Lord God of hosts …

Communion Antiphon   Cf. Mt 2:2

**We have seen his star in the East,
and have come with gifts to adore the Lord.**

Prayer after Communion
Go before us with heavenly light, O Lord,
always and everywhere,
that we may perceive with clear sight
and revere with true affection
the mystery in which you have willed us to participate.
Through Christ our Lord.

Solemn Blessing
The Priest invites people to bow down for the blessing.
May God, who has called you
out of darkness into his wonderful light,
pour out in kindness his blessing upon you
and make your hearts firm
in faith, hope and charity.
Amen.

And since in all confidence you follow Christ,
who today appeared in the world
as a light shining in darkness,
may God make you, too,
a light for your brothers and sisters.
Amen.

And so when your pilgrimage is ended,
may you come to him
whom the Magi sought as they followed the star
and whom they found with great joy, the Light from Light,
who is Christ the Lord.
Amen.

And may the blessing of almighty God,
the Father, and the Son, ✠ and the Holy Spirit,
come down on you and remain with you for ever.
Amen.

---

8 JANUARY

THE BAPTISM OF THE LORD

(Celebrated today in Ireland, England and Wales
and in Scotland on 9 January)

(In Scotland **The Ephipahy of the Lord**
is celebrated today – page 69)

*Begin by recalling some special moments between yourself and your
parents. Did you ever hear from them the equivalent of "This is my
son, my daughter, the beloved: my favour rests on you"? In Jesus'
ministry, on several occasions, he felt such a word from his Abba,
his Father. His baptism by John was one such moment, as was the
Transfiguration later on. Such deep love and affirmation grounded
him as a human being and as God's prophet to the people of Israel.
Our sense of calling grows out of our relationship with the Father,
whose beloved we are, whose favour we enjoy.*

Entrance Antiphon   Cf. Mt 3:16-17
**After the Lord was baptized, the heavens were opened,
and the Spirit descended upon him like a dove,
and the voice of the Father thundered:
This is my beloved Son, with whom I am well pleased.**

Greeting, Penitential Rite, Gloria – pages 7-13.

Collect
Almighty ever-living God,
who, when Christ had been baptized in the River Jordan
and as the Holy Spirit descended upon him,

solemnly declared him your beloved Son,
grant that your children by adoption,
reborn of water and the Holy Spirit,
may always be well pleasing to you.
Through our Lord Jesus Christ, your Son,
who lives and reigns with you in the unity of the Holy Spirit,
one God, for ever and ever.

    Or:

O God, whose Only Begotten Son
has appeared in our very flesh,
grant, we pray, that we may be inwardly transformed
through him whom we recognize as outwardly like ourselves.
Who lives and reigns with you in the unity of the Holy Spirit,
one God, for ever and ever.

FIRST READING   Is 42:1-4.6-7

A reading from the prophet Isaiah.
Here is my servant in whom my soul delights.

Thus says the Lord:
    Here is my servant whom I uphold,
    my chosen one in whom my soul delights.
    I have endowed him with my spirit
    that he may bring true justice to the nations.
    He does not cry out or shout aloud,
    or make his voice heard in the streets.
    He does not break the crushed reed,
    nor quench the wavering flame.
    Faithfully he brings true justice;
    he will neither waver, nor be crushed
    until true justice is established on earth,
    for the islands are awaiting his law.
    I, the Lord, have called you to serve the cause of right;
    I have taken you by the hand and formed you;
    I have appointed you as covenant of the people and light of
        the nations,
    to open the eyes of the blind,
    to free captives from prison,
    and those who live in darkness from the dungeon.

The word of the Lord.

RESPONSORIAL PSALM   Ps 28:1-4.9-10

℟ **The Lord will bless his people with peace.**

1. O give the Lord you sons of God,
    give the Lord glory and power;
    give the Lord the glory of his name.
    Adore the Lord in his holy court. ℟

2. The Lord's voice resounding on the waters,
    the Lord on the immensity of waters;
    the voice of the Lord, full of power,
    the voice of the Lord, full of splendour. ℟

3. The God of glory thunders.
    In his temple they all cry: 'Glory!'
    The Lord sat enthroned over the flood;
    the Lord sits as king for ever. ℟

SECOND READING   Acts 10:34-38

A reading from the Acts of the Apostles.
God anointed him with the Holy Spirit.

Peter addressed Cornelius and his household: 'The truth I have now come to realise' he said 'is that God does not have favourites, but that anybody of any nationality who fears God and does what is right is acceptable to him.

'It is true, God sent his word to the people of Israel, and it was to them that the good news of peace was brought by Jesus Christ – but Jesus Christ is Lord of all men. You must have heard about the recent happenings in Judaea; about Jesus of Nazareth and how he began in Galilee, after John had been preaching baptism. God had anointed him with the Holy Spirit and with power, and because God was with him, Jesus went about doing good and curing all who had fallen into the power of the devil.'

The word of the Lord.

GOSPEL ACCLAMATION   Mk 9:7

Alleluia, alleluia!
The heavens opened and the Father's voice resounded:
'This is my Son, the Beloved. Listen to him.'
Alleluia!

GOSPEL   Mt 3:13-17

A reading from the holy Gospel according to Matthew.

As soon as Jesus was baptised he saw the Spirit of God coming down on him.

Jesus came from Galilee to the Jordan to be baptised by John. John tried to dissuade him. 'It is I who need baptism from you,' he said 'and yet you come to me!' But Jesus replied, 'Leave it like this for the time being; it is fitting that we should, in this way, do all that righteousness demands.' At this, John gave in to him.

As soon as Jesus was baptised he came up from the water, and suddenly the heavens opened and he saw the Spirit of God descending like a dove and coming down on him. And a voice spoke from heaven, 'This is my Son, the Beloved; my favour rests on him.'

The Gospel of the Lord.

Profession of Faith – pages 14-15.

Prayer over the Offerings
Accept, O Lord, the offerings
we have brought to honour the revealing of your beloved Son,
so that the oblation of your faithful
may be transformed into the sacrifice of him
who willed in his compassion
to wash away the sins of the world.
Who lives and reigns for ever and ever.

Preface: The Baptism of the Lord
The Lord be with you.
And with your spirit.

Lift up your hearts.
We lift them up to the Lord.

Let us give thanks to the Lord our God.
It is right and just.

It is truly right and just, our duty and our salvation,
always and everywhere to give you thanks,
Lord, holy Father, almighty and eternal God.

For in the waters of the Jordan
you revealed with signs and wonders a new Baptism,
so that through the voice that came down from heaven
we might come to believe in your Word dwelling among us,

and by the Spirit's descending in the likeness of a dove
we might know that Christ your Servant
has been anointed with the oil of gladness
and sent to bring the good news to the poor.

And so, with the Powers of heaven,
we worship you constantly on earth,
and before your majesty
without end we acclaim:

Holy, Holy, Holy Lord God of hosts …

Communion Antiphon   Jn 1:32.34
**Behold the One of whom John said:
I have seen and testified that this is the Son of God.**

Prayer after Communion
Nourished with these sacred gifts,
we humbly entreat your mercy, O Lord,
that, faithfully listening to your Only Begotten Son,
we may be your children in name and in truth.
Through Christ our Lord.

Solemn Blessing – pages 57-59.

───────── 15 JANUARY ─────────
SECOND SUNDAY IN ORDINARY TIME

*In John's Gospel, the first thing that any human being says of Jesus
is found on the lips of John the Baptist: Look, there is the Lamb of
God. We think naturally and correctly of the Passover lamb and of
the Passover, the feast which marks the liberation of Israel. To be set
free is a wonderful experience and I could reflect on how I experience
my freedom in Christ. From what have I been set free? (For example,
fear of death, the risk of absurdity, sins and false directions in life…).
Even more important, for what have I been set free?*

Entrance Antiphon   Ps 65:4
**All the earth shall bow down before you, O God,
and shall sing to you,
shall sing to your name, O Most High!**

Greeting, Penitential Rite, Gloria – pages 7-13.

Collect

Almighty ever-living God,
who govern all things,
both in heaven and on earth,
mercifully hear the pleading of your people
and bestow your peace on our times.
Through our Lord Jesus Christ, your Son,
who lives and reigns with you in the unity of the Holy Spirit,
one God, for ever and ever.

FIRST READING   Is 49:3.5-6

A reading from the prophet Isaiah.

*I will make you the light of the nations so that my salvation may reach to the
ends of the earth.*

The Lord said to me, 'Yor are my servant, Israel,
in whom I shall be glorified';
I was honoured in the eyes of the Lord,
my God was my strength.
And now the Lord has spoken,
he who formed me in the womb to be his servant,
to bring Jacob back to him,
to gather Israel to him:

> 'It is not enough for you to be my servant,
> to restore the tribes of Jacob and bring back the survivors
>   of Israel;
> I will make you the light of the nations
> so that my salvation may reach to the ends of the earth.'

The word of the Lord.

RESPONSORIAL PSALM   Ps 39:2.4.7-10

℟ **Here I am, Lord!**
   I come to do your will.

1. I waited, I waited for the Lord
   and he stooped down to me;
   he heard my cry.
   He put a new song into my mouth,
   praise of our God. ℟

2. You do not ask for sacrifice and offerings,
   but an open ear.

You do not ask for holocaust and victim.
Instead, here am I. ℟

3. In the scroll of the book it stands written
   that I should do your will.
   My God, I delight in your law
   in the depth of my heart. ℟

4. Your justice I have proclaimed
   in the great assembly.
   My lips I have not sealed;
   you know it, O Lord. ℟

SECOND READING   1 Cor 1:1-3

A reading from the first letter of St Paul to the Corinthians.
May God our Father and the Lord Jesus Christ send you grace and peace.

I, Paul, appointed by God to be an apostle, together with
brother Sosthenes, send greetings to the church of God in
Corinth, to the holy people of Jesus Christ, who are called to
take their place among all the saints everywhere who pray to
our Lord Jesus Christ; for he is their Lord no less than ours. May
God our Father and the Lord Jesus Christ send you grace and
peace.

    The word of the Lord.

GOSPEL ACCLAMATION   Lk 19:38.2:14

Alleluia, alleluia!
Blessings on the King who comes,
in the name of the Lord!
Peace in heaven
and glory in the highest heavens! Alleluia!
    Or: Jn 1:14.12

Alleluia, alleluia!
The Word was made flesh and lived among us;
to all who did accept him
he gave power to become children of God.
Alleluia!

GOSPEL   Jn 1:29-34

A reading from the holy Gospel according to John.
Look, there is the lamb of God that takes away the sin of the world.

Seeing Jesus coming towards him, John said, 'Look, there
is the lamb of God that takes away the sin of the world. This

is the one I spoke of when I said: A man is coming after me who ranks before me because he existed before me. I did not know him myself, and yet it was to reveal him to Israel that I came baptising with water.' John also declared, 'I saw the Spirit coming down on him from heaven like a dove and resting on him. I did not know him myself, but he who sent me to baptise with water had said to me, "The man on whom you see the Spirit come down and rest is the one who is going to baptise with the Holy Spirit." Yes, I have seen and I am the witness that he is the Chosen One of God.'

The Gospel of the Lord.

Profession of Faith – pages 14-15.

Prayer over the Offerings

Grant us, O Lord, we pray,
that we may participate worthily in these mysteries,
for whenever the memorial of this sacrifice is celebrated
the work of our redemption is accomplished.
Through Christ our Lord.

Preface I-VIII of Sundays in Ordinary Time – pages 23-26.

Communion Antiphon   Cf. Ps 22:5

**You have prepared a table before me,
and how precious is the chalice that quenches my thirst.**

    Or: 1 Jn 4:16

**We have come to know and to believe
in the love that God has for us.**

Prayer after Communion

Pour on us, O Lord, the Spirit of your love,
and in your kindness
make those you have nourished
by this one heavenly Bread
one in mind and heart.
Through Christ our Lord.

Solemn Blessing – pages 57-59.

22 JANUARY
THIRD SUNDAY IN ORDINARY TIME

The heart of Jesus' proclamation is given in today's Gospel. As is often noted, the word "repent" is not the best translation of the original Greek and it would be better to use some other expression such as "convert." It really means a new way of looking at everything, a new mind or outlook. It may of course include being sorry about the past, but the real energy is towards the future: "convert and put your trust in the Good News." We could put it like this: from what are we called to conversion is important; more important is towards what are we being called?

Entrance Antiphon   Cf. Ps 95:1.6

O sing a new song to the Lord;
sing to the Lord, all the earth.
In his presence are majesty and splendour,
strength and honour in his holy place.

Greeting, Penitential Rite, Gloria – pages 7-13.

Collect

Almighty ever-living God,
direct our actions according to your good pleasure,
that in the name of your beloved Son
we may abound in good works.
Through our Lord Jesus Christ, your Son,
who lives and reigns with you in the unity of the Holy Spirit,
one God, for ever and ever.

FIRST READING   Is 8:23-9:3

A reading from the prophet Isaiah.
In Galilee of the nations the people has seen a great light.

In days past the Lord humbled the land of Zebulun and the land of Naphtali, but in days to come he will confer glory on the Way of the Sea on the far side of Jordan, province of the nations.

The people that walked in darkness
has seen a great light;
on those who live in a land of deep shadow
a light has shone.
You have made their gladness greater,
you have made their joy increase;

they rejoice in your presence
as men rejoice at harvest time,
as men are happy when they are dividing the spoils.

For the yoke that was weighing on him,
the bar across his shoulders,
the rod of his oppressor,
these you break as on the day of Midian.

   The word of the Lord.

RESPONSORIAL PSALM   Ps 26:1.4.13-14

℟ **The Lord is my light and my help.**

1. The Lord is my light and my help;
   whom shall I fear?
   The Lord is the stronghold of my life;
   before whom shall I shrink? ℟

2. There is one thing I ask of the Lord,
   for this I long,
   to live in the house of the Lord,
   all the days of my life,
   to savour the sweetness of the Lord,
   to behold his temple. ℟

3. I am sure I shall see the Lord's goodness
   in the land of the living.
   Hope in him, hold firm and take heart.
   Hope in the Lord! ℟

SECOND READING   1 Cor 1:10-13.17

A reading from the first letter of St Paul to the Corinthians.

Make up the differences between you instead of disagreeing among yourselves.

I appeal to you, brothers, for the sake of our Lord Jesus Christ,
to make up the differences between you, and instead of
disagreeing among yourselves, to be united again in your belief
and practice. From what Chloe's people have been telling me,
my dear brothers, it is clear that there are serious differences
among you. What I mean are all these slogans that you have,
like: 'I am for Paul', 'I am for Apollos', 'I am for Cephas', 'I am
for Christ'. Has Christ been parcelled out? Was it Paul that was
crucified for you? Were you baptised in the name of Paul?

   For Christ did not send me to baptise, but to preach the

Good News, and not to preach that in the terms of philosophy in which the crucifixion of Christ cannot be expressed.

The word of the Lord.

GOSPEL ACCLAMATION   Cf. Mt 4:23
Alleluia, alleluia!
Jesus proclaimed the Good News of the kingdom,
and cured all kinds of sickness among the people.
Alleluia!

GOSPEL   Mt 4:12-23

(For Shorter Form, read between ♦ ♦).

A reading from the holy Gospel according to Matthew.

He went and settled in Capernaum: in this way the prophecy of Isaiah was to be fulfilled.

♦Hearing that John had been arrested Jesus went back to Galilee, and leaving Nazareth he went and settled in Capernaum, a lakeside town on the borders of Zebulun and Naphtali. In this way the prophecy of Isaiah was to be fulfilled:

Land of Zebulun! Land of Naphtali!
Way of the sea on the far side of Jordan,
Galilee of the nations!
The people that lived in darkness
has seen a great light;
on those who dwell in the land and shadow of death
a light has dawned.

From that moment Jesus began his preaching with the message, 'Repent, for the kingdom of heaven is close at hand.'♦

As he was walking by the Sea of Galilee he saw two brothers, Simon, who was called Peter, and his brother Andrew; they were making a cast in the lake with their net, for they were fishermen. And he said to them, 'Follow me and I will make you fishers of men.' And they left their nets at once and followed him.

Going on from there he saw another pair of brothers, James son of Zebedee and his brother John; they were in their boat with their father Zebedee, mending their nets, and he called them. At once, leaving the boat and their father, they followed him.

He went round the whole of Galilee teaching in their synagogues, proclaiming the Good News of the kingdom and curing all kinds of diseases and sickness among the people.

The Gospel of the Lord.

Profession of Faith – pages 14-15.

Prayer over the Offerings

Accept our offerings, O Lord, we pray,
and in sanctifying them
grant that they may profit us for salvation.
Through Christ our Lord.

Preface I-VIII of Sundays in Ordinary Time – pages 23-26.

Communion Antiphon   Cf. Ps 33:6

**Look towards the Lord and be radiant;
let your faces not be abashed.**

    Or: Jn 8:12

**I am the light of the world, says the Lord;
whoever follows me will not walk in darkness,
but will have the light of life.**

Prayer after Communion

Grant, we pray, almighty God,
that, receiving the grace
by which you bring us to new life,
we may always glory in your gift.
Through Christ our Lord.

Solemn Blessing – pages 57-59.

29 JANUARY
FOURTH SUNDAY IN ORDINARY TIME

Matthew's gospel was written with a particular community or church in mind. In this sense, it is a community book. It provided the basis on which a group could build its life and structures. It also allowed the members to develop an understanding of the relationship between the past, the present and the future.

Entrance Antiphon   Ps 105:47

Save us, O Lord our God!
And gather us from the nations,
to give thanks to your holy name,
and make it our glory to praise you.

Greeting, Penitential Rite, Gloria – pages 7-13.

Collect

Grant us, Lord our God,
that we may honour you with all our mind,
and love everyone in truth of heart.
Through our Lord Jesus Christ, your Son,
who lives and reigns with you in the unity of the Holy Spirit,
one God, for ever and ever.

FIRST READING   Zp 2:3;3:12-13

A reading from the prophet Zephaniah.
In your midst I will leave a humble and a lowly people.

Seek the Lord
all you, the humble of the earth,
who obey his commands.
Seek integrity, seek humility:
you may perhaps find shelter
on the day of the anger of the Lord.
In your midst I will leave
a humble and lowly people,
and those who are left in Israel will seek refuge in the name of
    the Lord.
They will do no wrong,
will tell no lies;
and the perjured tongue will no longer
be found in their mouths.

But they will be able to graze and rest
with no one to disturb them.

The word of the Lord.

RESPONSORIAL PSALM   Ps 145:7-10

℟ **How happy are the poor in spirit;**
  theirs is the kingdom of heaven.

1. It is the Lord who keeps faith for ever,
    who is just to those who are oppressed.
    It is he who gives bread to the hungry,
    the Lord, who sets prisoners free. ℟

2. It is the Lord who gives sight to the blind,
    who raises up those who are bowed down,
    the Lord, who protects the stranger
    and upholds the widow and orphan. ℟

3. It is the Lord who loves the just
    but thwarts the path of the wicked.
    The Lord will reign for ever,
    Zion's God, from age to age. ℟

SECOND READING   1 Cor 1:26-31

A reading from the first letter of St Paul to the Corinthians.

God chose what is foolish by human reckoning.

Take yourselves, brothers, at the time when you were called: how
many of you were wise in the ordinary sense of the word, how
many were influential people, or came from noble families?
No, it was to shame the wise that God chose what is foolish by
human reckoning, and to shame what is strong that he chose
what is weak by human reckoning; those whom the world
thinks common and contemptible are the ones that God has
chosen — those who are nothing at all to show up those who
are everything. The human race has nothing to boast about to
God, but you, God has made members of Christ Jesus and by
God's doing he has become our wisdom, and our virtue, and
our holiness, and our freedom. As scripture says: if anyone wants
to boast, let him boast about the Lord.

The word of the Lord.

GOSPEL ACCLAMATION   Mt 11:25

Alleluia, alleluia!
Blessed are you, Father,
Lord of heaven and earth,
for revealing the mysteries of the kingdom
to mere children.
Alleluia!

        Or   Mt 5:12

Alleluia, alleluia!
Rejoice and be glad:
your reward will be great in heaven.
Alleluia!

GOSPEL   Mt 5:1-12

A reading from the holy Gospel according to Matthew.

How happy are the poor in spirit.

Seeing the crowds, Jesus went up the hill. There he sat down and was joined by his disciples. Then he began to speak. This is what he taught them:

'How happy are the poor in spirit;
theirs is the kingdom of heaven.
Happy the gentle:
they shall have the earth for their heritage.
Happy those who mourn:
they shall be comforted.
Happy those who hunger and thirst for what is right:
they shall be satisfied.
Happy the merciful:
they shall have mercy shown them.
Happy the pure in heart:
they shall see God.
Happy the peacemakers:
they shall be called sons of God.
Happy those who are persecuted in the cause of right:
theirs is the kingdom of heaven.

'Happy are you when people abuse you and persecute you and speak all kinds of calumny against you on my account. Rejoice and be glad, for your reward will be great in heaven.'

The Gospel of the Lord.

Profession of Faith – pages 14-15.

Prayer over the Offerings

O Lord, we bring to your altar
these offerings of our service:
be pleased to receive them, we pray,
and transform them
into the Sacrament of our redemption.
Through Christ our Lord.

Preface of Sundays in Ordinary Time I-VIII – pages 23-26.

Communion Antiphon   Ps 30:17-18

Let your face shine on your servant.
Save me in your merciful love.
O Lord, let me never be put to shame, for I call on you.

Or   Mt 5:3-4

Blessed are the poor in spirit,
for theirs is the kingdom of heaven.
Blessed are the meek, for they shall possess the land.

Prayer after Communion

Nourished by these redeeming gifts,
we pray, O Lord,
that through this help to eternal salvation
true faith may ever increse.
Through Christ our Lord.

Solemn Blessing –pages 57-59.

5 FEBRUARY
FIFTH SUNDAY IN ORDINARY TIME

*We can easily see how Jesus should be the light of the world. Even
though the words are familiar, we are perhaps unaccustomed to
reflecting on ourselves as the light of the world and salt of the earth.
This is an act of profound trust in us by God. Jesus has faith in us to
be bearers of his Good News in our time. How are we to be that? Not
first by our words or even by our deeds. We are the light and salt on
account of who we are as disciples. As the Gospel text puts it, a city
built on a hilltop cannot be hidden. We cannot help being seen as his
disciples, for that is who we are.*

Entrance Antiphon   Ps 94:6-7

**O come, let us worship God
and bow low before the God who made us,
for he is the Lord our God.**

Greeting, Penitential Rite, Gloria – pages 7-13.

Collect

Keep your family safe, O Lord, with unfailing care,
that, relying solely on the hope of heavenly grace,
they may be defended always by your protection.
Through our Lord Jesus Christ, your Son,
who lives and reigns with you in the unity of the Holy Spirit,
one God, for ever and ever.

FIRST READING   Is 58:7-10

A reading from the prophet Isaiah.
Then will your light shine like the dawn.

Thus says the Lord:

Share your bread with the hungry,
and shelter the homeless poor,
clothe the man you see to be naked
and turn not from your own kin.
Then will your light shine like the dawn
and your wound be quickly healed over.
Your integrity will go before you
and the glory of the Lord behind you.
Cry, and the Lord will answer;

call, and he will say, 'I am here.'
If you do away with the yoke,
the clenched fist, the wicked word,
if you give your bread to the hungry,
and relief to the oppressed,
your light will rise in the darkness,
and your shadows become like noon.

The word of the Lord.

RESPONSORIAL PSALM   Ps 111:4-9

℞ **The good man is a light in the darkness for the upright.**

1. He is a light in the darkness for the upright:
   he is generous, merciful and just.
   The good man takes pity and lends,
   he conducts his affairs with honour. ℞

2. The just man will never waver:
   he will be remembered for ever.
   He has no fear of evil news;
   with a firm heart he trusts in the Lord. ℞

3. With a steadfast heart he will not fear;
   open-handed, he gives to the poor;
   his justice stands firm for ever.
   His head will be raised in glory. ℞

SECOND READING   1 Cor 2:1-5

A reading from the first letter of St Paul to the Corinthians.

During my stay with you, the only knowledge I claimed to have was about Jesus as the crucified Christ.

When I came to you, brothers, it was not with any show of oratory or philosophy, but simply to tell you what God had guaranteed. During my stay with you, the only knowledge I claimed to have was about Jesus, and only about him as the crucified Christ. Far from relying on any power of my own, I came among you in great 'fear and trembling' and in my speeches and sermons that I gave, there were none of the arguments that belong to philosophy; only a demonstration of the power of the Spirit. And I did this so that your faith should not depend on human philosophy but on the power of God.

The word of the Lord.

GOSPEL ACCLAMATION   Jn 8:12
Alleluia, alleluia!
I am the light of the world, says the Lord,
anyone who follows me
will have the light of life.
Alleluia!

GOSPEL   Mt 5:13-16
A reading from the holy Gospel according to Matthew.
You are the light of the world.

Jesus said to his disciples: 'You are the salt of the earth. But if
the salt becomes tasteless, what can make it salty again? It is
good for nothing, and can only be thrown out to be trampled
underfoot by men.

'You are the light of the world. A city built on a hill-top
cannot be hidden. No one lights a lamp to put it under a tub;
they put it on the lamp-stand where it shines for everyone in
the house. In the same way your light must shine in the sight of
men, so that, seeing your good works, they may give praise to
your Father in heaven.'

The Gospel of the Lord.

Profession of Faith – pages 14-15.

Prayer over the Offerings
O Lord our God,
who once established these created things
to sustain us in our frailty,
grant, we pray,
that they may become for us now
the Sacrament of eternal life.
Through Christ our Lord.

Preface I-VIII of Sundays in Ordinary Time – pages 23-26.

Communion Antiphon   Cf. Ps 106:8-9
Let them thank the Lord for his mercy,
his wonders for the children of men
for he satisfies the thirsty soul,
and the hungry he fills with good things.

     Or: Mt 5:5-6
Blessed are those who mourn, for they shall be consoled.

Blessed are those who hunger and thirst for righteousness, for they shall have their fill.

Prayer after Communion

O God, who have willed that we be partakers
in the one Bread and the one Chalice,
grant us, we pray, so to live
that, made one in Christ,
we may joyfully bear fruit
for the salvation of the world.
Through Christ our Lord.

Solemn Blessing – pages 57-59.

=== 12 FEBRUARY ===

SIXTH SUNDAY IN ORDINARY TIME

It is clear already in the Old Testament that it is not our misdeeds which accuse us before God, but our hearts, fractured and divided as they are. Consistent with Israelite teaching, Jesus insists that we go deeper than our external deeds. The important question is what is going on in our hearts, the source of inner thoughts and motivations? The teaching is presented using various examples, presented sometimes with great simplicity, other times with irony and wit.

Entrance Antiphon   Cf. Ps 30:3-4

**Be my protector, O God,
a mighty stronghold to save me.
For you are my rock, my stronghold!
Lead me, guide me, for the sake of your name.**

Greeting, Penitential Rite, Gloria – pages 7-13.

Collect

O God, who teach us that you abide
in hearts that are just and true,
grant that we may be so fashioned by your grace
as to become a dwelling pleasing to you.
Through our Lord Jesus Christ, your Son,
who lives and reigns with you in the unity of the Holy Spirit,
one God, for ever and ever.

FIRST READING   Eccles 15:15-20

A reading from the book of Ecclesiasticus.

He never commanded anyone to be godless.

If you wish, you can keep the commandments,
to behave faithfully is within your power.
He has set fire and water before you;
put out your hand to whichever you prefer.
Man has life and death before him;
whichever a man likes better will be given him.
For vast is the wisdom of the Lord;
he is almighty and all-seeing.
His eyes are on those who fear him,
he notes every action of man.
He never commanded anyone to be godless,
he has given no one permission to sin.

  The word of the Lord.

RESPONSORIAL PSALM   Ps 118:1-2.4-5.17-18.33-34

℟ **They are happy who follow God's law!**

1. They are happy whose life is blameless,
    who follow God's law!
    They are happy those who do his will,
    seeking him with all their hearts. ℟

2. You have laid down your precepts
    to be obeyed with care.
    May my footsteps be firm
    to obey your statutes. ℟

3. Bless your servant and I shall live
    and obey your word.
    Open my eyes that I may consider
    the wonders of your law. ℟

4. Teach me the demands of your statutes
    and I will keep them to the end.
    Train me to observe your law,
    to keep it with my heart. ℟

SECOND READING   1 Cor 2:6-10

A reading from the first letter of St Paul to the Corinthians.

God predestined wisdom to be for our glory before the ages began.

We have a wisdom to offer those who have reached maturity:

not a philosophy of our age, it is true, still less of the masters of our age, which are coming to their end. The hidden wisdom of God which we teach in our mysteries is the wisdom that God predestined to be for our glory before the ages began. It is a wisdom that none of the masters of this age have ever known, or they would not have crucified the Lord of Glory; we teach what scripture calls: the things that no eye has seen and no ear has heard, things beyond the mind of man, all that God has prepared for those who love him.

These are the very things that God has revealed to us through the Spirit, for the Spirit reaches the depths of everything, even the depths of God.

The word of the Lord.

GOSPEL ACCLAMATION   1 S 3:9; Jn 6:68
Alleluia, alleluia!
Speak, Lord, your servant is listening:
you have the message of eternal life.
Alleluia!
   Or: Cf. Mt 11:25
Alleluia, alleluia!
Blessed are you, Father,
Lord of heaven and earth,
for revealing the mysteries of the kingdom
to mere children.
Alleluia!

GOSPEL   Mt 5:17-37

(For Shorter Form, read between ♦ ♦).

A reading from the holy Gospel according to Matthew.
You have learnt how it was said to your ancestors; but I say this to you.

| ♦Jesus said to his disciples:♦ 'Do not imagine that I have come to abolish the Law or the Prophets. I have come not to abolish them but to complete them. I tell you solemnly, till heaven and earth disappear, not one dot, one little stroke, shall disappear from the Law until its purpose is achieved. Therefore, the man who infringes even one of the least of these commandments and teaches others to do the same will be considered the least in the kingdom of heaven; but the man who keeps them and teaches them will be considered great in the kingdom of heaven.

'For ♦I tell you, if your virtue goes no deeper than that of the scribes and the Pharisees, you will never get into the kingdom of heaven.

'You have learnt how it was said to our ancestors: You must not kill; and if anyone does kill he must answer for it before the court. But I say this to you: anyone who is angry with his brother will answer for it before the court;♦ if a man calls his brother "Fool" he will answer for it before the Sanhedrin; and if a man calls him "Renegade" he will answer for it in hell fire. So then, if you are bringing your offering to the altar and there remember that your brother has something against you, leave your offering there before the altar, go and be reconciled with your brother first, and then come back and present your offering. Come to terms with your opponent in good time while you are still on the way to the court with him, or he may hand you over to the judge and the judge to the officer, and you will be thrown into prison. I tell you solemnly, you will not get out till you have paid the last penny.

♦You have learnt how it was said: You must not commit adultery. But I say this to you: if a man looks at a woman lustfully, he has already committed adultery with her in his heart.♦ If your right eye should cause you to sin, tear it out and throw it away; for it will do you less harm to lose one part of you than to have your whole body thrown into hell. And if your right hand should cause you to sin, cut it off and throw it away; for it will do you less harm to lose one part of you than to have your whole body go to hell.

'It has also been said: Anyone who divorces his wife must give her a writ of dismissal. But I say this to you: everyone who divorces his wife, except for the case of fornication, makes her an adulteress; and anyone who marries a divorced woman commits adultery.

♦'Again, you have learnt how it was said to our ancestors: You must not break your oath, but must fulfil your oaths to the Lord. But I say this to you: do not swear at all,♦ either by heaven, since that is God's throne; or by the earth, since that is his footstool; or by Jerusalem, since that is the city of the great king. Do not swear by your own head either, since you cannot turn a single hair white or black. ♦All you need say is "Yes" if you mean yes,

"No" if you mean no; anything more than this comes from the evil one.' ✦

The Gospel of the Lord.

Profession of Faith – pages 14-15.

Prayer over the Offerings

May this oblation, O Lord, we pray,
cleanse and renew us
and may it become for those who do your will
the source of eternal reward.
Through Christ our Lord.

Preface of Sundays in Ordinary Time I-VIII – pages 23-26.

Communion Antiphon   Cf. Ps 77:29-30

They ate and had their fill,
and what they craved the Lord gave them;
they were not disappointed in what they craved.

    Or: Jn 3:16

God so loved the world
that he gave his Only Begotten Son,
so that all who believe in him may not perish,
but may have eternal life.

Prayer after Communion

Having fed upon these heavenly delights,
we pray, O Lord,
that we may always long
for that food by which we truly live.
Through Christ our Lord.

Solemn Blessing – pages 57-59.

19 FEBRUARY
SEVENTH SUNDAY IN ORDINARY TIME

Today's gospel continues the challenge from last week to go deeper into the heart, the seat of hidden thoughts and desires. The call to conversion is a call to give just as we have received: we are loved and so should love; we are forgiven and so should forgive; we are consoled and so should console and so forth. Why is that? Because the love, the forgiveness, etc., that we have received becomes truly "me" only when I pass it on. Only then have I experienced the message of the prophet: I will remove from your body the heart of stone and give you a heart of flesh (Ezk 36:26).

Entrance Antiphon   Ps 12:6

O Lord, I trust in your merciful love.
My heart will rejoice in your salvation.
I will sing to the Lord who has been bountiful with me.

Greeting, Penitential Rite, Gloria – pages 7-13.

Collect
Grant, we pray, almighty God,
that, always pondering spiritual things,
we may carry out in both word and deed
that which is pleasing to you.
Through our Lord Jesus Christ, your Son,
who lives and reigns with you in the unity of the Holy Spirit,
one God, for ever and ever.

FIRST READING   Lv 19:1-2.17-18
A reading from the book of Leviticus.
You must love your neighbour as yourself.

The Lord spoke to Moses; he said: 'Speak to the whole community of the sons of Israel and say to them: "Be holy, for I, the Lord your God, am holy.

"You must not bear hatred for your brother in your heart. You must openly tell him, your neighbour, of his offence; this way you will not take a sin upon yourself. You must not exact vengeance, nor must you bear a grudge against the children of your people. You must love your neighbour as yourself. I am the Lord."'

The word of the Lord.

RESPONSORIAL PSALM   Ps 102:1-4.8.10.12-13

℟ **The Lord is compassion and love.**

1. My soul, give thanks to the Lord,
    all my being, bless his holy name.
    My soul, give thanks to the Lord
    and never forget all his blessings. ℟

2. It is he who forgives all your guilt,
    who heals every one of your ills,
    who redeems your life from the grave,
    who crowns you with love and compassion. ℟

3. The Lord is compassion and love,
    slow to anger and rich in mercy.
    He does not treat us according to our sins
    nor repay us according to our faults. ℟

4. As far as the east is from the west
    so far does he remove our sins.
    As a father has compassion on his sons,
    the Lord has pity on those who fear him. ℟

SECOND READING   1 Cor 3:16-23

A reading from the first letter of St Paul to the Corinthians.

All are your servants, but you belong to Christ and Christ belongs to God.

Didn't you realize that you were God's temple and that the Spirit of God was living among you? If anybody should destroy the temple of God, God will destroy him, because the temple of God is sacred; and you are that temple.

Make no mistake about it: if any one of you thinks of himself as wise, in the ordinary sense of the word, then he must learn to be a fool before he really can be wise. Why? Because the wisdom of this world is foolishness to God. As scripture says: The Lord knows wise men's thoughts: he knows how useless they are, or again: God is not convinced by the arguments of the wise. So there is nothing to boast about in anything human: Paul, Apollos, Cephas, the world, life and death, the present and the future, are all your servants; but you belong to Christ and Christ belongs to God.

The word of the Lord.

GOSPEL ACCLAMATION   Jn 14:23

Alleluia, alleluia!
If anyone loves me he will keep my word,
and my Father will love him,
and we shall come to him.
Alleluia!

   Or: 1 Jn 2:5

Alleluia, alleluia!
When anyone obeys what Christ has said,
God's love comes to perfection in him.
Alleluia!

GOSPEL   Mt 5:38-48

A reading from the holy Gospel according to Matthew.
Love your enemies.

Jesus said to his disciples: 'You have learnt how it was said:
Eye for eye and tooth for tooth. But I say this to you: offer the
wicked man no resistance. On the contrary, if anyone hits you
on the right cheek, offer him the other as well; if a man takes
you to law and would have your tunic, let him have your cloak
as well. And if anyone orders you to go one mile, go two miles
with him. Give to anyone who asks, and if anyone wants to
borrow, do not turn away.

   'You have learnt how it was said: You must love your
neighbour and hate your enemy. But I say this to you: love your
enemies and pray for those who persecute you; in this way you
will be sons of your Father in heaven, for he causes his sun to
rise on bad men as well as good, and his rain to fall on honest
and dishonest men alike. For if you love those who love you,
what right have you to claim any credit? Even the tax collectors
do as much, do they not? And if you save your greetings for your
brothers, are you doing anything exceptional? Even the pagans
do as much, do they not? You must therefore be perfect as your
heavenly Father is perfect.'

   The Gospel of the Lord.

Profession of Faith – pages 14-15.

Prayer over the Offerings
As we celebrate your mysteries, O Lord,
with the observance that is your due,

we humbly ask you,
that what we offer to the honour of your majesty
may profit us for salvation.
Through Christ our Lord.

Preface of Sundays in Ordinary Time I-VIII – pages 23-26.

Communion Antiphon   Ps 9:2-3
**I will recount all your wonders,
I will rejoice in you and be glad,
and sing psalms to your name, O Most High.**
　　Or: Jn 11:27
**Lord, I have come to believe that you are the Christ,
the Son of the living God, who is coming into this world.**

Prayer after Communion
Grant, we pray, almighty God,
that we may experience the effects of the salvation
which is pledged to us by these mysteries.
Through Christ our Lord.

Solemn Blessing – pages 57-59.

22 FEBRUARY
ASH WEDNESDAY

Our word "Lent" comes from an old English word lencten, meaning to lengthen or to grow longer. These days, at least in the Northern Hemisphere, each day there are two minutes more light in the morning and two minutes more light in the evening. So, "Lent" really means springtime. This tells us precisely what is supposed to happen in this springtime of the faith: new shoots, spring growth, signs of life and joy. So, whatever I undertake this Lent, may it lead to a new springtime of faith for me and my community.

Entrance Antiphon   Ws 11:24.25.27

**You are merciful to all, O Lord,
and despise nothing that you have made.
You overlook people's sins, to bring them to repentance,
and you spare them, for you are the Lord our God.**

The Penitential Act is omitted, and the Distribution of Ashes takes its place – see below. The Gloria is not said.

Collect

Grant, O Lord, that we may begin with holy fasting
this campaign of Christian service,
so that, as we take up battle against spiritual evils,
we may be armed with weapons of self-restraint.
Through our Lord Jesus Christ, your Son,
who lives and reigns with you in the unity of the Holy Spirit,
one God, for ever and ever.

FIRST READING   Jl 2:12-18

A reading from the prophet Joel.

Let your hearts be broken, not your garments torn.

'Now, now – it is the Lord who speaks –
come back to me with all your heart,
fasting, weeping, mourning.'
Let your hearts be broken not your garments torn,
turn to the Lord your God again,
for he is all tenderness and compassion,
slow to anger, rich in graciousness,
and ready to relent.
Who knows if he will not turn again, will not relent,

will not leave a blessing as he passes,
oblation and libation
for the Lord your God?
Sound the trumpet in Zion!
Order a fast,
proclaim a solemn assembly,
call the people together,
summon the community,
assemble the elders,
gather the children,
even the infants at the breast.
Let the bridegroom leave his bedroom
and the bride her alcove.
Between vestibule and altar let the priests,
the ministers of the Lord, lament.
Let them say,
'Spare your people, Lord!
Do not make your heritage a thing of shame,
a byword for the nations.
Why should it be said among the nations,
"Where is their God?" '
Then the Lord, jealous on behalf of his land,
took pity on his people.

The word of the Lord.

RESPONSORIAL PSALM   Ps 50:3-6.12-14.17

℟ **Have mercy on us, O Lord, for we have sinned.**

1. Have mercy on me, God, in your kindness.
    In your compassion blot out my offence.
    O wash me more and more from my guilt
    and cleanse me from my sin. ℟

2. My offences truly I know them;
    my sin is always before me.
    Against you, you alone, have I sinned:
    what is evil in your sight I have done. ℟

3. A pure heart create for me, O God,
    put a steadfast spirit within me.
    Do not cast me away from your presence,
    nor deprive me of your holy spirit. ℟

4. Give me again the joy of your help;
    with a spirit of fervour sustain me.
    O Lord, open my lips
    and my mouth shall declare your praise.

SECOND READING   2 Cor 5:20–6:2

A reading from the second letter of St Paul to the Corinthians.

Be reconciled to God… now is the favourable time.

We are ambassadors for Christ; it is as though God were
appealing through us, and the appeal that we make in Christ's
name is: be reconciled to God. For our sake God made the
sinless one into sin, so that in him we might become the
goodness of God. As his fellow workers, we beg you once again
not to neglect the grace of God that you have received. For he
says: At the favourable time, I have listened to you; on the day of
salvation I came to your help. Well, now is the favourable time;
this is the day of salvation.

The word of the Lord.

GOSPEL ACCLAMATION   Ps 50:12.14

Praise to you, O Christ, king of eternal glory!
A pure heart create for me, O God,
and give me again the joy of your help.
Praise to you, O Christ, king of eternal glory!

   Or: Cf. Ps 94:8

Praise to you, O Christ, king of eternal glory!
Harden not your hearts today,
but listen to the voice of the Lord.
Praise to you, O Christ, King of eternal glory!

GOSPEL   Mt 6:1-6.16-18

A reading from the holy Gospel according to Matthew.

Your Father, who sees all that is done in secret, will reward you.

Jesus said to his disciples:

   'Be careful not to parade your good deeds before men to
attract their notice; by doing this you will lose all reward from
your Father in heaven. So when you give alms, do not have it
trumpeted before you; this is what the hypocrites do in the
synagogues and in the streets to win men's admiration. I tell you
solemnly, they have had their reward. But when you give alms,
your left hand must not know what your right is doing; your

almsgiving must be secret, and your Father who sees all that is done in secret will reward you.

'And when you pray, do not imitate the hypocrites: they love to say their prayers standing up in the synagogues and at the street corners for people to see them. I tell you solemnly, they have had their reward. But when you pray go to your private room and, when you have shut your door, pray to your Father who is in that secret place, and your Father who sees all that is done in secret will reward you.

'When you fast do not put on a gloomy look as the hypocrites do: they pull long faces to let men know they are fasting. I tell you solemnly, they have had their reward. But when you fast, put oil on your head and wash your face, so that no one will know you are fasting except your Father who sees all that is done in secret; and your Father who sees all that is done in secret will reward you.'

The Gospel of the Lord.

Blessing and Distribution of Ashes

After the Homily, the Priest, standing with hands joined, says:

Dear brethren (brothers and sisters),
let us humbly ask God our Father
that he be pleased to bless with the abundance of his grace
these ashes, which we will put on our heads in penitence.

After a brief prayer in silence, and, with hands extended, he continues:

O God, who are moved by acts of humility
and respond with forgiveness to works of penance,
lend your merciful ear to our prayers
and in your kindness pour out the grace of your ✠ blessing
on your servants who are marked with these ashes,
that, as they follow the Lenten observances,
they may be worthy to come with minds made pure
to celebrate the Paschal Mystery of your Son.
Through Christ our Lord.
Amen.

Or:

O God, who desire not the death of sinners,
but their conversion,
mercifully hear our prayers

and in your kindness be pleased to bless ✠ these ashes,
which we intend to receive upon our heads,
that we, who acknowledge we are but ashes
and shall return to dust,
may, through a steadfast observance of Lent,
gain pardon for sins and newness of life
after the likeness of your Risen Son.
Who lives and reigns for ever and ever.
Amen.

He sprinkles the ashes with holy water, without saying anything.

Then the Priest places ashes on the head of all those present who come
to him, and says to each one:

Repent, and believe in the Gospel.

Or:

Remember that you are dust, and to dust you shall return.

Meanwhile, the following are sung:

Antiphon 1

Let us change our garments to sackcloth and ashes,
let us fast and weep before the Lord,
that our God, rich in mercy, might forgive us our sins.

Antiphon 2   Cf. Jl 2:17; Est 4:17

Let the priests, the ministers of the Lord,
stand between the porch and the altar and weep and cry out:
Spare, O Lord, spare your people;
do not close the mouths of those who sing your praise,
  O Lord.

Antiphon 3   Ps 50:3

Blot out my transgressions, O Lord.

This may be repeated after each verse of Psalm 50 (Have mercy on me,
O God).

Responsory   Cf. Ba 3:2; Ps 78:9

℣ Let us correct our faults which we have committed in
   ignorance, let us not be taken unawares by the day of our
   death, looking in vain for leisure to repent.
℟ **Hear us, O Lord, and show us your mercy, for we have**
   sinned against you.

℣ Help us, O God our Saviour; for the sake of your name, O Lord, set us free.

℟ **Hear us, O Lord …**

Another appropriate chant may also be sung.

After the distribution of ashes, the Priest washes his hands and proceeds to the Universal Prayer, and continues the Mass in the usual way.

The Profession of Faith is not said.

Prayer over the Offerings

As we solemnly offer
the annual sacrifice for the beginning of Lent,
we entreat you, O Lord,
that, through works of penance and charity,
we may turn away from harmful pleasures
and, cleansed from our sins, may become worthy
to celebrate devoutly the Passion of your Son.
Who lives and reigns for ever and ever.

Preface III or IV of Lent – pages 20-21.

Communion Antiphon Cf. Ps 1:2-3

**He who ponders the law of the Lord day and night
will yield fruit in due season.**

Prayer after Communion

May the Sacrament we have received sustain us, O Lord,
that our Lenten fast may be pleasing to you
and be for us a healing remedy.
Through Christ our Lord.

Prayer over the People

Pour out a spirit of compunction, O God,
on those who bow before your majesty,
and by your mercy may they merit the rewards you promise
to those who do penance.
Through Christ our Lord.

26 FEBRUARY
FIRST SUNDAY OF LENT

The temptations in today's Gospel are not at all temptations to this or that sin but rather fundamental options which matter for the direction of life. Jesus was tempted in the course of his ministry to choose another way of being God's prophet, the Messiah or anointed. In a less spectacular way, we too can be attracted by choices which shape the way our life unfolds. We ask ourselves, what do I live on? What's my true goal? Where is my nourishment? My humanity is more than food and drink. Only the Word of God truly nourishes and illuminates.

Entrance Antiphon   Cf. Ps 90:15-16

When he calls on me, I will answer him;
I will deliver him and give him glory,
I will grant him length of days.

Greeting, Penitential Rite – pages 7-12.

The **Gloria** is not said.

Collect

Grant, almighty God,
through the yearly observances of holy Lent,
that we may grow in understanding
of the riches hidden in Christ
and by worthy conduct pursue their effects.
Through our Lord Jesus Christ, your Son,
who lives and reigns with you in the unity of the Holy Spirit,
one God, for ever and ever.

FIRST READING   Gn 2:7-9;3:1-7

A reading from the book of Genesis.

The creation and the sin of our first parents.

The Lord God fashioned man of dust from the soil. Then he breathed into his nostrils a breath of life, and thus man became a living being.

The Lord God planted a garden in Eden which is in the east, and there he put the man he had fashioned. The Lord God caused to spring up from the soil every kind of tree, enticing to look at and good to eat, with the tree of life and the tree of the knowledge of good and evil in the middle of the garden.

The serpent was the most subtle of all the wild beasts that the Lord God had made. It asked the woman, 'Did God really say you were not to eat from any of the trees in the garden?' The woman answered the serpent, 'We may eat the fruit of the trees in the garden. But of the fruit of the tree in the middle of the garden God said, "You must not eat it, nor touch it, under pain of death." ' Then the serpent said to the woman, 'No! You will not die! God knows in fact that on the day you eat it your eyes will be opened and you will be like gods, knowing good and evil.' The woman saw that the tree was good to eat and pleasing to the eye, and that it was desirable for the knowledge that it could give. So she took some of its fruit and ate it. She gave some also to her husband who was with her, and he ate it. Then the eyes of both of them were opened and they realised that they were naked. So they sewed fig-leaves together to make themselves loin-cloths.

The word of the Lord.

RESPONSORIAL PSALM   Ps 50:3-6.12-14.17

℟ **Have mercy on us, O Lord, for we have sinned.**

1. Have mercy on me, God, in your kindness.
    In your compassion blot out my offence.
    O wash me more and more from my guilt
    and cleanse me from my sin. ℟

2. My offences truly I know them;
    my sin is always before me.
    Against you, you alone have I sinned;
    what is evil in your sight I have done. ℟

3. A pure heart create for me, O God,
    put a steadfast spirit within me.
    Do not cast me away from your presence,
    nor deprive me of your holy spirit.

4. Give me again the joy of your help;
    with a spirit of fervour sustain me.
    O Lord, open my lips
    and my mouth shall declare your praise. ℟

SECOND READING   Rm 5:12-19

(For Shorter Form, read between ♦ ♦).

A reading from the letter of St Paul to the Romans.

However great the number of sins committed, grace was even greater.

♦Sin entered the world through one man, and through sin death, and thus death has spread through the whole human race because everyone has sinned.♦ Sin existed in the world long before the Law was given. There was no law and so no one could be accused of the sin of 'law-breaking,' yet death reigned over all from Adam to Moses, even though their sin, unlike that of Adam, was not a matter of breaking a law.

Adam prefigured the One to come, but the gift itself considerably outweighed the fall. If it is certain that through one man's fall so many died, it is even more certain that divine grace, coming through the one man, Jesus Christ, came to so many as an abundant free gift. The results of the gift also outweigh the results of one man's sin: for after one single fall came judgement with a verdict of condemnation, now after many falls comes grace with its verdict of acquittal. ♦If it is certain that death reigned over everyone as the consequence of one man's fall, it is even more certain that one man, Jesus Christ, will cause everyone to reign in life who receives the free gift that he does not deserve, of being made righteous. Again, as one man's fall brought condemnation on everyone, so the good act of one man brings everyone life and makes them justified. As by one man's disobedience many were made sinners, so by one man's obedience many will be made righteous.♦

The word of the Lord.

GOSPEL ACCLAMATION   Mt 4:4

Praise to you, O Christ, king of eternal glory!
Man does not live on bread alone,
but on every word that comes from the mouth of God.
Praise to you, O Christ, king of eternal glory!

GOSPEL   Mt 4:1-11

A reading from the holy Gospel according to Matthew.

Jesus fasts for forty days and is tempted.

Jesus was led by the Spirit out into the wilderness to be tempted by the devil. He fasted for forty days and forty nights, after which he was very hungry, and the tempter came and said to him, 'If you are the Son of God, tell these stones to turn into loaves.' But he replied, 'Scripture says:

> Man does not live on bread alone
> but on every word that comes from the mouth of God.'

The devil then took him to the holy city and made him stand on the parapet of the Temple. 'If you are the Son of God' he said 'throw yourself down; for scripture says:

> He will put you in his angels' charge,
> and they will support you on their hands
> in case you hurt your foot against a stone.'

Jesus said to him, 'Scripture also says:

> You must not put the Lord your God to the test.'

Next, taking him to a very high mountain, the devil showed him all the kingdoms of the world and their splendour. 'I will give you all these', he said, 'if you fall at my feet and worship me.' Then Jesus replied, 'Be off, Satan! For scripture says:

> You must worship the Lord your God,
> and serve him alone.'

Then the devil left him, and angels appeared and looked after him.

> The Gospel of the Lord.

Profession of Faith – pages 14-15.

Prayer over the Offerings
Give us the right dispositions, O Lord, we pray,
to make these offerings,
for with them we celebrate the beginning
of this venerable and sacred time.
Through Christ our Lord.

Preface: The Temptation of the Lord
The Lord be with you.
And with your spirit.

Lift up your hearts.
We lift them up to the Lord.

Let us give thanks to the Lord our God.
It is right and just.

It is truly right and just, our duty and our salvation,
always and everywhere to give you thanks,
Lord, holy Father, almighty and eternal God,
through Christ our Lord.

By abstaining forty long days from earthly food,
he consecrated through his fast
the pattern of our Lenten observance,
and, by overturning all the snares of the ancient serpent,
taught us to cast out the leaven of malice,
so that, celebrating worthily the Paschal Mystery,
we might pass over at last to the eternal paschal feast.

And so, with the company of Angels and Saints,
we sing the hymn of your praise,
as without end we acclaim:

Holy, Holy, Holy Lord God of hosts …

Communion Antiphon   Mt 4:4

One does not live by bread alone,
but by every word that comes forth from the mouth of God.
    Or: Cf. Ps 90:4

The Lord will conceal you with his pinions,
and under his wings you will trust.

Prayer after Communion

Renewed now with heavenly bread,
by which faith is nourished, hope increased,
and charity strengthened,
we pray, O Lord,
that we may learn to hunger for Christ,
the true and living Bread,
and strive to live by every word
which proceeds from your mouth.
Through Christ our Lord.

Prayer over the People

May bountiful blessing, O Lord, we pray,
come down upon your people,
that hope may grow in tribulation,
virtue be strengthened in temptation,
and eternal redemption be assured.
Through Christ our Lord.

1 MARCH
SAINT DAVID
Bishop, Patron of Wales

We have received the faith from the generation just before us, and they from the one just before them, and so forth back to the time of St David and beyond. Our first attitude should be one of gratitude, thanking God for his gifts over time and in the present moment. And because every believer is both disciple and evangelist, we can ask ourselves who we in our turn are passing on the word of life.

Entrance Antiphon   Is 52:7

**How beautiful upon the mountains are the feet of him who brings glad tidings of peace,
bearing good news, announcing salvation!**

Greeting, Penitential Rite, Gloria – pages 7-13.

Collect

O God, who graciously bestowed on your
    Bishop Saint David of Wales
the virtue of wisdom and the gift of eloquence,
and made him an example of prayer and pastoral zeal;
grant that, through his intercession,
your Church may ever prosper and render you joyful praise.
Through our Lord Jesus Christ, your Son,
who lives and reigns with you in the unity of the Holy Spirit,
one God for ever and ever.

FIRST READING   Ph 3:8-14

A reading from the letter of St Paul to the Philippians.

I am racing for the finish, for the prize to which God calls us upwards to receive in Christ Jesus.

I believe nothing can happen that will outweigh the supreme advantage of knowing Christ Jesus my Lord. For him I have accepted the loss of everything, and I look on everything as so much rubbish if only I can have Christ and be given a place in him. I am no longer trying for perfection by my own efforts, the perfection that comes from the Law, but I want only the perfection that comes through faith in Christ, and is from God and based on faith. All I want is to know Christ and the power of his resurrection and to share his sufferings by reproducing the pattern of his death. That is the way I can hope to take my place in the resurrection of the dead. Not that I have become perfect yet: I have not yet won, but I am still running, trying to capture the prize for which Christ Jesus captured me. I can assure you my brothers, I am far from thinking that I have already won. All I can say is that I forget the past and I strain ahead for what is still to come; I am racing for the finish, for the prize to which God calls us upwards to receive in Christ Jesus.

The word of the Lord.

RESPONSORIAL PSALM   Ps 1:1-4.6

℟ **Happy the man who has placed
his trust in the Lord.**

1. Happy indeed is the man
    who follows not the counsel of the wicked,
    nor lingers in the way of sinners
    nor sits in the company of scorners,
    but whose delight is the law of the Lord
    and who ponders his law day and night. ℟

2. He is like a tree that is planted
    beside the flowing waters,
    that yields its fruit in due season
    and whose leaves shall never fade;
    and all that he does shall prosper. ℟

3. Not so are the wicked, not so!
    For they like winnowed chaff
    shall be driven away by the wind;
    for the Lord guards the way of the just
    but the way of the wicked leads to doom. ℟

GOSPEL ACCLAMATION   Jn 8:31-32

**Alleluia, alleluia!
If you make my word your home
you will indeed be my disciples,
and you will learn the truth, says the Lord.
Alleluia!**

GOSPEL   Mt 5:13-16

A reading from the holy Gospel according to Matthew.

You are the light of the world.

Jesus said to his disciples: 'You are the salt of the earth. But if salt becomes tasteless, what can make it salty again? It is good for nothing, and can only be thrown out to be trampled underfoot by men.

'You are the light of the world. A city built on a hill-top cannot be hidden. No one lights a lamp to put it under a tub; they put it on the lamp-stand where it shines for everyone in the house. In the same way your light must shine in the sight of men, so that, seeing your good works, they may give the praise to your Father in heaven.'

The Gospel of the Lord.

Profession of Faith – pages 14-15.

Prayer over the Offerings

Look with favour, O Lord, we pray,
on the offerings we set upon this sacred altar
on the feast day of the Bishop Saint David,
that, bestowing on us your pardon,
our oblations may give honour to your name.
Through Christ our Lord.

Preface I of Saints

The Lord be with you.
And with your spirit.

Lift up your hearts.
We lift them up to the Lord.

Let us give thanks to the Lord our God.
It is right and just.

It is truly right and just, our duty and our salvation,
always and everywhere to give you thanks,
Lord, holy Father, almighty and eternal God.

For you are praised in the company of your Saints
and in crowning their merits, you crown your own gifts.
By their way of life you offer us an example,
by communion with them you give us companionship,
by their intercession, sure support,
so that, encouraged by so great a cloud of witnesses,
we may run as victors in the race before us
and win with them the imperishable crown of glory,
through Christ our Lord.

And so, with the Angels and Archangels,
and with the great multitude of the Saints,
we sing the hymn of your praise,
as without end we acclaim:

Holy, Holy, Holy Lord God of hosts …

Communion Antiphon   1 Cor 1:23-24

**We proclaim Christ crucified,
Christ, the power of God, and the wisdom of God.**

Prayer after Communion

We pray, almighty God,
that we, who are fortified by the power of this Sacrament,
may learn through the example of your Bishop Saint David
to seek you always above all things
and to bear in this world the likeness of the New Man.
Through Christ our Lord.

━━━━━━━━━ 5 MARCH ━━━━━━━━━
SECOND SUNDAY OF LENT

*Every so often, we catch a glimpse of the "something more" that God
has in store for us. These fleeting experiences are to be treasured: the
birth of my first child, falling in love, a sense of "being held" by God's
presence. Such experiences may help us approach the Transfiguration.
Like all transcendent experiences, it is fleeting and yet it etches a
memory and leaves a longing. What should we do? Practise listening
to him. Be not afraid. We cannot always be "on the mountain" and
yet what happens on the heights can help us on the lowlands of the
everyday.*

Entrance Antiphon   Cf. Ps 26:8-9

**Of you my heart has spoken: Seek his face.
It is your face, O Lord, that I seek;
hide not your face from me.**

          Or: Cf. Ps 24:6.2.22

**Remember your compassion, O Lord,
and your merciful love, for they are from of old.
Let not our enemies exult over us.
Redeem us, O God of Israel, from all our distress.**

Greeting, Penitential Rite – pages 7-12.
The Gloria is not said.

Collect

O God, who have commanded us
to listen to your beloved Son,
be pleased, we pray,
to nourish us inwardly by your word,
that, with spiritual sight made pure,
we may rejoice to behold your glory.
Through our Lord Jesus Christ, your Son,
who lives and reigns with you in the unity of the Holy Spirit,
one God, for ever and ever.

FIRST READING   Gn 12:1-4

A reading from the book of Genesis.
The call of Abraham, the father of God's people.

The Lord said to Abram, 'Leave your country, your family and
your father's house, for the land I will show you. I will make you
a great nation; I will bless you and make your name so famous
that it will be used as a blessing.

'I will bless those who bless you:
I will curse those who slight you.
All the tribes of the earth
shall bless themselves by you.'

So Abram went as the Lord told him.

The word of the Lord.

RESPONSORIAL PSALM   Ps 32:4-5.18-20.22

℟ **May your love be upon us, O Lord,
as we place all our hope in you.**

1. The word of the Lord is faithful
   and all his works to be trusted.
   The Lord loves justice and right
   and fills the earth with his love. ℟

2. The Lord looks on those who revere him,
   on those who hope in his love,
   to rescue their souls from death,
   to keep them alive in famine. ℟

3.   Our soul is waiting for the Lord.
     The Lord is our help and our shield.
     May your love be upon us, O Lord,
     as we place all our hope in you. ℟

SECOND READING   2 Tm 1:8-10

A reading from the second letter of St Paul to Timothy.
God calls and enlightens us.

With me, bear the hardships for the sake of the Good News,
relying on the power of God who has saved us and called us
to be holy – not because of anything we ourselves have done
but for his own purpose and by his own grace. This grace had
already been granted to us, in Christ Jesus, before the beginning
of time, but it has only been revealed by the Appearing of our
saviour Christ Jesus. He abolished death, and he has proclaimed
life and immortality through the Good News.

     The word of the Lord.

GOSPEL ACCLAMATION   Mt 17:5

Glory and praise to you, O Christ!
From the bright cloud the Father's voice was heard:
'This is my Son, the Beloved. Listen to him!'
Glory and praise to you, O Christ!

GOSPEL   Mt 17:1-9

A reading from the holy Gospel according to Matthew.
His face shone like the sun.

Jesus took with him Peter and James and his brother John and
led them up a high mountain where they could be alone. There
in their presence he was transfigured; his face shone like the sun
and his clothes became as white as the light. Suddenly Moses
and Elijah appeared to them; they were talking with him. Then
Peter spoke to Jesus. 'Lord,' he said 'it is wonderful for us to
be here; if you wish, I will make three tents here, one for you,
one for Moses and one for Elijah.' He was still speaking when
suddenly a bright cloud covered them with shadow, and from
the cloud there came a voice which said, 'This is my Son, the
Beloved; he enjoys my favour. Listen to him.' When they heard
this, the disciples fell on their faces, overcome with fear. But
Jesus came up and touched them. 'Stand up,' he said 'do not

be afraid.' And when they raised their eyes they saw no one but only Jesus.

As they came down from the mountain Jesus gave them this order. 'Tell no one about the vision until the Son of Man has risen from the dead.'

The Gospel of the Lord.

Profession of Faith – pages 14-15.

Prayer over the Offerings

May this sacrifice, O Lord, we pray,
cleanse us of our faults
and sanctify your faithful in body and mind
for the celebration of the paschal festivities.
Through Christ our Lord.

Preface: The Transfiguration of the Lord

The Lord be with you.
And with your spirit.

Lift up your hearts.
We lift them up to the Lord.

Let us give thanks to the Lord our God.
It is right and just.

It is truly right and just, our duty and our salvation,
always and everywhere to give you thanks,
Lord, holy Father, almighty and eternal God,
through Christ our Lord.

For after he had told the disciples of his coming Death,
on the holy mountain he manifested to them his glory,
to show, even by the testimony of the law and the prophets,
that the Passion leads to the glory of the Resurrection.

And so, with the Powers of heaven,
we worship you constantly on earth,
and before your majesty
without end we acclaim:

Holy, Holy, Holy Lord God of hosts …

Communion Antiphon   Mt 17:5
This is my beloved Son, with whom I am well pleased; listen to him.

Prayer after Communion

As we receive these glorious mysteries,
we make thanksgiving to you, O Lord,
for allowing us while still on earth
to be partakers even now of the things of heaven.
Through Christ our Lord.

Prayer over the People

Bless your faithful, we pray, O Lord,
with a blessing that endures for ever,
and keep them faithful
to the Gospel of your Only Begotten Son,
so that they may always desire and at last attain
that glory whose beauty he showed in his own Body,
to the amazement of his Apostles.
Through Christ our Lord.

═══════ 12 MARCH ═══════

THIRD SUNDAY OF LENT

*Today we are greatly helped by the wonderful Gospel of the Woman at
the Well. On the third attempt, Jesus finally gets through to her but
after that there is no stopping her. She represents us: what do I thirst
for? What is the most important thing in my life? Where do I now
find God? By relentless challenge and resolute honesty, we too can be
led to that encounter with Jesus, which changes everything, "giving
life a new horizon and a decisive direction". May we come to believe
because we have heard him ourselves and we know that he really is
the saviour of the world.*

Entrance Antiphon   Cf. Ps 24:15-16

My eyes are always on the Lord,
for he rescues my feet from the snare.
Turn to me and have mercy on me,
for I am alone and poor.

    Or: Cf. Ezk 36:23-26

When I prove my holiness among you,
I will gather you from all the foreign lands;
and I will pour clean water upon you

and cleanse you from all your impurities,
and I will give you a new spirit, says the Lord.

Greeting, Penitential Rite – pages 7-12.

The Gloria is not said.

Collect

O God, author of every mercy and of all goodness,
who in fasting, prayer and almsgiving
have shown us a remedy for sin,
look graciously on this confession of our lowliness,
that we, who are bowed down by our conscience,
may always be lifted up by your mercy.
Through our Lord Jesus Christ, your Son
who lives and reigns with you in the unity of the Holy Spirit,
one God, for ever and ever.

FIRST READING   Ex 17:3-7

A reading from the book of Exodus.

Give us water to drink.

Tormented by thirst, the people complained against Moses.
'Why did you bring us out of Egypt?' they said. 'Was it so that
I should die of thirst, my children too, and my cattle?' Moses
appealed to the Lord. 'How am I to deal with this people?' he
said. 'A little more and they will stone me!' The Lord said to
Moses, 'Take with you some of the elders of Israel and move on
to the forefront of the people; take in your hand the staff with
which you struck the river, and go. I shall be standing before you
there on the rock, at Horeb. You must strike the rock, and water
will flow from it for the people to drink.' This is what Moses did,
in the sight of the elders of Israel. The place was named Massah
and Meribah because of the grumbling of the sons of Israel and
because they put the Lord to the test by saying, 'Is the Lord with
us, or not?'

The word of the Lord.

RESPONSORIAL PSALM   Ps 94:1-2.6-9

℟ O that today you would listen to his voice:
   'Harden not your hearts.'

1. Come, ring out our joy to the Lord;
    hail the rock who saves us.

Let us come before him, giving thanks,
with songs let us hail the Lord. ℟

2. Come in; let us bow and bend low;
let us kneel before the God who made us
for he is our God and we
the people who belong to his pasture,
the flock that is led by his hand. ℟

3. O that today you would listen to his voice!
'Harden not your hearts as at Meribah,
as on that day at Massah in the desert
when your fathers put me to the test;
when they tried me, though they saw my work.' ℟

SECOND READING   Rm 5:1-2.5-8

A reading from the letter of St Paul to the Romans.

The love of God has been poured into our hearts by the Holy Spirit which has been given us.

Through our Lord Jesus Christ by faith we are judged righteous
and at peace with God, since it is by faith and through Jesus that
we have entered this state of grace in which we can boast about
looking forward to God's glory. This hope is not deceptive,
because the love of God has been poured into our hearts by the
Holy Spirit which has been given us. We were still helpless when
at his appointed moment Christ died for sinful men. It is not
easy to die even for a good man – though of course for someone
really worthy, a man might be prepared to die – but what proves
that God loves us is that Christ died for us while we were still
sinners.

The word of the Lord.

GOSPEL ACCLAMATION   Jn 4:42.15

Glory to you, O Christ, you are the Word of God!
Lord, you are really the saviour of the world;
give me the living water, so that I may never get thirsty.
Glory to you, O Christ, you are the Word of God!

GOSPEL   Jn 4:5-42

(For Shorter Form, read between ♦ ♦).

A reading from the holy Gospel according to John.

A spring of water welling up to eternal life.

|♦Jesus came to the Samaritan town called Sychar, near the land

that Jacob gave to his son Joseph. Jacob's well is there and Jesus,
tired by the journey, sat straight down by the well. It was about
the sixth hour. When a Samaritan woman came to draw water,
Jesus said to her, 'Give me a drink.' His disciples had gone into
the town to buy food. The Samaritan woman said to him,
'What? You are a Jew and you ask me, a Samaritan, for a drink?'
– Jews, in fact, do not associate with Samaritans. Jesus replied:

> 'If you only knew what God is offering
> and who it is that is saying to you:
> Give me a drink,
> you would have been the one to ask,
> and he would have given you living water.'

'You have no bucket, sir,' she answered 'and the well is deep:
how could you get this living water? Are you a greater man than
our father Jacob who gave us this well and drank from it himself
with his sons and his cattle?' Jesus replied:

> 'Whoever drinks this water
> will get thirsty again;
> but anyone who drinks the water that I shall give
> will never be thirsty again:
> the water that I shall give
> will turn into a spring inside him, welling up to eternal life.'

'Sir,' said the woman, 'give me some of that water, so that I may
never get thirsty and never have to come here again to draw
water.'◆ 'Go and call your husband' said Jesus to her 'and come
back here.' The woman answered, 'I have no husband.' He said
to her, 'You are right to say, "I have no husband"; for although
you have had five, the one you have now is not your husband.
You spoke the truth there.' ◆'I see you are a prophet, sir' said
the woman. 'Our fathers worshipped on this mountain, while
you say that Jerusalem is the place where one ought to worship.'
Jesus said:

> 'Believe me, woman, the hour is coming
> when you will worship the Father
> neither on this mountain nor in Jerusalem.
> You worship what you do not know;
> we worship what we know;
> for salvation comes from the Jews.
> But the hour will come – in fact it is here already –

when true worshippers will worship the Father in spirit
  and truth:
that is the kind of worshipper
the Father wants.
God is spirit,
and those who worship
must worship in spirit and truth.'

The woman said to him, 'I know that Messiah – that is,
Christ – is coming; and when he comes he will tell us
everything.' 'I who am speaking to you,' said Jesus 'I am he.'◀

At this point his disciples returned, and were surprised to
find him speaking to a woman, though none of them asked,
'What do you want from her?' or, 'Why are you talking to her?'
The woman put down her water jar and hurried back to the
town to tell the people, 'Come and see a man who has told me
everything I ever did; I wonder if he is the Christ?' This brought
people out of the town and they started walking towards him.

Meanwhile, the disciples were urging him, 'Rabbi, do have
something to eat;' but he said, 'I have food to eat that you
do not know about.' So the disciples asked one another, 'Has
someone been bringing him food?' But Jesus said:

'My food
is to do the will of the one who sent me,
and to complete his work.
Have you not got a saying:
Four months and then the harvest?
Well, I tell you:
Look around you, look at the fields;
already they are white, ready for harvest!
Already the reaper is being paid his wages,
already he is bringing in the grain for eternal life,
and thus sower and reaper rejoice together.
For here the proverb holds good:
one sows, another reaps;
I sent you to reap
a harvest you had not worked for.
Others worked for it;
and you have come into the rewards of their trouble.'

◀Many Samaritans of that town had believed in him on the
strength of the woman's testimony when she said, 'He told me

all I have ever done,' so, when the Samaritans came up to him, they begged him to stay with them. He stayed for two days, and when he spoke to them many more came to believe; and they said to the woman, 'Now we no longer believe because of what you told us; we have heard him ourselves and we know that he really is the saviour of the world.'◄

The Gospel of the Lord.

Profession of Faith – pages 14-15.

Prayer over the Offerings

Be pleased, O Lord, with these sacrificial offerings,
and grant that we who beseech pardon for our own sins,
may take care to forgive our neighbour.
Through Christ our Lord.

Preface: The Samaritan Woman

The Lord be with you.
And with your spirit.

Lift up your hearts.
We lift them up to the Lord.

Let us give thanks to the Lord our God.
It is right and just.

It is truly right and just, our duty and our salvation,
always and everywhere to give you thanks,
Lord, holy Father, almighty and eternal God,
through Christ our Lord.

For when he asked the Samaritan woman for water to drink,
he had already created the gift of faith within her
and so ardently did he thirst for her faith,
that he kindled in her the fire of divine love.

And so we, too, give you thanks
and with the Angels
praise your mighty deeds, as we acclaim:

Holy, Holy, Holy Lord God of hosts …

Communion Antiphon   Jn 4:13-14
**For anyone who drinks it, says the Lord,
the water I shall give will become in him
a spring welling up to eternal life.**

Prayer after Communion

As we receive the pledge
of things yet hidden in heaven
and are nourished while still on earth
with the Bread that comes from on high,
we humbly entreat you, O Lord,
that what is being brought about in us in mystery
may come to true completion.
Through Christ our Lord.

Prayer over the People

Direct, O Lord, we pray, the hearts of your faithful,
and in your kindness grant your servants this grace:
that, abiding in the love of you and their neighbour,
they may fulfil the whole of your commands.
Through Christ our Lord.

17 MARCH

SAINT PATRICK

Patron of Ireland

It would no doubt take the modest St Patrick by surprise to know how widely his feast is celebrated and marked! We know something of the man himself from the few documents which have come down to us. His return to those who enslaved him shows great character; even more outstanding is his commitment to Jesus Christ, the Scriptures (his writings are full of allusions), and to his calling as apostle and evangelist. The spark of faith has shone among the Irish, sometimes brightly, sometimes dimly, ever since. Let us mark the feast with thanksgiving and renewed faith.

Entrance Antiphon   Gn 12:1-2

Go from your country and your kindred and your father's
    house to the land that I will show you.
I will make of you a great nation, and I will bless you,
and make your name great, so that you will be a blessing.

Greeting, Penitential Rite, Gloria – pages 7-13.

Collect

Lord, through the work of Saint Patrick in Ireland
we have come to acknowledge the mystery of the one true God
and give thanks for our salvation in Christ;
grant by his prayers
that we who celebrate this festival
may keep alive the fire of faith he kindled.
Through our Lord Jesus Christ, your Son,
who lives and reigns with you in the unity of the Holy Spirit,
one God, for ever and ever.

FIRST READING   Sir 39:6-10

A reading from the book of Ecclesiasticus.

His memory will not disappear, generation after generation his name will live.

If it is the will of the great Lord,
the scholar will be filled with the spirit of understanding,
he will shower forth words of wisdom,
and in prayer give thanks to the Lord.
He will grow upright in purpose and learning,
he will ponder the Lord's hidden mysteries.
He will display the instruction he has received,
taking his pride in the Law of the Lord's covenant.
Many will praise his understanding,
and it will never be forgotten.
His memory will not disappear,
generation after generation his name will live.
Nations will proclaim his wisdom,
the assembly will celebrate his praises.

> The word of the Lord.

RESPONSORIAL PSALM   Ps 115:12-19

℟ **How can I repay the Lord for his goodness to me?**

1. How can I repay the Lord
   for his goodness to me?
   The cup of salvation I will raise;
   I will call on the Lord's name. ℟

2. My vows to the Lord I will fulfil
   before all his people.
   O precious in the eyes of the Lord
   is the death of his faithful. ℟

3. Your servant, Lord, your servant am I;
    you have loosened my bonds.
    A thanksgiving sacrifice I make;
    I will call on the Lord's name. ℞

4. My vows to the Lord I will fulfil
    before all his people,
    in the courts of the house of the Lord,
    in your midst, O Jerusalem. ℞

SECOND READING   2 Tm 4:1-8

A reading from the second letter of St Paul to Timothy.
Convince, rebuke and encourage, with the utmost patience in teaching.

Before God and before Christ Jesus who is to be judge of the
living and the dead, I put this duty to you, in the name of his
Appearing and of his kingdom: proclaim the message and,
welcome or unwelcome, insist on it. Refute falsehood, correct
error, call to obedience – but do all with patience and with the
intention of teaching. The time is sure to come when, far from
being content with sound teaching, people will be avid for the
latest novelty and collect themselves a whole series of teachers
according to their own tastes; and then, instead of listening to
the truth, they will turn to myths. Be careful always to choose
the right course; be brave under trials; make the preaching of the
Good News your life's work, in thoroughgoing service.

   As for me, my life is already being poured away as a libation,
and the time has come for me to be gone. I have fought the
good fight to the end; I have run the race to the finish; I
have kept the faith; all there is to come now is the crown of
righteousness reserved for me, which the Lord, the righteous
judge, will give me on that Day; and not only to me but to all
those who have longed for his Appearing.

   The word of the Lord.

GOSPEL ACCLAMATION   Jm 1:21

Glory to you, O Christ, you are the Word of God!
Accept and submit to the word which has been planted in you
     and can save your souls.
Glory to you, O Christ, you are the Word of God!

GOSPEL   Mt 13:24-32

A reading from the holy Gospel according to Matthew.

It is the smallest of all the seeds, but when it has grown it is the greatest of shrubs.

Jesus put a parable before the crowds, 'The kingdom of heaven may be compared to a man who sowed good seed in his field. While everybody was asleep his enemy came, sowed darnel all among the wheat and made off. When the new wheat sprouted and ripened, the darnel appeared as well. The owner's servants went to him and said, "Sir, was it not good seed that you sowed in your field? If so, where does the darnel come from?" "Some enemy has done this," he answered. And the servants said, "Do you want us to go and weed it out?" But he said, "No, because when you weed out the darnel you might pull up the wheat with it. Let them both grow till the harvest; and at harvest time I shall say to the reapers: First collect the darnel and tie it in bundles to be burnt, then gather the wheat into my barn."'

He put another parable before them: 'The kingdom of heaven is like a mustard seed which a man took and sowed in his field. It is the smallest of all the seeds, but when it has grown it is the biggest of shrubs and becomes a tree, so that the birds of the air can come and shelter in its branches.'

The Gospel of the Lord.

Profession of Faith – pages 14-15.

Prayer over the Offerings

Lord, accept this pure sacrifice
which, through the labours of Saint Patrick,
your grateful people make
to the glory of your name.
Through Christ our Lord.

Preface

The Lord be with you.
And with your spirit.

Lift up your hearts.
We lift them up to the Lord.

Let us give thanks to the Lord our God.
It is right and just.

It is truly right and just, our duty and our salvation,
always and everywhere to give you thanks,
Lord, holy Father, almighty and eternal God,
and to proclaim your greatness with due praise
as we honour Saint Patrick.

For you drew him through daily prayer
in captivity and hardship
to know you as a loving Father.

You chose him out of all the world
to return to the land of his captors,
that they might acknowledge Jesus Christ, their Redeemer.

In the power of your Spirit you directed his paths
to win the sons and daughters of the Irish
to the service of the Triune God.

And so, with the Angels and Archangels,
and with the great multitude of the Saints,
we sing the hymn of your praise,
as without end we acclaim:

Holy, Holy, Holy Lord God of hosts …

Communion Antiphon   Mt 8:11

**Many will come from east and west
and sit down with Abraham, Isaac and Jacob
at the feast in the kingdom of heaven, says the Lord.**

Prayer after Communion

Strengthen us, O Lord, by this sacrament
so that we may profess the faith taught by Saint Patrick
and to proclaim it in our way of living.
Through Christ our Lord.

Solemn Blessing

The Priest invites people to bow down for the blessing.

May God the Father, who called us together
to celebrate the solemnity of Saint Patrick,
bless you, protect you, and keep you faithful.
Amen.

May Christ the Lord, the High King of Heaven,
be near you at all times and shield you from evil.
Amen.

May the Holy Spirit, who is the source of all holiness,
make you rich in the love of God's people.
Amen.

And may the blessing of almighty God,
the Father, and the Son, ✠ and the Holy Spirit,
come down on you and remain with you for ever.
Amen.

=== 19 MARCH ===

FOURTH SUNDAY OF LENT

*How we respond to pressure can vary very much from person to
person. In John's gospel there are two related stories of blind men
being healed, one in chapter 5, and the other in chapter 9 found in
today's reading. The man at the pool eventually betrays Jesus. The
man born blind resists pressure and even grows on the strength of it.
Part of his energy comes from his experience – no matter what others
may say about Jesus, he himself once was blind and now he sees! His
courageous attachment to what he knows from his personal encounter
with Jesus leads eventually to a full act of faith.*

Entrance Antiphon   Cf. Is 66:10-11
Rejoice, Jerusalem, and all who love her.
Be joyful, all who were in mourning;
exult and be satisfied at her consoling breast.

Greeting, Penitential Rite – pages 7-12.
The Gloria is not said.

Collect
O God, who through your Word
reconcile the human race to yourself in a wonderful way,
grant, we pray,
that with prompt devotion and eager faith
the Christian people may hasten
towards the solemn celebrations to come.
Through our Lord Jesus Christ, your Son,
who lives and reigns with you in the unity of the Holy Spirit,
one God, for ever and ever.

FIRST READING   1 Sam 16:1.6-7.10-13

A reading from the first book of Samuel.

David is anointed king of Israel.

The Lord said to Samuel, 'Fill your horn with oil and go. I am sending you to Jesse of Bethlehem, for I have chosen myself a king among his sons'. When Samuel arrived, he caught sight of Eliab and thought, 'Surely the Lord's anointed one stands there before him', but the Lord said to Samuel, 'Take no notice of his appearance or his height for I have rejected him; God does not see as man sees; man looks at appearances but the Lord looks at the heart'. Jesse presented his seven sons to Samuel, but Samuel said to Jesse, 'The Lord has not chosen these'. He then asked Jesse, 'Are these all the sons you have?' He answered, 'There is still one left, the youngest; he is out looking after the sheep'. Then Samuel said to Jesse, 'Send for him; we will not sit down to eat until he comes'. Jesse had him sent for, a boy of fresh complexion, with fine eyes and pleasant bearing. The Lord said, 'Come, anoint him, for this is the one'. At this, Samuel took the horn of oil and anointed him where he stood with his brothers; and the spirit of the Lord seized on David and stayed with him from that day on.

The word of the Lord.

RESPONSORIAL PSALM   Ps 22

℟ **The Lord is my shepherd;**
   there is nothing I shall want.

1. The Lord is my shepherd;
    there is nothing I shall want.
    Fresh and green are the pastures
    where he gives me repose.
    Near restful waters he leads me,
    to revive my drooping spirit. ℟

2. He guides me along the right path;
    he is true to his name.
    If I should walk in the valley of darkness
    no evil would I fear.
    You are there with your crook and your staff;
    with these you give me comfort. ℟

3. You have prepared a banquet for me
   in the sight of my foes.
   My head you have anointed with oil;
   my cup is overflowing. ℞

4. Surely goodness and kindness shall follow me
   all the days of my life.
   In the Lord's own house shall I dwell
   for ever and ever. ℞

SECOND READING   Ep 5:8-14

A reading from the letter of St Paul to the Ephesians.

Rise from the dead and Christ will shine on you.

You were darkness once, but now you are light in the Lord;
be like children of light, for the effects of the light are seen in
complete goodness and right living and truth. Try to discover
what the Lord wants of you, having nothing to do with the futile
works of darkness but exposing them by contrast. The things
which are done in secret are things that people are ashamed
even to speak of; but anything exposed by the light will be
illuminated and anything illuminated turns into light. That is
why it is said:

Wake up from your sleep,
rise from the dead,
and Christ will shine on you.

The word of the Lord.

GOSPEL ACCLAMATION   Jn 8:12

Glory to you, O Christ, you are the Word of God!
I am the light of the world, says the Lord;
anyone who follows me will have the light of life.
Glory to you, O Christ, you are the Word of God!

GOSPEL   Jn 9:1-41

(For Shorter Form, read between ◆ ◆).

A reading from the holy Gospel according to John.

He went off and washed himself, and came away with his sight restored.

◆As Jesus went along, he saw a man who had been blind from
birth.◆ His disciples asked him, 'Rabbi, who sinned, this man or
his parents, for him to have been born blind?' 'Neither he nor
his parents sinned,' Jesus answered 'he was born blind so that
the works of God might be displayed in him.

'As long as the day lasts
I must carry out the work of the one who sent me;
the night will soon be here when no one can work.
As long as I am in the world
I am the light of the world.'

Having said this, ◆he spat on the ground, made a paste with the spittle, put this over the eyes of the blind man and said to him, 'Go and wash in the Pool of Siloam' (a name that means 'sent'). So the blind man went off and washed himself, and came away with his sight restored.

His neighbours and people who earlier had seen him begging said, 'Isn't this the man who used to sit and beg?' Some said, 'Yes, it is the same one.' Others said, 'No, he only looks like him'. The man himself said, 'I am the man'.◆ So they said to him, 'Then how do your eyes come to be open?' 'The man called Jesus' he answered 'made a paste, daubed my eyes with it and said to me, "Go and wash at Siloam"; so I went, and when I washed I could see'. They asked, 'Where is he?' 'I don't know' he answered.

◆They brought the man who had been blind to the Pharisees. It had been a sabbath day when Jesus made the paste and opened the man's eyes, so when the Pharisees asked him how he had come to see, he said, 'He put a paste on my eyes, and I washed, and I can see'. Then some of the Pharisees said, 'This man cannot be from God: he does not keep the sabbath.' Others said, 'How could a sinner produce signs like this?' And there was disagreement among them. So they spoke to the blind man again, 'What have you to say about him yourself, now that he has opened your eyes?' 'He is a prophet' replied the man.◆

However, the Jews would not believe that the man had been blind and had gained his sight, without first sending for his parents and asking them, 'Is this man really your son who you say was born blind? If so how is it that he is now able to see?' His parents answered, 'We know he is our son and we know he was born blind, but we don't know how it is that he can see now, or who opened his eyes. He is old enough: let him speak for himself.' His parents spoke like this out of fear of the Jews, who had already agreed to expel from the synagogue anyone who should acknowledge Jesus as the Christ. This was why his parents said, 'He is old enough; ask him.'

So the Jews again sent for the man and said to him, 'Give glory to God! For our part, we know that this man is a sinner.' The man answered, 'I don't know if he is a sinner; I only know that I was blind and now I can see.' They said to him, 'What did he do to you? How did he open your eyes?' He replied, 'I have told you once and you wouldn't listen. Why do you want to hear it all again? Do you want to become his disciples too?' At this they hurled abuse at him: 'You can be his disciple,' they said 'we are disciples of Moses: we know that God spoke to Moses, but as for this man, we don't know where he comes from.' The man replied, 'Now here is an astonishing thing! He has opened my eyes and you don't know where he comes from! We know that God doesn't listen to sinners, but God does listen to men who are devout and do his will. Ever since the world began it is unheard of for anyone to open the eyes of a man who was born blind; if this man were not from God, he couldn't do a thing'. ▶'Are you trying to teach us,' they replied, 'and you a sinner through and through, since you were born!' And they drove him away.

Jesus heard they had driven him away, and when he found him he said to him, 'Do you believe in the Son of Man?' 'Sir,' the man replied 'tell me who he is so that I may believe in him.' Jesus said, 'You are looking at him; he is speaking to you'. The man said, 'Lord, I believe', and worshipped him.◀

Jesus said:
'It is for judgement
that I have come into this world,
so that those without sight may see
and those with sight turn blind.'

Hearing this, some Pharisees who were present said to him, 'We are not blind, surely?' Jesus replied:

'Blind? If you were,
you would not be guilty,
but since you say, "We see",
your guilt remains.'

The Gospel of the Lord.

Profession of Faith – pages 14-15.

Prayer over the Offerings

We place before you with joy these offerings,
which bring eternal remedy, O Lord,
praying that we may both faithfully revere them
and present them to you, as is fitting,
for the salvation of all the world.
Through Christ our Lord.

Preface: The Man Born Blind

The Lord be with you.
And with your spirit.

Lift up your hearts.
We lift them up to the Lord.

Let us give thanks to the Lord our God.
It is right and just.

It is truly right and just, our duty and our salvation,
always and everywhere to give you thanks,
Lord, holy Father, almighty and eternal God,
through Christ our Lord.

By the mystery of the Incarnation,
he has led the human race that walked in darkness
into the radiance of the faith
and has brought those born in slavery to ancient sin
through the waters of regeneration
to make them your adopted children.

Therefore, all creatures of heaven and earth
sing a new song in adoration,
and we, with all the host of Angels,
cry out, and without end acclaim:

Holy, Holy, Holy Lord God of hosts …

Communion Antiphon   Cf. Jn 9:11,38

**The Lord anointed my eyes: I went, I washed,
I saw and I believed in God.**

Prayer after Communion

O God, who enlighten everyone who comes into this world,
illuminate our hearts, we pray,
with the splendour of your grace,
that we may always ponder

what is worthy and pleasing to your majesty
and love you in all sincerity.
Through Christ our Lord.

Prayer over the People

Look upon those who call to you, O Lord,
and sustain the weak;
give life by your unfailing light
to those who walk in the shadow of death,
and bring those rescued by your mercy from every evil
to reach the highest good.
Through Christ our Lord.

---

26 MARCH

FIFTH SUNDAY OF LENT

John's Gospel puts before the believer a grand array of 'I Am'
sentences, rooted in the name of God in Exodus 3:14, I am who I
am. I am the bread of life (Jn 6:35, 48, 51); I am the light of the
world (Jn 8:12; 9:5); I am the gate for the sheep (Jn 10:7, 9); I am
the good shepherd (Jn 10:11, 14); I am the resurrection and the life
(Jn 11:25); I am the way, and the truth, and the life (Jn 14:6); I am
the true vine (Jn 15:1, 5). Altogether, they constitute a resounding
reminder that we believe first of all, and above all, in a person, not in
a philosophy.

Entrance Antiphon   Cf. Ps 42:1-2

Give me justice, O God,
and plead my cause against a nation that is faithless.
From the deceitful and cunning rescue me,
for you, O God, are my strength.

Greeting, Penitential Rite – pages 7-12.

The Gloria is not said.

Collect

By your help, we beseech you, Lord our God,
may we walk eagerly in that same charity
with which, out of love for the world,
your Son handed himself over to death.

Through our Lord Jesus Christ, your Son,
who lives and reigns with you in the unity of the Holy Spirit,
one God, for ever and ever.

FIRST READING   Ezk 37:12-14

A reading from the prophet Ezekiel.

I shall put my spirit in you, and you will live.

The Lord says this: I am now going to open your graves; I mean
to raise you from your graves, my people, and lead you back to
the soil of Israel. And you will know that I am the Lord, when
I open your graves and raise you from your graves, my people.
And I shall put my spirit in you, and you will live, and I shall
resettle you on your own soil; and you will know that I, the
Lord, have said and done this – it is the Lord who speaks.

The word of the Lord.

RESPONSORIAL PSALM   Ps 129

℟ **With the Lord there is mercy
   and fullness of redemption.**

1. Out of the depths I cry to you, O Lord,
    Lord, hear my voice!
    O let your ears be attentive
    to the voice of my pleading. ℟

2. If you, O Lord, should mark our guilt,
    Lord, who would survive?
    But with you is found forgiveness:
    for this we revere you. ℟

3. My soul is waiting for the Lord,
    I count on his word.
    My soul is longing for the Lord
    more than watchman for daybreak.
    (Let the watchman count on daybreak
    and Israel on the Lord.) ℟

4. Because with the Lord there is mercy
    and fullness of redemption,
    Israel indeed he will redeem
    from all its iniquity. ℟

SECOND READING

Rm 8:8-11

A reading from the letter of St Paul to the Romans.

The Spirit of him who raised Jesus from the dead is living in you.

People who are interested only in unspiritual things can never be pleasing to God. Your interests, however, are not in the unspiritual, but in the spiritual, since the Spirit of God has made his home in you. In fact, unless you possessed the Spirit of Christ you would not belong to him. Though your body may be dead it is because of sin, but if Christ is in you then your spirit is life itself because you have been justified; and if the Spirit of him who raised Jesus from the dead is living in you, then he who raised Jesus from the dead will give life to your own mortal bodies through his Spirit living in you.

The word of the Lord.

GOSPEL ACCLAMATION

Jn 11:25-26

Glory and praise to you, O Christ!
I am the resurrection and the life, says the Lord;
whoever believes in me will never die.
Glory and praise to you, O Christ!

GOSPEL

Jn 11:1-45

(For Shorter Form, read between ♦ ♦).

A reading from the holy Gospel according to John.

I am the resurrection and the life.

There was a man named Lazarus who lived in the village of Bethany with two sisters, Mary and Martha, and he was ill. It was the same Mary, the sister of the sick man Lazarus, who anointed the Lord with ointment and wiped his feet with her hair. ♦The sisters sent this message to Jesus, 'Lord, the man you love is ill.' On receiving the message, Jesus said, 'This sickness will end not in death but in God's glory, and through it the Son of God will be glorified.'

Jesus loved Martha and her sister and Lazarus, yet when he heard that Lazarus was ill he stayed where he was for two more days before saying to the disciples, 'Let us go to Judaea.'♦ The disciples said, 'Rabbi, it is not long since the Jews wanted to stone you; are you going back again?' Jesus replied:

'Are there not twelve hours in the day?
A man can walk in the day-time without stumbling

because he has the light of this world to see by;
but if he walks at night he stumbles,
because there is no light to guide him.'

He said that and then added, 'Our friend Lazarus is resting, I
am going to wake him.' The disciples said to him 'Lord, if he is
able to rest he is sure to get better.' The phrase Jesus used referred
to the death of Lazarus, but they thought that by 'rest' he meant
'sleep', so Jesus put it plainly, 'Lazarus is dead, and for your sake
I am glad I was not there because now you will believe. But let
us go to him.' Then Thomas – known as the Twin – said to the
other disciples, 'Let us go too, and die with him.'

◆On arriving, Jesus found that Lazarus had been in the tomb
for four days already.◆ Bethany is only about two miles from
Jerusalem, and many Jews had come to Martha and Mary to
sympathise with them over their brother. ◆When Martha heard
that Jesus had come she went to meet him. Mary remained
sitting in the house. Martha said to Jesus, 'If you had been here,
my brother would not have died, but I know that, even now,
whatever you ask of God, he will grant you.' 'Your brother' said
Jesus to her 'will rise again.' Martha said, 'I know he will rise
again at the resurrection on the last day.' Jesus said:

'I am the resurrection and the life.
If anyone believes in me, even though he dies he will live,
and whoever lives and believes in me
will never die.
Do you believe this?

'Yes, Lord,' she said 'I believe that you are the Christ, the Son of
God, the one who was to come into this world.'◆

When she had said this, she went and called her sister Mary,
saying in a low voice, 'The Master is here and wants to see you.'
Hearing this, Mary got up quickly and went to him. Jesus had
not yet come into the village; he was still at the place where
Martha had met him. When the Jews who were in the house
sympathising with Mary saw her get up so quickly and go out,
they followed her, thinking that she was going to the tomb to
weep there.

Mary went to Jesus, and as soon as she saw him she threw
herself at his feet, saying, 'Lord, if you had been here, my
brother would not have died.' At the sight of her tears, and those

of the Jews who followed her, ⟡Jesus said in great distress, with a sigh that came straight from the heart, 'Where have you put him?' They said, 'Lord, come and see.' Jesus wept; and the Jews said, 'See how much he loved him!' But there were some who remarked, 'He opened the eyes of the blind man, could he not have prevented this man's death?' Still sighing, Jesus reached the tomb: it was a cave with a stone to close the opening. Jesus said, 'Take the stone away.' Martha said to him 'Lord, by now he will smell; this is the fourth day.' Jesus replied 'Have I not told you that if you believe you will see the glory of God?' So they took away the stone. Then Jesus lifted up his eyes and said:

'Father, I thank you for hearing my prayer.
I knew indeed that you always hear me.
But I speak
for the sake of all these who stand round me,
so that they may believe it was you who sent me.'

When he had said this, he cried in a loud voice, 'Lazarus, here! Come out!' The dead man came out, his feet and hands bound with bands of stuff and a cloth round his face. Jesus said to them, 'Unbind him, let him go free.'

Many of the Jews who had come to visit Mary and had seen what he did believed in him.⟡

The Gospel of the Lord.

Profession of Faith – pages 14-15.

Prayer over the Offerings

Hear us, almighty God,
and, having instilled in your servants
the teachings of the Christian faith,
graciously purify them
by the working of this sacrifice.
Through Christ our Lord.

Preface: Lazarus

The Lord be with you.
And with your spirit.

Lift up your hearts.
We lift them up to the Lord.

Let us give thanks to the Lord our God.
It is right and just.

It is truly right and just, our duty and our salvation,
always and everywhere to give you thanks,
Lord, holy Father, almighty and eternal God,
through Christ our Lord.

For as true man he wept for Lazarus his friend
and as eternal God raised him from the tomb,
just as, taking pity on the human race,
he leads us by sacred mysteries to new life.

Through him the host of Angels adores your majesty
and rejoices in your presence for ever.
May our voices, we pray, join with theirs
in one chorus of exultant praise, as we acclaim:

Holy, Holy, Holy Lord God of hosts …

Communion Antiphon   Cf. Jn 11:26

**Everyone who lives and believes in me
will not die for ever, says the Lord.**

Prayer after Communion

We pray, almighty God,
that we may always be counted among the members of Christ,
in whose Body and Blood we have communion.
Who lives and reigns for ever and ever.

Prayer over the People

Bless, O Lord, your people,
who long for the gift of your mercy,
and grant that what, at your prompting, they desire
they may receive by your generous gift.
Through Christ our Lord.

2 APRIL

PALM SUNDAY OF THE PASSION OF THE LORD

There is a core similarity between the four accounts of the death of Jesus in the New Testament. However, they differ in sequence and in details, allowing various understandings of the cross to unfold. Because the death of Jesus was and is such a deeply mysterious and indeed perplexing event, different dimensions are explored and laid bare by different New Testament writers. Matthew, Luke and John all bring forward somehow the resurrection into the story of Jesus' death. None is more dramatic than Matthew, who introduces not one but two earthquakes at this point.

THE COMMEMORATION OF THE LORD'S ENTRANCE INTO JERUSALEM

First Form: The Procession

The congregation assembles at a smaller church or other suitable place other than inside the church to which the procession will go. The faithful hold branches in their hands.

The Priest, accompanied by other ministers, approach the place where the people are gathered. Meanwhile, the following antiphon or another appropriate chant is sung.

Antiphon   Mt 21:9

Hosanna to the Son of David;
blessed is he who comes in the name of the Lord,
    the King of Israel.
Hosanna in the highest.

    Or:

Hosanna filio David: benedictus qui venit in nomine Domini.
Rex Israel: Hosanna in excelsis.

The Priest greets the people in these or similar words:

Dear brethren (brothers and sisters),
since the beginning of Lent until now
we have prepared our hearts by penance and charitable works.
Today we gather together to herald with the whole Church
the beginning of the celebration
of our Lord's Paschal Mystery,
that is to say, of his Passion and Resurrection.

For it was to accomplish this mystery
that he entered his own city of Jerusalem.
Therefore, with all faith and devotion,
let us commemorate
the Lord's entry into the city for our salvation,
following in his footsteps,
so that, being made by his grace partakers of the Cross,
we may have a share also in his Resurrection and in his life.

After the address, the Priest says one of the following prayers.

Let us pray.

Almighty ever-living God,
sanctify ✠ these branches with your blessing,
that we, who follow Christ the King in exultation,
may reach the eternal Jerusalem through him.
Who lives and reigns for ever and ever.
Amen.

> Or:

Increase the faith of those who place their hope in you, O God,
and graciously hear the prayers of those who call on you,
that we, who today hold high these branches
to hail Christ in his triumph,
may bear fruit for you by good works accomplished in him.
Who lives and reigns for ever and ever.
Amen.

He sprinkles the branches with holy water without saying anything.

The Gospel concerning the Lord's entrance is proclaimed.

GOSPEL   Mt 21:1-11

A reading from the holy Gospel according to Matthew.
Blessings on him who comes in the name of the Lord!

When they were near Jerusalem and had come in sight of
Bethphage on the Mount of Olives, Jesus sent two disciples,
saying to them, 'Go to the village facing you, and you will
immediately find a tethered donkey and a colt with her. Untie
them and bring them to me. If anyone says anything to you,
you are to say, "The Master needs them and will send them back
directly."' This took place to fulfil the prophecy:

> Say to the daughter of Zion:
> Look, your king comes to you;

he is humble, he rides on a donkey
and on a colt, the foal of a beast of burden.

So the disciples went out and did as Jesus had told them. They brought the donkey and the colt, then they laid their cloaks on their backs and he sat on them. Great crowds of people spread their cloaks on the road, while others were cutting branches from the trees and spreading them in his path. The crowds who went in front of him and those who followed were all shouting:

'Hosanna to the Son of David!
Blessings on him who comes in the name of the Lord!
Hosanna in the highest heavens!'

And when he entered Jerusalem, the whole city was in turmoil. 'Who is this?' people asked, and the crowds answered, 'This is the prophet Jesus from Nazareth in Galilee.'

The Gospel of the Lord.

After the Gospel, an invitation may be given in these or similar words.

Dear brethren (brothers and sisters),
like the crowds who acclaimed Jesus in Jerusalem,
let us go forth in peace.

Or:

Let us go forth in peace.

In the name of Christ. Amen.

The Procession to the church where Mass will be celebrated then sets off in the usual way.

As the Procession moves forward, the following or other suitable chants in honour of Christ the King are sung by the choir and people.

Antiphon 1

**The children of the Hebrews, carrying olive branches,
went to meet the Lord, crying out and saying:
Hosanna in the highest.**

If appropriate, this antiphon is repeated between the strophes of the following Psalm.

Psalm 23

The Lord's is the earth and its fullness,*
the world, and those who dwell in it.
It is he who set it on the seas;*
on the rivers he made it firm.

The antiphon is repeated.

Who shall climb the mountain of the Lord?*
The clean of hands and pure of heart,
whose soul is not set on vain things,†
who has not sworn deceitful words.*

The antiphon is repeated.

Blessings from the Lord shall he receive,*
and right reward from the God who saves him.
Such are the people who seek him,*
who seek the face of the God of Jacob.

The antiphon is repeated.

O gates, lift high your heads;†
grow higher, ancient doors.*
Let him enter, the king of glory!
Who is this king of glory?*
The Lord, the mighty, the valiant;
the Lord, the valiant in war.

The antiphon is repeated.

O gates, lift high your heads;†
grow higher, ancient doors.*
Let him enter, the king of glory!
Who is this king of glory?*
He, the Lord of hosts,
he is the king of glory.

The antiphon is repeated.

Antiphon 2

**The children of the Hebrews
    spread their garments on the road,
crying out and saying: Hosanna to the Son of David;
blessed is he who comes in the name of the Lord.**

If appropriate, this antiphon is repeated between the strophes of the
following Psalm.

Psalm 46

All peoples, clap your hands.*
Cry to God with shouts of joy!
For the Lord, the Most high, is awesome,*
the great king over all the earth.

The antiphon is repeated

He humbles peoples under us *
and nations under our feet.
Our heritage he chose for us, *
the pride of Jacob whom he loves.
God goes up with shouts of joy. *
The Lord goes up with trumpet blast.

The antiphon is repeated

Sing praise for God; sing praise! *
Sing praise to our king; sing praise!
God is king of all earth. *
Sing praise with all your skill.

The antiphon is repeated

God reigns over the nations. *
God sits upon his holy throne.
The princes of the peoples are assembled
with the people of the God of Abraham. †
The rulers of the earth belong to God, *
who is greatly exalted.

The antiphon is repeated.

Hymn to Christ the King

Chorus:

**Glory and honour and praise be to you, Christ,
    King and Redeemer,
to whom young children cried out loving Hosannas with joy.**

All repeat: **Glory and honour …**

Chorus:

Israel's King are you, King David's magnificent offspring;
you are the ruler who come blest in the name of the Lord.

All repeat: **Glory and honour …**

Chorus:

Heavenly hosts on high unite in singing your praises;
men and women on earth and all creation join in.

All repeat: **Glory and honour …**

Chorus:

Bearing branches of palm, Hebrews came crowding to greet you;
see how with prayers and hymns we come to pay you our vows.

All repeat: **Glory and honour …**

Chorus:
They offered gifts of praise to you, so near to your Passion;
see how we sing this song now to you reigning on high.

All repeat: **Glory and honour …**

Chorus:
Those you were pleased to accept; now accept our gifts of
     devotion,
good and merciful King, lover of all that is good.

All repeat: **Glory and honour …**

As the procession enters the church, there is sung the following
responsory or another chant, which should speak of the Lord's entrance.

℣   As the Lord entered the holy city, the children of the
    Hebrews proclaimed the resurrection of life.

℞   **Waving their branches of palm, they cried: Hosanna in the
    Highest.**

℣   When the people heard that Jesus was coming to Jerusalem,
    they went out to meet him.

℞   **Waving their branches …**

The Priest goes to the chair, says the Collect of the Mass, and then
continues the Mass in the usual way.

Second Form: The Solemn Entrance

When a procession outside the church cannot take place, the entrance of
the Lord is celebrated inside the church by means of a Solemn Entrance
before the principal Mass.

Holding branches in their hands, the faithful gather either outside, in
front of the church door, or inside the church itself.

While the Priest approaches the appointed place, the antiphon **Hosanna**
or another appropriate chant is sung. Then the blessing of branches and
the proclamation of the Gospel of the Lord's entrance into Jerusalem
take place as above.

Arriving at the altar, the Priest says the Collect of the Mass, and then
continues the Mass in the usual way.

Third Form: The Simple Entrance

If the Solemn Entrance is not held, the memorial of the Lord's entrance into Jerusalem takes place by means of a Simple Entrance.

While the Priest proceeds to the altar, the Entrance Antiphon with its Psalm (see below) or another chant on the same theme is sung. The Mass continues in the usual way.

Entrance Antiphon   Cf. Jn 12:1.12-13; Ps 23:9-10

Six days before the Passover,
when the Lord came into the city of Jerusalem,
the children ran to meet him;
in their hands they carried palm branches
and with a loud voice cried out:

*Hosanna in the highest!
Blessed are you, who have come in your abundant mercy!

O gates, lift high your heads;
grow higher, ancient doors.
Let him enter, the king of glory!
Who is this king of glory?
He, the Lord of hosts,
he is the king of glory.

*Hosanna in the highest!
Blessed are you, who have come in your abundant mercy!

——————— AT THE MASS ———————

Collect

Almighty ever-living God,
who as an example of humility for the human race to follow
caused our Saviour to take flesh and submit to the Cross,
graciously grant that we may heed his lesson of patient suffering
and so merit a share in his Resurrection.
Who lives and reigns with you in the unity of the Holy Spirit,
one God, for ever and ever.

FIRST READING   Is 50:4-7

A reading from the prophet Isaiah.
I did not cover my face against insult – I know I shall not be shamed.

The Lord has given me
a disciple's tongue.

So that I may know how to reply to the wearied
he provides me with speech.
Each morning he wakes me to hear,
to listen like a disciple.
The Lord has opened my ear.

For my part, I made no resistance,
neither did I turn away.
I offered my back to those who struck me,
my cheeks to those who tore at my beard;
I did not cover my face
against insult and spittle.

The Lord comes to my help,
so that I am untouched by the insults.
So, too, I set my face like flint;
I know I shall not be shamed.

> The word of the Lord.

RESPONSORIAL PSALM   Ps 21:8-9.17-20.23-24

℟ **My God, my God,
   why have you forsaken me?**

1. All who see me deride me.
    They curl their lips, they toss their heads.
    'He trusted in the Lord, let him save him:
    let him release him if this is his friend.' ℟

2. Many dogs have surrounded me,
    a band of the wicked beset me.
    They tear holes in my hands and my feet,
    I can count every one of my bones. ℟

3. They divide my clothing among them.
    They cast lots for my robe.
    O Lord, do not leave me alone,
    my strength, make haste to help me! ℟

4. I will tell of your name to my brethren
    and praise you where they are assembled.
    'You who fear the Lord give him praise;
    all sons of Jacob, give him glory.
    Revere him, Israel's sons.' ℟

SECOND READING   Ph 2:6-11

A reading from the letter of St Paul to the Philippians.

He humbled himself, but God raised him high.

His state was divine,
yet Christ Jesus did not cling
to his equality with God
but emptied himself
to assume the condition of a slave,
and became as men are;
and being as all men are,
he was humbler yet,
even to accepting death,
death on a cross.
But God raised him high
and gave him the name
which is above all other names
so that all beings
in the heavens, on earth and in the underworld,
should bend the knee at the name of Jesus
and that every tongue should acclaim
Jesus Christ as Lord,
to the glory of God the Father.

    The word of the Lord.

GOSPEL ACCLAMATION   Ph 2:8-9

Praise to you, O Christ, King of eternal glory!
Christ was humbler yet,
even to accepting death,
death on a cross.
But God raised him high
and gave him the name which is above all names.
Praise to you, O Christ, king of eternal glory.

GOSPEL   Mt 26:14-27:66

(For Shorter Form, read between ♦ ◀).

[N. Narrator; J. Jesus; O. other single speaker; C. the 'crowd' – bold types]

The passion of our Lord Jesus Christ according to Matthew.

N.   One of the Twelve, the man called Judas Iscariot, went to
     the chief priests and said:

O. What are you prepared to give me if I hand him over to you?

N. They paid him thirty silver pieces, and from that moment he looked for an opportunity to betray him.

Now on the first day of Unleavened Bread the disciples came to Jesus to say,

C. **Where do you want us to make the preparations for you to eat the passover?**

N. He replied:

J. Go to so-and-so in the city and say to him, 'The Master says: My time is near. It is at your house that I am keeping Passover with my disciples'.

N. The disciples did what Jesus told them and prepared the Passover. When the evening came he was at table with the twelve disciples. And while they were eating he said:

J. I tell you solemnly, one of you is about to betray me.

N. They were greatly distressed and started asking him in turn,

O. Not I, Lord, surely?

N. He answered:

J. Someone who has dipped his hand into the dish with me, will betray me. The Son of Man is going to his fate, as the scriptures say he will, but alas for that man by whom the Son of Man is betrayed! Better for that man if he had never been born!

N. Judas, who was to betray him, asked in his turn,

O. Not I, Rabbi, surely?

N. Jesus answered:

J. They are your own words.

N. Now as they were eating, Jesus took some bread, and when he had said the blessing he broke it and gave it to the disciples and said:

J. Take it and eat; this is my body.

N. Then he took a cup, and when he had returned thanks he gave it to them saying:

J. Drink all of you from this, for this is my blood, the blood of the covenant, which is to be poured out for many for the forgiveness of sins. From now on, I tell you, I shall not drink wine until the day I drink the new wine with you in the kingdom of my Father.

N. After psalms had been sung they left for the Mount of Olives. Then Jesus said to them,

J. You will all lose faith in me this night, for the scripture says: I shall strike the shepherd and the sheep of the flock will be scattered. But after my resurrection I shall go before you to Galilee.

N. At this, Peter said:

O. Though all lose faith in you, I will never lose faith.

N. Jesus answered him,

J. I tell you solemnly, this very night, before the cock crows, you will have disowned me three times.

N. Peter said to him,

O. Even if I have to die with you, I will never disown you.

N. · And all the disciples said the same.

Then Jesus came with them to a small estate called Gethsemane; and he said to his disciples,

J. Stay here while I go over there to pray.

N. He took Peter and the two sons of Zebedee with him. And sadness came over him, and great distress. Then he said to them:

J. My soul is sorrowful to the point of death. Wait here and keep awake with me.

N. And going on a little further he fell on his face and prayed:

J. My Father, if it is possible let this cup pass me by. Nevertheless, let it be as you, not I, would have it.

N. He came back to the disciples and found them sleeping, and he said to Peter:

J. So you had not the strength to keep awake with me one hour? You should be awake, and praying not to be put to the test. The spirit is willing, but the flesh is weak.

N. Again, a second time, he went away and prayed:

J. My father, if this cup cannot pass by without my drinking it, your will be done!

N. And he came again back and found them sleeping, their eyes were so heavy. Leaving them there, he went away again and prayed for the third time, repeating the same words. Then he came back to the disciples and said to them,

J.   You can sleep on now and take your rest. Now the hour has
     come when the Son of Man is to be betrayed into the hands
     of sinners. Get up! Let us go! My betrayer is already close at
     hand.

N.   He was still speaking when Judas, one of the Twelve,
     appeared, and with him a large number of men armed with
     swords and clubs, sent by the chief priests and elders of the
     people. Now the traitor had arranged a sign with them. He
     had said:

O.   'The one I kiss, he is the man. Take him in charge.'

N.   So he went straight up to Jesus and said:

O.   Greetings, Rabbi,

N.   and kissed him. Jesus said to him,

J.   My friend, do what you are here for.

N.   Then they came forward, seized Jesus and took him in
     charge. At that, one of the followers of Jesus grasped his
     sword and drew it; he struck out at the high priest's servant,
     and cut off his ear. Jesus then said:

J.   Put your sword back, for all who draw the sword will die
     by the sword. Or do you think that I cannot appeal to my
     Father who would promptly send more than twelve legions
     of angels to my defence? But then, how would the scriptures
     be fulfilled that say this is the way it must be?

N.   It was at this time that Jesus said to the crowds:

J.   Am I a brigand, that you had to set out to capture me with
     swords and clubs? I sat teaching in the Temple day after day
     and you never laid hands on me.

N.   Now all this happened to fulfil the prophecies in scripture.
     Then all the disciples deserted him and ran away.

     The men who had arrested Jesus led him off to Caiaphas
     the high priest, where the scribes and the elders were
     assembled. Peter followed him at a distance, and when he
     reached the high priest's palace, he went in and sat down
     with the attendants to see what the end would be.

     The chief priests and the whole Sanhedrin were looking
     for evidence against Jesus, however false, on which they
     might pass the death-sentence. But they could not find any,
     though several lying witnesses came forward. Eventually two
     stepped forward and made a statement,

O.   This man said: 'I have power to destroy the Temple of God and in three days build it up'.

N.   The high priest then stood up and said to him:

O.   Have you no answer to that? What is this evidence these men are bringing against you?

N.   But Jesus was silent. And the high priest said to him:

O.   I put you on oath by the living God to tell us if you are the Christ, the Son of God.

N.   Jesus answered:

J.   The words are your own. Moreover, I tell you that from this time onward you will see the Son of Man seated at the right hand of the Power and coming on the clouds of heaven.

N.   At this, the high priest tore his clothes and said:

O.   He has blasphemed. What need of witnesses have we now? There! You have just heard the blasphemy. What is your opinion?

N.   They answered:

C.   **He deserves to die.**

N.   Then they spat in his face and hit him with their fists; others said as they struck him:

C.   Play the prophet, Christ! Who hit you then?

N.   Meanwhile Peter was sitting outside in the courtyard, and a servant-girl came up to him and said:

O.   You too were with Jesus the Galilean.

N.   But he denied it in front of them all, saying:

O.   I do not know what you are talking about.

N.   When he went out to the gateway another servant-girl saw him and said to the people there:

O.   This man was with Jesus the Nazarene.

N.   And again, with an oath, he denied it,

O.   I do not know the man.

N.   A little later the bystanders came up and said to Peter:

C.   **You are one of them for sure! Why, your accent gives you away.**

N.   Then he started calling down curses on himself and swearing:

O.   I do not know the man.

N. At that moment the cock crew, and Peter remembered what Jesus had said, 'Before the cock crows you will have disowned me three times.' And he went outside and wept bitterly.

When morning came, all the chief priests and the elders of the people met in council to bring about the death of Jesus. They had him bound, and led him away to hand him over to Pilate, the governor. When he found that Jesus had been condemned, Judas his betrayer was filled with remorse and took the thirty pieces of silver back to the chief priests and elders, saying:

O. I have sinned. I have betrayed innocent blood.

N. They replied:

C. **What is that to us? That is your concern.**

N. And flinging down the silver pieces in the sanctuary he made off, and went and hanged himself. The chief priests picked up the silver pieces and said:

C. **It is against the Law to put this into the treasury; it is blood money.**

N. So they discussed the matter and bought the potter's field with it as a graveyard for foreigners, and this is why the field is called the Field of Blood today. The words of the prophet Jeremiah were then fulfilled: And they took the thirty silver pieces, the sum at which the precious One was priced by children of Israel, and they gave them for the potter's field, just as the Lord directed me.

◆Jesus, then, was brought before the governor, and the governor put to him this question:

O. Are you the king of the Jews?

N. Jesus replied:

J. It is you who say it.

N. But when he was accused by the chief priests and the elders he refused to answer at all. Pilate then said to him:

O. Do you not hear how many charges they have brought against you?

N. But to the governor's complete amazement, he offered no reply to any of the charges.

At festival time it was the governor's practice to release a prisoner for the people, anyone they chose. Now there was at that time a notorious prisoner whose name was Barabbas. So when the crowd gathered, Pilate said to them,

O.   Which do you want me to release for you: Barabbas or Jesus who is called Christ?

N.   For Pilate knew it was out of jealousy that they had handed him over. Now as he was seated in the chair of judgement, his wife sent him a message,

O.   Have nothing to do with that man; I have been upset all day by a dream I had about him.

N.   The chief priests and the elders, however, had persuaded the crowd to demand the release of Barabbas and the execution of Jesus. So when the governor spoke and asked them:

O.   Which of the two do you want me to release for you?

N.   They said:

C.   **Barabbas.**

N.   Pilate said to them:

O.   What am I to do with Jesus who is called Christ?

N.   They all said:

C.   **Let him be crucified!**

N.   Pilate asked:

O.   Why? What harm has he done?

N.   But they shouted all the louder,

C.   **Let him be crucified!**

N.   Then Pilate saw that he was making no impression, that in fact a riot was imminent. So he took some water, washed his hands in front of the crowd and said:

O.   I am innocent of this man's blood. It is your concern.

N.   And the people, to a man, shouted back:

C.   **His blood be on us and on our children!**

N.   Then he released Barabbas for them. He ordered Jesus to be first scourged and then handed over to be crucified.

The governor's soldiers took Jesus with them into the Praetorium and collected the whole cohort round him. Then they stripped him and made him wear a scarlet cloak, and having twisted some thorns into a crown they put this on his head and placed a reed in his right hand. To make fun of him they knelt to him saying:

C. **Hail, king of the Jews!**

N. And they spat on him and took the reed and struck him on the head with it. And when they had finished making fun of him, they took off the cloak and dressed him in his own clothes and led him away to crucify him.

On their way out, they came across a man from Cyrene, Simon by name, and enlisted him to carry his cross. When they had reached a place called Golgotha, that is, the place of the skull, they gave him wine to drink. When they had finished crucifying him they shared out his clothing by casting lots, and then sat down and stayed there keeping guard over him. Above his head was placed the charge against him; it read: 'This is Jesus, the King of the Jews'. At the same time two robbers were crucified with him, one on the right and one on the left.

The passers-by jeered at him; they shook their heads and said:

C. **So you would destroy the Temple and rebuild it in three days! Then save yourself! If you are God's son, come down from the cross!**

N. The chief priests with the scribes and the elders mocked him in the same way, saying:

C. **He saved others; he cannot save himself. He is the King of Israel; let him come down from the cross now, and we will believe in him. He put his trust in God; now let God rescue him if he wants him. For he did say, 'I am the son of God'.**

N. Even the robbers who were crucified with him taunted him in the same way.

From the sixth hour there was darkness over all the land until the ninth hour. And about the ninth hour, Jesus cried out in a loud voice:

J. Eli, Eli, lama sabachthani?

N. That is: 'My God, my God, why have you deserted me?' When some of those who stood there heard this, they said:

C. **The man is calling on Elijah,**

N. and one of them quickly ran to get a sponge which he dipped in vinegar and, putting it on a reed, gave it him to drink. The rest of them said:

C. **Wait! See if Elijah will come to save him.**

N. But Jesus, again crying out in a loud voice, yielded up his spirit.

(All kneel and pause a moment.)

N. At that, the veil of the Temple was torn in two from top to bottom; the earth quaked; the rocks were split; the tombs opened and the bodies of many holy men rose from the dead, and these, after his resurrection, came out of the tombs, entered the Holy City and appeared to a number of people.

  Meanwhile the centurion, together with the others guarding Jesus, had seen the earthquake and all that was taking place, and they were terrified and said:

C. **In truth this was a son of God.◀**

N. And many women were there, watching from a distance, the same women who had followed Jesus from Galilee and looked after him. Among them were Mary of Magdala, Mary the mother of James and Joseph, and the mother of Zebedee's sons.

  When it was evening, there came a rich man of Arimathaea called Joseph, who had himself become a disciple of Jesus. This man went to Pilate and asked for the body of Jesus. Pilate thereupon ordered it to be handed over. So Joseph took the body, wrapped it in a clean shroud and put it in his own new tomb which he had hewn out of the rock. He then rolled a large stone across the entrance of the tomb and went away. Now Mary of Magdala and the other Mary were there, sitting opposite the sepulchre.

  Next day, that is, when Preparation Day was over, the chief priests and the Pharisees went in a body to Pilate and said to him,

C. **Your Excellency, we recall that this impostor said, while he was still alive, 'After three days I shall rise again'. Therefore give the order to have the sepulchre kept secure until the third day, for fear his disciples come and steal him away and tell the people, 'He has risen from the dead'. This last piece of fraud would be worse than what went before.**

N. Pilate said to them:

O.   You may have your guards. Go and make all as secure as you know how.

N.   So they went and made the sepulchre secure, putting seals on the stone and mounting a guard.

Profession of Faith – pages 14-15.

Prayer over the Offerings

Through the Passion of your Only Begotten Son, O Lord,
may our reconciliation with you be near at hand,
so that, though we do not merit it by our own deeds,
yet by this sacrifice made once for all,
we may feel already the effects of your mercy.
Through Christ our Lord.

Preface: The Passion of the Lord

The Lord be with you.
And with your spirit.

Lift up your hearts.
We lift them up to the Lord.

Let us give thanks to the Lord our God.
It is right and just.

It is truly right and just, our duty and our salvation,
always and everywhere to give you thanks,
Lord, holy Father, almighty and eternal God,
through Christ our Lord.

For, though innocent, he suffered willingly for sinners
and accepted unjust condemnation to save the guilty.
His Death has washed away our sins,
and his Resurrection has purchased our justification.

And so, with all the Angels,
we praise you, as in joyful celebration we acclaim:

Holy, Holy, Holy Lord God of hosts …

Communion Antiphon   Mt 26:42

**Father, if this chalice cannot pass without my drinking it,
your will be done.**

Prayer after Communion

Nourished with these sacred gifts,
we humbly beseech you, O Lord,

that, just as through the death of your Son
you have brought us to hope for what we believe,
so by his Resurrection
you may lead us to where you call.
Through Christ our Lord.

Prayer over the People

Look, we pray, O Lord, on this your family,
for whom our Lord Jesus Christ
did not hesitate to be delivered into the hands of the wicked
and submit to the agony of the Cross.
Who lives and reigns for ever and ever.

═══════════════ 6 APRIL ═══════════════
THURSDAY OF THE LORD'S SUPPER

*The services of the Easter Triduum are presented as one liturgical
event over three days. The Mass this evening ends in silence; Friday's
service begins and ends in silence; The Vigil begins, however, with the
sign of the Cross and ends with the great Thanks be to God, alleluia,
alleluia! At each stage, while reflecting on different stages, we are
invited to keep the whole Paschal Mystery present in our minds.*

─────────── AT THE EVENING MASS ───────────

Entrance Antiphon   Cf. Gal 6:14

**We should glory in the Cross of our Lord Jesus Christ,
in whom is our salvation, life and resurrection,
through whom we are saved and delivered.**

Greeting, Penitential Rite, Gloria – pages 7-13.

Collect

O God, who have called us to participate
in this most sacred Supper,
in which your Only Begotten Son,
when about to hand himself over to death,
entrusted to the Church a sacrifice new for all eternity,
the banquet of his love,
grant, we pray,
that we may draw from so great a mystery,

the fullness of charity and of life.
Through our Lord Jesus Christ, your Son,
who lives and reigns with you in the unity of the Holy Spirit,
one God, for ever and ever.

FIRST READING   Ex 12:1-8.11-14

A reading from the book of Exodus.

Instructions concerning the Passover meal.

The Lord said to Moses and Aaron in the land of Egypt, 'This month is to be the first of all the others for you, the first month of your year. Speak to the whole community of Israel and say, "On the tenth day of this month each man must take an animal from the flock, one for each family: one animal for each household. If the household is too small to eat the animal, a man must join with his neighbour, the nearest to his house, as the number of persons requires. You must take into account what each can eat in deciding the number for the animal. It must be an animal without blemish, a male one year old; you may take it from either sheep or goats. You must keep it till the fourteenth day of the month when the whole assembly of the community of Israel shall slaughter it between the two evenings. Some of the blood must then be taken and put on the two doorposts and the lintel of the houses where it is eaten. That night, the flesh is to be eaten, roasted over the fire; it must be eaten with unleavened bread and bitter herbs. You shall eat it like this: with a girdle round your waist, sandals on your feet, a staff in your hand. You shall eat it hastily: it is a passover in honour of the Lord. That night, I will go through the land of Egypt and strike down all the first-born in the land of Egypt, man and beast alike, and I shall deal out punishment to all the gods of Egypt, I am the Lord. The blood shall serve to mark the houses that you live in. When I see the blood I will pass over you and you shall escape the destroying plague when I strike the land of Egypt. This day is to be a day of remembrance for you, and you must celebrate it as a feast in the Lord's honour. For all generations you are to declare it a day of festival, for ever".'

The word of the Lord.

RESPONSORIAL PSALM   Ps 115:12-13.15-18

℟ **The blessing-cup that we bless**
   is a communion with the blood of Christ.

1. How can I repay the Lord
   for his goodness to me?
   The cup of salvation I will raise;
   I will call on the Lord's name. ℟

2. O precious in the eyes of the Lord
   is the death of his faithful.
   Your servant, Lord, your servant am I;
   you have loosened my bonds. ℟

3. A thanksgiving sacrifice I make:
   I will call on the Lord's name.
   My vows to the Lord I will fulfil
   before all his people. ℟

SECOND READING   1 Cor 11:23-26

A reading from the first letter of St Paul to the Corinthians.

Every time you eat this bread and drink this cup, you are proclaiming the death of the Lord.

This is what I received from the Lord, and in turn passed on to you: that on the same night that he was betrayed, the Lord Jesus took some bread, and thanked God for it and broke it, and he said, 'This is my body, which is for you; do this as a memorial of me.' In the same way he took the cup after supper, and said, 'This cup is the new covenant in my blood. Whenever you drink it, do this as a memorial of me.' Until the Lord comes, therefore, every time you eat this bread and drink this cup, you are proclaiming his death.

The word of the Lord.

GOSPEL ACCLAMATION   Jn 13:34

Praise and honour to you, Lord Jesus!
I give you a new commandment:
love one another just as I have loved you, says the Lord.
Praise and honour to you, Lord Jesus!

GOSPEL   Jn 13:1-15

A reading from the holy Gospel according to John.

Now he showed how perfect his love was.

It was before the festival of the Passover, and Jesus knew that the hour had come for him to pass from this world to the Father. He had always loved those who were his in the world, but now he showed how perfect his love was.

They were at supper, and the devil had already put it into the mind of Judas Iscariot son of Simon, to betray him. Jesus knew that the Father had put everything into his hands, and that he had come from God and was returning to God, and he got up from table, removed his outer garment and, taking a towel, wrapped it round his waist; he then poured water into a basin and began to wash the disciples' feet and to wipe them with the towel he was wearing.

He came to Simon Peter, who said to him, 'Lord, are you going to wash my feet?' Jesus answered, 'At the moment you do not know what I am doing, but later you will understand.' 'Never!' said Peter. 'You shall never wash my feet.' Jesus replied, 'If I do not wash you, you can have nothing in common with me.' 'Then, Lord,' said Simon Peter 'not only my feet, but my hands and my head as well!' Jesus said, 'No one who has taken a bath needs washing, he is clean all over. You too are clean, though not all of you are.' He knew who was going to betray him, that was why he said, 'though not all of you are.'

When he had washed their feet and put on his clothes again he went back to the table. 'Do you understand,' he said, 'what I have done to you? You call me Master and Lord, and rightly; so I am. If I, then, the Lord and Master, have washed your feet, you should wash each other's feet. I have given you an example so that you may copy what I have done to you.'

The Gospel of the Lord.

The Washing of Feet

After the Homily, where a pastoral reason suggests it, the Washing of Feet follows.

Meanwhile some of the following antiphons or other appropriate chants are sung.

Antiphon 1   Cf. Jn 13:4.5.15

**After the Lord had risen from supper,
he poured water into a basin
and began to wash the feet of his disciples:
he left them this example.**

Antiphon 2   Cf. Jn 13:12.13.15

**The Lord Jesus, after eating supper with his disciples,
washed their feet and said to them:**

Do you know what I, your Lord and Master,
    have done for you?
I have given you an example, that you should do likewise.

Antiphon 3   Jn 13:6.7.8

Lord, are you to wash my feet? Jesus said to him in answer:
If I do not wash your feet, you will have no share with me.

V. So he came to Simon Peter and Peter said to him:

    – Lord, are you to wash my feet …

V. What I am doing, you do not know for now,
    but later you will come to know.

    – Lord, are you to wash my feet …

Antiphon 4   Cf. Jn 13:14

If I, your Lord and Master, have washed your feet,
how much more should you wash each other's feet?

Antiphon 5   Jn 13:35

This is how all will know that you are my disciples:
if you have love for one another.

V. Jesus said to his disciples:

    – This is how all will know …

Antiphon 6   Jn 13:34

I give you a new commandment,
that you love one another
as I have loved you, says the Lord.

Antiphon 7   1 Cor 13:13

Let faith, hope and charity, these three, remain among you,
but the greatest of these is charity.

V. Now faith, hope and charity, these three, remain;
    but the greatest of these is charity.

    – Let faith, hope and charity …

The Profession of Faith is not said.

The Liturgy of the Eucharist

At the beginning of the Liturgy of the Eucharist, there may be a
procession of the faithful in which gifts for the poor may be presented
with the bread and wine.

Meanwhile the following, or another appropriate chant, is sung.

Ant. **Where true charity is dwelling, God is present there.**

V.   By the love of Christ we have been brought together:
V.   let us find in him our gladness and our pleasure;
V.   may we love him and revere him, God the living,
V.   and in love respect each other with sincere hearts.

Ant. **Where true charity is dwelling, God is present there.**

V.   So when we as one are gathered all together,
V.   let us strive to keep our minds free of division;
V.   may there be an end to malice, strife and quarrels,
V.   and let Christ our God be dwelling here among us.

Ant. **Where true charity is dwelling, God is present there.**

V.   May your face thus be our vision, bright in glory,
V.   Christ our God, with all the blessed Saints in heaven:
V.   such delight is pure and faultless, joy unbounded,
V.   which endures through countless ages world without end.
        Amen.

Prayer over the Offerings

Grant us, O Lord, we pray,
that we may participate worthily in these mysteries,
for whenever the memorial of this sacrifice is celebrated
the work of our redemption is accomplished.
Through Christ our Lord.

Preface I of the Most Holy Eucharist

The Lord be with you.
And with your spirit.

Lift up your hearts.
We lift them up to the Lord.

Let us give thanks to the Lord our God.
It is right and just.

It is truly right and just, our duty and our salvation,
always and everywhere to give you thanks,
Lord, holy Father, almighty and eternal God,
through Christ our Lord.

For he is the true and eternal Priest,
who instituted the pattern of an everlasting sacrifice,
and was the first to offer himself as the saving Victim,
commanding us to make this offering as his memorial.

As we eat his flesh that was sacrificed for us,
we are made strong,
and, as we drink his Blood that was poured out for us,
we are washed clean.

And so, with Angels and Archangels,
with Thrones and Dominions,
and with all the hosts and Powers of heaven,
we sing the hymn of your glory,
as without end we acclaim:

Holy, Holy, Holy Lord God of hosts …

Communion Antiphon   1 Cor 11:24-25

**This is the Body that will be given up for you;
this is the Chalice of the new covenant in my Blood,
    says the Lord;
do this, whenever you receive it, in memory of me.**

Prayer after Communion

Grant, almighty God,
that, just as we are renewed
by the Supper of your Son in this present age,
so we may enjoy his banquet for all eternity.
Who lives and reigns for ever and ever.

The Transfer of the Most Blessed Sacrament

After the Prayer after Communion, takes place the solemn transfer of
the Blessed Sacrament. During the procession the hymn Pange, lingua
or some other eucharistic chant is sung.

Pange, lingua gloriosi
Corporis mysterium,
Sanguinisque pretiosi,
Quem in mundi pretium
Fructus ventris generosi
Rex effudit gentium.

Nobis datus, nobis natus
Ex intacta virgine,
Et in mundo conversatus
Sparso verbi semine,
Sui moras incolatus
Miro clausit ordine.

In supremae nocte coenae,
Recumbens cum fratribus,
Observata lege plene
Cibis in legalibus,
Cibum turbae duodenae
Se dat suis manibus.

Verbum caro, panem verum,
Verbo carnem efficit:
Fitque sanguis Christi merum:
Et si sensus deficit,
Ad firmandum cor sincerum
Sola fides sufficit

When the procession reaches the place of repose, the Priest places the ciborium in the tabernacle. Then he puts incense in the thurible and, kneeling, incenses the Blessed Sacrament, while **Tantum ergo sacramentum** is sung. The tabernacle of repose is then closed.

Tantum ergo sacramentum	Genitori, Genitoque
Veneremur cernui:	Laus et jubilatio,
Et antiquum documentum	Salus, honor, virtus quoque
Novo cedat ritui;	Sit et benedictio:
Praestet fides supplementum	Procedenti ab utroque
Sensuum defectui.	Compar sit laudatio. Amen.

After a period of adoration in silence, the Priest and the ministers genuflect and return to the sacristy.

At an appropriate time, the altar is stripped and, if possible, the crosses are removed from the church. It is expedient that any crosses which remain in the church be veiled.

The faithful are invited to continue adoration before the Blessed Sacrament for a suitable length of time during the night, according to local circumstances, but after midnight the adoration should take place without solemnity.

──────────── 7 APRIL ────────────

FRIDAY OF THE PASSION OF THE LORD
(Good Friday)

In today's Gospel, Jesus dies with the words: "It is accomplished." This Gospel begins with the words "In the beginning" and in John 20 we are told that the Risen Lord "breathed on" the apostles. These details remind us consistently of Genesis 1-2, where we read, "In the beginning God created heaven and earth" (Gen 1:1); "on the seventh day God had completed the work he had been doing" (Gen 2:2); blew the breath of life into his nostrils, (Gen 2:7). The evangelist is teaching us "if anyone is in Christ, there is a new creation" (2 Cor 5:17).

All pray silently for a while. Then the Priest says, omitting the invitation **Let us pray.**

Prayer
Remember your mercies, O Lord,
and with your eternal protection sanctify your servants,

for whom Christ your Son,
by the shedding of his Blood,
established the Paschal Mystery.
Who lives and reigns for ever and ever.

Or:

O God, who by the Passion of Christ your Son, our Lord,
abolished the death inherited from ancient sin
by every succeeding generation,
grant that just as, being conformed to him,
we have borne by the law of nature
the image of the man of earth,
so by the sanctification of grace
we may bear the image of the Man of heaven.
Through Christ our Lord.
Amen.

First Part:
The Liturgy of the Word

FIRST READING   Is 52:13–53:12

A reading from the prophet Isaiah.
He was pierced through for our faults.

See, my servant will prosper,
he shall be lifted up, exalted, rise to great heights.

As the crowds were appalled on seeing him
– so disfigured did he look
that he seemed no longer human –
so will the crowds be astonished at him,
and kings stand speechless before him;
for they shall see something never told
and witness something never heard before:
'Who could believe what we have heard,
and to whom has the power of the Lord been revealed?'

Like a sapling he grew up in front of us,
like a root in arid ground.
Without beauty, without majesty (we saw him),
no looks to attract our eyes;
a thing despised and rejected by men,
a man of sorrows and familiar with suffering,

a man to make people screen their faces;
he was despised and we took no account of him.

And yet ours were the sufferings he bore,
ours the sorrows he carried.
But we, we thought of him as someone punished,
struck by God, and brought low.
Yet he was pierced through for our faults,
crushed for our sins.
On him lies a punishment that brings us peace,
and through his wounds we are healed.

We had all gone astray like sheep,
each taking his own way,
and the Lord burdened him
with the sins of all of us.
Harshly dealt with, he bore it humbly,
he never opened his mouth,
like a lamb that is led to the slaughter-house,
like a sheep that is dumb before its shearers
never opening its mouth.

By force and by law he was taken;
would anyone plead his cause?
Yes, he was torn away from the land of the living;
for our faults struck down in death.
They gave him a grave with the wicked,
a tomb with the rich,
though he had done no wrong
and there had been no perjury in his mouth.
The Lord has been pleased to crush him with suffering.
If he offers his life in atonement,
he shall see his heirs, he shall have a long life
and through him what the Lord wishes will be done.

His soul's anguish over
he shall see the light and be content.
By his sufferings shall my servant justify many,
taking their faults on himself.

Hence I will grant whole hordes for his tribute,
he shall divide the spoil with the mighty,
for surrendering himself to death
and letting himself be taken for a sinner,

while he was bearing the faults of many
and praying all the time for sinners.

The word of the Lord.

RESPONSORIAL PSALM   Ps 30:2-6.12-13.15-17.25

℟ **Father, into your hands I commend my spirit.**

1. In you, O Lord, I take refuge.
   Let me never be put to shame.
   In your justice, set me free.
   Into your hands I commend my spirit.
   It is you who will redeem me, Lord. ℟

2. In the face of all my foes
   I am a reproach,
   an object of scorn to my neighbours
   and of fear to my friends. ℟.

3. Those who see me in the street
   run far away from me.
   I am like a dead man, forgotten in men's hearts,
   like a thing thrown away. ℟

4. But as for me, I trust in you, Lord,
   I say: 'You are my God.'
   My life is in your hands, deliver me
   from the hands of those who hate me. ℟

5. Let your face shine on your servant.
   Save me in your love.
   Be strong, let your heart take courage,
   all who hope in the Lord. ℟

SECOND READING   Heb 4:14-16; 5:7-9

A reading from the letter to the Hebrews.

He learnt to obey through suffering and became for all who obey him the source of eternal salvation.

Since in Jesus, the Son of God, we have the supreme high priest who has gone through to the highest heaven, we must never let go of the faith that we have professed. For it is not as if we had a high priest who was incapable of feeling our weaknesses with us; but we have one who has been tempted in every way that we are, though he is without sin. Let us be confident, then, in approaching the throne of grace, that we shall have mercy from him and find grace when we are in need of help.

During his life on earth, he offered up prayer and entreaty, aloud and in silent tears, to the one who had the power to save him out of death, and he submitted so humbly that his prayer was heard. Although he was Son, he learnt to obey through suffering; but having been made perfect, he became for all who obey him the source of eternal salvation.

The word of the Lord.

GOSPEL ACCLAMATION   Ph 2:8-9

Glory and praise to you, O Christ!
Christ was humbler yet,
even to accepting death, death on a cross.
But God raised him high
and gave him the name that is above all names.
Glory and praise to you, O Christ!

GOSPEL   Jn 18:1–19:42

(N. Narrator; J. Jesus; O. other individual voices; C. the 'crowd' – **bold types**.)

The passion of our Lord Jesus Christ according to John.

N. Jesus left with his disciples and crossed the Kedron valley. There was a garden there, and he went into it with his disciples. Judas the traitor knew the place well, since Jesus had often met his disciples there, and he brought the cohort to this place together with a detachment of guards sent by the chief priests and the Pharisees, all with lanterns and torches and weapons. Knowing everything that was going to happen to him, Jesus then came forward and said,

J. Who are you looking for?

N. They answered,

C. **Jesus the Nazarene.**

N. He said,

J. I am he.

N. Now Judas the traitor was standing among them. When Jesus said, 'I am he', they moved back and fell to the ground. He asked them a second time,

J. Who are you looking for?

N. They said,

C. **Jesus the Nazarene.**

N. Jesus replied,

J. I have told you that I am he. If I am the one you are looking for, let these others go.

N. This was to fulfil the words he had spoken, 'Not one of those you gave me have I lost.'

Simon Peter, who carried a sword, drew it and wounded the high priest's servant, cutting off his right ear. The servant's name was Malchus. Jesus said to Peter,

J. Put your sword back in its scabbard; am I not to drink the cup that the Father has given me?

N. The cohort and its captain and the Jewish guards seized Jesus and bound him. They took him first to Annas, because Annas was the father-in-law of Caiaphas, who was high priest that year. It was Caiaphas who had suggested to the Jews, 'It is better for one man to die for the people.'

Simon Peter, with another disciple, followed Jesus. This disciple, who was known to the high priest, went with Jesus into the high priest's palace, but Peter stayed outside the door. So the other disciple, the one known to the high priest, went out, spoke to the woman who was keeping the door and brought Peter in. The maid on duty at the door said to Peter,

O. Aren't you another of that man's disciples?

N. He answered,

O. I am not.

N. Now it was cold, and the servants and guards had lit a charcoal fire and were standing there warming themselves; so Peter stood there too, warming himself with the others.

The high priest questioned Jesus about his disciples and his teaching. Jesus answered,

J. I have spoken openly for all the world to hear; I have always taught in the synagogue and in the Temple where all the Jews meet together: I have said nothing in secret. But why ask me? Ask my hearers what I taught: they know what I said.

N. At these words, one of the guards standing by gave Jesus a slap in the face, saying,

O. Is that the way to answer the high priest?

N. Jesus replied,

J. If there is something wrong in what I said, point it out; but if there is no offence in it, why do you strike me?

N. Then Annas sent him, still bound, to Caiaphas the high priest.

As Simon Peter stood there warming himself, someone said to him,

O. Aren't you another of his disciples?

N. He denied it saying,

O. I am not.

N. One of the high priest's servants, a relation of the man whose ear Peter had cut off, said,

O. Didn't I see you in the garden with him?

N. Again Peter denied it; and at once a cock crew.

They then led Jesus from the house of Caiaphas to the Prætorium. It was now morning. They did not go into the Prætorium themselves or they would be defiled and unable to eat the passover. So Pilate came outside to them and said,

O. What charge do you bring against this man?

N. They replied,

C. **If he were not a criminal, we should not be handing him over to you.**

N. Pilate said,

O. Take him yourselves, and try him by your own Law.

N. The Jews answered,

C. **We are not allowed to put a man to death.**

N. This was to fulfil the words Jesus had spoken indicating the way he was going to die.

So Pilate went back into the Prætorium and called Jesus to him, and asked,

O. Are you the king of the Jews?

N. Jesus replied,

J. Do you ask this of your own accord, or have others spoken to you about me?

N. Pilate answered,

O. Am I a Jew? It is your own people and the chief priests who have handed you over to me: what have you done?'

N. Jesus replied,

J. Mine is not a kingdom of this world; if my kingdom were of this world, my men would have fought to prevent my being surrendered to the Jews. But my kingdom is not of this kind.

N. Pilate said,

O. So you are a king then?

N. Jesus answered,

J. It is you who say it. Yes, I am a king. I was born for this, I came into the world for this: to bear witness to the truth; and all who are on the side of truth listen to my voice.

N. Pilate said,

O. Truth? What is that?

N. And with that he went out again to the Jews and said,

O. I find no case against him. But according to a custom of yours I should release one prisoner at the Passover; would you like me, then, to release the king of the Jews?

N. At this they shouted:

C. **Not this man, but Barabbas.**

N. Barabbas was a brigand.

Pilate then had Jesus taken away and scourged; and after this, the soldiers twisted some thorns into a crown and put it on his head, and dressed him in a purple robe. They kept coming up to him and saying,

C. **Hail, king of the Jews!**

N. and they slapped him in the face.

Pilate came outside again and said to them,

O. Look, I am going to bring him out to you to let you see that I find no case.

N. Jesus then came out wearing the crown of thorns and the purple robe. Pilate said,

O. Here is the man.

N. When they saw him the chief priests and the guards shouted,

C. **Crucify him! Crucify him!**

N. Pilate said,

O. Take him yourselves and crucify him: I can find no case against him.

N. The Jews replied,

C. **We have a Law, and according to that Law he ought to die, because he has claimed to be the Son of God.**

N. When Pilate heard them say this his fears increased. Re-entering the Prætorium, he said to Jesus,

O. Where do you come from?

N. But Jesus made no answer. Pilate then said to him,

O. Are you refusing to speak to me? Surely you know I have power to release you and I have power to crucify you?

N. Jesus replied,

J. You would have no power over me if it had not been given you from above; that is why the one who handed me over to you has the greater guilt.

N. From that moment Pilate was anxious to set him free, but the Jews shouted,

C. **If you set him free you are no friend of Caesar's; anyone who makes himself king is defying Caesar.**

N. Hearing these words, Pilate had Jesus brought out, and seated himself on the chair of judgement at a place called the Pavement, in Hebrew Gabbatha. It was Passover Preparation Day, about the sixth hour. Pilate said to the Jews,

O. Here is your king.

N. They said,

C. **Take him away, take him away! Crucify him!**

N. Pilate said,

O. Do you want me to crucify your king?

N. The chief priests answered,

C. **We have no king except Caesar.**

N. So in the end Pilate handed him over to them to be crucified.

They then took charge of Jesus, and carrying his own cross he went out of the city to the place of the skull or, as it was called in Hebrew, Golgotha, where they crucified him with two others, one on either side with Jesus in the middle. Pilate wrote out a notice and had it fixed to the cross; it ran: 'Jesus the Nazarene, King of the Jews'. This notice was read by many of the Jews, because the place where Jesus was

N. crucified was not far from the city, and the writing was in Hebrew, Latin and Greek. So the Jewish chief priests said to Pilate,

C. **You should not write "King of the Jews", but "This man said: I am King of the Jews".**

N. Pilate answered,

O. What I have written, I have written.

N. When the soldiers had finished crucifying Jesus they took his clothing and divided it into four shares, one for each soldier. His undergarment was seamless, woven in one piece from neck to hem; so they said to one another,

C. **Instead of tearing it, let's throw dice to decide who is to have it.**

N. In this way the words of scripture were fulfilled:

> They shared out my clothing among them.
> They cast lots for my clothes.

This is exactly what the soldiers did.

Near the cross of Jesus stood his mother and his mother's sister, Mary the wife of Clopas, and Mary of Magdala. Seeing his mother and the disciple he loved standing near her, Jesus said to his mother,

J. Woman, this is your son.

N. Then to the disciple he said,

J. This is your mother.

N. And from that moment the disciple made a place for her in his home.

After this, Jesus knew that everything had now been completed, and to fulfil the scripture perfectly he said:

J. I am thirsty.

N. A jar full of vinegar stood there, so putting a sponge soaked in vinegar on a hyssop stick they held it up to his mouth. After Jesus had taken the vinegar he said,

J. It is accomplished;

N. and bowing his head he gave up the spirit.

All kneel and pause a moment.

N. It was Preparation Day, and to prevent the bodies remaining on the cross during the sabbath – since that sabbath was a day of special solemnity – the Jews asked Pilate to have the legs broken and the bodies taken away. Consequently the soldiers came and broke the legs of the first man who had been crucified with him and then of the other. When they came to Jesus, they found he was already dead, and so instead of breaking his legs one of the soldiers pierced his side with a lance; and immediately there came out blood and water. This is the evidence of one who saw it – trustworthy evidence, and he knows he speaks the truth – and he gives it so that you may believe as well. Because all this happened to fulfil the words of scripture:

Not one bone of his will be broken,

and again, in another place scripture says:

They will look on the one whom they have pierced.

After this, Joseph of Arimathaea, who was a disciple of Jesus – though a secret one because he was afraid of the Jews – asked Pilate to let him remove the body of Jesus. Pilate gave permission, so they came and took it away. Nicodemus came as well – the same one who had first come to Jesus at night-time – and he brought a mixture of myrrh and aloes, weighing about a hundred pounds. They took the body of Jesus and wrapped it with the spices in linen cloths, following the Jewish burial custom. At the place where he had been crucified there was a garden, and in this garden a new tomb in which no one had yet been buried. Since it was the Jewish Day of Preparation and the tomb was near at hand, they laid Jesus there.

───────── THE SOLEMN INTERCESSIONS ─────────

I. For Holy Church

Let us pray, dearly beloved, for the holy Church of God,
that our God and Lord be pleased to give her peace,
to guard her and to unite her throughout the whole world
and grant that, leading our life in tranquillity and quiet,
we may glorify God the Father almighty.

Prayer in silence. Then the Priest says:

Almighty ever-living God,
who in Christ revealed your glory to all the nations,
watch over the works of your mercy,
that your Church, spread throughout all the world,

may persevere with steadfast faith in confessing your name.
Through Christ our Lord.
Amen.

II. For the Pope

Let us pray also for our most Holy Father Pope N.,
that our God and Lord,
who chose him for the Order of Bishops,
may keep him safe and unharmed for the Lord's holy Church,
to govern the holy People of God.

Prayer in silence. Then the Priest says:

Almighty ever-living God,
by whose decree all things are founded,
look with favour on our prayers
and in your kindness protect the Pope chosen for us,
that, under him, the Christian people,
governed by you their maker,
may grow in merit by reason of their faith.
Through Christ our Lord.
Amen.

III. For all orders and degrees of the faithful

Let us pray also for our Bishop N.,
for all Bishops, Priests, and Deacons of the Church
and for the whole of the faithful people.

Prayer in silence. Then the Priest says:

Almighty ever-living God,
by whose Spirit the whole body of the Church
is sanctified and governed,
hear our humble prayer for your ministers,
that, by the gift of your grace,
all may serve you faithfully.
Through Christ our Lord.
Amen.

IV. For catechumens

Let us pray also for (our) catechumens,
that our God and Lord
may open wide the ears of their inmost hearts
and unlock the gates of his mercy,
that, having received forgiveness of all their sins

through the waters of rebirth,
they, too, may be one with Christ Jesus our Lord.

Prayer in silence. Then the Priest says:

Almighty ever-living God,
who make your Church ever fruitful with new offspring,
increase the faith and understanding of (our) catechumens,
that, reborn in the font of Baptism,
they may be added to the number of your adopted children.
Through Christ our Lord.
Amen.

V. For the unity of Christians

Let us pray also for all our brothers and sisters
    who believe in Christ,
that our God and Lord may be pleased,
as they live the truth,
to gather them together and keep them in his one Church.

Prayer in silence. Then the Priest says:

Almighty ever-living God,
who gather what is scattered
and keep together what you have gathered,
look kindly on the flock of your Son,
that those whom one Baptism has consecrated
may be joined together by integrity of faith
and united in the bond of charity.
Through Christ our Lord.
Amen.

VI. For the Jewish people

Let us pray also for the Jewish people,
to whom the Lord our God spoke first,
that he may grant them to advance in love of his name
and in faithfulness to his covenant.

Prayer in silence. Then the Priest says:

Almighty ever-living God,
who bestowed your promises on Abraham and his descendants,
graciously hear the prayers of your Church,
that the people you first made your own
may attain the fullness of redemption.
Through Christ our Lord.
Amen.

VII. For those who do not believe in Christ

Let us pray also for those who do not believe in Christ,
that, enlightened by the Holy Spirit,
they, too, may enter on the way of salvation.

Prayer in silence. Then the Priest says:

Almighty ever-living God,
grant to those who do not confess Christ
that, by walking before you with a sincere heart,
they may find the truth
and that we ourselves, being constant in mutual love
and striving to understand more fully the mystery of your life,
may be made more perfect witnesses to your love in the world.
Through Christ our Lord.
Amen.

VIII. For those who do not believe in God

Let us pray also for those who do not acknowledge God,
that, following what is right in sincerity of heart,
they may find the way to God himself.

Prayer in silence. Then the Priest says:

Almighty ever-living God,
who created all people
to seek you always by desiring you
and, by finding you, come to rest,
grant, we pray,
that, despite every harmful obstacle,
all may recognize the signs of your fatherly love
and the witness of the good works
done by those who believe in you,
and so in gladness confess you,
the one true God and Father of our human race.
Through Christ our Lord.
Amen.

IX. For those in public office

Let us pray also for those in public office,
that our God and Lord
may direct their minds and hearts according to his will
for the true peace and freedom of all.

Prayer in silence. Then the Priest says:

Almighty ever-living God,
in whose hand lies every human heart
and the rights of peoples,
look with favour, we pray,
on those who govern with authority over us,
that throughout the whole world,
the prosperity of peoples,
the assurance of peace,
and freedom of religion
may through your gift be made secure.
Through Christ our Lord.
Amen.

X. For those in tribulation

Let us pray, dearly beloved,
to God the Father almighty,
that he may cleanse the world of all errors,
banish disease, drive out hunger,
unlock prisons, loosen fetters,
granting to travellers safety, to pilgrims return,
health to the sick, and salvation to the dying.

Prayer in silence. Then the Priest says:

Almighty ever-living God,
comfort of mourners, strength of all who toil,
may the prayers of those who cry out in any tribulation
come before you,
that all may rejoice,
because in their hour of need
your mercy was at hand.
Through Christ our Lord.
Amen.

SECOND PART:
THE ADORATION OF THE HOLY CROSS

The solemn Adoration of the Holy Cross takes place in three stages.

The Showing of the Holy Cross

First Form

The Priest, standing before the altar and facing the people, receives the Cross, uncovers a little of its upper part and elevates it while beginning the **Ecce lignum Crucis** (**Behold the wood of the Cross**). All respond, **Come, let us adore**. At the end of the singing, all kneel and for a brief moment adore in silence.

Behold the wood of the Cross,
on which hung the salvation of the world.
Come, let us adore.

Then the Priest uncovers the right arm of the Cross and again, raising up the Cross, begins,

Behold the wood of the Cross,
on which hung the salvation of the world.
Come, let us adore.

Finally, he uncovers the Cross entirely and, raising it up, begins,

Behold the wood of the Cross,
on which hung the salvation of the world.
Come, let us adore.

Second Form

The Priest goes to the door of the church, where he receives the unveiled Cross. Then the procession sets off through the church to the sanctuary. Near the door, in the middle of the church, and before the entrance of the sanctuary, the one who carries the Cross elevates it, singing, **Behold the wood of the Cross**, to which all respond, **Come, let us adore**. After each response all kneel and for a brief moment adore in silence, as above.

The Adoration of the Holy Cross

While the adoration of the Holy Cross is taking place, the antiphon **Crucem tuam adoramus** (**We adore your Cross, O Lord**), the Reproaches, the hymn **Crux fidelis** (**Faithful Cross**) or other suitable chants are sung, during which all who have already adored the Cross remain seated.

Chants to be sung during the Adoration of the Holy Cross.

Antiphon
We adore your Cross, O Lord,
we praise and glorify your holy Resurrection,
for behold, because of the wood of a tree
joy has come to the whole world.

Cf. Ps 66:2

May God have mercy on us and bless us;
may he let his face shed its light upon us
and have mercy on us.

And the antiphon is repeated: **We adore …**

The Reproaches

Numbers 1 and 2 indicate first and second choir.

I

1 and 2   My people, what have I done to you?
   Or how have I grieved you? Answer me!
1   Because I led you out of the land of Egypt,
  you have prepared a Cross for your Saviour.

1   Hagios o Theos,

2   Holy is God,

1   Hagios Ischyros,

2   Holy and Mighty,

1   Hagios Athanatos, eleison himas.

2   Holy and Immortal One, have mercy on us.

1 and 2   Because I led you out through the desert forty years
   and fed you with manna and brought you into a land
     of plenty,
   you have prepared a Cross for your Saviour.

1   Hagios o Theos,

2   Holy is God,

1   Hagios Ischyros,

2   Holy and Mighty,

1   Hagios Athanatos, eleison himas.

2   Holy and Immortal One, have mercy on us.

1 and 2   What more should I have done for you and have not
          done?
     Indeed, I planted you as my most beautiful chosen vine and
     you have turned very bitter for me,
     for in my thirst you gave me vinegar to drink
     and with a lance you pierced your Saviour's side.

1   Hagios o Theos,

2   Holy is God,

1   Hagios Ischyros,

2   Holy and Mighty,

1   Hagios Athanatos, eleison himas.

2   Holy and Immortal One, have mercy on us.

II

Cantors:
I scourged Egypt for your sake with its firstborn sons,
and you scourged me and handed me over.

1 and 2 repeat:
My people, what have I done to you?
Or how have I grieved you? Answer me!

Cantors:
I led you out from Egypt as Pharaoh lay sunk in the Red Sea,
and you handed me over to the chief priests.

1 and 2 repeat:
My people …

Cantors:
I opened up the sea before you,
and you opened my side with a lance.

1 and 2 repeat:
My people …

Cantors:
I went before you in a pillar of cloud,
and you led me into Pilate's palace.

1 and 2 repeat:
My people …

Cantors:
I fed you with manna in the desert,
and on me you rained blows and lashes.

1 and 2 repeat:
My people …

Cantors:
I gave you saving water from the rock to drink,
and for drink you gave me gall and vinegar.

1 and 2 repeat:
My people …

Cantors:
I struck down for you the kings of the Canaanites,
and you struck my head with a reed.

1 and 2 repeat:
My people …

Cantors:
I put in your hand a royal sceptre,
and you put on my head a crown of thorns.

1 and 2 repeat:
My people …

Cantors:
I exalted you with great power,
and you hung me on the scaffold of the Cross.

1 and 2 repeat:
My people …

Hymn

All:
Faithful Cross the Saints rely on,
Noble tree beyond compare!
Never was there such a scion,
Never leaf or flower so rare.
Sweet the timber, sweet the iron,
Sweet the burden that they bear!

Cantors:
Sing, my tongue, in exultation
Of our banner and device!

Make a solemn proclamation
Of a triumph and its price:
How the Saviour of creation
Conquered by his sacrifice!

All:

Faithful Cross the Saints rely on,
Noble tree beyond compare!
Never was there such a scion,
Never leaf or flower so rare.

Cantors:

For, when Adam first offended,
Eating that forbidden fruit,
Not all hopes of glory ended
With the serpent at the root:
Broken nature would be mended
By a second tree and shoot.

All:

Sweet the timber, sweet the iron,
Sweet the burden that they bear!

Cantors:

Thus the tempter was outwitted
By a wisdom deeper still:
Remedy and ailment fitted,
Means to cure and means to kill;
That the world might be acquitted,
Christ would do his Father's will.

All:

Faithful Cross the Saints rely on,
Noble tree beyond compare!
Never was there such a scion,
Never leaf or flower so rare.

Cantors:

So the Father, out of pity
For our self-inflicted doom,
Sent him from the heavenly city
When the holy time had come:
He, the Son and the Almighty,
Took our flesh in Mary's womb.

All:
Sweet the timber, sweet the iron,
Sweet the burden that they bear!

Cantors:
Hear a tiny baby crying,
Founder of the seas and strands;
See his virgin Mother tying
Cloth around his feet and hands;
Find him in a manger lying
Tightly wrapped in swaddling-bands!

All:
Faithful Cross the Saints rely on,
Noble tree beyond compare!
Never was there such a scion,
Never leaf or flower so rare.

Cantors:
So he came, the long-expected,
Not in glory, not to reign;
Only born to be rejected,
Choosing hunger, toil and pain,
Till the scaffold was erected
And the Paschal Lamb was slain.

All:
Sweet the timber, sweet the iron,
Sweet the burden that they bear!

Cantors:
No disgrace was too abhorrent:
Nailed and mocked and parched he died;
Blood and water, double warrant,
Issue from his wounded side,
Washing in a mighty torrent
Earth and stars and oceantide.

All:
Faithful Cross the Saints rely on,
Noble tree beyond compare!
Never was there such a scion,
Never leaf or flower so rare.

Cantors:

Lofty timber, smooth your roughness,
Flex your boughs for blossoming;
Let your fibres lose their toughness,
Gently let your tendrils cling;
Lay aside your native gruffness,
Clasp the body of your King!

All:

Sweet the timber, sweet the iron,
Sweet the burden that they bear!

Cantors:

Noblest tree of all created,
Richly jewelled and embossed:
Post by Lamb's blood consecrated;
Spar that saves the tempest-tossed;
Scaffold-beam which, elevated,
Carries what the world has cost!

All:

Faithful Cross the Saints rely on,
Noble tree beyond compare!
Never was there such a scion,
Never leaf or flower so rare.

The following conclusion is never to be omitted:

All:

Wisdom, power, and adoration
To the blessed Trinity
For redemption and salvation
Through the Paschal Mystery,
Now, in every generation,
And for all eternity. Amen.

THIRD PART:
HOLY COMMUNION

The Priest brings the Blessed Sacrament back from the place of repose to
the altar, while all stand in silence.

Then the Priest says:

At the Saviour's command
and formed by divine teaching,
we dare to say:

Our Father, who art in heaven,
hallowed be thy name;
thy kingdom come,
thy will be done
on earth as it is in heaven.
Give us this day our daily bread,
and forgive us our trespasses,
as we forgive those who trespass against us;
and lead us not into temptation,
but deliver us from evil.

Deliver us, Lord, we pray, from every evil,
graciously grant peace in our days,
that, by the help of your mercy,
we may be always free from sin
and safe from all distress,
as we await the blessed hope
and the coming of our Saviour, Jesus Christ.

**For the kingdom, the power and the glory are yours
now and for ever.**

May the receiving of your Body and Blood,
Lord Jesus Christ,
not bring me to judgement and condemnation,
but through your loving mercy
be for me protection in mind and body
and a healing remedy.

Behold the Lamb of God,
behold him who takes away the sins of the world.
Blessed are those called to the supper of the Lamb.

**Lord, I am not worthy
that you should enter under my roof,
but only say the word
and my soul shall be healed.**

After the Communion a brief silence may be observed. Then the Priest says:

Let us pray.

Almighty ever-living God,
who have restored us to life
by the blessed Death and Resurrection of your Christ,
preserve in us the work of your mercy,

that, by partaking of this mystery,
we may have a life unceasingly devoted to you.
Through Christ our Lord.
Amen.

Prayer over the People

The Priest invites people to bow down for the blessing.

May abundant blessing, O Lord, we pray,
descend upon your people,
who have honoured the Death of your Son
in the hope of their resurrection:
may pardon come,
comfort be given,
holy faith increase,
and everlasting redemption be made secure.
Through Christ our Lord.
Amen.

All depart in silence.

8 APRIL
THE EASTER VIGIL IN THE HOLY NIGHT

This is our Passover, the night of nights and the feast of feasts. Let us celebrate and rejoice, therefore! To help our feelings catch up with our convictions, on this holy night we use fire and darkness and water, readings and songs to mark and to evoke the great events of our salvation. We bring to the feast whatever is "dark" in our own lives, whatever is in need of light and healing. As the angel said, there is no need to be afraid. Like the women at the tomb, may we go away filled with awe and great joy. On this night, may the risen Lord come to meet us.

FIRST PART:
THE SOLEMN BEGINNING OF THE VIGIL
OR LUCERNARIUM

The Blessing of the Fire and Preparation of the Candle

The lights of the church are extinguished. Fire is prepared in a suitable place outside the church. When the people have assembled the priest goes there with the ministers, one of whom carries the Easter candle.

The Priest and the faithful sign themselves while the Priest says: **In the name of the Father, and of the Son, and of the Holy Spirit**, and then he greets the assembled people in the usual way and briefly instructs them in these or similar words:

Dear brethren (brothers and sisters),
on this most sacred night,
in which our Lord Jesus Christ
passed over from death to life,
the Church calls upon her sons and daughters,
scattered throughout the world,
to come together to watch and pray.
If we keep the memorial
of the Lord's paschal solemnity in this way,
listening to his word and celebrating his mysteries,
then we shall have the sure hope
of sharing his triumph over death
and living with him in God.

Then the Priest blesses the fire, saying with hands extended:

Let us pray.

O God, who through your Son
bestowed upon the faithful the fire of your glory,
sanctify ✠ this new fire, we pray,
and grant that,
by these paschal celebrations,
we may be so inflamed with heavenly desires,
that with minds made pure
we may attain festivities of unending splendour.
Through Christ our Lord.
Amen.

After the blessing of the new fire, one of the ministers brings the paschal
candle to the Priest, who cuts a cross into the candle with a stylus. Then
he makes the Greek letter Alpha above the cross, the letter Omega below
and the four numerals of the current year, saying meanwhile:

1. Christ yesterday and today;
2. the Beginning and the End;
3. the Alpha;
4. and the Omega.
5. All time belongs to him;
6. and all the ages.
7. To him be glory and power;
8. through every age and for ever. Amen.

A

2 | 0

2 | 3

Ω

The Priest may insert five grains of incense into the candle in the form
of a cross, meanwhile saying:

1. By his holy
2. and glorious wounds,
3. may Christ the Lord
4. guard us
5. and protect us. Amen.

1

4 2 5

3

The Priest lights the paschal candle from the new fire, saying:

May the light of Christ rising in glory
dispel the darkness of our hearts and minds.

Procession

When the candle has been lit, one of the ministers takes burning coals from the fire and places them in the thurible, and the Priest puts incense into it in the usual way. The Deacon or, if there is no Deacon, another suitable minister, takes the paschal candle and a procession forms. The thurifer with the smoking thurible precedes the Deacon or other minister who carries the paschal candle. After them follows the Priest with the ministers and the people, all holding in their hands unlit candles.

At the door of the church the Deacon, raising up the candle, sings:

The Light of Christ.

And all reply:

Thanks be to God.

The Priest lights his candle from the flame of the paschal candle.

Then the Deacon moves forward to the middle of the church and raising up the candle, sings a second time:

The Light of Christ.

And all reply:

Thanks be to God.

All light their candles from the flame of the paschal candle and continue in procession.

When the Deacon arrives before the altar, he stands facing the people, raises up the candle and sings a third time:

The Light of Christ.

And all reply:

Thanks be to God.

And lights are lit throughout the church, except for the altar candles.

The Easter Proclamation (Exsultet)

(The Proclamation may also be sung in the shorter form – see page 209).

Longer Form of the Easter Proclamation
Exult, let them exult, the hosts of heaven,
exult, let Angel ministers of God exult,
let the trumpet of salvation
sound aloud our mighty King's triumph!
Be glad, let earth be glad, as glory floods her,
ablaze with light from her eternal King,

let all corners of the earth be glad,
knowing an end to gloom and darkness.
Rejoice, let Mother Church also rejoice,
arrayed with the lightning of his glory,
let this holy building shake with joy,
filled with the mighty voices of the peoples.

(Therefore, dearest friends,
standing in the awesome glory of this holy light,
invoke with me, I ask you,
the mercy of God almighty,
that he, who has been pleased to number me,
though unworthy, among the Levites,
may pour into me his light unshadowed,
that I may sing this candle's perfect praises.)

(The Lord be with you.
And with your spirit.)

Lift up your hearts.
We lift them up to the Lord.

Let us give thanks to the Lord our God.
It is right and just.

It is truly right and just,
with ardent love of mind and heart
and with devoted service of our voice,
to acclaim our God invisible, the almighty Father,
and Jesus Christ, our Lord, his Son, his Only Begotten.

Who for our sake paid Adam's debt to the eternal Father,
and, pouring out his own dear Blood,
wiped clean the record of our ancient sinfulness.

These, then, are the feasts of Passover,
in which is slain the Lamb, the one true Lamb,
whose Blood anoints the doorposts of believers.

This is the night,
when once you led our forebears, Israel's children,
from slavery in Egypt
and made them pass dry-shod through the Red Sea.

This is the night
that with a pillar of fire
banished the darkness of sin.

This is the night
that even now, throughout the world,
sets Christian believers apart from worldly vices
and from the gloom of sin,
leading them to grace
and joining them to his holy ones.

This is the night,
when Christ broke the prison-bars of death
and rose victorious from the underworld.

Our birth would have been no gain,
had we not been redeemed.
O wonder of your humble care for us!
O love, O charity beyond all telling,
to ransom a slave you gave away your Son!

O truly necessary sin of Adam,
destroyed completely by the Death of Christ!

O happy fault
that earned so great, so glorious a Redeemer!

O truly blessed night,
worthy alone to know the time and hour
when Christ rose from the underworld!

This is the night
of which it is written:
The night shall be as bright as day,
dazzling is the night for me,
and full of gladness.

The sanctifying power of this night
dispels wickedness, washes faults away,
restores innocence to the fallen, and joy to mourners,
drives out hatred, fosters concord, and brings down the mighty.

On this, your night of grace, O holy Father,
accept this candle, a solemn offering,
the work of bees and of your servants' hands,
an evening sacrifice of praise,
this gift from your most holy Church.

But now we know the praises of this pillar,
which glowing fire ignites for God's honour,
a fire into many flames divided,

yet never dimmed by sharing of its light,
for it is fed by melting wax,
drawn out by mother bees
to build a torch so precious.

O truly blessed night,
when things of heaven are wed to those of earth,
and divine to the human.

Therefore, O Lord,
we pray you that this candle,
hallowed to the honour of your name,
may persevere undimmed,
to overcome the darkness of this night.
Receive it as a pleasing fragrance,
and let it mingle with the lights of heaven.
May this flame be found still burning
by the Morning Star:
the one Morning Star who never sets,
Christ your Son,
who, coming back from death's domain,
has shed his peaceful light on humanity,
and lives and reigns for ever and ever.
Amen.

Shorter Form of the Easter Proclamation

Exult, let them exult, the hosts of heaven,
exult, let Angel ministers of God exult,
let the trumpet of salvation
sound aloud our mighty King's triumph!
Be glad, let earth be glad, as glory floods her,
ablaze with light from her eternal King,
let all corners of the earth be glad,
knowing an end to gloom and darkness.
Rejoice, let Mother Church also rejoice,
arrayed with the lightning of his glory,
let this holy building shake with joy,
filled with the mighty voices of the peoples.

(The Lord be with you.
And with your spirit.)

Lift up your hearts.
We lift them up to the Lord.

Let us give thanks to the Lord our God.
It is right and just.

It is truly right and just,
with ardent love of mind and heart
and with devoted service of our voice,
to acclaim our God invisible, the almighty Father,
and Jesus Christ, our Lord, his Son, his Only Begotten.

Who for our sake paid Adam's debt to the eternal Father,
and, pouring out his own dear Blood,
wiped clean the record of our ancient sinfulness.

These then are the feasts of Passover,
in which is slain the Lamb, the one true Lamb,
whose Blood anoints the doorposts of believers.

This is the night,
when once you led our forebears, Israel's children,
from slavery in Egypt
and made them pass dry-shod through the Red Sea.

This is the night
that with a pillar of fire
banished the darkness of sin.

This is the night
that even now, throughout the world,
sets Christian believers apart from worldly vices
and from the gloom of sin,
leading them to grace
and joining them to his holy ones.

This is the night,
when Christ broke the prison-bars of death
and rose victorious from the underworld.

O wonder of your humble care for us!
O love, O charity beyond all telling,
to ransom a slave you gave away your Son!

O truly necessary sin of Adam,
destroyed completely by the Death of Christ!

O happy fault
that earned so great, so glorious a Redeemer!
The sanctifying power of this night

dispels wickedness, washes faults away,
restores innocence to the fallen, and joy to mourners.

O truly blessed night,
when things of heaven are wed to those of earth,
and divine to the human.

On this, your night of grace, O holy Father,
accept this candle, a solemn offering,
the work of bees and of your servants' hands,
an evening sacrifice of praise,
this gift from your most holy Church.

Therefore, O Lord,
we pray you that this candle,
hallowed to the honour of your name,
may persevere undimmed,
to overcome the darkness of this night.
Receive it as a pleasing fragrance,
and let it mingle with the lights of heaven.
May this flame be found still burning
by the Morning Star:
the one Morning Star who never sets,
Christ your Son,
who, coming back from death's domain,
has shed his peaceful light on humanity,
and lives and reigns for ever and ever.
Amen.

SECOND PART:
THE LITURGY OF THE WORD

After setting aside their candles, all sit. Before the readings begin, the Priest instructs the people in these or similar words:

Dear brethren (brothers and sisters),
now that we have begun our solemn Vigil,
let us listen with quiet hearts to the Word of God.
Let us meditate on how God in times past saved his people
and in these, the last days, has sent us his Son as our Redeemer.
Let us pray that our God may complete this paschal
    work of salvation
by the fullness of redemption.

Then the readings follow. A reader goes to the ambo and proclaims the reading. Afterwards a psalmist or a cantor sings or says the Psalm with the people making the response. Then all rise, the Priest says, **Let us pray** and, after all have prayed for a while in silence, he says the prayer corresponding to the reading. In place of the Responsorial Psalm a period of sacred silence may be observed, in which case the pause after **Let us pray** is omitted.

FIRST READING   Gn 1:1–2:2
(For Shorter Form, read between ♦ ♦).

A reading from the book of Genesis.

God saw all he had made, and indeed it was very good.

| ♦In the beginning God created the heavens and the earth. ♦ Now the earth was a formless void, there was darkness over the deep, and God's spirit hovered over the water.

God said, 'Let there be light', and there was light. God saw that light was good, and God divided light from darkness. God called light 'day', and darkness he called 'night'. Evening came and morning came: the first day.

God said, 'Let there be a vault in the waters to divide the waters in two.' And so it was. God made the vault, and it divided the waters above the vault from the waters under the vault. God called the vault 'heaven'. Evening came and morning came: the second day.

God said, 'Let the waters under heaven come together into a single mass, and let dry land appear.' And so it was. God called the dry land 'earth' and the mass of waters 'seas', and God saw that it was good.

God said, 'Let the earth produce vegetation: seed-bearing plants, and fruit trees bearing fruit with their seed inside, on the earth.' And so it was. The earth produced vegetation: plants bearing seed in their several kinds, and trees bearing fruit with their seed inside in their several kinds. God saw that it was good. Evening came and morning came: the third day.

God said, 'Let there be lights in the vault of heaven to divide day from night, and let them indicate festivals, days and years. Let them be lights in the vault of heaven to shine on the earth.' And so it was. God made the two great lights: the greater light to govern the day, the smaller light to govern the night, and the stars. God set them in the vault of heaven to shine on the earth, to govern the day and the night and to divide light from darkness. God saw that it was good. Evening came and morning came: the fourth day.

God said, 'Let the waters teem with living creatures, and let birds fly above the earth within the vault of heaven.' And so it was. God created great sea-serpents and every kind of living creature with which the waters teem, and every kind of winged creature. God saw that it was good. God blessed them, saying, 'Be fruitful, multiply, and fill the waters of the seas; and let the birds multiply upon the earth.' Evening came and morning came: the fifth day.

God said, 'Let the earth produce every kind of living creature: cattle, reptiles, and every kind of wild beast.' And so it was. God made every kind of wild beast, every kind of cattle, and every kind of land reptile. God saw that it was good.

♦ God said, 'Let us make man in our own image, in the likeness of ourselves, and let them be masters of the fish of the sea, the birds of heaven, the cattle, all the wild beasts and all the reptiles that crawl upon the earth.'

God created man in the image of himself,
in the image of God he created him,
male and female he created them.

God blessed them, saying to them, 'Be fruitful, multiply, fill the earth and conquer it. Be masters of the fish of the sea, the birds of heaven and all living animals on the earth.' God said, 'See, I give you all the seed-bearing plants that are upon the whole earth, and all the trees with seed-bearing fruit; this shall be your food. To all wild beasts, all birds of heaven and all living reptiles on the earth I give all the foliage of plants for food.' And so it was. God saw all he had made, and indeed it was very good. ♦ Evening came and morning came: the sixth day.

Thus heaven and earth were completed with all their array. On the seventh day God completed the work he had been doing. He rested on the seventh day after all the work he had been doing.

The word of the Lord.

RESPONSORIAL PSALM   Ps 103:1-2.5-6.10.12-14.24.35

℟ **Send forth your spirit, O Lord,
and renew the face of the earth.**

1. Bless the Lord, my soul!
   Lord God, how great you are,
   clothed in majesty and glory,
   wrapped in light as in a robe! ℟

2. You founded the earth on its base,
   to stand firm from age to age.
   You wrapped it with the ocean like a cloak:
   the waters stood higher than the mountains. ℟

3. You make springs gush forth in the valleys:
   they flow in between the hills.
   On their banks dwell the birds of heaven;
   from the branches they sing their song. ℟

4. From your dwelling you water the hills;
   earth drinks its fill of your gift.
   You make the grass grow for the cattle
   and the plants to serve man's needs. ℟

5. How many are your works, O Lord!
   In wisdom you have made them all.
   The earth is full of your riches.
   Bless the Lord, my soul! ℟

ALTERNATIVE PSALM   Ps 32:4-7.12-13.20.22

℟ **The Lord fills the earth with his love.**

1. The word of the Lord is faithful
   and all his works to be trusted.
   The Lord loves justice and right
   and fills the earth with his love. ℟

2. By his word the heavens were made,
   by the breath of his mouth all the stars.
   He collects the waves of the ocean;
   he stores up the depths of the sea. ℟

3. They are happy, whose God is the Lord,
   the people he has chosen as his own.
   From the heavens the Lord looks forth,
   he sees all the children of men. ℟

4. Our soul is waiting for the Lord.
   The Lord is our help and our shield.
   May your love be upon us, O Lord,
   as we place all our hope in you. ℟

All stand for the prayer.

Let us pray.

Almighty ever-living God,
who are wonderful in the ordering of all your works,
may those you have redeemed understand
that there exists nothing more marvellous
than the world's creation in the beginning
except that, at the end of the ages,
Christ our Passover has been sacrificed.
Who lives and reigns for ever and ever.
Amen.

Or, On the creation of man:

O God, who wonderfully created human nature
and still more wonderfully redeemed it,
grant us, we pray,
to set our minds against the enticements of sin,
that we may merit to attain eternal joys.
Through Christ our Lord.
Amen.

SECOND READING   Gn 22:1-18

(For Shorter Form, read between ♦ ♦).

A reading from the book of Genesis.
The sacrifice of Abraham, our father in faith.

♦ God put Abraham to the test. 'Abraham, Abraham,' he called. 'Here I am' he replied. 'Take your son,' God said, 'your only child Isaac, whom you love, and go to the land of Moriah. There you shall offer him as a burnt-offering, on a mountain I will point out to you.' ♦

Rising early next morning Abraham saddled his ass and took with him two of his servants and his son Isaac. He chopped wood for the burnt-offering and started on his journey to the place God had pointed out to him. On the third day Abraham looked up and saw the place in the distance. Then Abraham said to his servants, 'Stay here with the donkey. The boy and I will go over there; we will worship and come back to you.'

Abraham took the wood for the burnt-offering, loaded it on Isaac, and carried in his own hands the fire and the knife. Then the two of them set out together. Isaac spoke to his father

Abraham, 'Father', he said. 'Yes, my son', he replied. 'Look,' he said 'here are the fire and the wood, but where is the lamb for the burnt-offering?' Abraham answered, 'My son, God himself will provide the lamb for the burnt-offering.' Then the two of them went on together.

♦When they arrived at the place God had pointed out to him, Abraham built an altar there, and arranged the wood. Then he bound his son Isaac and put him on the altar on top of the wood. Abraham stretched out his hand and seized the knife to kill his son.

But the angel of the Lord called to him from heaven, 'Abraham, Abraham' he said. 'I am here' he replied. 'Do not raise your hand against the boy' the angel said. 'Do not harm him, for now I know you fear God. You have not refused me your son, your only son.' Then looking up, Abraham saw a ram caught by its horns in a bush. Abraham took the ram and offered it as a burnt-offering in place of his son. ♦

Abraham called this place 'The Lord provides', and hence the saying today: On the mountain the Lord provides.

♦The angel of the Lord called Abraham a second time from heaven. 'I swear by my own self – it is the Lord who speaks – because you have done this, because you have not refused me your son, your only son, I will shower blessings on you, I will make your descendants as many as the stars of heaven and the grains of sand on the seashore. Your descendants shall gain possession of the gates of their enemies. All the nations of the earth shall bless themselves by your descendants, as a reward for your obedience.'♦

The word of the Lord.

RESPONSORIAL PSALM   Ps 15:5.8-11

℟ **Preserve me, God, I take refuge in you.**

1. O Lord, it is you who are my portion and cup;
    it is you yourself who are my prize.
    I keep the Lord ever in my sight:
    since he is at my right hand, I shall stand firm. ℟

2. And so my heart rejoices, my soul is glad;
    even my body shall rest in safety.
    For you will not leave my soul among the dead,
    nor let your beloved know decay. ℟

3.   You will show me the path of life,
     the fullness of joy in your presence,
     at your right hand happiness for ever. ℟

All stand for the prayer.

Let us pray.

O God, supreme Father of the faithful,
who increase the children of your promise
by pouring out the grace of adoption
throughout the whole world
and who through the Paschal Mystery
make your servant Abraham father of nations,
as once you swore,
grant, we pray,
that your peoples may enter worthily
into the grace to which you call them.
Through Christ our Lord.
Amen.

The following reading is obligatory.

THIRD READING   Ex 14:15–15:1

A reading from the book of Exodus.
The sons of Israel went on dry ground right into the sea.

The Lord said to Moses, 'Why do you cry to me so? Tell sons of
Israel to march on. For yourself, raise your staff and stretch out
your hand over the sea and part it for the sons of Israel to walk
through the sea on dry ground. I for my part will make the heart
of the Egyptians so stubborn that they will follow them. So shall
I win myself glory at the expense of Pharaoh, of all his army, his
chariots, his horsemen. And when I have won glory for myself,
at the expense of Pharaoh and his chariots and his army, the
Egyptians will learn that I am the Lord.'

     Then the angel of the Lord, who marched at the front of
the army of Israel, changed station and moved to their rear.
The pillar of cloud changed station from the front to the rear
of them, and remained there. It came between the camp of the
Egyptians and the camp of Israel. The cloud was dark, and the
night passed without the armies drawing any closer the whole
night long. Moses stretched out his hand over the sea. The Lord
drove back the sea with a strong easterly wind all night, and

he made dry land of the sea. The waters parted and the sons of Israel went on dry ground right into the sea, walls of water to right and to left of them. The Egyptians gave chase: after them they went, right into the sea, all Pharaoh's horses, his chariots, and his horsemen. In the morning watch, the Lord looked down on the army of the Egyptians from the pillar of fire and of cloud, and threw the army into confusion. He so clogged their chariot wheels that they could scarcely make headway. 'Let us flee from the Israelites,' the Egyptians cried 'the Lord is fighting for them against the Egyptians!' 'Stretch out your hand over the sea,' the Lord said to Moses 'that the waters may flow back on the Egyptians and their chariots and their horsemen.' Moses stretched out his hand over the sea and, as day broke, the sea returned to its bed. The fleeing Egyptians marched right into it, and the Lord overthrew the Egyptians in the very middle of the sea. The returning waters overwhelmed the chariots and the horsemen of Pharaoh's whole army, which had followed the Israelites into the sea; not a single one of them was left. But the sons of Israel had marched through the sea on dry ground, walls of water to right and to left of them. That day, the Lord rescued Israel from the Egyptians, and Israel saw the Egyptians lying dead on the shore. Israel witnessed the great act that the Lord had performed against the Egyptians, and the people venerated the Lord; they put their faith in the Lord and in Moses, his servant.

It was then that Moses and the sons of Israel sang this song in honour of the Lord:

The Responsorial Psalm follows immediately.

RESPONSORIAL PSALM   Ex 15:1-6.17-18

℟ **I will sing to the Lord, glorious his triumph!**

1. I will sing to the Lord, glorious his triumph!
    Horse and rider he has thrown into the sea!
    The Lord is my strength, my song, my salvation.
    This is my God and I extol him,
    my father's God and I give him praise. ℟

2. The Lord is a warrior! The Lord is his name.
    The chariots of Pharaoh he hurled into the sea,
    the flower of his army is drowned in the sea.
    The deeps hide them; they sank like a stone. ℟

3. Your right hand, Lord, glorious in its power,
   your right hand, Lord, has shattered the enemy.
   In the greatness of your glory you crushed the foe. ℟

4. You will lead your people and plant them on your
        mountain,
   the place, O Lord, where you have made your home,
   the sanctuary, Lord, which your hands have made.
   The Lord will reign for ever and ever. ℟

All stand for the prayer.

Let us pray.

O God, whose ancient wonders
remain undimmed in splendour even in our day,
for what you once bestowed on a single people,
freeing them from Pharaoh's persecution
by the power of your right hand,
now you bring about as the salvation of the nations
through the waters of rebirth,
grant, we pray, that the whole world
may become children of Abraham
and inherit the dignity of Israel's birthright.
Through Christ our Lord.
Amen.

Or:

O God, who by the light of the New Testament
have unlocked the meaning
of wonders worked in former times,
so that the Red Sea prefigures the sacred font
and the nation delivered from slavery
foreshadows the Christian people,
grant, we pray, that all nations,
obtaining the privilege of Israel by merit of faith,
may be reborn by partaking of your Spirit.
Through Christ our Lord.
Amen.

FOURTH READING   Is 54:5-14

A reading from the prophet Isaiah.
With everlasting love the Lord your redeemer has taken pity on you.

Thus says the Lord:

Now your creator will be your husband,
his name, the Lord of hosts;
your redeemer will be the Holy One of Israel,
he is called the God of the whole earth.
Yes, like a forsaken wife, distressed in spirit,
the Lord calls you back.
Does a man cast off the wife of his youth?
says your God.

I did forsake you for a brief moment,
but with great love will I take you back.
In excess of anger, for a moment
I hid my face from you.
But with everlasting love I have taken pity on you,
says the Lord, your redeemer.

I am now as I was in the days of Noah
when I swore that Noah's waters
should never flood the world again.
So now I swear concerning my anger with you
and the threats I made against you;
for the mountains may depart,
the hills be shaken,
but my love for you will never leave you
and my covenant of peace with you will never be shaken,
says the Lord who takes pity on you.

Unhappy creature, storm-tossed, disconsolate,
see, I will set your stones on carbuncles
and your foundations on sapphires.
I will make rubies your battlements,
your gates crystal,
and your entire wall precious stones.
Your sons will all be taught by the Lord.
The prosperity of your sons will be great.
You will be founded on integrity;
remote from oppression, you will have nothing to fear;
remote from terror, it will not approach you.
The word of the Lord.

RESPONSORIAL PSALM   Ps 29:2.4-6.11-13

℟ **I will praise you, Lord, you have rescued me.**

1. I will praise you, Lord, you have rescued me
   and have not let my enemies rejoice over me.
   O Lord, you have raised my soul from the dead,
   restored me to life from those who sink into the grave. ℟

2. Sing psalms to the Lord, you who love him,
   give thanks to his holy name.
   His anger lasts but a moment; his favour through life.
   At night there are tears, but joy comes with dawn. ℟

3. The Lord listened and had pity.
   The Lord came to my help.
   For me you have changed my mourning into dancing,
   O Lord my God, I will thank you for ever. ℟

All stand for the prayer.

Let us pray.

Almighty ever-living God,
surpass, for the honour of your name,
what you pledged to the Patriarchs by reason of their faith,
and through sacred adoption increase the children of your
   promise,
so that what the Saints of old never doubted would come to pass
your Church may now see in great part fulfilled.
Through Christ our Lord.
Amen.

FIFTH READING   Is 55:1-11

A reading from the prophet Isaiah.

Come to me and your soul will live, and I will make an everlasting covenant with you.

Thus says the Lord:

> Oh, come to the water all you who are thirsty;
> though you have no money, come!
> Buy corn without money, and eat,
> and, at no cost, wine and milk.
> Why spend money on what is not bread,
> your wages on what fails to satisfy?
> Listen, listen to me, and you will have good things to eat
> and rich food to enjoy.
> Pay attention, come to me;
> listen, and your soul will live.

With you I will make an everlasting covenant
out of the favours promised to David.
See, I have made of you a witness to the peoples,
a leader and a master of the nations.
See, you will summon a nation you never knew,
those unknown will come hurrying to you,
for the sake of the Lord your God,
of the Holy One of Israel who will glorify you.

Seek the Lord while he is still to be found,
call to him while he is still near.
Let the wicked man abandon his way,
the evil man his thoughts.
Let him turn back to the Lord who will take pity on him,
to our God who is rich in forgiving;
for my thoughts are not your thoughts,
my ways not your ways – it is the Lord who speaks.
Yes, the heavens are as high above earth
as my ways are above your ways,
my thoughts above your thoughts.

Yes, as the rain and the snow come down from the heavens and
do not return without watering the earth, making it yield and
giving growth to provide seed for the sower and bread for the
eating, so the word that goes from my mouth does not return to
me empty, without carrying out my will and succeeding in what
it was sent to do.

The word of the Lord.

RESPONSORIAL PSALM   Is 12:2-6

℞ **With joy you will draw water**
   from the wells of salvation.

1. Truly God is my salvation,
   I trust, I shall not fear.
   For the Lord is my strength, my song,
   he became my saviour.
   With joy you will draw water
   from the wells of salvation. ℞

2. Give thanks to the Lord, give praise to his name!
   Make his mighty deeds known to the peoples,
   declare the greatness of his name. ℞

3. Sing a psalm to the Lord
   for he has done glorious deeds,
   make them known to all the earth!
   People of Zion, sing and shout for joy
   for great in your midst is the Holy One of Israel. ℟

All stand for the prayer.

Let us pray.

Almighty ever-living God,
sole hope of the world,
who by the preaching of your Prophets
unveiled the mysteries of this present age,
graciously increase the longing of your people,
for only at the prompting of your grace
do the faithful progress in any kind of virtue.
Through Christ our Lord.
Amen.

SIXTH READING   Ba 3:9-15.31–4:4

A reading from the prophet Baruch.

In the radiance of the Lord make your way to light.

Listen, Israel, to commands that bring life;
hear, and learn what knowledge means.
Why, Israel, why are you in the country of your enemies,
growing older and older in an alien land,
sharing defilement with the dead,
reckoned with those who go to Sheol?
Because you have forsaken the fountain of wisdom.
Had you walked in the way of God,
you would have lived in peace for ever.
Learn where knowledge is, where strength,
where understanding, and so learn
where length of days is, where life,
where the light of the eyes and where peace.
But who has found out where she lives,
who has entered her treasure house?

But the One who knows all knows her,
he has grasped her with his own intellect,
he has set the earth firm for ever
and filled it with four-footed beasts,
he sends the light – and it goes,

he recalls it – and trembling it obeys;
the stars shine joyfully at their set times:
when he calls them, they answer, 'Here we are';
they gladly shine for their creator.
It is he who is our God,
no other can compare with him.
He has grasped the whole way of knowledge,
and confided it to his servant Jacob,
to Israel his well-beloved;
so causing her to appear on earth
and move among men.

This is the book of the commandments of God,
the Law that stands for ever;
those who keep her live,
those who desert her die.
Turn back, Jacob, seize her,
in her radiance make your way to light:
do not yield your glory to another,
your privilege to a people not your own.
Israel, blessed are we:
what pleases God has been revealed to us.

>   The word of the Lord.

RESPONSORIAL PSALM   Ps 18:8-11

℟ **You have the message of eternal life, O Lord.**

1. The law of the Lord is perfect,
    it revives the soul.
    The rule of the Lord is to be trusted,
    it gives wisdom to the simple. ℟

2. The precepts of the Lord are right,
    they gladden the heart.
    The command of the Lord is clear,
    it gives light to the eyes. ℟

3. The fear of the Lord is holy,
    abiding for ever.
    The decrees of the Lord are truth
    and all of them just. ℟

4. They are more to be desired than gold,
    than the purest of gold

and sweeter are they than honey,
than honey from the comb. ℟

Let us pray.

O God, who constantly increase your Church
by your call to the nations,
graciously grant
to those you wash clean in the waters of Baptism
the assurance of your unfailing protection.
Through Christ our Lord.
Amen.

SEVENTH READING   Ezk 36:16-28
A reading from the prophet Ezekiel.
I shall pour clean water over you, and I shall give you a new heart.

The word of the Lord was addressed to me as follows: 'Son of man, the members of the House of Israel used to live in their own land, but they defiled it by their conduct and actions. I then discharged my fury at them because of the blood they shed in their land and the idols with which they defiled it. I scattered them among the nations and dispersed them in foreign countries. I sentenced them as their conduct and actions deserved. And now they have profaned my holy name among the nations where they have gone, so that people say of them, "These are the people of the Lord; they have been exiled from his land." But I have been concerned about my holy name, which the House of Israel has profaned among the nations where they have gone. And so, say to the House of Israel, "The Lord says this: I am not doing this for your sake, House of Israel, but for the sake of my holy name, which you have profaned among the nations where you have gone. I mean to display the holiness of my great name, which has been profaned among the nations, which you have profaned among them. And the nations will learn that I am the Lord – it is the Lord who speaks – when I display my holiness for your sake before their eyes. Then I am going to take you from among the nations and gather you together from all the foreign countries, and bring you home to your own land. I shall pour clean water over you and you will be cleansed; I shall cleanse you of all your defilement and all your idols. I shall give you a new heart, and put a new spirit in you; I shall remove the heart of stone from your bodies and give you a heart of flesh instead. I shall put my spirit in you, and make you keep my laws and sincerely respect my observances. You will live in the land which I gave your ancestors. You shall be my people and I will be your God." '

The word of the Lord.

RESPONSORIAL PSALM   Ps 41:3.5; 42:3.4

℟ Like the deer that yearns for running streams,
   so my soul is yearning for you, my God.

1. My soul is thirsting for God,
    the God of my life;
    when can I enter and see
    the face of God? ℟

2. These things will I remember
    as I pour out my soul:
    how I would lead the rejoicing crowd
    into the house of God,
    amid cries of gladness and thanksgiving,
    the throng wild with joy. ℟

3. O send forth your light and your truth;
    let these be my guide.
    Let them bring me to your holy mountain
    to the place where you dwell. ℟

4. And I will come to the altar of God,
    the God of my joy.
    My redeemer, I will thank you on the harp,
    O God, my God. ℟

If a Baptism takes place, the Responsorial Psalm which follows the Fifth Reading above (page 223) is used or Ps 50 as follows.

RESPONSORIAL PSALM   Ps 50:12-15.18-19

℟ A pure heart create for me, O God.

1. A pure heart create for me, O God,
    put a steadfast spirit within me.
    Do not cast me away from your presence,
    nor deprive me of your holy spirit. ℟

2. Give me again the joy of your help;
   with a spirit of fervour sustain me,
   that I may teach transgressors your ways
   and sinners may return to you. ℟

3. For in sacrifice you take no delight,
   burnt offering from me you would refuse,
   my sacrifice, a contrite spirit.
   A humbled, contrite heart you will not spurn. ℟

All stand for the prayer.

Let us pray.

O God of unchanging power and eternal light,
look with favour on the wondrous mystery of the whole Church
and serenely accomplish the work of human salvation,
which you planned from all eternity;
may the whole world know and see
that what was cast down is raised up,
what had become old is made new,
and all things are restored to integrity through Christ,
just as by him they came into being.
Who lives and reigns for ever and ever.
Amen.

Or:

O God, who by the pages of both Testaments
instruct and prepare us to celebrate the Paschal Mystery,
grant that we may comprehend your mercy,
so that the gifts we receive from you this night
may confirm our hope of the gifts to come.
Through Christ our Lord.
Amen.

After the last reading from the Old Testament with its Responsorial
Psalm and its prayer, the altar candles are lit, and the Priest intones the
hymn Gloria in excelsis Deo (Glory to God in the highest), which is
taken up by all, while bells are rung, according to local custom.

Collect

Let us pray.

O God, who make this most sacred night radiant
with the glory of the Lord's Resurrection,
stir up in your Church a spirit of adoption,

so that, renewed in body and mind,
we may render you undivided service.
Through our Lord Jesus Christ, your Son,
who lives and reigns with you in the unity of the Holy Spirit,
one God, for ever and ever.

EPISTLE   Rm 6:3-11

A reading from the letter of St Paul to the Romans.
Christ, having been raised from the dead, will never die again.

When we were baptized in Christ Jesus we were baptized in his
death; in other words, when we were baptized we went into the
tomb with him and joined him in death, so that as Christ was
raised from the dead by the Father's glory, we too might live a
new life.

If in union with Christ we have imitated his death, we shall
also imitate him in his resurrection. We must realise that our
former selves have been crucified with him to destroy this sinful
body and to free us from the slavery of sin. When a man dies, of
course, he has finished with sin.

But we believe that having died with Christ we shall return
to life with him: Christ, as we know, having been raised from
the dead will never die again. Death has no power over him any
more. When he died, he died, once for all, to sin, so his life
now is life with God; and in that way, you too must consider
yourselves to be dead to sin but alive for God in Christ Jesus.

The word of the Lord.

After the Epistle all rise. The Priest solemnly intones the **Alleluia** which
is repeated by all.

RESPONSORIAL PSALM   Ps 117:1-2.16-17.22-23

℟ **Alleluia, alleluia, alleluia!**

1. Give thanks to the Lord for he is good,
    for his love has no end.
    Let the sons of Israel say:
    'His love has no end.' ℟

2. The Lord's right hand has triumphed;
    his right hand raised me up.
    I shall not die, I shall live
    and recount his deeds. ℟

3. The stone which the builders rejected
    has become the corner stone.
    This is the work of the Lord,
    a marvel in our eyes. ℟

GOSPEL   Mt 28:1-10

A reading from the holy Gospel according to Matthew.

He has risen from the dead and now he is going before you into Galilee.

After the sabbath, and towards dawn on the first day of the week, Mary of Magdala and the other Mary went to visit the sepulchre. And all at once there was a violent earthquake, for the angel of the Lord, descending from heaven, came and rolled away the stone and sat on it. His face was like lightning, his robe white as snow. The guards were so shaken, so frightened of him, that they were like dead men. But the angel spoke; and he said to the women, 'There is no need for you to be afraid. I know you are looking for Jesus, who was crucified. He is not here, for he has risen, as he said he would. Come and see the place where he lay, then go quickly and tell his disciples, "He has risen from the dead and now he is going before you to Galilee; it is there you will see him." Now I have told you.' Filled with awe and great joy the women came quickly away from the tomb and ran to tell the disciples.

And there, coming to meet them, was Jesus. 'Greetings' he said. And the women came up to him and, falling down before him, clasped his feet. Then Jesus said to them, 'Do not be afraid; go and tell my brothers that they must leave for Galilee; they will see me there.'

The Gospel of the Lord.

THIRD PART:
BAPTISMAL LITURGY

The Priest goes with the ministers to the baptismal font, if this can be seen by the faithful. Otherwise a vessel with water is placed in the sanctuary.

Catechumens, if there are any, are called forward and presented by their godparents in front of the assembled Church or, if they are small children, are carried by their parents and godparents.

The Priest makes an introductory statement in these or similar words.

If there are candidates to be baptized:

Dearly beloved,
with one heart and one soul, let us by our prayers
come to the aid of these our brothers and sisters
    in their blessed hope,
so that, as they approach the font of rebirth,
the almighty Father may bestow on them
all his merciful help.

If the font is to be blessed, but no one is to be baptized:

Dearly beloved,
let us humbly invoke upon this font
the grace of God the almighty Father,
that those who from it are born anew
may be numbered among the children of adoption in Christ.

All present stand and answer. If there is no one to be baptized and the font is not to be blessed the litany is omitted, and the Blessing of Water takes place at once (see page 234).

Lord, have mercy,	**Lord, have mercy.**
Christ, have mercy,	**Christ, have mercy.**
Lord, have mercy,	**Lord, have mercy.**
Holy Mary, Mother of God,	**pray for us.**
Saint Michael,	"
Holy angels of God,	"
Saint John the Baptist,	"
Saint Joseph,	"
Saint Peter and Saint Paul,	"
Saint Andrew,	"
Saint John,	"
Saint Mary Magdalene,	"
Saint Stephen,	"
Saint Ignatius of Antioch,	"
Saint Lawrence,	"
Saint Perpetua and Saint Felicity,	"
Saint Agnes,	"
Saint Gregory,	"
Saint Augustine,	"
Saint Athanasius,	"
Saint Basil,	"
Saint Martin,	"
Saint Benedict,	"
Saint Francis and Saint Dominic,	"

Saint Francis Xavier,   "
Saint John Vianney,   "
Saint Catherine of Siena,   "
Saint Teresa of Jesus,   "
All holy men and women, Saints of God,   "
Lord, be merciful,   **Lord, deliver us, we pray.**
From all evil,   "
From every sin,   "
From everlasting death,   "
By your Incarnation,   "
By your Death and Resurrection,   "
By the outpouring of the Holy Spirit,   "
Be merciful to us sinners,   **Lord, we ask you, hear our prayer.**

If there are candidates to be baptized:

Bring these chosen ones to new birth through the grace of
    Baptism,   **Lord, we ask you, hear our prayer.**

If there is no one to be baptized:

Make this font holy by your grace for the new birth of your
    children,   **Lord, we ask you, hear our prayer.**
Jesus, Son of the living God, **Lord, we ask you, hear our prayer.**
Christ, hear us.   **Christ, hear us.**
Christ, graciously hear us.   **Christ, graciously hear us.**

If there are candidates to be baptized, the Priest says the following
prayer:

Almighty ever-living God,
be present by the mysteries of your great love
and send forth the spirit of adoption
to create the new peoples
brought to birth for you in the font of Baptism,
so that what is to be carried out by our humble service
may be brought to fulfilment by your mighty power.
Through Christ our Lord.
Amen.

Blessing of Baptismal Water

The Priest then blesses the baptismal water, saying the following prayer:

O God, who by invisible power
accomplish a wondrous effect
through sacramental signs

and who in many ways have prepared water, your creation,
to show forth the grace of Baptism;

O God, whose Spirit
in the first moments of the world's creation
hovered over the waters,
so that the very substance of water
would even then take to itself the power to sanctify;

O God, who by the outpouring of the flood
foreshadowed regeneration,
so that from the mystery of one and the same element of water
would come an end to vice and a beginning of virtue;

O God, who caused the children of Abraham
to pass dry-shod through the Red Sea,
so that the chosen people,
set free from slavery to Pharaoh,
would prefigure the people of the baptized;

O God, whose Son,
baptized by John in the waters of the Jordan,
was anointed with the Holy Spirit,
and, as he hung upon the Cross,
gave forth water from his side along with blood,
and after his Resurrection, commanded his disciples:
"Go forth, teach all nations, baptizing them
in the name of the Father and of the Son
    and of the Holy Spirit,"
look now, we pray, upon the face of your Church
and graciously unseal for her the fountain of Baptism.

May this water receive by the Holy Spirit
the grace of your Only Begotten Son,
so that human nature, created in your image
and washed clean through the Sacrament of Baptism
from all the squalor of the life of old,
may be found worthy to rise to the life of newborn children
through water and the Holy Spirit.

And, if appropriate, lowering the paschal candle into the water either
once or three times, he continues:
May the power of the Holy Spirit,
O Lord, we pray,

come down through your Son
into the fullness of this font,

and, holding the candle in the water, he continues:

so that all who have been buried with Christ
by Baptism into death
may rise again to life with him.
Who lives and reigns with you in the unity of the Holy Spirit,
one God, for ever and ever.
Amen.

Then the candle is lifted out of the water, as the people acclaim:

**Springs of water, bless the Lord;
praise and exalt him above all for ever.**

Those who are to be baptized renounce the devil individually. Then they are questioned about their faith and are baptized. Adults are confirmed immediately after baptism if a bishop, or a priest with the faculty to confirm, is present.

The Blessing of Water

If no one present is to be baptized and the font is not to be blessed, the Priest introduces the faithful to the blessing of water, saying:

Dear brothers and sisters,
let us humbly beseech the Lord our God
to bless this water he has created,
which will be sprinkled upon us
as a memorial of our Baptism.
May he graciously renew us,
that we may remain faithful to the Spirit
whom we have received.

And after a brief pause in silence, he proclaims the following prayer:

Lord our God,
in your mercy be present to your people
who keep vigil on this most sacred night,
and, for us who recall the wondrous work of our creation
and the still greater work of our redemption,
graciously bless this water.
For you created water to make the fields fruitful
and to refresh and cleanse our bodies.
You also made water the instrument of your mercy:

for through water you freed your people from slavery
and quenched their thirst in the desert;
through water the Prophets proclaimed the new covenant
you were to enter upon with the human race;
and last of all,
through water, which Christ made holy in the Jordan,
you have renewed our corrupted nature
in the bath of regeneration.
Therefore, may this water be for us
a memorial of the Baptism we have received,
and grant that we may share
in the gladness of our brothers and sisters,
who at Easter have received their Baptism.
Through Christ our Lord.
Amen.

The Renewal of Baptismal Promises

When the Rite of Baptism (and Confirmation) has been completed or, if this has not taken place, after the blessing of water, all stand, holding lighted candles in their hands, and renew the promise of baptismal faith, unless this has already been done together with those to be baptized.

The Priest addresses the faithful in these or similar words:

Dear brethren (brothers and sisters),
through the Paschal Mystery
we have been buried with Christ in Baptism,
so that we may walk with him in newness of life.
And so, now that our Lenten observance is concluded,
let us renew the promises of Holy Baptism,
by which we once renounced Satan and his works
and promised to serve God in the holy Catholic Church.

And so I ask you:

Do you renounce Satan?
I do.

And all his works?
I do.

And all his empty show?
I do.

Or:

Do you renounce sin,
so as to live in the freedom of the children of God?
I do.

Do you renounce the lure of evil,
so that sin may have no mastery over you?
I do.

Do you renounce Satan,
the author and prince of sin?
I do.

Then the Priest continues:

Do you believe in God,
the Father almighty,
Creator of heaven and earth?
I do.

Do you believe in Jesus Christ,
his only Son, our Lord,
who was born of the Virgin Mary,
suffered death and was buried,
rose again from the dead
and is seated at the right hand of the Father?
I do.

Do you believe in the Holy Spirit,
the holy Catholic Church,
the communion of saints,
the forgiveness of sins,
the resurrection of the body,
and life everlasting?
I do.

And the Priest concludes:

And may almighty God, the Father of our Lord Jesus Christ,
who has given us new birth by water and the Holy Spirit
and bestowed on us forgiveness of our sins,
keep us by his grace,
in Christ Jesus our Lord,
for eternal life.
Amen.

The Priest sprinkles the people with the blessed water, while all sing:

Antiphon

**I saw water flowing from the Temple,
from its right-hand side, alleluia;
and all to whom this water came were saved
and shall say: Alleluia, alleluia.**

Another chant that is baptismal in character may also be sung.

FOURTH PART:
THE LITURGY OF THE EUCHARIST

Prayer over the Offerings

Accept, we ask, O Lord,
the prayers of your people
with the sacrificial offerings,
that what has begun in the paschal mysteries
may, by the working of your power,
bring us to the healing of eternity.
Through Christ our Lord.

Preface I of Easter

The Lord be with you.
And with your spirit.

Lift up your hearts.
We lift them up to the Lord.

Let us give thanks to the Lord our God.
It is right and just.

It is truly right and just, our duty and our salvation,
at all times to acclaim you, O Lord,
but on this night above all
to laud you yet more gloriously,
when Christ our Passover has been sacrificed.

For he is the true Lamb
who has taken away the sins of the world;
by dying he has destroyed our death,
and by rising, restored our life.

Therefore, overcome with paschal joy,
every land, every people exults in your praise
and even the heavenly Powers, with the angelic hosts,
sing together the unending hymn of your glory,
as they acclaim:

Holy, Holy, Holy Lord God of hosts …

Communion Antiphon   1 Cor 5:7-8

Christ our Passover has been sacrificed;
therefore let us keep the feast
with the unleavened bread of purity and truth, alleluia.

Prayer after Communion

Pour out on us, O Lord, the Spirit of your love,
and in your kindness make those you have nourished
by this paschal Sacrament
one in mind and heart.
Through Christ our Lord.

Solemn Blessing

The Priest invites people to bow down for the blessing.

May almighty God bless you
through today's Easter Solemnity
and, in his compassion,
defend you from every assault of sin.
Amen.

And may he, who restores you to eternal life
in the Resurrection of his Only Begotten,
endow you with the prize of immortality.
Amen.

Now that the days of the Lord's Passion have drawn to a close,
may you who celebrate the gladness of the Paschal Feast
come with Christ's help, and exulting in spirit,
to those feasts that are celebrated in eternal joy.
Amen.

And may the blessing of almighty God,
the Father, and the Son, ✠ and the Holy Spirit,
come down on you and remain with you for ever.
Amen.

To dismiss the people the Deacon or, if there is no Deacon, the Priest
himself sings or says:

Go forth, the Mass is ended, alleluia, alleluia.

- Or:

Go in peace, alleluia, alleluia.

Thanks be to God, alleluia, alleluia.

9 APRIL
EASTER SUNDAY
OF THE RESURRECTION OF THE LORD

*Details in today's Gospel encourage us to think of the resurrection
as the gift of God's love. The cloth around Jesus' head – so carefully
mentioned – takes us back to the raising of Lazarus and the words of
the witnesses, "See how he loved him!" (Jn 11:36). It is the disciple
whom Jesus loved who first comes to faith. In a word, coming to
resurrection faith is a movement of the heart, that is, letting ourselves
be so loved by God and loving in return.*

Entrance Antiphon   Cf. Ps 138:18.5-6

I have risen, and I am with you still, alleluia.
You have laid your hand upon me, alleluia.
Too wonderful for me, this knowledge, alleluia, alleluia.

    Or: Lk 24:34; Cf. Rv 1:6

The Lord is truly risen, alleluia.
To him be glory and power
for all the ages of eternity, alleluia, alleluia.

Greeting, Penitential Rite, Gloria – pages 7-13.

Collect

O God, who on this day,
through your Only Begotten Son,
have conquered death
and unlocked for us the path to eternity,
grant, we pray, that we who keep
the solemnity of the Lord's Resurrection
may, through the renewal brought by your Spirit,
rise up in the light of life.
Through our Lord Jesus Christ, your Son,
who lives and reigns with you in the unity of the Holy Spirit,
one God, for ever and ever.

FIRST READING   Acts 10:34.37-43

A reading from the Acts of the Apostles.
We have eaten and drunk with him after his resurrection.

Peter addressed Cornelius and his household: 'You must have
heard about the recent happenings in Judaea: about Jesus of

Nazareth and how he began in Galilee, after John had been preaching baptism. God had anointed him with the Holy Spirit and with power, and because God was with him, Jesus went about doing good and curing all who had fallen into the power of the devil. Now I, and those with me, can witness to everything he did throughout the country-side of Judaea and in Jerusalem itself: and also to the fact that they killed him by hanging him on a tree, yet three days afterwards God raised him to life and allowed him to be seen, not by the whole people but only by certain witnesses God had chosen beforehand. Now we are those witnesses – we have eaten and drunk with him after his resurrection from the dead – and he has ordered us to proclaim this to his people and to tell them that God has appointed him to judge everyone, alive or dead. It is to him that all the prophets bear this witness: that all who believe in Jesus will have their sins forgiven through his name.'

The word of the Lord.

RESPONSORIAL PSALM   Ps 117:1-2.16-17.22-23

℞ **This day was made by the Lord;
we rejoice and are glad.**

Or:

Alleluia, alleluia, alleluia!

1. Give thanks to the Lord for he is good,
    for his love has no end.
    Let the sons of Israel say:
    'His love has no end.' ℞

2. The Lord's right hand has triumphed;
    his right hand raised me up.
    I shall not die, I shall live
    and recount his deeds. ℞

3. The stone which the builders rejected
    has become the corner stone.
    This is the work of the Lord,
    a marvel in our eyes. ℞

SECOND READING   Col 3:1-4

A reading from the letter of St Paul to the Colossians.
You must look for the things that are in heaven, where Christ is.

Since you have been brought back to true life with Christ, you must look for the things that are in heaven, where Christ is, sitting at God's right hand. Let your thoughts be on heavenly things, not on the things that are on the earth, because you have died, and now the life you have is hidden with Christ in God. But when Christ is revealed – and he is your life – you too will be revealed in all your glory with him.

The word of the Lord.

Alternative Second Reading   (1 Cor 5:6-8)

A reading from the first letter of St Paul to the Corinthians.

Get rid of the old yeast, make yourselves into a completely new batch of bread.

You must know how even a small amount of yeast is enough to leaven all the dough, so get rid of all the old yeast, and make yourselves into a completely new batch of bread, unleavened as you are meant to be. Christ, our passover, has been sacrificed; let us celebrate the feast, by getting rid of all the old yeast of evil and wickedness, having only the unleavened bread of sincerity and truth.

The word of the Lord.

Sequence

Christians, to the Paschal Victim offer sacrifice and praise.
The sheep are ransomed by the Lamb;
and Christ, the undefiled,
hath sinners to his Father reconciled.
Death with life contended; combat strangely ended!
Life's own Champion, slain, yet lives to reign.
Tell us, Mary: say what thou didst see upon the way.
The tomb the Living did enclose;
I saw Christ's glory as he rose!
The angels there attesting,
shroud with grave-clothes resting.
Christ, my hope, has risen: he goes before you into Galilee.
That Christ is truly risen from the dead we know.
Victorious king, thy mercy show!

GOSPEL ACCLAMATION   1 Cor 5:7-8

Alleluia, alleluia!
Christ, our passover, has been sacrificed;

let us celebrate the feast then, in the Lord.
Alleluia!

GOSPEL   Jn 20:1-9

(Instead of the following Gospel, that of the Easter Vigil may be used).

A reading from the holy Gospel according to John.

He must rise from the dead.

It was very early on the first day of the week and still dark, when Mary of Magdala came to the tomb. She saw that the stone had been moved away from the tomb and came running to Simon Peter and the other disciple, the one Jesus loved. 'They have taken the Lord out of the tomb' she said 'and we don't know where they have put him.'

So Peter set out with the other disciple to go to the tomb. They ran together, but the other disciple, running faster than Peter, reached the tomb first; he bent down and saw the linen cloths lying on the ground, but did not go in. Simon Peter who was following now came up, went right into the tomb, saw the linen cloths on the ground, and also the cloth that had been over his head; this was not with the linen cloths but rolled up in a place by itself. Then the other disciple who had reached the tomb first also went in; he saw and he believed. Till this moment they had failed to understand the teaching of scripture, that he must rise from the dead.

The Gospel of the Lord.

The rite of the Renewal of Baptismal Promises (page 222) is desirable after the homily. The Profession of Faith is then omitted.

Prayer over the Offerings

Exultant with paschal gladness, O Lord,
we offer the sacrifice
by which your Church
is wondrously reborn and nourished.
Through Christ our Lord.

Preface I of Easter

The Lord be with you.
And with your spirit.

Lift up your hearts.
We lift them up to the Lord.

Let us give thanks to the Lord our God.
It is right and just.

It is truly right and just, our duty and our salvation,
at all times to acclaim you, O Lord,
but on this day above all
to laud you yet more gloriously,
when Christ our Passover has been sacrificed.

For he is the true Lamb
who has taken away the sins of the world;
by dying he has destroyed our death,
and by rising, restored our life.

Therefore, overcome with paschal joy,
every land, every people exults in your praise
and even the heavenly Powers, with the angelic hosts,
sing together the unending hymn of your glory,
as they acclaim:

Holy, Holy, Holy Lord God of hosts ...

Communion Antiphon   1 Cor 5:7-8

**Christ our Passover has been sacrificed, alleluia;
therefore let us keep the feast with the unleavened bread
of purity and truth, alleluia, alleluia.**

Prayer after Communion

Look upon your Church, O God,
with unfailing love and favour,
so that, renewed by the paschal mysteries,
she may come to the glory of the resurrection.
Through Christ our Lord.

Solemn Blessing – page 225.

16 APRIL

SECOND SUNDAY OF EASTER

(Sunday of Divine Mercy)

Mercy and merciful are words which speak to heart and rightly so because we all need from time to time the experience of mercy and compassion, not only from our neighbour, but from God himself. We see something of that mercy in today's Gospel: Thomas is unable to come to faith and Jesus reaches out to him, inviting him to touch him. The climax of the story is the "beatitude" which closes it: Happy are those who have not seen and yet believe!

Entrance Antiphon   1 Pt 2:2

**Like newborn infants, you must long for the pure, spiritual milk,
that in him you may grow to salvation, alleluia.**

    Or: 4 Ezra 2:36-37

**Receive the joy of your glory, giving thanks to God,
who has called you into the heavenly kingdom, alleluia.**

Greeting, Penitential Rite, Gloria – pages 7-13.

Collect

God of everlasting mercy,
who, in the very recurrence of the paschal feast
kindle the faith of the people you have made your own,
increase, we pray, the grace you have bestowed,
that all may grasp and rightly understand
in what font they have been washed,
by whose Spirit they have been reborn,
by whose Blood they have been redeemed.
Through our Lord Jesus Christ, your Son,
who lives and reigns with you in the unity of the Holy Spirit,
one God, for ever and ever.

FIRST READING   Acts 2:42-47

A reading from the Acts of the Apostles.

The faithful all lived together and owned everything in common.

The whole community remained faithful to the teaching of the apostles, to the brotherhood, to the breaking of bread and to the prayers.

The many miracles and signs worked through the apostles made a deep impression on everyone.

The faithful all lived together and owned everything in common; they sold their goods and possessions and shared out the proceeds among themselves according to what each one needed.

They went as a body to the Temple every day but met in their houses for the breaking of bread; they shared their food gladly and generously; they praised God and were looked up to by everyone. Day by day the Lord added to their community those destined to be saved.

The word of the Lord.

RESPONSORIAL PSALM   Ps 117:2-4.13-15.22-24

℟ **Give thanks to the Lord for he is good,
    for his love has no end.**

     Or:

    Alleluia, alleluia, alleluia!

1. Let the sons of Israel say:
    'His love has no end.'
    Let the sons of Aaron say:
    'His love has no end,'
    Let those who fear the Lord say:
    'His love has no end.' ℟

2. I was thrust, thrust down and falling
    but the Lord was my helper.
    The Lord is my strength and my song;
    he was my saviour.
    There are shouts of joy and victory
    in the tents of the just. ℟

3. The stone which the builders rejected
    has become the corner stone.
    This is the work of the Lord,
    a marvel in our eyes.
    This day was made by the Lord;
    we rejoice and are glad. ℟

SECOND READING   1 Pt 1:3-9

A reading from the first letter of St Peter

In his great mercy he has given us a new birth as his sons by raising Jesus from the dead.

Blessed be God the Father of our Lord Jesus Christ, who in his great mercy has given us a new birth as his sons, by raising Jesus Christ from the dead, so that we have a sure hope and the promise of an inheritance that can never be spoilt or soiled and never fade away, because it is being kept for you in the heavens. Through your faith, God's power will guard you until the salvation which had been prepared is revealed at the end of time. This is a cause of great joy for you, even though you may for a short time have to bear being plagued by all sorts of trials; so that, when Jesus Christ is revealed, your faith will have been tested and proved like gold – only it is more precious than gold, which is corruptible even though it bears testing by fire – and then you will have praise and glory and honour. You did not see him, yet you love him; and still without seeing him, you are already filled with joy so glorious that it cannot be described, because you believe; and you are sure of the end to which your faith looks forward, that is, the salvation of your souls.

The word of the Lord.

GOSPEL ACCLAMATION   Jn 20:29

Alleluia, alleluia!
Jesus said: 'You believe because you can see me.
Happy are those who have not seen and yet believe.' Alleluia!

GOSPEL   Jn 20:19-31

A reading from the holy Gospel according to John.

Eight days later, Jesus came.

In the evening of that same day, the first day of the week, the doors were closed in the room where the disciples were, for fear of the Jews. Jesus came and stood among them. He said to them, 'Peace be with you,' and showed them his hands and his side. The disciples were filled with joy when they saw the Lord, and he said to them again, 'Peace be with you.

'As the Father sent me,
so am I sending you.'

After saying this he breathed on them and said:

'Receive the Holy Spirit.
For those whose sins you forgive,
they are forgiven;
for those whose sins you retain,
they are retained.'

Thomas, called the Twin, who was one of the Twelve, was not with them when Jesus came. When the disciples said, 'We have seen the Lord', he answered, 'Unless I see the holes that the nails made in his hands and can put my finger into the holes they made, and unless I can put my hand into his side, I refuse to believe.' Eight days later the disciples were in the house again and Thomas was with them. The doors were closed, but Jesus came in and stood among them. 'Peace be with you' he said. Then he spoke to Thomas, 'Put your finger here; look, here are my hands. Give me your hand; put it into my side. Doubt no longer but believe.' Thomas replied, 'My Lord and my God!' Jesus said to him:

'You believe because you can see me.
Happy are those who have not seen and yet believe.'

There were many other signs that Jesus worked and the disciples saw, but they are not recorded in this book. These are recorded so that you may believe that Jesus is the Christ, the Son of God, and that believing this you may have life through his name.

The Gospel of the Lord.

Profession of Faith – pages 14-15.

Prayer over the Offerings
Accept, O Lord, we pray,
the oblations of your people
(and of those you have brought to new birth),
that, renewed by confession of your name and by Baptism,
they may attain unending happiness.
Through Christ our Lord.

Preface I of Easter – page 230.

Communion Antiphon   Cf. Jn 20:27
**Bring your hand and feel the place of the nails,
and do not be unbelieving but believing, alleluia.**

Prayer after Communion

Grant, we pray, almighty God,
that our reception of this paschal Sacrament
may have a continuing effect
in our minds and hearts.
Through Christ our Lord.

Solemn Blessing – page 225.

Solemn Blessing – page 225.

═══════════ 23 APRIL ═══════════

THIRD SUNDAY OF EASTER

*We come to Easter faith by acknowledging the hungers of the heart
("our own hope had been"), by searching the scriptures ("our hearts
burning within us"), by holding on to the story of the first disciples
and witness of the women, by the Eucharist ("the breaking of the
bread") and by sharing our faith ("they told their story"). Is there
more? As the story starts, he stops them. Towards the end of the story,
they stop him from walking out of their lives, perhaps for ever. The
moment of desire leads to the moment of recognition and a life-
changing encounter.*

Entrance Antiphon   Ps 65:1-2

**Cry out with joy to God, all the earth;
O sing to the glory of his name.
O render him glorious praise, alleluia.**

Greeting, Penitential Rite, Gloria – pages 7-13.

Greeting, Penitential Rite, Gloria – pages 7-13.

Collect

May your people exult for ever, O God,
in renewed youthfulness of spirit,
so that, rejoicing now in the restored glory of our adoption,
we may look forward in confident hope
to the rejoicing of the day of resurrection.
Through our Lord Jesus Christ, your Son,
who lives and reigns with you in the unity of the Holy Spirit,
one God, for ever and ever.

FIRST READING   Acts 2:14.22-33

A reading from the Acts of the Apostles.

It was impossible for him to be held in the power of Hades.

On the day of Pentecost Peter stood up with the Eleven and addressed the crowd in a loud voice: 'Men of Israel, listen to what I am going to say: Jesus the Nazarene was a man commended to you by God by the miracles and portents and signs that God worked through him when he was among you, as you all know. This man, who was put into your power by the deliberate intention and foreknowledge of God, you took and had crucified by men outside the Law. You killed him, but God raised him to life, freeing him from the pangs of Hades; for it was impossible for him to be held in its power since, as David says of him:

I saw the Lord before me always,
for with him at my right hand nothing can shake me.
So my heart was glad
and my tongue cried out with joy;
my body, too, will rest in the hope
that you will not abandon my soul to Hades
nor allow your holy one to experience corruption.
You have made known the way of life to me,
you will fill me with gladness through your presence.

'Brothers, no one can deny that the patriarch David himself is dead and buried: his tomb is still with us. But since he was a prophet, and knew that God had sworn him an oath to make one of his descendants succeed him on the throne, what he foresaw and spoke about was the resurrection of the Christ: he is the one who was not abandoned to Hades, and whose body did not experience corruption. God raised this man Jesus to life, and all of us are witnesses to that. Now raised to the heights by God's right hand, he has received from the Father the Holy Spirit, who was promised, and what you see and hear is the outpouring of that Spirit.'

The word of the Lord.

RESPONSORIAL PSALM   Ps 15:1-2.5.7-11

℟ **Show us, Lord, the path of life.**

Or:

Alleluia!

1. Preserve me, God, I take refuge in you.
   I say to the Lord: 'You are my God.'
   O Lord, it is you who are my portion and cup;
   it is you yourself who are my prize. ℟

2. I will bless the Lord who gives me counsel,
   who even at night directs my heart.
   I keep the Lord ever in my sight:
   since he is at my right hand, I shall stand firm.

3. And so my heart rejoices, my soul is glad;
   even my body shall rest in safety.
   For you will not leave my soul among the dead,
   nor let your beloved know decay. ℟

4. You will show me the path of life,
   the fullness of joy in your presence,
   at your right hand happiness for ever. ℟

SECOND READING   1 Pt 1:17-21

A reading from the first letter of St Peter.

Your ransom was paid in the precious blood of a lamb without spot or stain, namely, Christ.

If you are acknowledging as your Father one who has no favourites and judges everyone according to what he has done, you must be scrupulously careful as long as you are living away from your home. Remember, the ransom that was paid to free you from the useless way of life your ancestors handed down was not paid in anything corruptible, neither in silver nor gold, but in the precious blood of a lamb without spot or stain, namely Christ; who, though known since before the world was made, has been revealed only in our time, the end of the ages, for your sake. Through him you now have faith in God, who raised him from the dead and gave him glory for that very reason – so that you would have faith and hope in God.

    The word of the Lord.

GOSPEL ACCLAMATION   Cf. Lk 24:32

Alleluia, alleluia!
Lord Jesus, explain the scriptures to us.
Make our hearts burn within us as you talk to us
Alleluia!

GOSPEL   Lk 24:13-35

A reading from the holy Gospel according to Luke.

They recognised him at the breaking of bread.

Two of the disciples of Jesus were on their way to a village called Emmaus, seven miles from Jerusalem, and they were talking together about all that had happened. Now as they talked this over, Jesus himself came up and walked by their side; but something prevented them from recognising him. He said to them, 'What matters are you discussing as you walk along?' They stopped short, their faces downcast.

Then one of them, called Cleopas, answered him, 'You must be the only person staying in Jerusalem who does not know the things that have been happening there these last few days.' 'What things?' he asked. 'All about Jesus of Nazareth' they answered 'who proved he was a great prophet by the things he said and did in the sight of God and of the whole people; and how our chief priests and our leaders handed him over to be sentenced to death, and had him crucified. Our own hope had been that he would be the one to set Israel free. And this is not all: two whole days have gone by since it all happened; and some women from our group have astounded us: they went to the tomb in the early morning, and when they did not find the body, they came back to tell us they had seen a vision of angels who declared he was alive. Some of our friends went to the tomb and found exactly as the women had reported, but of him they saw nothing.'

Then he said to them, 'You foolish men! So slow to believe the full message of the prophets! Was it not ordained that the Christ should suffer and so enter into his glory?' Then, starting with Moses and going through all the prophets, he explained to them the passages throughout the scriptures that were about himself.

When they drew near to the village to which they were going, he made as if to go on; but they pressed him to stay with them. 'It is nearly evening' they said 'and the day is almost over.' So he went in to stay with them. Now while he was with them at the table, he took the bread and said the blessing; then he broke it and handed it to them. And their eyes were opened and they recognised him; but he had vanished from their sight. Then they said to each other, 'Did not our hearts burn within us as he talked to us on the road and explained the scriptures to us?'

They set out that instant and returned to Jerusalem. There they found the Eleven assembled together with their companions, who said to them, 'Yes, it is true. The Lord has risen and has appeared to Simon.' Then they told their story of what had happened on the road and how they had recognised him at the breaking of bread.

The Gospel of the Lord.

Profession of Faith – pages 14-15.

Prayer over the Offerings
Receive, O Lord, we pray,
these offerings of your exultant Church,
and, as you have given her cause for such great gladness,
grant also that the gifts we bring
may bear fruit in perpetual happiness.
Through Christ our Lord.

Preface II-V of Easter – pages 21-22.

Communion Antiphon   Lk 24:35
**The disciples recognised the Lord Jesus
in the breaking of the bread, alleluia.**

Prayer after Communion
Look with kindness upon your people, O Lord,
and grant, we pray,
that those you were pleased to renew by eternal mysteries
may attain in their flesh
the incorruptible glory of the resurrection.
Through Christ our Lord.

Solemn Blessing – page 57.

24 APRIL
SAINT GEORGE
Martyr, Patron of England

The patron of England and a martyr, very little is known about the life of George. His historical existence, though it has sometimes been disputed, is now generally accepted. It is likely that he suffered before the time of Constantine in the fourth century, but it wasn't until the sixth century that devotion to him became popular. In 1415 his feast became one of the chief holydays in England. It was around this time that St George's arms, a red cross on a white background, became a kind of uniform for soldiers.

Entrance Antiphon   Cf. Mt 25:34

Rejoice, you Saints, in the presence of the Lamb;
a kingdom has been prepared for you
from the foundation of the world, alleluia.

    Or: Ps 90:13

On the asp and the viper you will tread,
and trample the young lion and the dragon, alleluia.

Greeting, Penitential Rite, Gloria – pages 7-13.

Collect
God of hosts,
who so kindled the fire of charity
in the heart of Saint George your martyr,
that he bore witness to the risen Lord
both by his life and by his death;
grant us through his intercession, we pray,
the same faith and power of love,
that we who rejoice in his triumph
may be led to share with him
in the fullness of the resurrection.
Through our Lord Jesus Christ, your Son,
who lives and reigns with you in the unity of the Holy Spirit,
one God, for ever and ever.

FIRST READING   Apoc 12:10-12

A reading from the book of the Apocalypse.

In the face of death they would not cling to life.

I, John, heard a voice shout from heaven, 'Victory and power
and empire for ever have been won by our God, and all
authority for his Christ, now that the persecutor, who accused
our brothers day and night before our God, has been brought
down. They have triumphed over him by the blood of the Lamb
and by the witness of their martyrdom, because even in the face
of death they would not cling to life. Let the heavens rejoice and
all who live there.'

The word of the Lord.

RESPONSORIAL PSALM   Ps 125

℞ **Those who are sowing in tears**
    will sing when they reap.

1. When the Lord delivered Zion from bondage,
    it seemed like a dream.
    Then was our mouth filled with laughter,
    on our lips there were songs. ℞

2. The heathens themselves said:
    'What marvels the Lord worked for them!'
    What marvels the Lord worked for us!
    Indeed we were glad.

3. Deliver us, O Lord, from our bondage
    as streams in dry land.
    Those who are sowing in tears
    will sing when they reap.

4. They go out, they go out, full of tears,
    carrying seed for the sowing;
    they come back, they come back, full of song,
    carrying their sheaves. ℞

GOSPEL ACCLAMATION

Alleluia, alleluia!
Happy the man who stands firm,
for he has proved himself,
and will win the crown of life.
Alleluia!

GOSPEL   Jn 15:18-21

A reading from the holy Gospel according to John.
If they persecuted me, they will persecute you.

Jesus said to his disciples:

'If the world hates you,
remember that it hated me before you.
If you belonged to the world,
the world would love you as its own;
but because you do not belong to the world,
because my choice withdrew you from the world,
therefore the world hates you.
Remember the words I said to you:
A servant is not greater than his master.
If they persecuted me,
they will persecute you too;
if they kept my word,
they will keep yours as well.
But it will be on my account that they will do this,
because they do not know the one who sent me.'

The Gospel of the Lord.

Prayer over the Offerings
Receive, we pray, O Lord,
the sacrifice of conciliation and praise,
which we offer to your majesty
in commemoration of the blessed Martyr Saint George,
that it may lead us to forgiveness
and confirm us in constant thanksgiving.
Through Christ our Lord.

Preface I of Holy Martyrs
The Lord be with you.
And with your spirit.

Lift up your hearts.
We lift them up to the Lord.

Let us give thanks to the Lord our God.
It is right and just.

It is truly right and just, our duty and our salvation,
always and everywhere to give you thanks,
Lord, holy Father, almighty and eternal God.

For the blood of your blessed Martyr St George,
poured out like Christ's to glorify your name,
shows forth your marvellous works,
by which in our weakness you perfect your power
and on the feeble bestow strength to bear you witness,
through Christ our Lord.

And so, with the Powers of heaven,
we worship you constantly on earth,
and before your majesty
without end we acclaim:

Holy, Holy, Holy Lord God of hosts …

Communion Antiphon   Cf. 2 Tm 2:11-12

**If we have died with Christ, we shall also live with him;
if we persevere, we shall also reign with him, alleluia.**

Prayer after Communion

Rejoicing on this festival day, O Lord,
we have received your heavenly gifts;
grant, we pray,
that we who in this divine banquet
proclaim the death of your Son
may merit with Saint George to be partakers
in his resurrection and glory.
Through Christ our Lord.

30 APRIL
FOURTH SUNDAY OF EASTER
(Day of Prayer for Vocations)

What is distinctive about our faith as Christians? We do not believe in a system of ideas or even in a higher ethics: we believe in a person, who gives life "a new horizon and a decisive direction" (Benedict XVI). John's Gospel makes this clear with its great 'I Am' sentences, one of which we hear today: "I am the gate." Naturally, we ask, the gate to what? The gate to life to the full. The risk today is to set our expectations low, to be happy with less. But the Gospel calls not to be half alive, but to be fully alive. Let us enter by the gate himself, because the gate to life is always open.

Entrance Antiphon   Cf. Ps 32:5-6

The merciful love of the Lord fills the earth;
by the word of the Lord the heavens were made, alleluia.

Greeting, Penitential Rite, Gloria – pages 7-13.

Collect

Almighty ever-living God,
lead us to a share in the joys of heaven,
so that the humble flock may reach
where the brave Shepherd has gone before.
Who lives and reigns with you in the unity of the Holy Spirit,
one God, for ever and ever.

FIRST READING   Acts 2:14.36-41

A reading from the Acts of the Apostles.
God has made him both Lord and Christ.

On the day of Pentecost Peter stood up with the Eleven and addressed the crowd with a loud voice: 'The whole House of Israel can be certain that God has made this Jesus whom you crucified both Lord and Christ.'

Hearing this, they were cut to the heart and said to Peter and the apostles, 'What must we do, brothers?' 'You must repent,' Peter answered 'and every one of you must be baptised in the name of Jesus Christ for the forgiveness of sins, and you will receive the gift of the Holy Spirit. The promise that was made is for you and your children, and for all those who are far away, for all those whom the Lord our God will call to himself.' He spoke to them for a long time using many arguments, and he urged them, 'Save yourselves from this perverse generation.' They were convinced by his arguments, and they accepted what he said and were baptised. That very day about three thousand were added to their number.

The word of the Lord.

RESPONSORIAL PSALM   Ps 22:1-6

℟ **The Lord is my shepherd;**
   there is nothing I shall want.

         Or:

   Alleluia!

1. The Lord is my shepherd;
    there is nothing I shall want.
    Fresh and green are the pastures
    where he gives me repose.
    Near restful waters he leads me,
    to revive my drooping spirit. ℟

2. He guides me along the right path;
    he is true to his name.
    If I should walk in the valley of darkness
    no evil would I fear.
    You are there with your crook and your staff;
    with these you give me comfort. ℟

3. You have prepared a banquet for me
    in the sight of my foes.
    My head you have anointed with oil;
    my cup is overflowing. ℟

4. Surely goodness and kindness shall follow me
    all the days of my life.
    In the Lord's own house shall I dwell
    for ever and ever. ℟

SECOND READING   1 Pt 2:20-25

A reading from the first letter of St Peter.
You have come back to the shepherd of your souls.

The merit, in the sight of God, is in bearing punishment patiently when you are punished after doing your duty.

This, in fact, is what you are called to do, because Christ suffered for you and left an example for you to follow the way he took. He had not done anything wrong, and there had been no perjury in his mouth. He was insulted and did not retaliate with insults; when he was tortured he made no threats but he put his trust in the righteous judge. He was bearing our faults in his own body on the cross, so that we might die to our faults and live for holiness; through his wounds you have been healed. You had gone astray like sheep but now you have come back to the shepherd and guardian of your souls.

The word of the Lord.

GOSPEL ACCLAMATION   Jn 10:14

Alleluia, alleluia!
I am the good shepherd, says the Lord;
I know my own sheep and my own know me.
Alleluia!

GOSPEL   Jn 10:1-10

A reading from the holy Gospel according to John.

I am the gate of the sheepfold.

Jesus said: 'I tell you most solemnly, anyone who does not enter the sheepfold through the gate, but gets in some other way is a thief and a brigand. The one who enters through the gate is the shepherd of the flock; the gatekeeper lets him in, the sheep hear his voice, one by one he calls his own sheep and leads them out. When he has brought out his flock, he goes ahead of them, and the sheep follow because they know his voice. They never follow a stranger but run away from him: they do not recognise the voice of strangers.'

Jesus told them this parable but they failed to understand what he meant by telling it to them.

So Jesus spoke to them again:

'I tell you most solemnly,
I am the gate of the sheepfold.
All others who have come
are thieves and brigands;
but the sheep took no notice of them.
I am the gate.
Anyone who enters through me will be safe:
he will go freely in and out

and be sure of finding pasture.
The thief comes
only to steal and kill and destroy.
I have come
so that they may have life
and have it to the full.'
The Gospel of the Lord.

Profession of Faith – pages 14-15.

Prayer over the Offerings
Grant, we pray, O Lord,
that we may always find delight in these paschal mysteries,
so that the renewal constantly at work within us
may be the cause of our unending joy.
Through Christ our Lord.

Preface II-V of Easter – pages 21-22.

Communion Antiphon
The Good Shepherd has risen,
who laid down his life for his sheep
and willingly died for his flock, alleluia.

Prayer after Communion
Look upon your flock, kind Shepherd,
and be pleased to settle in eternal pastures
the sheep you have redeemed
by the Precious Blood of your Son.
Who lives and reigns for ever and ever.

Solemn Blessing – page 57.

7 MAY
FIFTH SUNDAY OF EASTER

Jesus is our Way, our Truth and our Life. As the Gospel says, to have eternal life is to believe in him whom God has sent (Jn 5:24; 17:3). This is a reality for us now and it guides our life, in matters great and small. At the core of this reality is trust, that is, the capacity to entrust all that we have and are to the living God and to his Son, raised from the dead. It is not an accident that the phrase "I believe" occurs no fewer than ninety-eight times in the Fourth Gospel.

Entrance Antiphon   Cf. Ps 97:1-2

**O sing a new song to the Lord,
for he has worked wonders;
in the sight of the nations
he has shown his deliverance, alleluia.**

Greeting, Penitential Rite, Gloria – pages 7-13.

Collect

Almighty ever-living God,
constantly accomplish the Paschal Mystery within us,
that those you were pleased to make new in Holy Baptism
may, under your protective care, bear much fruit
and come to the joys of life eternal.
Through our Lord Jesus Christ, your Son,
who lives and reigns with you in the unity of the Holy Spirit,
one God, for ever and ever.

FIRST READING   Acts 6:1-7

A reading from the Acts of the Apostles.

They elected seven men full of the Holy Spirit.

About this time, when the number of disciples was increasing, the Hellenists made a complaint against the Hebrews: in the daily distribution their own widows were being overlooked. So the Twelve called a full meeting of the disciples and addressed them, 'It would not be right for us to neglect the word of God so as to give out food; you, brothers, must select from among yourselves seven men of good reputation, filled with the Spirit and with wisdom; we will hand over this duty to them, and continue to devote ourselves to prayer and to the service of the word.' The whole assembly approved of this proposal and elected Stephen, a man full of faith and of the Holy Spirit, together with Philip, Prochorus, Nicanor, Timon, Parmenas, and Nicolaus of Antioch, a convert to Judaism. They presented these to the apostles, who prayed and laid their hands on them.

The word of the Lord continued to spread: the number of disciples in Jerusalem was greatly increased, and a large group of priests made their submission to the faith.

The word of the Lord.

RESPONSORIAL PSALM   Ps 32:1-2.4-5.18-19

℟ **May your love be upon us, O Lord,
as we place all our hope in you.**

> Or:

Alleluia!

1. Ring out your joy to the Lord, O you just;
   for praise is fitting for loyal hearts.
   Give thanks to the Lord upon the harp,
   with a ten-stringed lute sing him songs. ℟

2. For the word of the Lord is faithful
   and all his works to be trusted.
   The Lord loves justice and right
   and fills the earth with his love. ℟

3. The Lord looks on those who revere him,
   on those who hope in his love,
   to rescue their souls from death,
   to keep them alive in famine. ℟

SECOND READING   1 Pt 2:4-9

A reading from the first letter of St Peter.

But you are a chosen race, a royal priesthood.

The Lord is the living stone, rejected by men but chosen by God and precious to him; set yourselves close to him so that you too, the holy priesthood that offers the spiritual sacrifices which Jesus Christ has made acceptable to God, may be living stones making a spiritual house. As scripture says: See how I lay in Zion a precious cornerstone that I have chosen and the man who rests his trust on it will not be disappointed. That means that for you who are believers, it is precious; but for unbelievers, the stone rejected by the builders has proved to be the keystone, a stone to stumble over, a rock to bring men down. They stumble over it because they do not believe in the word; it was the fate in store for them.

But you are a chosen race, a royal priesthood, a consecrated nation, a people set apart to sing the praises of God who called you out of the darkness into his wonderful light.

The word of the Lord.

GOSPEL ACCLAMATION   Jn 14:6

Alleluia, alleluia!
Jesus said: 'I am the Way, the Truth and the Life.
No one can come to the Father except through me.'
Alleluia!

GOSPEL   Jn 14:1-12

A reading from the holy Gospel according to John.

I am the Way, the Truth and the Life.

Jesus said to his disciples:

'Do not let your hearts be troubled.
Trust in God still, and trust in me.
There are many rooms in my Father's house;
if there were not, I should have told you.
I am now going to prepare a place for you,
and after I have gone and prepared you a place,
I shall return to take you with me;
so that where I am
you may be too.

You know the way to the place where I am going.'

Thomas said, 'Lord, we do not know where you are going, so how can we know the way?' Jesus said:

'I am the Way, the Truth and the Life.
No one can come to the Father except through me.
If you know me, you know my Father too.
From this moment you know him and have seen him.'

Philip said, 'Lord, let us see the Father and then we shall be satisfied.' 'Have I been with you all this time, Philip,' said Jesus to him 'and you still do not know me?

'To have seen me is to have seen the Father,
so how can you say, "Let us see the Father"?
Do you not believe

that I am in the Father and the Father is in me?
The words I say to you I do not speak as from myself:
it is the Father, living in me, who is doing this work.
You must believe me when I say
that I am in the Father and the Father is in me;
believe it on the evidence of this work, if for no other reason.
'I tell you most solemnly,
whoever believes in me
will perform the same works as I do myself,
he will perform even greater works,
because I am going to the Father.'

The Gospel of the Lord.

Profession of Faith – pages 14-15.

Prayer over the Offerings
O God, who by the wonderful exchange
    effected in this sacrifice
have made us partakers of the one supreme Godhead,
grant, we pray,
that, as we have come to know your truth,
we may make it ours by a worthy way of life.
Through Christ our Lord.

Preface II-V of Easter – pages 21-22.

Communion Antiphon   Jn 15:1.5
**I am the true vine and you are the branches, says the Lord.
Whoever remains in me, and I in him,
bears fruit in plenty, alleluia.**

Prayer after Communion
Graciously be present to your people, we pray, O Lord,
and lead those you have imbued with heavenly mysteries
to pass from former ways to newness of life.
Through Christ our Lord.

Solemn Blessing – page 57.

14 MAY
SIXTH SUNDAY OF EASTER

The following words, attributed to Pedro Arrupe SJ, may up-lift and inspire. "Nothing is more practical than finding God, that is, than falling in love, in a quite absolute, final way. What you are in love with, what seizes your imagination, will affect everything. It will decide what will get you out of bed in the morning, what you will do with your evening, how you will spend your weekends, what you read, who you know, what breaks your heart, and what amazes you with joy and gratitude. Fall in love, stay in love and it will decide everything."

Entrance Antiphon   Cf. Is 48:20

**Proclaim a joyful sound and let it be heard;
proclaim to the ends of the earth:
The Lord has freed his people, alleluia.**

Greeting, Penitential Rite, Gloria – pages 7-13.

Collect

Grant, almighty God,
that we may celebrate with heartfelt devotion
    these days of joy,
which we keep in honour of the risen Lord,
and that what we relive in remembrance
we may always hold to in what we do.
Through our Lord Jesus Christ, your Son,
who lives and reigns with you in the unity of the Holy Spirit,
one God, for ever and ever.

FIRST READING   Acts 8:5-8.14-17

A reading from the Acts of the Apostles.

They laid hands on them, and they received the Holy Spirit.

Philip went to a Samaritan town and proclaimed the Christ to them. The people united in welcoming the message Philip preached, either because they had heard of the miracles he worked or because they saw them for themselves. There were, for example, unclean spirits that came shrieking out of many who were possessed, and several paralytics and cripples were cured. As a result there was great rejoicing in that town.

When the apostles in Jerusalem heard that Samaria had accepted the word of God, they sent Peter and John to them, and they went down there, and prayed for the Samaritans to receive the Holy Spirit, for as yet he had not come down on any of them: they had only been baptised in the name of the Lord Jesus. Then they laid hands on them, and they received the Holy Spirit.

The word of the Lord.

RESPONSORIAL PSALM   Ps 65:1-7.16-20

℟ **Cry out with joy to God all the earth.**

    Or:

    Alleluia!

1. Cry out with joy to God all the earth,
   O sing to the glory of his name.
   O render him glorious praise.
   Say to God: 'How tremendous your deeds! ℟

2. 'Before you all the earth shall bow;
   shall sing to you, sing to your name!'
   Come and see the works of God,
   tremendous his deeds among men. ℟

3. He turned the sea into dry land,
   they passed through the river dry-shod.
   Let our joy then be in him;
   he rules for ever by his might. ℟

4. Come and hear, all who fear God.
   I will tell what he did for my soul:
   Blessed be God who did not reject my prayer
   nor withhold his love from me. ℟

SECOND READING   1 Pt 3:15-18

A reading from the first letter of St Peter.

In the body he was put to death, in the spirit he was raised to life.

Reverence the Lord Christ in your hearts, and always have your answer ready for people who ask you the reason for the hope that you all have. But give it with courtesy and respect and with a clear conscience, so that those who slander you when you are living a good life in Christ may be proved wrong in the accusations that they bring. And if it is the will of God that you should suffer, it is better to suffer for doing right than for doing wrong.

Why, Christ himself, innocent though he was, had died once for sins, died for the guilty, to lead us to God. In the body he was put to death, in the spirit he was raised to life.

The word of the Lord.

GOSPEL ACCLAMATION   Jn 14:23

Alleluia, alleluia!
Jesus said: 'If anyone loves me he will keep my word,
and my Father will love him, and we shall come to him.'
Alleluia!

GOSPEL   Jn 14:15-21

A reading from the holy Gospel according to John.
I shall ask the Father and he will give you another Advocate.

Jesus said to his disciples:

'If you love me you will keep my commandments.
I shall ask the Father,
and he will give you another Advocate
to be with you for ever,
that Spirit of truth
whom the world can never receive
since it neither sees nor knows him;
but you know him,
because he is with you, he is in you.
I will not leave you orphans;
I will come back to you.
In a short time the world will no longer see me;
but you will see me,
because I live and you will live.
On that day
you will understand that I am in my Father
and you in me and I in you.
Anybody who receives my commandments and keeps them
will be one who loves me;
and anybody who loves me will be loved by my Father,
and I shall love him and show myself to him.'

The Gospel of the Lord.

Profession of Faith – pages 14-15.

Prayer over the Offerings

May our prayers rise up to you, O Lord,
together with the sacrificial offerings,
so that, purified by your graciousness,
we may be conformed to the mysteries of your mighty love.
Through Christ our Lord.

Preface II-V of Easter – pages 21-22.

Communion Antiphon   Jn 14:15-16

**If you love me, keep my commandments, says the Lord,
and I will ask the Father and he will send you another
    Paraclete,
to abide with you for ever, alleluia.**

Prayer after Communion

Almighty ever-living God,
who restore us to eternal life in the Resurrection of Christ,
increase in us, we pray, the fruits of this paschal Sacrament
and pour into our hearts the strength of this saving food.
Through Christ our Lord.

Solemn Blessing – page 57.

18 or 21 MAY
THE ASCENSION OF THE LORD

(Celebrated in Ireland on 21 May
and in England, Wales and Scotland on 18 May)

(In England, Wales and Scotland **Seventh Sunday of Easter**
is celebrated on 21 May – page 261)

*We could ask, 'how is the Risen Lord with us?' The New Testament
and the Church tradition offer a rich array of "presences." Christ
is present in the neighbour in need, in creation, and wherever the
disciples gather, in the word proclaimed, in the sacrament celebrated
through the Holy Spirit. Perhaps we do not always feel this presence,
but the words of Jesus are a guarantee that no matter what is going
on in my life or my community or my Church, he is with us, our
Emmanuel.*

Entrance Antiphon   Acts 1:11

Men of Galilee, why gaze in wonder at the heavens?
This Jesus whom you saw ascending into heaven
will return as you saw him go, alleluia.

Greeting, Penitential Rite, Gloria – pages 7-13.

Collect

Gladden us with holy joys, almighty God,
and make us rejoice with devout thanksgiving,
for the Ascension of Christ your Son
is our exaltation,
and, where the Head has gone before in glory,
the Body is called to follow in hope.
Through our Lord Jesus Christ, your Son,
who lives and reigns with you in the unity of the Holy Spirit,
one God, for ever and ever.

    Or:

Grant, we pray, almighty God,
that we, who believe that your Only Begotten Son,
    our Redeemer,
ascended this day to the heavens,
may in spirit dwell already in heavenly realms.
Who lives and reigns with you in the unity of the Holy Spirit,
one God, for ever and ever.

FIRST READING   Acts 1:1-11

A reading from the Acts of the Apostles.

He was lifted up while they looked on.

In my earlier work, Theophilus, I dealt with everything Jesus had done and taught from the beginning until the day he gave his instructions to the apostles he had chosen through the Holy Spirit, and was taken up to heaven. He had shown himself alive to them after his Passion by many demonstrations: for forty days he had continued to appear to them and tell them about the kingdom of God. When he had been at table with them, he had told them not to leave Jerusalem, but to wait there for what the Father had promised. 'It is,' he had said, 'what you have heard me speak about: John baptised with water but you, not many days from now, will be baptised with the Holy Spirit.'

   Now having met together, they asked him, 'Lord, has the time come? Are you going to restore the kingdom to Israel?' He replied, 'It is not for you to know times or dates that the Father has decided by his own authority, but you will receive power when the Holy Spirit comes on you, and then you will be my witnesses not only in Jerusalem but throughout Judaea and Samaria, and indeed to the ends of the earth.'

   As he said this he was lifted up while they looked on, and a cloud took him from their sight. They were still staring into the sky when suddenly two men in white were standing near them and they said, 'Why are you men from Galilee standing here looking into the sky? Jesus who has been taken up from you into heaven, this same Jesus will come back in the same way as you have seen him go there.'

   The word of the Lord.

RESPONSORIAL PSALM   Ps 46:2-3.6-7.8-9

℟   **God goes up with shouts of joy;**
    the Lord goes up with trumpet blast.

        Or:

    Alleluia!

1. All peoples, clap your hands,
    cry to God with shouts of joy!
    For the Lord, the Most High, we must fear,
    great king over all the earth.   ℟

2. God goes up with shouts of joy;
   the Lord goes up with trumpet blast.
   Sing praise for God, sing praise,
   sing praise to our king, sing praise. ℞

3. God is king of all the earth.
   Sing praise with all your skill.
   God is king over the nations;
   God reigns on his holy throne. ℞

SECOND READING   Ep 1:17-23

A reading from the letter of St Paul to the Ephesians.

He made him sit at his right hand in heaven.

May the God of our Lord Jesus Christ, the Father of glory, give you a spirit of wisdom and perception of what is revealed, to bring you to full knowledge of him. May he enlighten the eyes of your mind so that you can see what hope his call holds for you, what rich glories he has promised the saints will inherit and how infinitely great is the power that he has exercised for us believers. This you can tell from the strength of his power at work in Christ, when he used it to raise him from the dead and to make him sit at his right hand, in heaven, far above every Sovereignty, Authority, Power, or Domination, or any other name that can be named, not only in this age, but also in the age to come. He has put all things under his feet, and made him as the ruler of everything, the head of the Church; which is his body, the fullness of him who fills the whole creation.

     The word of the Lord.

GOSPEL ACCLAMATION   Mt 28:19.20

Alleluia, alleluia!
Go, make disciples of all the nations;
I am with you always; yes, to the end of time. Alleluia!

GOSPEL   Mt 28:16-20

A reading from the holy Gospel according to Matthew.

All authority in heaven and on earth has been given to me.

The eleven disciples set out for Galilee, to the mountain where Jesus had arranged to meet them. When they saw him they fell down before him, though some hesitated. Jesus came up and spoke to them. He said, 'All authority in heaven and on earth has been given to me. Go, therefore, make disciples of all the nations; baptise them in the name of the Father and of the Son and of the Holy Spirit, and teach them to observe all the commands I gave you. And know that I am with you always; yes, to the end of time.'

The Gospel of the Lord.

Profession of Faith – pages 14-15.

Prayer over the Offerings

We offer sacrifice now in supplication, O Lord,
to honour the wondrous Ascension of your Son:
grant, we pray,
that through this most holy exchange
we, too, may rise up to the heavenly realms.
Through Christ our Lord.

Preface I of the Ascension of the Lord

The Lord be with you.
And with your spirit.

Lift up your hearts.
We lift them up to the Lord.

Let us give thanks to the Lord our God.
It is right and just.

It is truly right and just, our duty and our salvation,
always and everywhere to give you thanks,
Lord, holy Father, almighty and eternal God.

For the Lord Jesus, the King of glory,
conqueror of sin and death,
ascended (today) to the highest heavens,
as the Angels gazed in wonder.

Mediator between God and man,
judge of the world and Lord of hosts,
he ascended, not to distance himself from our lowly state
but that we, his members, might be confident of following
where he, our Head and Founder, has gone before.

Therefore, overcome with paschal joy,
every land, every people exults in your praise
and even the heavenly Powers, with the angelic hosts,
sing together the unending hymn of your glory,
as they acclaim:

Holy, Holy, Holy Lord God of hosts …

Communion Antiphon   Mt 28:20

**Behold, I am with you always,
even to the end of the age, alleluia.**

Prayer after Communion

Almighty ever-living God,
who allow those on earth to celebrate divine mysteries,
grant, we pray,
that Christian hope may draw us onward
to where our nature is united with you.
Through Christ our Lord.

Solemn Blessing

The Priest invites people to bow down for the blessing.

May almighty God bless you,
for on this very day his Only Begotten Son
pierced the heights of heaven
and unlocked for you the way
to ascend to where he is.
Amen.

May he grant that,
as Christ after his Resurrection
was seen plainly by his disciples,
so when he comes as Judge
he may show himself merciful to you for all eternity.
Amen.

And may you, who believe he is seated
with the Father in his majesty,
know with joy the fulfilment of his promise
to stay with you until the end of time.
Amen.

And may the blessing of almighty God,
the Father, and the Son, ✠ and the Holy Spirit,
come down on you and remain with you for ever.
Amen.

21 MAY

SEVENTH SUNDAY OF EASTER

(Celebrated in England, Wales and Scotland)

To understand the death of Jesus is to see that he opened his arms on the cross to embrace in unity and love all of God's people and to form them into his body, the Church. God's will is that we stand before him, not as isolated individuals, but as a united people, the universal Church. This week the Church prays for a renewal of Pentecost which will bring an ever deeper understanding of the Church.

Entrance Antiphon   Cf. Ps 26:7-9

**O Lord, hear my voice, for I have called to you;
of you my heart has spoken: Seek his face;
hide not your face from me, alleluia.**

Greeting, Penitential Rite, Gloria – pages 7-13.

Collect

Graciously hear our supplications, O Lord,
so that we, who believe that the Saviour of the human race
is with you in your glory,
may experience, as he promised,
until the end of the world,
his abiding presence among us.
Who lives and reigns with you in the unity of the Holy Spirit,
one God, for ever and ever.

FIRST READING   Acts 1:12-14

A reading from the Acts of the Apostles.

All joined in continuous prayer.

After Jesus was taken up into heaven, the apostles went back from the Mount of Olives, as it is called, to Jerusalem, a short distance away, no more than a sabbath walk; and when they reached the city they went to the upper room where they were staying; there were Peter and John, James and Andrew, Philip and Thomas, Bartholomew and Matthew, James son of Alphaeus and Simon the Zealot, and Jude son of James. All these joined in continuous prayer, together with several women, including Mary the mother of Jesus, and with his brothers.

The word of the Lord.

RESPONSORIAL PSALM   Ps 26:1,4,7-8. R. v.13

℟ I am sure I shall see the Lord's goodness in the land
    of the living.

Or:

Alleluia!

1. The Lord is my light and my help;
   whom shall I fear?
   The Lord is the stronghold of my life;
   before whom shall I shrink? ℟

2. There is one thing I ask of the Lord,
   for this I long,
   to live in the house of the Lord,
   all the days of my life,
   to savour the sweetness of the Lord,
   to behold his temple. ℟

3. O Lord, hear my voice when I call;
   have mercy and answer.
   Of you my heart has spoken;
   'Seek his face.' ℟

SECOND READING   4:13-16

A reading from the first letter of St Peter.

It is a blessing for you when they insult you for bearing the name of Christ.

If you can have some share in the sufferings of Christ, be glad,
because you will enjoy a much greater gladness when his glory is
revealed. It is a blessing for you when they insult you for bearing
the name of Christ, because it means that you have the Spirit
of glory, the Spirit of God resting on you. None of you should
ever deserve to suffer for being a murderer, a thief, a criminal
or an informer; but if anyone of you should suffer for being a
Christian, then he is not to be ashamed of it; he should thank
God that he has been called one.

The word of the Lord.

GOSPEL ACCLAMATION   Cf. Jn 14:18

Alleluia, alleluia!
I will not leave you orphans, says the Lord;
I will come back to you,
and your hearts will be full of joy.
Alleluia!

GOSPEL 17:1-11

A reading from the holy Gospel according to John.

Father, glorify your Son.

Jesus raised his eyes to heaven and said:

'Father, the hour has come:
glorify your Son
so that your Son may glorify you;
and, through the power over all mankind that you have
     given him,
let him give eternal life to all those you have entrusted
     to him.
And eternal life is this:
to know you,
the only true God,
and Jesus Christ whom you have sent.
I have glorified you on earth
and finished the work
that you gave me to do.
Now, Father, it is time for you to glorify me
with that glory I had with you
before ever the world was.
I have made your name known
to the men you took from the world to give me.
They were yours and you gave them to me,
and they have kept your word.
Now at last they know
that all you have given me comes indeed from you;
for I have given them
the teaching you gave to me,
and they have truly accepted this, that I came from you,
and have believed that it was you who sent me.
I pray for them;
I am not praying for the world
but for those you have given me,
because they belong to you:
all I have is yours
and all you have is mine,
and in them I am glorified.
I am not in the world any longer,
but they are in the world,

and I am coming to you.'
The Gospel of the Lord.

Profession of Faith – pages 14-15.

Prayer over the Offerings

Accept, O Lord, the prayers of your faithful
with the sacrificial offerings,
that through these acts of devotedness
we may pass over to the glory of heaven.
Through Christ our Lord.

Preface II-V of Easter – pages 21-22.

Communion Antiphon   Jn 17:22
**Father, I pray that they may be one
as we also are one, alleluia.**

Prayer after Communion

Hear us, O God our Saviour,
and grant us confidence,
that through these sacred mysteries
there will be accomplished in the body of the whole Church
what has already come to pass in Christ her Head.
Who lives and reigns for ever and ever.

Solemn Blessing – page 57.

PENTECOST SUNDAY

— At the Vigil Mass —

"Come, Holy Spirit!" Where truth, love, goodness, peace, kindness, wisdom, courage, patience, and many others of his fruits are present, there the Spirit is active. In so many different ways, the Spirit reminds the world of the Gospel.

Entrance Antiphon   Rm 5:5; Cf. 8:11
The love of God has been poured into our hearts through the Spirit of God dwelling within us, alleluia.

Greeting, Penitential Rite, Gloria – pages 7-13.

Collect
Almighty ever-living God,
who willed the Paschal Mystery
to be encompassed as a sign in fifty days,
grant that from out of the scattered nations
the confusion of many tongues
may be gathered by heavenly grace
into one great confession of your name.
Through our Lord Jesus Christ, your Son,
who lives and reigns with you in the unity of the Holy Spirit,
one God, for ever and ever.

Or:

Grant, we pray, almighty God,
that the splendour of your glory
may shine forth upon us
and that, by the bright rays of the Holy Spirit,
the light of your light may confirm the hearts
of those born again by your grace.
Through our Lord Jesus Christ, your Son,
who lives and reigns with you in the unity of the Holy Spirit,
one God, for ever and ever.

FIRST READING   Gn 11:1-9
A reading from the book of Genesis.
It was named Babel because there the language of the whole earth was confused.

Throughout the earth men spoke the same language, with the same vocabulary. Now as they moved eastwards they found a plain in the land of Shinar where they settled. They said to one another, 'Come, let us make bricks and bake them in the fire.' – For stone they used bricks, and for mortar they used bitumen. – 'Come,' they said, 'let us build ourselves a town and a tower with its top reaching heaven. Let us make a name for ourselves, so that we may not be scattered about the whole earth.'

Now the Lord came down to see the town and the tower that the sons of man had built. 'So they are all a single people with a single language!' said the Lord. 'This is but the start of their undertakings! There will be nothing too hard for them to do. Come, let us go down and confuse their language on the spot so that they can no longer understand one another.' The Lord scattered them thence over the whole face of the earth, and they stopped building the town. It was named Babel therefore, because there the Lord confused the language of the whole earth. It was from there that the Lord scattered them over the whole face of the earth.

The word of the Lord.

RESPONSORIAL PSALM   Ps 103:1-2.24.27-30.35

℟ **Send forth your Spirit, O Lord,
   and renew the face of the earth.**

>   Or:

>   **Alleluia!**

1. Bless the Lord, my soul!
   Lord God, how great you are,
   clothed in majesty and glory,
   wrapped in light as in a robe! ℟

2. How many are your works, O Lord!
   In wisdom you have made them all.
   The earth is full of your riches.
   Bless the Lord, my soul.

3. All of these look to you
   to give them their food in due season.
   You give it, they gather it up:
   you open your hand, they have their fill.

4. You take back your spirit, they die,
   returning to the dust from which they came.
   You send forth your spirit, they are created;
   and you renew the face of the earth. ℟

SECOND READING   Rm 8:22-27

A reading from the letter of St Paul to the Romans.

The Spirit himself expresses our plea in a way that could never be put into words.

From the beginning till now the entire creation, as we know, has been groaning in one great act of giving birth; and not only creation, but all of us who possess the first-fruits of the Spirit, we too groan inwardly as we wait for our bodies to be set free. For we must be content to hope that we shall be saved – our salvation is not in sight, we should not have to be hoping for it if it were – but, as I say, we must hope to be saved since we are not saved yet – it is something we must wait for with patience.

The Spirit too comes to help us in our weakness. For when we cannot choose words in order to pray properly, the Spirit himself expresses our plea in a way that could never be put into words, and God who knows everything in our hearts knows perfectly well what he means, and that the pleas of the saints expressed by the Spirit are according to the mind of God.

The word of the Lord.

GOSPEL ACCLAMATION

Alleluia, alleluia!
Come, Holy Spirit, fill the hearts of your faithful
and kindle in them the fire of your love.
Alleluia!

GOSPEL   Jn 7:37-39

A reading from the holy Gospel according to John.

From his breast shall flow fountains of living water.

On the last day and greatest day of the festival, Jesus stood there and cried out:

'If any man is thirsty, let him come to me!
Let the man come and drink who believes in me!'

As scripture says: From his breast shall flow fountains of living water.

He was speaking of the Spirit which those who believed in

him were to receive; for there was no Spirit as yet because Jesus
had not yet been glorified.

The Gospel of the Lord.

Profession of Faith – pages 14-15.

Prayer over the Offerings
Pour out upon these gifts the blessing of your Spirit,
we pray, O Lord,
so that through them your Church may be imbued with such
    love
that the truth of your saving mystery
may shine forth for the whole world.
Through Christ our Lord.

Preface of Pentecost – page 272.

Communion Antiphon   Jn 7:37
On the last day of the festival, Jesus stood and cried out:
If anyone is thirsty, let him come to me and drink, alleluia.

Prayer after Communion
May these gifts we have consumed
benefit us, O Lord,
that we may always be aflame with the same Spirit,
whom you wondrously poured out on your Apostles.
Through Christ our Lord.

Solemn Blessing – page 273.

———— At the Mass during the Day ————

Shalom – peace – is one of those wonderful words which speaks
directly to the hearts and needs of us all. In the Old Testament,
shalom already has a rich meaning: physical health, prosperity, good
relationship and fertility. The shalom of the Risen Lord includes his
love, his offer of forgiveness of sins and his gift of freedom from death
and the fear of death. We live these gifts through the indwelling of the
Holy Spirit, the gift of the Risen Christ.

Entrance Antiphon   Ws 1:7
The Spirit of the Lord has filled the whole world
and that which contains all things
understands what is said, alleluia.

Or: Rm 5:5; Cf. 8:11

**The love of God has been poured into our hearts
through the Spirit of God dwelling within us, alleluia.**

Greeting, Penitential Rite, Gloria – pages 7-13.

Collect

O God, who by the mystery of today's great feast
sanctify your whole Church in every people and nation,
pour out, we pray, the gifts of the Holy Spirit
across the face of the earth
and, with the divine grace that was at work
when the Gospel was first proclaimed,
fill now once more the hearts of believers.
Through our Lord Jesus Christ, your Son,
who lives and reigns with you in the unity of the Holy Spirit,
one God, for ever and ever.

FIRST READING   Acts 2:1-11

A reading from the Acts of the Apostles.

They were all filled with the Holy Spirit and began to speak.

When Pentecost day came round, the apostles had all met in
one room, when suddenly they heard what sounded like a
powerful wind from heaven, the noise of which filled the entire
house in which they were sitting; and something appeared to
them that seemed like tongues of fire; these separated and came
to rest on the head of each of them. They were all filled with the
Holy Spirit, and began to speak foreign languages as the Spirit
gave them the gift of speech.

Now there were devout men living in Jerusalem from every
nation under heaven, and at this sound they all assembled, each
one bewildered to hear these men speaking his own language.
They were amazed and astonished. 'Surely' they said 'all these
men speaking are Galileans? How does it happen that each of
us hears them in his own native language? Parthians, Medes and
Elamites; people from Mesopotamia, Judaea and Cappadocia,
Pontus and Asia, Phrygia and Pamphylia, Egypt and the parts of
Libya round Cyrene; as well as visitors from Rome – Jews and
proselytes alike – Cretans and Arabs; we hear them preaching in
our own language about the marvels of God.'

The word of the Lord.

RESPONSORIAL PSALM   Ps 103:1.24.29-31.34

℞ **Send forth your Spirit, O Lord,**
   and renew the face of the earth.

        Or:

   Alleluia!

1. Bless the Lord, my soul!
   Lord God, how great you are,
   How many are your works, O Lord!
   The earth is full of your riches. ℞

2. You take back your spirit, they die,
   returning to the dust from which they came.
   You send forth your spirit, they are created;
   and you renew the face of the earth. ℞

3. May the glory of the Lord last for ever!
   May the Lord rejoice in his works!
   May my thoughts be pleasing to him.
   I find my joy in the Lord.

SECOND READING   1 Cor 12:3-7.12-13

A reading from the first letter of St Paul to the Corinthians.

In the one Spirit we were all baptised.

No one can say, 'Jesus is Lord' unless he is under the influence of
the Holy Spirit.

   There is a variety of gifts but always the same Spirit; there
are all sorts of service to be done, but always to the same Lord;
working in all sorts of different ways in different people, it is the
same God who is working in all of them. The particular way in
which the Spirit is given to each person is for a good purpose.

   Just as a human body, though it is made up of many parts,
is a single unit because all these parts, though many, make one
body, so it is with Christ. In the one Spirit we were all baptised,
Jews as well as Greeks, slaves as well as citizens, and one Spirit
was given to us all to drink.

   The word of the Lord.

SEQUENCE

(The sequence may be said or sung).

Holy Spirit, Lord of light,
From the clear celestial height
Thy pure beaming radiance give.

Come, thou Father of the poor,
Come with treasures which endure;
Come, thou light of all that live!

Thou, of all consolers best,
Thou, the soul's delightful guest,
Dost refreshing peace bestow.

Thou in toil art comfort sweet;
Pleasant coolness in the heat;
Solace in the midst of woe.

Light immortal, light divine,
Visit thou these hearts of thine,
And our inmost being fill:

If thou take thy grace away,
Nothing pure in man will stay;
All his good is turned to ill.

Heal our wounds, our strength renew;
On our dryness pour thy dew;
Wash the stains of guilt away:

Bend the stubborn heart and will;
Melt the frozen, warm the chill;
Guide the steps that go astray.

Thou, on us who evermore
Thee confess and thee adore,
With thy sevenfold gifts descend:

Give us comfort when we die;
Give us life with thee on high;
Give us joys that never end.

GOSPEL ACCLAMATION

Alleluia, alleluia!
Come, Holy Spirit, fill the hearts of your faithful,
and kindle in them the fire of your love.
Alleluia!

GOSPEL   Jn 20:19-23

A reading from the holy Gospel according to John.

As the Father sent me, so am I sending you: receive the Holy Spirit.

In the evening of the first day of the week, the doors were closed
in the room where the disciples were, for fear of the Jews. Jesus

came and stood among them. He said to them, 'Peace be with you,' and showed them his hands and his side. The disciples were filled with joy when they saw the Lord, and he said to them again, 'Peace be with you'.

> 'As the Father sent me,
> so am I sending you.'

After saying this he breathed on them and said:

> 'Receive the Holy Spirit.
> For those whose sins you forgive,
> they are forgiven;
> for those whose sins you retain,
> they are retained.'

The Gospel of the Lord

Profession of Faith – pages 14-15.

Prayer over the Offerings

Grant, we pray, O Lord,
that, as promised by your Son,
the Holy Spirit may reveal to us more abundantly
the hidden mystery of this sacrifice
and graciously lead us into all truth.
Through Christ our Lord.

Preface: The Mystery of Pentecost

The Lord be with you.
And with your spirit.

Lift up your hearts.
We lift them up to the Lord.

Let us give thanks to the Lord our God.
It is right and just.

It is truly right and just, our duty and our salvation,
always and everywhere to give you thanks,
Lord, holy Father, almighty and eternal God.

For, bringing your Paschal Mystery to completion,
you bestowed the Holy Spirit today
on those you made your adopted children
by uniting them to your Only Begotten Son.
This same Spirit, as the Church came to birth,
opened to all peoples the knowledge of God

and brought together the many languages of the earth
in profession of the one faith.

Therefore, overcome with paschal joy,
every land, every people exults in your praise
and even the heavenly Powers, with the angelic hosts,
sing together the unending hymn of your glory as they acclaim:
Holy, Holy, Holy Lord God of hosts …

Communion Antiphon   Ac 2:4.11
**They were all filled with the Holy Spirit
and spoke of the marvels of God, alleluia.**

Prayer after Communion
O God, who bestow heavenly gifts upon your Church,
safeguard, we pray, the grace you have given,
that the gift of the Holy Spirit poured out upon her
may retain all its force
and that this spiritual food
may gain her abundance of eternal redemption.
Through Christ our Lord.

Solemn Blessing
The Priest invites people to bow down for the blessing.
May God, the Father of lights,
who was pleased to enlighten the disciples' minds
by the outpouring of the Spirit, the Paraclete,
grant you gladness by his blessing
and make you always abound with the gifts of the same Spirit.
Amen.

May the wondrous flame that appeared above the disciples,
powerfully cleanse your hearts from every evil
and pervade them with its purifying light.
Amen.

And may God, who has been pleased to unite many tongues
in the profession of one faith,
give you perseverance in that same faith
and, by believing, may you journey from hope to clear vision.
Amen.

And may the blessing of almighty God,
the Father, and the Son, ✠ and the Holy Spirit,
come down on you and remain with you for ever.
Amen.

━━━━━━━━━━━ 4 JUNE ━━━━━━━━━━━

THE MOST HOLY TRINITY

The Trinity is not first of all a puzzle, which in principle could be solved, but rather a mystery, a relationship which is first of all lived, never exhausted and only inadequately spoken of in words. This is true of any of the significant relationships in our lives and true therefore all the more so of God. Within the mystery of that relationship, we recognise God, from whom we come, in whom we live and move and have our being. We recognise the Son, the Way, the Truth and the Life. We recognise the Spirit, who helps us to pray when we do not know how to pray as we ought.

Entrance Antiphon
**Blest be God the Father,
and the Only Begotten Son of God,
and also the Holy Spirit,
for he has shown us his merciful love.**

Greeting, Penitential Rite, Gloria – pages 7-13.

Collect
God our Father, who by sending into the world
the Word of truth and the Spirit of sanctification
made known to the human race your wondrous mystery,
grant us, we pray, that in professing the true faith,
we may acknowledge the Trinity of eternal glory
and adore your Unity, powerful in majesty.
Through our Lord Jesus Christ, your Son,
who lives and reigns with you in the unity of the Holy Spirit,
one God, for ever and ever.

FIRST READING   Ex 34:4-6.8-9
A reading from the book of Exodus.
Lord, a God of tenderness and compassion.

With the two tablets of stone in his hands, Moses went up the mountain of Sinai in the early morning as the Lord had commanded him. And the Lord descended in the form of a cloud, and Moses stood with him there.

He called on the name of the Lord. The Lord passed before him and proclaimed, 'Lord, Lord, a God of tenderness and compassion, slow to anger, rich in kindness and faithfulness.' And Moses bowed down to the ground at once and worshipped. 'If I have indeed won your favour, Lord,' he said 'let my Lord come with us, I beg. True, they are a headstrong people, but forgive us our faults and our sins, and adopt us as your heritage.'

The word of the Lord.

RESPONSORIAL PSALM   Dn 3:52-56

℞ **To you glory and praise for evermore.**

1. You are blest, Lord God of our fathers. ℞
   Blest your glorious holy name. ℞

2. You are blest in the temple of your glory. ℞
   You are blest on the throne of your kingdom. ℞

3. You are blest who gaze into the depths. ℞
   You are blest in the firmament of heaven. ℞

SECOND READING   2 Cor 13:11-13

A reading from the second letter of St Paul to the Corinthians.

The grace of Jesus Christ, the love of God, and the fellowship of the Holy Spirit.

Brothers, we wish you happiness; try to grow perfect; help one another. Be united; live in peace, and the God of love and peace will be with you.

Greet one another with the holy kiss. All the saints send you greetings.

The grace of the Lord Jesus Christ, the love of God and the fellowship of the Holy Spirit be with you all.

The word of the Lord.

GOSPEL ACCLAMATION   Cf. Rv 1:8

Alleluia, alleluia!
Glory be to the Father, and to the Son, and to the Holy Spirit, the God who is, who was, and who is to come.
Alleluia!

GOSPEL   Jn 3:16-18

A reading from the holy Gospel according to John.
God sent his Son so that through him the world might be saved.

Jesus said to Nicodemus,

> 'God loved the world so much
> that he gave his only Son,
> so that everyone who believes in him may not be lost
> but may have eternal life.
> For God sent his Son into the world
> not to condemn the world,
> but so that through him the world might be saved.
> No one who believes in him will be condemned;
> but whoever refuses to believe is condemned already,
> because he has refused to believe
> in the name of God's only Son.'

The Gospel of the Lord.

Profession of Faith – pages 14-15.

Prayer over the Offerings

Sanctify by the invocation of your name,
we pray, O Lord our God,
this oblation of our service,
and by it make of us an eternal offering to you.
Through Christ our Lord.

Preface: The Mystery of the Most Holy Trinity

The Lord be with you.
And with your spirit.

Lift up your hearts.
We lift them up to the Lord.

Let us give thanks to the Lord our God.
It is right and just.

It is truly right and just, our duty and our salvation,
always and everywhere to give you thanks,
Lord, holy Father, almighty and eternal God.

For with your Only Begotten Son and the Holy Spirit
you are one God, one Lord:
not in the unity of a single person,
but in a Trinity of one substance.

For what you have revealed to us of your glory
we believe equally of your Son
and of the Holy Spirit,
so that, in the confessing of the true and eternal Godhead,
you might be adored in what is proper to each Person,
their unity in substance,
and their equality in majesty.

For this is praised by Angels and Archangels,
Cherubim, too, and Seraphim,
who never cease to cry out each day,
as with one voice they acclaim:

Holy, Holy, Holy Lord God of hosts …

Communion Antiphon   Ga 4:6

Since you are children of God,
God has sent into your hearts the Spirit of his Son,
the Spirit who cries out: Abba, Father.

Prayer after Communion

May receiving this Sacrament, O Lord our God,
bring us health of body and soul,
as we confess your eternal holy Trinity and undivided Unity.
Through Christ our Lord.

11 JUNE
THE MOST HOLY BODY AND BLOOD OF CHRIST
(Corpus Christi)

Jesus himself practised open table-fellowship, to express God's unconditional love and acceptance. Before he died, he spoke words over the bread and the wine, words which disclosed the meaning of his death and resurrection. When St Paul wrote to the Corinthians about the Lord's Supper, he had to remind them that the sacrament is meant to be a communion among all who celebrate it and to have a practical effect in our lives. As Benedict XVI wrote: "A Eucharist which does not pass over into the concrete practice of love is essentially fragmented" (God is Love).

Entrance Antiphon   Cf. Ps 80:17

**He fed them with the finest wheat
and satisfied them with honey from the rock.**

Greeting, Penitential Rite, Gloria – pages 7-13.

Collect

O God, who in this wonderful Sacrament
have left us a memorial of your Passion,
grant us, we pray,
so to revere the sacred mysteries of your Body and Blood
that we may always experience in ourselves
the fruits of your redemption.
Who live and reign with God the Father
in the unity of the Holy Spirit,
one God, for ever and ever.

FIRST READING   Deut 8:2-3.14-16

A reading from the book of Deuteronomy.

He fed you with manna which neither you nor your fathers had known.

Moses said to the people: 'Remember how the Lord your God led you for forty years in the wilderness, to humble you, to test you and to know your inmost heart – whether you would keep his commandments or not. He humbled you, he made you feel hunger, he fed you with manna which neither you nor your fathers had known, to make you understand that man does not live on bread alone but that man lives on everything that comes from the mouth of the Lord.

'Do not then forget the Lord your God who brought you out of the land of Egypt, out of the house of slavery: who guided you through this vast and dreadful wilderness, a land of fiery serpents, scorpions, thirst; who in this waterless place brought you water from the hardest rock; who in this wilderness fed you with manna that your fathers had not known.'

The word of the Lord.

RESPONSORIAL PSALM   Ps 147:12-15.19-20

℞ **O praise the Lord, Jerusalem!**

    Or:

    Alleluia!

1. O praise the Lord, Jerusalem!
    Zion, praise your God!
    He has strengthened the bars of your gates,
    he has blessed the children within you. ℞

2. He established peace on your borders,
    he feeds you with finest wheat.
    He sends out his word to the earth
    and swiftly runs his command. ℞

3. He makes his word known to Jacob,
    to Israel his laws and decrees.
    He has not dealt thus with other nations;
    he has not taught them his decrees. ℞

SECOND READING   1 Cor 10:16-17

A reading from the first letter of St Paul to the Corinthians.

That there is only one loaf means that, though there are many of us, we form a single body.

The blessing-cup that we bless is a communion with the blood of Christ, and the bread that we break is a communion with the body of Christ. The fact that there is only one loaf means that, though there are many of us, we form a single body because we all have a share in this one loaf.

The word of the Lord.

SEQUENCE (Shorter Form)

(The Sequence may be said or sung)

Behold the bread of angels, sent
For pilgrims in their banishment,
The bread for God's true children meant,
    That may not unto dogs be given:

Oft in the olden types foreshadowed;
In Isaac on the altar bowed,
And in the ancient paschal food,
    And in the manna sent from heaven.

Come then, good shepherd, bread divine,
Still show to us Thy mercy sign;
Oh, feed us still, still keep us Thine
So may we see Thy glories shine
    In fields of immortality;

O Thou, the wisest, mightiest, best,
Our present food, our future rest,
Come, make us each Thy chosen guest,
Co-heirs of Thine, and comrades blest
    With saints whose dwelling is with Thee.

GOSPEL ACCLAMATION   Jn 6:51-52

Alleluia, alleluia!
I am the living bread which has come down from heaven,
says the Lord.
Anyone who eats this bread will live for ever.
Alleluia!

GOSPEL   Jn 6:51-58

A reading from the holy Gospel according to John.
My flesh is real food and my blood is real drink.

Jesus said to the Jews:

    'I am the living bread which has come down from heaven.
    Anyone who eats this bread will live for ever;
    and the bread that I shall give
    is my flesh, for the life of the world.'

    Then the Jews started arguing with one another: 'How can
this man give us his flesh to eat?' they said. Jesus replied:

    'I tell you most solemnly,

if you do not eat the flesh of the Son of Man
and drink his blood,
you will not have life in you.
Anyone who does eat my flesh and drink my blood
has eternal life,
and I shall raise him up on the last day.
For my flesh is real food
and my blood is real drink.
He who eats my flesh and drinks my blood
lives in me
and I live in him.
As I, who am sent by the living Father,
myself draw life from the Father,
so whoever eats me will draw life from me.
This is the bread come down from heaven;
not like the bread our ancestors ate:
they are dead,
but anyone who eats this bread will live for ever.'

The Gospel of the Lord.

Profession of Faith – pages 14-15.

Prayer over the Offerings

Grant your Church, O Lord, we pray,
the gifts of unity and peace,
whose signs are to be seen in mystery
in the offerings we here present.
Through Christ our Lord.

Preface II of the Most Holy Eucharist

The Lord be with you.
And with your spirit.

Lift up your hearts.
We lift them up to the Lord.

Let us give thanks to the Lord our God.
It is right and just.

It is truly right and just, our duty and our salvation,
always and everywhere to give you thanks,
Lord, holy Father, almighty and eternal God,
through Christ our Lord.

For at the Last Supper with his Apostles,
establishing for the ages to come the saving memorial of
     the Cross,
he offered himself to you as the unblemished Lamb,
the acceptable gift of perfect praise.

Nourishing your faithful by this sacred mystery,
you make them holy, so that the human race,
bounded by one world,
may be enlightened by one faith
and united by one bond of charity.

And so, we approach the table of this wondrous Sacrament,
so that, bathed in the sweetness of your grace,
we may pass over to the heavenly realities here foreshadowed.

Therefore, all creatures of heaven and earth
sing a new song in adoration,
and we, with all the host of Angels,
cry out, and without end we acclaim:

Holy, Holy, Holy Lord God of hosts …

Communion Antiphon   Jn 6:57
Whoever eats my flesh and drinks my blood
remains in me and I in him, says the Lord.

Prayer after Communion
Grant, O Lord, we pray,
that we may delight for all eternity
in that share in your divine life,
which is foreshadowed in the present age
by our reception of your precious Body and Blood.
Who live and reign for ever and ever.

18 JUNE

ELEVENTH SUNDAY IN ORDINARY TIME

Matthew's Gospel values the Hebrew Scriptures for their prophetic material. For Matthew, Jesus fulfils in his life the Old testament prophecies. He portrays Jesus as closely resembling Moses, being pursued from his infancy and now the giver of a New Law. Jesus establishes a new code of life for the people of God.

Entrance Antiphon   Cf. Ps 26:7,9

OLord, hear my voice, for I have called to you; be my help. Do not abandon or forsake me, O God, my Saviour!

Greeting, Penitential Rite, Gloria – pages 7-13.

Collect

O God, strength of those who hope in you,
graciously hear our pleas,
and, since without you mortal frailty can do nothing,
grant us always the help of your grace,
that in following your commands
we may please you by our resolve and our deeds.
Through our Lord Jesus Christ, your Son,
who lives and reigns with you in the unity of the Holy Spirit,
one God, for ever and ever.

FIRST READING   Ex 19:2-6

A reading from the book of Exodus.

I will count you a kingdom of priests, a consecrated nation.

From Rephidim the Israelites set out again; and when they reached the wilderness of Sinai, there in the wilderness they pitched their camp; there facing the mountain Israel pitched camp.

Moses then went up to God, and the Lord called to him from the mountain, saying, 'Say this to the House of Jacob, declare this to the sons of Israel, "You yourselves have seen what I did with the Egyptians, how I carried you on eagle's wings and brought you to myself. From this you know that now, if you obey my voice and hold fast to my covenant, you of all the nations shall be my very own, for all the earth is mine. I will count you a kingdom of priests, a consecrated nation."'

The word of the Lord.

RESPONSORIAL PSALM   Ps 99:1-3,5. R. v.3

℟ **We are his people:**
   the sheep of his flock.

1. Cry out with joy to the Lord, all the earth.
   Serve the Lord with gladness.
   Come before him, singing for joy. ℟

2. Know that he, the Lord, is God.
   He made us, we belong to him,
   we are his people, the sheep of his flock. ℟

3. Indeed, how good is the Lord,
   eternal his merciful love.
   He is faithful from age to age. ℟

SECOND READING   Rom 5:6-11

A reading from the letter of St Paul to the Romans.

*Now that we have been reconciled by the death of his Son, surely we may
count on being saved by the life of his Son.*

We were still helpless when at his appointed moment Christ
died for sinful men. It is not easy to die even for a good man
– though of course for someone really worthy, a man mighty
be prepared to die – but what proves that God loves us is that
Christ died for us while we were still sinners. Having died to
make us righteous, is it likely that he would now fail to save
us from God's anger? When we were reconciled to God by
the death of his Son, we were still enemies; now that we have
been reconciled, surely we may count on being saved by the
life of his Son? Not merely because we have been reconciled
but because we are filled with joyful trust in God through our
Lord Jesus Christ, through whom we have already gained our
reconciliation.

   The word of the Lord.

GOSPEL ACCLAMATION   Jn 10:27

Alleluia, alleluia!
The sheep that belong to me listen to my voice,
says the Lord,
I know them and they follow me.
Alleluia!

   Or: Mk 1:15

Alleluia, alleluia!

The kingdom of God is close at hand.
Repent, and believe the Good News.
Alleluia!

GOSPEL   Mat 9:36-10:8

A reading from the holy Gospel according to Matthew.

He summoned his twelve disciples and sent them out.

When Jesus saw the crowds he felt sorry for them because they were harassed and dejected, like sheep without a shepherd. Then he said to his disciples, 'The harvest is rich but the labourers are few, so ask the Lord of the harvest to send labourers to his harvest.'

He summoned his twelve disciples, and gave them authority over unclean spirits with power to cast them out and to cure all kinds of diseases and sickness.

These are the names of the twelve apostles: first, Simon who is called Peter, and his brother Andrew; James the son of Zebedee, and his brother John; Philip and Bartholomew; Thomas, and Matthew the tax collector; James the son of Alphaeus, and Thaddaeus; Simon the Zealot and Judas Iscariot, the one who was to betray him. These twelve Jesus sent out, instructing them as follows:

'Do not turn your steps to pagan territory, and do not enter any Samaritan town; go rather to the lost sheep of the House of Israel. And as you go, proclaim that the kingdom of heaven is close at hand. Cure the sick, raise the dead, cleanse the lepers, cast out devils. You received without charge, give without charge.'

The Gospel of the Lord.

Profession of Faith – pages 14-15

Prayer over the Offerings
O God, who in the offerings presented here
provide for the twofold needs of human nature,
nourishing us with food
and renewing us with your Sacrament,
grant, we pray,
that the sustenance they provide
may not fail us in body or in spirit.
Through Christ our Lord.

Preface I-VIII of Sundays in Ordinary Time – pages 23-26.

Communion Antiphon   Ps 26:4

There is one thing I ask of the Lord, only this do I seek:
to live in the house of the Lord all the days of my life.

    Or: Jn 17:11

Holy Father, keep in your name those you have given me,
that they may be one as we are one, says the Lord.

Prayer after Communion

As this reception of your Holy Communion, O Lord,
foreshadows the union of the faithful in you,
so may it bring about unity in your Church.
Through Christ our Lord.

===== 25 JUNE =====

TWELFTH SUNDAY IN ORDINARY TIME

Death and imprisonment for Christ are realities for many Christians
even in these times. But we who live in more tolerant societies can be
frightened by the erosion of faith and the de-christianising of values.
To be a genuine Christian means standing apart at times. Christ calls
us to take a stand, to be for him or else against. To live the Christian
ideal in marriage and in business requires courage. Jesus says to all,
"Be not afraid." And in the end he will stand up for those who are
faithful.

Entrance Antiphon   Cf. Ps 27:8-9

The Lord is the strength of his people,
a saving refuge for the one he has anointed.
Save your people, Lord, and bless your heritage,
and govern them for ever.

Collect

Grant, O Lord,
that we may always revere and love your holy name,
for you never deprive of your guidance
those you set firm on the foundation of your love.
Through our Lord Jesus Christ, your Son,
who lives and reigns with you in the unity of the Holy Spirit,
one God, for ever and ever.

FIRST READING   (Jr 20:10-13)

A reading from the prophet Jeremiah.

He has delivered the soul of the needy from the hands of evil men.

Jeremiah said:

> I hear so many disparaging me,
> '"Terror from every side!"
> Denounce him! Let us denounce him!'
> All those who used to be my friends
> watched for my downfall,
> 'Perhaps he will be seduced into error.
> Then we will master him
> and take our revenge!'
> But the Lord is at my side, a mighty hero;
> my opponents will stumble, mastered,
> confounded by their failure;
> everlasting, unforgettable disgrace will be theirs.
> But you, Lord of Hosts, you who probe with justice,
> who scrutinise the loins and heart,
> let me see the vengeance you will take on them,
> for I have committed my cause to you.
> Sing to the Lord,
> praise the Lord,
> for he has delivered the soul of the needy
> from the hands of evil men.
>
> This is the word of the Lord.

RESPONSORIAL PSALM   (Ps 68:8-10.14.17.33-35)

℟ **In your great love, answer me, O God.**

1. It is for you that I suffer taunts,
   that shame covers my face,
   that I have become a stranger to my brothers,
   an alien to my own mother's sons.
   I burn with zeal for your house
   and taunts against you fall on me. ℟

2. This is my prayer to you,
   my prayer for your favour.
   In your great love, answer me, O God,
   with your help that never fails:
   Lord, answer, for your love is kind;
   in your compassion, turn towards me. ℟

3. The poor when they see it will be glad
    and God-seeking hearts will revive;
    for the Lord listens to the needy;
    and does not spurn his servants in their chains.
    Let the heavens and the earth give him praise,
    the sea and all its living creatures. ℟

SECOND READING   (Rm 5:12-15)

A reading from the letter of St Paul to the Romans.

The gift considerably outweighed the fall.

Sin entered the world through one man, and through sin
death, and thus death has spread through the whole human
race because everyone has sinned. Sin existed in the world long
before the Law was given. There was no law and so no one could
be accused of the sin of 'law-breaking', yet death reigned over
all from Adam to Moses, even though their sin, unlike that of
Adam, was not a matter of breaking a law.

Adam prefigured the One to come, but the gift itself
considerably outweighed the fall. If it is certain that through one
man's fall so many died, it is even more certain that divine grace,
coming through the one man, Jesus Christ, came to so many as
an abundant free gift.

This is the word of the Lord.

GOSPEL ACCLAMATION   (Jn 1:14.12)

Alleluia, alleluia!
The Word was made flesh and lived among us;
to all who did accept him
he gave power to become children of God.
Alleluia!

   Or: (Jn 15:26-27)

Alleluia, alleluia!
The Spirit of truth will be my witness;
and you too will be my witnesses.
Alleluia!

GOSPEL   (Mt 10:26-33)

A reading from the holy Gospel according to Matthew.

Do not be afraid of those who kill the body.

Jesus instructed the Twelve as follows: 'Do not be afraid. For
everything that is now covered will be uncovered, and everything

now hidden will be made clear. What I say to you in the dark, tell in the daylight; what you hear in whispers, proclaim from the house-tops.

'Do not be afraid of those who kill the body but cannot kill the soul; fear him rather who can destroy both body and soul in hell. Can you not buy two sparrows for a penny? And yet not one falls to the ground without your Father knowing. Why, every hair on your head has been counted. So there is no need to be afraid; you are worth more than hundreds of sparrows.

'So if anyone declares himself for me in the presence of men, I will declare myself for him in the presence of my Father in heaven. But the one who disowns me in the presence of men, I will disown in the presence of my Father in heaven.'

This is the Gospel of the Lord.

Profession of Faith – pages 14-15

Prayer over the Offerings
Receive, O Lord, the sacrifice of conciliation and praise
and grant that, cleansed by its action,
we may make offering of a heart pleasing to you.
Through Christ our Lord.

Preface I-VIII of Sundays in Ordinary Time – pages 23-26.

Communion Antiphon   Ps 144:15
The eyes of all look to you, Lord,
and you give them their food in due season.

    Or: Jn 10:11,15
I am the Good Shepherd,
and I lay down my life for my sheep, says the Lord.

Prayer after Communion
Renewed and nourished
by the Sacred Body and Precious Blood of your Son,
we ask of your mercy, O Lord,
that what we celebrate with constant devotion
may be our sure pledge of redemption.
Through Christ our Lord.

Solemn Blessing – pages 57-59.

29 JUNE
SS PETER AND PAUL, APOSTLES

——————— At the Vigil Mass ———————

Peter was a humble fisherman. Paul was a persecutor of the first
Christians. But they were chosen to become the pillars of our faith,
which they sealed with their martyrdom in Rome.

Entrance Antiphon

Peter the Apostle, and Paul the teacher of the Gentiles,
these have taught us your law, O Lord.

Greeting, Penitential Rite, Gloria – pages 7-13.

Collect

Grant, we pray, O Lord our God,
that we may be sustained
by the intercession of the blessed Apostles Peter and Paul,
that, as through them you gave your Church
the foundations of her heavenly office,
so through them you may help her to eternal salvation.
Through our Lord Jesus Christ, your Son,
who lives and reigns with you in the unity of the Holy Spirit,
one God, for ever and ever.

FIRST READING   Acts 3:1-10

A reading from the Acts of the Apostles.

I will give you what I have: in the name of Jesus stand up and walk!

Once, when Peter and John were going up to the Temple for
the prayers at the ninth hour, it happened that there was a man
being carried past. He was a cripple from birth; and they used
to put him down every day near the Temple entrance called the
Beautiful Gate so that he could beg from the people going in.
When this man saw Peter and John on their way into the Temple
he begged from them. Both Peter and John looked straight
at him and said, 'Look at us.' He turned to them expectantly,
hoping to get something from them, but Peter said, 'I
have neither silver nor gold, but I will give you what I have: in the
name of Jesus Christ the Nazarene, walk!' Peter then took him
by the hand and helped him to stand up. Instantly his feet
and ankles became firm, he jumped up, stood, and began to

walk, and he went with them into the Temple, walking and jumping and praising God. Everyone could see him walking and praising God, and they recognised him as the man who used to sit begging at the Beautiful Gate of the Temple. They were all astonished and unable to explain what had happened to him.

The word of the Lord.

RESPONSORIAL PSALM   Ps 18:2-5

℟ **Their word goes forth through all the earth.**

1. The heavens proclaim the glory of God
   and the firmament shows forth the work of his hands.
   Day unto day takes up the story
   and night unto night makes known the message. ℟

2. No speech, no word, no voice is heard
   yet their span extends through all the earth,
   their words to the utmost bounds of the world. ℟

SECOND READING   Ga 1:11-20

A reading from the letter of St Paul to the Galatians.

God specially chose me while I was still in my mother's womb.

The Good News I preached is not a human message that I was given by men, it is something I learnt only through a revelation of Jesus Christ. You must have heard of my career as a practising Jew, how merciless I was in persecuting the Church of God, how much damage I did to it, how I stood out among other Jews of my generation, and how enthusiastic I was for the traditions of my ancestors.

Then God, who had specially chosen me while I was still in my mother's womb, called me through his grace and chose to reveal his Son to me, so that I might preach the Good News about him to the pagans. I did not stop to discuss this with any human being, nor did I go up to Jerusalem to see those who were already apostles before me, but I went off to Arabia at once and later went straight back from there to Damascus. Even when after three years I went up to Jerusalem to visit Cephas and stayed with him for fifteen days, I did not see any of the other apostles; I only saw James, the brother of the Lord, and I swear before God that what I have just written is the literal truth.

The word of the Lord.

GOSPEL ACCLAMATION   Jn 21:17

Alleluia, alleluia!
Lord, you know everything;
you know I love you.
Alleluia!

GOSPEL   Jn 21:15-19

A reading from the holy Gospel according to John.

Feed my lambs, feed my sheep.

After Jesus had shown himself to his disciples, and eaten with
them, he said to Simon Peter, 'Simon son of John, do you love
me more than these others do?' He answered, 'Yes, Lord, you
know I love you.' Jesus said to him, 'Feed my lambs.' A second
time he said to him, 'Simon son of John, do you love me?' He
replied, 'Yes, Lord, you know I love you.' Jesus said to him, 'Look
after my sheep.' Then he said to him a third time, 'Simon, son
of John, do you love me?' Peter was upset that he asked him
the third time, "Do you love me?" and said, 'Lord, you know
everything; you know I love you.' Jesus said to him, 'Feed my
sheep.

> 'I tell you most solemnly,
> when you were young
> you put on your own belt
> and walked where you liked;
> but when you grow old
> you will stretch out your hands,
> and somebody else will put a belt round you
> and take you where you would rather not go.'

In these words he indicated the kind of death by which Peter
would give glory to God. After this he said, 'Follow me.'

The Gospel of the Lord.

Profession of Faith – pages 14-15.

Prayer over the Offerings

We bring offerings to your altar, O Lord,
as we glory in the solemn feast
of the blessed Apostles Peter and Paul,
so that the more we doubt our own merits,

the more we may rejoice that we are to be saved
by your loving kindness.
Through Christ our Lord.

Preface – page 332.

Communion Antiphon   Cf. Jn 21:15.17

**Simon, son of John, do you love me more than these?
Lord, you know everything; you know that I love you.**

Prayer after Communion

By this heavenly Sacrament, O Lord, we pray,
strengthen your faithful,
whom you have enlightened with the teaching of the Apostles.
Through Christ our Lord.

Solemn Blessing – page 333-334.

——————— At the Mass during the Day ———————

*The Church is like the human person: we are both body and spirit
at the same time. The body of Christ – which is what we are – has
both a bodily reality (membership, structure and sacraments) and a
spiritual reality (life of faith and prayer, the indwelling Spirit). The
institutional and the prophetic dimensions of Church are sometimes
in tension and that is quite normal. To be part of the living body of
Christ is to hear again Jesus' question, who do you say I am? As St
Paul reminds us, no one can say "Jesus is Lord" except by the Holy
Spirit (1 Cor 12:3).*

Entrance Antiphon

**These are the ones who, living in the flesh,
planted the Church with their blood;
they drank the chalice of the Lord
and became the friends of God.**

Greeting, Penitential Rite, Gloria – pages 7-13.

Collect

O God, who on the Solemnity of the Apostles Peter and Paul
give us the noble and holy joy of this day,
grant, we pray, that your Church
may in all things follow the teaching
of those through whom she received

the beginnings of right religion.
Through our Lord Jesus Christ, your Son,
who lives and reigns with you in the unity of the Holy Spirit,
one God, for ever and ever.

FIRST READING   Acts 12:1-11

A reading from the Acts of the Apostles.
Now I know the Lord really did save me from Herod.

King Herod started persecuting certain members of the Church.
He beheaded James the brother of John, and when he saw that
this pleased the Jews he decided to arrest Peter as well. This
was during the days of Unleavened Bread, and he put Peter in
prison, assigning four squads of four soldiers each to guard him
in turns. Herod meant to try Peter in public after the end of
Passover week. All the time Peter was under guard the Church
prayed to God for him unremittingly.

On the night before Herod was to try him, Peter was sleeping
between two soldiers, fastened with double chains, while guards
kept watch at the main entrance to the prison. Then suddenly
the angel of the Lord stood there, and the cell was filled with
light. He tapped Peter on the side and woke him. 'Get up!' he
said 'Hurry!' – and the chains fell from his hands. The angel
then said, 'Put on your belt and sandals.' After he had done this,
the angel next said, 'Wrap your cloak round you and follow me.'
Peter followed him, but had no idea that what the angel did was
all happening in reality; he thought he was seeing a vision. They
passed through two guard posts one after the other, and reached
the iron gate leading to the city. This opened of its own accord;
they went through it and had walked the whole length of one
street when suddenly the angel left him. It was only then that
Peter came to himself. 'Now I know it is all true,' he said. 'The
Lord really did send his angel and has saved me from Herod and
from all that the Jewish people were so certain would happen to
me.'

The word of the Lord.

RESPONSORIAL PSALM   Ps 33:2-9

℟ **From all my terrors the Lord set me free.**

Or:

The angel of the Lord rescues those who revere him.

1. I will bless the Lord at all times,
    his praise always on my lips;
    in the Lord my soul shall make its boast.
    The humble shall hear and be glad. ℟

2. Glorify the Lord with me.
    Together let us praise his name.
    I sought the Lord and he answered me;
    from all my terrors he set me free. ℟

3. Look towards him and be radiant;
    let your faces not be abashed.
    This poor man called; the Lord heard him
    and rescued him from all his distress. ℟

4. The angel of the Lord is encamped
    around those who revere him, to rescue them.
    Taste and see that the Lord is good.
    He is happy who seeks refuge in him. ℟

SECOND READING   2 Tm 4:6-8.17-18

A reading from the second letter of St Paul to Timothy.

All there is to come now is the crown of righteousness reserved for me.

My life is already being poured away as a libation, and the time
has come for me to be gone. I have fought the good fight to the
end; I have run the race to the finish; I have kept the faith; all
there is to come now is the crown of righteousness reserved for
me, which the Lord, the righteous judge, will give to me on that
Day; and not only to me but to all those who have longed for
his Appearing.

    The Lord stood by me and gave me power, so that through
me the whole message might be proclaimed for all the pagans to
hear; and so I was rescued from the lion's mouth. The Lord will
rescue me from all evil attempts on me, and bring me safely to
his heavenly kingdom. To him be glory for ever and ever. Amen.

    The word of the Lord.

GOSPEL ACCLAMATION   Mt 16:18

Alleluia, alleluia!
You are Peter and on this rock I will build my Church.
And the gates of the underworld can never hold out against it.
Alleluia!

GOSPEL Mt 16:13-19

A reading from the holy Gospel according to Matthew.

You are Peter, and I will give you the keys of the kingdom of heaven.

When Jesus came to the region of Caesarea Philippi he put this question to his disciples, 'Who do people say the Son of Man is?' And they said, 'Some say he is John the Baptist, some Elijah, and others Jeremiah or one of the prophets.' 'But you,' he said 'who do you say I am?' Then Simon Peter spoke up, 'You are the Christ,' he said 'the Son of the living God.' Jesus replied, 'Simon son of Jonah, you are a happy man! Because it was not flesh and blood that revealed this to you but my Father in heaven. So I now say to you: You are Peter and on this rock I will build my Church. And the gates of the underworld can never hold out against it. I will give you the keys of the kingdom of heaven: whatever you bind on earth shall be considered bound in heaven; whatever you loose on earth shall be considered loosed in heaven.'

The Gospel of the Lord.

Profession of Faith – pages 14-15.

Prayer over the Offerings

May the prayer of the Apostles, O Lord,
accompany the sacrificial gift
that we present to your name for consecration,
and may their intercession make us devoted to you
in celebration of the sacrifice.
Through Christ our Lord.

Preface: The Twofold Mission of Peter and Paul
in the Church

The Lord be with you.
And with your spirit.

Lift up your hearts.
We lift them up to the Lord.

Let us give thanks to the Lord our God.
It is right and just.

It is truly right and just, our duty and our salvation,
always and everywhere to give you thanks,
Lord, holy Father, almighty and eternal God.

For by your providence
the blessed Apostles Peter and Paul bring us joy:
Peter, foremost in confessing the faith,
Paul, its outstanding preacher,
Peter, who established the early Church
    from the remnant of Israel,
Paul, master and teacher of the Gentiles that you call.

And so, each in a different way
gathered together the one family of Christ;
and revered together throughout the world,
they share one Martyr's crown.

And therefore, with all the Angels and Saints,
we praise you, as without end we acclaim:

Communion Antiphon   Cf. Mt 16:16.18

**Peter said to Jesus: You are the Christ,
the Son of the living God.
And Jesus replied: You are Peter,
and upon this rock I will build my Church.**

Prayer after Communion

Grant us, O Lord,
who have been renewed by this Sacrament,
so to live in the Church,
that, persevering in the breaking of the Bread
and in the teaching of the Apostles,
we may be one heart and one soul,
made steadfast in your love.
Through Christ our Lord.

Solemn Blessing

The Priest invites people to bow down for the blessing.

May almighty God bless you,
for he has made you steadfast in Saint Peter's saving confession
and through it has set you on the solid rock of the
    Church's faith.
Amen.

And having instructed you
by the tireless preaching of Saint Paul,

may God teach you constantly by his example
to win brothers and sisters for Christ.
Amen.

So that by the keys of St Peter and the words of St Paul,
and by the support of their intercession,
God may bring us happily to that homeland
that Peter attained on a cross
and Paul by the blade of a sword.
Amen.

And may the blessing of almighty God,
the Father, and the Son, ✠ and the Holy Spirit,
come down on you and remain with you for ever.
Amen.

═══════════════ 2 JULY ═══════════════

13th SUNDAY IN ORDINARY TIME

Ce'ad mile fa'ilte, we say, and let us hope we mean it. Christ bids us welcome those who come in his name. This demands more than mere hospitability; it means openness to the other and to the message. Each member of the Church has received a mission so we must accept each other in a spirit of faith and love. Those whom Christ sends on an apostolic or prophetic ministry are to be listened to, whatever our natural feelings about them may be.

Entrance Antiphon   Ps 46:2

All peoples, clap your hands.
Cry to God with shouts of joy!

Greeting, Penitential Rite, Gloria – pages 7-13.

Collect

O God, who through the grace of adoption
chose us to be children of light,
grant, we pray,
that we may not be wrapped in the darkness of error
but always be seen to stand in the bright light of truth.
Through our Lord Jesus Christ, your Son,
who lives and reigns with you in the unity of the Holy Spirit,
one God, for ever and ever.

FIRST READING 2 Kgs 4:8-11.14-16

A reading from the second book of the Kings.

This is a holy man of God, let him rest there.

One day as Elisha was on his way to Shunem, a woman of rank who lived there pressed him to stay and eat there. After this he always broke his journey for a meal when he passed that way. She said to her husband, 'Look, I am sure the man who is constantly passing our way must be a holy man of God. Let us build him a small room on the roof, and put him a bed in it, and a table and chair and lamp; whenever he comes to us he can rest there.'

One day when he came, he retired to the upper room and lay down. 'What can be done for her?' he asked. Gehazi, his servant, answered, 'Well, she has no son and her husband is old.' Elisha said, 'Call her.' The servant called her and she stood at the door. 'This time next year,' Elisha said 'you will hold a son in your arms.'

The word of the Lord.

RESPONSORIAL PSALM Ps 88:2-3. 16-19

I will sing for ever of your love, O Lord.

1. I will sing for ever of your love, O Lord;
   through all ages my mouth will proclaim your truth.
   Of this I am sure, that your love lasts for ever,
   that your truth is firmly established as the heavens.

2. Happy the people who acclaim such a king,
   who walk, O Lord, in the light of your face,
   who find their joy every day in your name,
   who make your justice the source of their bliss.

3. For this is you, O Lord, who are the glory of their strength;
   it is by your favour that our might is exalted:
   for our ruler is in the keeping of the Lord;
   our king in the keeping of the Holy One of Israel.

SECOND READING Rom 6:3-4.8-11

A reading from the letter of St Paul to the Romans.

When we were baptised we went into the tomb with Christ, so that we too might live a new life.

When we were baptised in Christ Jesus we were baptised in his death; in other words, when we were baptised we went into the tomb with him and joined him in death, so that as Christ was raised from the dead by the Father's glory, we too might live a new life.

But we believe that having died with Christ we shall return to life with him: Christ, as we know, having been raised from the dead will never die again. Death has no power over him any more. When he died, he died, once for all, to sin, so his life now is life with God; and in that way, you too must consider yourselves to be dead to sin but alive for God in Christ Jesus.

The word of the Lord.

GOSPE ACCLAMATION   Cf Acts 16:14

Alleluia, alleluia!
Open our heart, O Lord,
to accept the words of your Son.
Alleluia!

Or: 1 Pt 2:9

Alleluia, alleluia!
You are a chosen race, a royal priesthood,
a people set apart to sing the praises of God
who called you out of darkness into his wonderful light.
Alleluia!

GOSPEL   Mt 10:37-42

A reading from the holy Gospel according to Matthew.

Anyone who does not take his cross and follows me is not worthy of me. Anyone who welcomes you welcomes me.

Jesus instructed the Twelve as follows: 'Anyone who prefers father or mother to me is not worthy of me. Anyone who prefers son or daughter to me is not worthy of me. Anhyone who does not take his cross and follow in my footsteps is not worthy of me. Anyhone who finds his life will lose it; anyone who loses his life for my sake will find it.

Anyone who welcomes you welcomes me; and those who welcome me welcome the one who sent me.

Anyone who welcomes a prophet because he is a prophet will have a prophet's reward; and anyone who welcomes a holy man because he is a holy man will have a holy man's reward.

If anyone gives so much as a cup of cold water to one of

these little ones because he is a disciple, then I tell you solemnly,
he will most certainly not lose his reward,'

   The Gospel of the Lord.

Prayer over the Offerings

O God, who graciously accomplish
the effects of your mysteries,
grant, we pray,
that the deeds by which we serve you
may be worthy of these sacred gifts.
Through Christ our Lord.

Preface I-VIII of Sundays in Ordinary Time – pages 23-26.

Communion Antiphon   Cf. Ps 102:1

Bless the Lord, O my soul,
and all within me, his holy name.

   Or: Jn 17:20-21

O Father, I pray for them, that they may be one in us,
that the world may believe that you have sent me,
**   says the Lord.**

Prayer after Communion

May this divine sacrifice we have offered and received
fill us with life, O Lord, we pray,
so that, bound to you in lasting charity,
we may bear fruit that lasts for ever.
Through Christ our Lord.

Solemn Blessing – pages 57-59.

9 JULY
FOURTEENTH SUNDAY IN ORDINARY TIME

The Lord understands us and knows us better than we know ourselves. O Lord, you have searched me and known me. You know when I sit down and when I rise up; you discern my thoughts from far away. You search out my path and my lying down, and are acquainted with all my ways (Ps 139:1-3). He knows what we are made of and so we can come confidently before him with our brokenness and need of his grace. It might be good during the Mass today to become aware of whatever is a burden to us now in our life and ask the Lord for his love and healing touch.

Entrance Antiphon   Cf. Ps 47:10-11

Your merciful love, O God,
we have received in the midst of your temple.
Your praise, O God, like your name,
reaches the ends of the earth;
your right hand is filled with saving justice.

Greeting, Penitential Rite, Gloria – pages 7-13.

Collect

O God, who in the abasement of your Son
have raised up a fallen world,
fill your faithful with holy joy,
for on those you have rescued from slavery to sin
you bestow eternal gladness.
Through our Lord Jesus Christ, your Son,
who lives and reigns with you in the unity of the Holy Spirit,
one God, for ever and ever.

FIRST READING   Zec 9:9-10

A reading from the prophet Zechariah.
See now, your king comes humbly to you.

The Lord says this:

'Rejoice heart and soul, daughter of Zion!
Shout with gladness, daughter of Jerusalem!
See now, your king comes to you;
he is victorious, he is triumphant,
humble and riding on a donkey,

on a colt, the foal of a donkey.
He will banish chariots from Ephraim
and horses from Jerusalem;
the bow of war will be banished.
He will proclaim peace for the nations.
His empire shall stretch from sea to sea,
from the River to the ends of the earth.'

The word of the Lord.

RESPONSORIAL PSALM   Ps 144:1-2.8-11.13-14

℟ **I will bless your name for ever,
O God my King.**

1. I will give you glory, O God my King,
    I will bless your name for ever.
    I will bless you day after day
    and praise your name for ever. ℟

2. The Lord is kind and full of compassion,
    slow to anger, abounding in love.
    How good is the Lord to all,
    compassionate to all his creatures. ℟

3. All your creatures shall thank you, O Lord,
    and your friends shall repeat their blessing.
    They shall speak of the glory of your reign
    and declare your might, O God. ℟

4. The Lord is faithful in all his words
    and loving in all his deeds.
    The Lord supports all who fall
    and raises all who are bowed down. ℟

SECOND READING   Rm 8:9.11-13

A reading from the letter of St Paul to the Romans.

If by the Spirit you put an end to the misdeeds of the body you will live.

Your interests are not in the unspiritual, but in the spiritual,
since the Spirit of God has made his home in you. In fact, unless
you possessed the Spirit of Christ you would not belong to him,
and if the Spirit of him who raised Jesus from the dead is living
in you, then he who raised Jesus from the dead will give life to
your own mortal bodies through his Spirit living in you.

So then, my brothers, there is no necessity for us to obey our
unspiritual selves or to live unspiritual lives. If you do live in

that way, you are doomed to die; but if by the Spirit you put an end to the misdeeds of the body you will live.

The word of the Lord.

GOSPEL ACCLAMATION   Cf. Mt 11:25
Alleluia, alleluia!
Blessed are you, Father, Lord of heaven and earth,
for revealing the mysteries of the kingdom to mere children.
Alleluia!

GOSPEL   Mt 11:25-30
A reading from the holy Gospel according to Matthew.
I am gentle and humble of heart.

Jesus exclaimed, 'I bless you, Father, Lord of heaven and of earth, for hiding these things from the learned and the clever and revealing them to mere children. Yes, Father, for that is what it pleased you to do. Everything has been entrusted to me by my Father; and no one knows the Son except the Father, just as no one knows the Father except the Son and those to whom the Son chooses to reveal him.

'Come to me, all you who labour and are overburdened, and I will give you rest. Shoulder my yoke and learn from me, for I am gentle and humble in heart, and you will find rest for your souls. Yes, my yoke is easy and my burden light.'

The Gospel of the Lord.

Profession of Faith – pages 14-15.

Prayer over the Offerings
May this oblation dedicated to your name
purify us, O Lord,
and day by day bring our conduct
closer to the life of heaven.
Through Christ our Lord.

Preface I-VIII of Sundays in Ordinary Time – pages 23-26.

Communion Antiphon   Ps 33:9
Taste and see that the Lord is good;
blessed the man who seeks refuge in him.
        Or: Mt 11:28
Come to me, all who labour and are burdened,
and I will refresh you, says the Lord.

Prayer after Communion

Grant, we pray, O Lord,
that, having been replenished by such great gifts,
we may gain the prize of salvation
and never cease to praise you.
Through Christ our Lord.

Solemn Blessing – pages 57-59.

———————————— 16 JULY ————————————

FIFTEENTH SUNDAY IN ORDINARY TIME

*The parable of the sower is told and explained by Jesus. It tells of
small, even careless, beginnings – the sower scatters the seeds all
over the place. As we see in nature, tiny seeds have an astonishing,
miraculous effect. Go back over your own experience and recall
something which began modestly but which in the end grew
surprisingly. The reign of God is like that – the modest beginnings of
Jesus' own preaching had tremendous effect.*

Entrance Antiphon   Cf. Ps 16:15

**As for me, in justice I shall behold your face;
I shall be filled with the vision of your glory.**

Greeting, Penitential Rite, Gloria – pages 7-13.

Collect

O God, who show the light of your truth
to those who go astray,
so that they may return to the right path,
give all who for the faith they profess
are accounted Christians
the grace to reject whatever is contrary to the name of Christ
and to strive after all that does it honour.
Through our Lord Jesus Christ, your Son
who lives and reigns with you in the unity of the Holy Spirit,
one God, for ever and ever.

FIRST READING   Is 55:10-11

A reading from the prophet Isaiah.
The rain makes the earth give growth.

Thus says the Lord: 'As the rain and the snow come down from the heavens and do not return without watering the earth, making it yield and giving growth to provide seed for the sower and bread for the eating, so the word that goes from my mouth does not return to me empty, without carrying out my will and succeeding in what it was sent to do.'

The word of the Lord.

RESPONSORIAL PSALM   Ps 64:10-14

℟ **Some seed fell into rich soil,
    and produced its crop.**

1. You care for the earth, give it water,
    you fill it with riches.
    Your river in heaven brims over
    to provide its grain. ℟

2. And thus you provide for the earth;
    you drench its furrows,
    you level it, soften it with showers,
    you bless its growth. ℟

3. You crown the year with your goodness.
    Abundance flows in your steps,
    in the pastures of the wilderness it flows. ℟

4. The hills are girded with joy,
    the meadows covered with flocks,
    the valleys are decked with wheat.
    They shout for joy, yes, they sing. ℟

SECOND READING   Rm 8:18-23

A reading from the letter of St Paul to the Romans.

The whole creation is eagerly waiting for God to reveal his sons.

I think that what we suffer in this life can never be compared to the glory, as yet unrevealed, which is waiting for us. The whole creation is eagerly waiting for God to reveal his sons. It was not for any fault on the part of creation that it was made unable to attain its purpose, it was made so by God; but creation still retains the hope of being freed, like us, from its slavery to decadence, to enjoy the same freedom and glory as the children of God. From the beginning till now the entire creation, as we know, has been groaning in one great act of giving birth; and not only creation, but all of us who possess the first-fruits of the

Spirit, we too groan inwardly as we wait for our bodies to be set free.

The word of the Lord.

GOSPEL ACCLAMATION   1 S 3:9; Jn 6:68
Alleluia, alleluia!
Speak, Lord, your servant is listening;
you have the message of eternal life.
Alleluia!
    Or:
Alleluia, alleluia!
The seed is the word of God, Christ the sower;
whoever finds this seed will remain for ever.
Alleluia!

GOSPEL   Mt 13:1-23
(For Shorter Form, read between ♦ ♦).
A reading from the holy Gospel according to Matthew.
A sower went out to sow.

♦Jesus left the house and sat by the lakeside, but such crowds gathered round him that he got into a boat and sat there. The people all stood on the beach, and he told them many things in parables.

He said, 'Imagine a sower going out to sow. As he sowed, some seeds fell on the edge of the path, and the birds came and ate them up. Others fell on patches of rock where they found little soil and sprang up straight away, because there was no depth of earth; but as soon as the sun came up they were scorched and, not having any roots, they withered away. Others fell among thorns, and the thorns grew up and chocked them. Others fell on rich soil and produced their crop, some a hundredfold, some sixty, some thirty. Listen, anyone who has ears!'♦

Then the disciples went up to him and asked, 'Why do you talk to them in parables?' 'Because' he replied 'the mysteries of the kingdom of heaven are revealed to you, but they are not revealed to them. For anyone who has will be given more, and he will have more than enough; but for anyone who has not, even what he has will be taken away. The reason I talk to them in parables is that they look without seeing and listen without hearing or understanding. So in their case this prophecy of Isaiah is being fulfilled:

You will listen and listen again, but not understand,
see and see again, but not perceive.
For the heart of this nation has grown coarse,
their ears are dull of hearing,
and they have shut their eyes,
for fear they should see with their eyes,
hear with their ears,
understand with their heart,
and be converted
and be healed by me.

'But happy are your eyes because they see, your ears because they hear! I tell you solemnly, many prophets and holy men longed to see what you see, and never saw it; to hear what you hear, and never heard it.

'You, therefore, are to hear the parable of the sower. When anyone hears the word of the kingdom without understanding, the evil one comes and carries off what was sown in his heart: this is the man who received the seed on the edge of the path. The one who received it on patches of rock is the man who hears the word and welcomes it at once with joy. But he has no root in him, he does not last; let some trial come, or some persecution on account of the word, and he falls away at once. The one who received the seed in thorns is the man who hears the word, but the worries of this world and the lure of riches choke the word and so he produces nothing. And the one who received the seed in rich soil is the man who hears the word and understands it; he is the one who yields a harvest and produces now a hundredfold, now sixty, now thirty.'◆

The Gospel of the Lord.

Profession of Faith – pages 14-15.

Prayer over the Offerings

Look upon the offerings of the Church, O Lord,
as she makes her prayer to you,
and grant that, when consumed by those who believe,
they may bring ever greater holiness.
Through Christ our Lord.

Preface I-VIII of Sundays in Ordinary Time – pages 23-26.

Communion Antiphon   Cf. Ps 83:4-5

The sparrow finds a home,
and the swallow a nest for her young:
by your altars, O Lord of hosts, my King and my God.
Blessed are they who dwell in your house,
for ever singing your praise.

    Or: Jn 6:57

Whoever eats my flesh and drinks my blood
remains in me and I in him, says the Lord.

Prayer after Communion

Having consumed these gifts, we pray, O Lord,
that, by our participation in this mystery,
its saving effects upon us may grow.
Through Christ our Lord.

Solemn Blessing – pages 57-59.

━━━━━━━━━━━━━━━ 23 JULY ━━━━━━━━━━━━━━━

SIXTEENTH SUNDAY IN ORDINARY TIME

The parable of the weeds among the wheat addresses the recurring
problem of believers who claim they can discern the righteous from the
wicked, thereby separating themselves from the rest to form a circle of
respectable people. Jesus himself ignores the social labels imposed by
the so-called pious and the respectable. The task of separating the good
from the bad is reserved for God, who will set things right in his own
time.

Entrance Antiphon   Ps 53:6.8

See, I have God for my help.
The Lord sustains my soul.
I will sacrifice to you with willing heart,
and praise your name, O Lord, for it is good.

Greeting, Penitential Rite, Gloria – pages 7-13.

Collect

Show favour, O Lord, to your servants
and mercifully increase the gifts of your grace,

that, made fervent in hope, faith and charity,
they may be ever watchful in keeping your commands.
Through our Lord Jesus Christ, your Son
who lives and reigns with you in the unity of the Holy Spirit,
one God, for ever and ever.

FIRST READING   Ws 12:13.16-19

A reading from the book of Wisdom.

After sin you will grant repentance.

There is no god, other than you, who cares for everything,
to whom you might have to prove that you never judged
    unjustly.
Your justice has its source in strength,
your sovereignty over all makes you lenient to all.
You show your strength when your sovereign power is
    questioned
and you expose the insolence of those who know it;
but, disposing of such strength, you are mild in judgement,
you govern us with great lenience,
for you have only to will, and your power is there.
By acting thus you have taught a lesson to your people
how the virtuous man must be kindly to his fellow men,
and you have given your sons the good hope
that after sin you will grant repentance.

    The word of the Lord.

RESPONSORIAL PSALM   Ps 85:5-6.9-10.15-16

℞ **O Lord, you are good and forgiving.**

1. O Lord, you are good and forgiving,
    full of love to all who call.
    Give heed, O Lord, to my prayer
    and attend to the sound of my voice. ℞

2. All the nations shall come to adore you
    and glorify your name, O Lord:
    for you are great and do marvellous deeds,
    you who alone are God. ℞

3. But you, God of mercy and compassion,
    slow to anger, O Lord,
    abounding in love and truth,
    turn and take pity on me. ℞

SECOND READING   Rm 8:26-27

A reading from the letter of St Paul to the Romans.

The Spirit expresses our plea in a way that could never be put into words.

The Spirit comes to help us in our weakness. For when we cannot choose words in order to pray properly, the Spirit himself expresses our plea in a way that could never be put into words, and God who knows everything in our hearts knows perfectly well what he means, and that the pleas of the saints expressed by the Spirit are according to the mind of God.

The word of the Lord.

GOSPEL ACCLAMATION   Cf. Ep 1:17.18

Alleluia, alleluia!
May the Father of our Lord Jesus Christ
enlighten the eyes of our mind,
so that we can see what hope his call holds for us.
Alleluia!

Or: Cf. Mt 11:25

Alleluia, alleluia!
Blessed are you, Father,
Lord of heaven and earth,
for revealing the mysteries of the kingdom
to mere children.
Alleluia!

GOSPEL   Mt 13:24-43

(For Shorter Form, read between ◗ ◖).

A reading from the holy Gospel according to Matthew.

Let them both grow till the harvest.

◗Jesus put a parable before the crowds, 'The kingdom of heaven may be compared to a man who sowed good seed in his field. While everybody was asleep his enemy came, sowed darnel all among the wheat, and made off. When the new wheat sprouted and ripened, the darnel appeared as well. The owner's servants went to him and said, "Sir, was it not good seed that you sowed in your field? If so, where does the darnel come from?" "Some enemy has done this," he answered. And the servants said, "Do you want us to go and weed it out?" But he said, "No, because when you weed out the darnel you might pull up the wheat with it. Let them both grow till the harvest; and at harvest time I shall say to the reapers: First collect the darnel and tie it in bundles to be burnt, then gather the wheat into my barn." ◀

He put another parable before them, 'The kingdom of heaven is like a mustard seed which a man took and sowed in his field. It is the smallest of all seeds, but when it has grown it is the biggest shrub of all and becomes a tree so that the birds of the air come and shelter in its branches.'

He told them another parable, 'The kingdom of heaven is like the yeast a woman took and mixed in with three measures of flour till it was leavened all through.'

In all this Jesus spoke to the crowds in parables; indeed, he would never speak to them except in parables. This was to fulfil the prophecy:

I will speak to you in parables
and expound things hidden since the foundation of the
    world.

Then, leaving the crowds, he went to the house; and his disciples came to him and said, 'Explain the parable about the darnel in the field to us.' He said in reply, 'The sower of the good seed is the Son of Man. The field is the world; the good seed is the subjects of the kingdom; the darnel, the subjects of the evil one; the enemy who sowed them, the devil; the harvest is the end of the world; the reapers are the angels. Well then, just as the darnel is gathered up and burnt in the fire, so it will be at the end of time. The Son of Man will send his angels and they will gather out of his kingdom all things that provoke offences and all who do evil, and throw them into the blazing furnace, where there will be weeping and grinding of teeth. Then the virtuous will shine like the sun in the kingdom of their Father. Listen, anyone who has ears!'

The Gospel of the Lord.

Profession of Faith – pages 14-15.

Prayer over the Offerings

O God, who in the one perfect sacrifice
brought to completion varied offerings of the law,
accept, we pray, this sacrifice from your faithful servants
and make it holy, as you blessed the gifts of Abel,
so that what each has offered to the honour of your majesty

may benefit the salvation of all.
Through Christ our Lord.

Preface I-VIII of Sundays in Ordinary Time – pages 23-26.

Communion Antiphon   Ps 110:4-5

**The Lord, the gracious, the merciful,
has made a memorial of his wonders;
he gives food to those who fear him.**

    Or: Rv 3:20

**Behold, I stand at the door and knock, says the Lord.
If anyone hears my voice and opens the door to me,
I will enter his house and dine with him, and he with me.**

Prayer after Communion

Graciously be present to your people, we pray, O Lord,
and lead those you have imbued with heavenly mysteries
to pass from former ways to newness of life.
Through Christ our Lord.

Solemn Blessing – pages 57-59.

─────────── 30 JULY ───────────

SEVENTEENTH SUNDAY IN ORDINARY TIME

*God loves us wholly and his grace touches every dimension of our
lives. Anyone who has made the discovery of faith, like the merchant
in search of fine pearls, is led to a discipleship costing not less than
everything. It can be daunting, of course, but it leads to life in
abundance (Jn 10:10).*

Entrance Antiphon   Cf. Ps 67:6-7.36

**God is in his holy place,
God who unites those who dwell in his house;
he himself gives might and strength to his people.**

Greeting, Penitential Rite, Gloria – pages 7-13.

Collect

O God, protector of those who hope in you,
without whom nothing has firm foundation, nothing is holy,
bestow in abundance your mercy upon us
and grant that, with you as our ruler and guide,

we may use the good things that pass
in such a way as to hold fast even now
to those that ever endure.
Through our Lord Jesus Christ, your Son,
who lives and reigns with you in the unity of the Holy Spirit,
one God, for ever and ever.

FIRST READING   1 Kgs 3:5.7-12
A reading from the first book of the Kings.
You have asked for a discerning judgement for yourself.

The Lord appeared to Solomon in a dream and said, 'Ask what
you would like me to give you.' Solomon replied, 'Lord, my
God, you have made your servant king in succession to David
my father. But I am a very young man, unskilled in leadership.
Your servant finds himself in the midst of this people of yours
that you have chosen, a people so many its numbers cannot be
counted or reckoned. Give your servant a heart to understand
how to discern between good and evil, for who could govern
this people of yours that is so great?' It pleased the Lord that
Solomon should have asked for this. 'Since you have asked
for this', the Lord said, 'and not asked for long life for yourself
or riches or the lives of your enemies, but have asked for a
discerning judgement for yourself, here and now I do what you
ask. I give you a heart wise and shrewd as none before you has
had and none will have after you.'

The word of the Lord.

RESPONSORIAL PSALM   Ps 118:57.72.76-77.127-130

℟ **Lord, how I love your law!**

1. My part, I have resolved, O Lord,
   is to obey your word.
   The law from your mouth means more to me
   than silver and gold. ℟

2. Let your love be ready to console me
   by your promise to your servant.
   Let your love come to me and I shall live
   for your law is my delight. ℟

3. That is why I love your commands
   more than finest gold.
   That is why I rule my life by your precepts:
   I hate false ways. ℟

4. Your will is wonderful indeed;
   therefore I obey it.
   The unfolding of your word gives light
   and teaches the simple. ℟

SECOND READING   Rm 8:28-30

A reading from the letter of St Paul to the Romans.

God intended us to become true images of his Son.

We know that by turning everything to their good God co-operates with all those who love him, with all those that he has called according to his purpose. They are the ones he chose specially long ago and intended to become true images of his Son, so that his Son might be the eldest of many brothers. He called those he intended for this; those he called he justified, and with those he justified he shared his glory.

   The word of the Lord.

GOSPEL ACCLAMATION   Jn 15:15

Alleluia, alleluia!
I call you friends, says the Lord,
because I have made known to you
everything I have learnt from my Father.
Alleluia!

   Or: Cf. Mt 11:25

Alleluia, alleluia!
Blessed are you, Father,
Lord of heaven and earth,
for revealing the mysteries of the kingdom
to mere children.
Alleluia!

GOSPEL   Mt 13:44-52

(For Shorter Form, read between ◗ ◖).

A reading from the holy Gospel according to Matthew.

He sells everything he owns and buys the field.

◗Jesus said to the crowds, 'The kingdom of heaven is like treasure hidden in a field which someone has found; he hides it again, goes off happy, sells everything he owns and buys the field.

   'Again, the kingdom of heaven is like a merchant looking for fine pearls; when he finds one of great value he goes and sells everything he owns and buys it.◖

'Again, the kingdom of heaven is like a dragnet cast into the sea that brings in a haul of all kinds. When it is full, the fishermen haul it ashore; then, sitting down, they collect the good ones in a basket and throw away those that are no use. This is how it will be at the end of time: the angels will appear and separate the wicked from the just to throw them into the blazing furnace where there will be weeping and grinding of teeth.

'Have you understood all this?' They said, 'Yes.' And he said to them, 'Well, then, every scribe who becomes a disciple of the kingdom of heaven is like a householder who brings out from his storeroom things both new and old.'

The Gospel of the Lord.

Profession of Faith – pages 14-15.

Prayer over the Offerings

Accept, O Lord, we pray, the offerings
which we bring from the abundance of your gifts,
that through the powerful working of your grace
these most sacred mysteries may sanctify
    our present way of life
and lead us to eternal gladness.
Through Christ our Lord.

Preface I-VIII of Sundays in Ordinary Time – pages 23-26.

Communion Antiphon   Ps 102:2

**Bless the Lord, O my soul,
and never forget all his benefits.**

        Or: Mt 5:7-8

**Blessed are the merciful, for they shall receive mercy.
Blessed are the clean of heart, for they shall see God.**

Prayer after Communion

We have consumed, O Lord, this divine Sacrament,
the perpetual memorial of the Passion of your Son;
grant, we pray, that this gift,
which he himself gave us with love beyond all telling,
may profit us for salvation.
Through Christ our Lord.

Solemn Blessing – pages 57-59.

6 AUGUST
THE TRANSFIGURATION OF THE LORD

The disciples had come to know Jesus well. But now he is changed before them, they seem truly to see the glory of God in his face. The veil is lifted for them on the inner life of the Blessed Trinity. The Father bears solemn testimony to the Son in their presence.

Entrance Antiphon   Cf. Mt 17:5

In a resplendent cloud the Holy Spirit appeared.
The Father's voice was heard: This is my beloved Son,
with whom I am well pleased. Listen to him.

Greeting, Penitential Rite, Gloria – pages 7-13.

Collect

O God, who in the glorious Transfiguration
of your Only Begotten Son
confirmed the mysteries of faith by the witness of the Fathers
and wonderfully prefigured our full adoption to sonship,
grant, we pray, to your servants,
that, listening to the voice of your beloved Son,
we may merit to become coheirs with him.
Who lives and reigns with you in the unity of the Holy Spirit,
one God, for ever and ever.
When this Feast falls on a Sunday, the Creed is said.

FIRST READING   Dan 7:9-10.13-14

A reading from the book of Daniel.

His robe was white as snow.

As I watched:
Thrones were set in place
and one of great age took his seat.
His robe was white as snow,
the hair of his head as pure as wool.
His throne was a blaze of flames,
its wheels were a burning fire.
A stream of fire poured out,
issuing from his presence.
A thousand times ten thousand stood before him.
A court was held and the books were opened.
I gazed into the visions of the night.

And I saw, coming on the clouds of heaven,
one like a son of man.
He came to the one of great age
and was led into his presence.
On him was conferred sovereignty,
glory and kingship,
and men of all peoples, nations and languages became his
servants.
His sovereignty is an eternal sovereignty
nor will his empire ever be destroyed.

The word of the Lord

RESPONSORIAL PSALM   Ps 96:1-2.5-6.9

℟ **The Lord is king,**
   most high above all the earth.

1. The Lord is king, let earth rejoice,
    let all the coastlands be glad.
    Cloud and darkness are his raiment;
    his throne, justice and right. ℟

2. The mountains melt like wax
    before the Lord of all the earth.
    The skies proclaim his justice;
    all peoples see his glory. ℟

3. For you indeed are the Lord
    most high above all the earth
    exalted far above all spirits. ℟

SECOND READING   1 Pt 1:16-19

A reading from the second letter of St Peter.

We heard this ourselves, spoken from heaven.

It was not any cleverly invented myths that we were repeating
when we brought you the knowledge of the power and the
coming of our Lord Jesus Christ; we had seen his majesty for
ourselves. He was honoured and glorified by God the Father,
when the Sublime Glory itself spoke to him and said, 'This is my
Son, the Beloved; he enjoys my favour.' We heard this ourselves,
spoken from heaven, when we were with him on the holy
mountain.

So we have confirmation of what was said in prophecies; and
you will be right to depend on prophecy and take it as a lamp

for lighing a way through the dark until the dawn comes and the morning star rises in your minds.

The word of the Lord.

GOSPEL ACCLAMATION   Mt 17:5
Alleluia, alleluia!
This is my Son, the Beloved,
he enjoys my favour;
listen to him.
Alleluia!

GOSPEL   Mt 17:1-9
A reading from the holy Gospel according to Matthew.
We heard this ourselves, spoken from heaven.

Jesus took with him Peter and James and his brother John and led them up a high mountain where they could be alone. There in their presence he was transfigured: his face shone like the sun and his clothes became as white as the light. Suddenly Moses and Elijah appeared to them; they were talking with him. Then Peter spoke to Jesus. 'Lord,' he said 'it is wonderful for us to be here; if you wish, I will make three tents here, one for you, one for Moses and one for Elijah.' He was still speaking when suddenly a bright cloud covered them with shadow, and from the cloud there came a voice which said, 'this is my Son; the Beloved; he enjoys my favour. Listen to him.' When they heard this, the disciples fell on their faces, overecome with fear. But Jesus came up and touched them. 'Stand up,' he said 'do not be afraid.' And when they raised their eyes they saw no one but only Jesus.

As they came down from the mountain Jesus gave them this order, 'Tell no one about the vision until the Son of Man has risen from the dead.'

The Gospel of the Lord.

Prayer over the Offerings
Sanctify, O Lord, we pray,
these offerings here made to celebrate
the glorious Transfiguration of your Only Begotten Son,
and by his radiant splendour
cleanse us from the stains of sin.
Through Christ our Lord.

Preface: The Mystery of the Transfiguration

The Lord be with you.
And with your spirit.

Lift up your hearts.
We lift them up to the Lord.

Let us give thanks to the Lord our God.
It is right and just.

It is truly right and just, our duty and our salvation,
always and everywhere to give you thanks,
Lord, holy Father, almighty and eternal God,
through Christ our Lord.

For he revealed his glory in the presence of chosen witnesses
and filled with the greatest splendour that bodily form
which he shares with all humanity,
that the scandal of the Cross
might be removed from the hearts of his disciples
and that he might show
how in the Body of the whole Church is to be fulfilled
what so wonderfully shone forth first in its Head.

And so, with the Powers of heaven,
we worship you constantly on earth,
and before your majesty
without end we acclaim:
Holy, Holy, Holy Lord God of hosts …

Communion Antiphon   Cf. 1 Jn 3:2
**When Christ appears, we shall be like him,
for we shall see him as he is.**

Prayer after Communion
May the heavenly nourishment we have received,
O Lord, we pray,
transform us into the likeness of your Son,
whose radiant splendour you willed to make manifest
in his glorious Transfiguration.
Who lives and reigns for ever and ever.

13 AUGUST
NINETEENTH SUNDAY IN ORDINARY TIME

"Do not be afraid" is one of those expressions which goes straight to the heart. Who has not sometimes been afraid? The command not to fear combines two things: firstly, it is a recognition that sometimes we are afraid; secondly, it proclaims that in the community of faith, with Jesus, God-with-us, our companion on the way, we ought really to be free from deep fear, because "all shall be well." Let us hear again the words, "Courage! It is I! Do not be afraid."

Entrance Antiphon   Cf. Ps 73:20.19.22.23

Look to your covenant, O Lord,
and forget not the life of your poor ones for ever.
Arise, O God, and defend your cause,
and forget not the cries of those who seek you.

Greeting, Penitential Rite, Gloria – pages 7-13.

Collect
Almighty ever-living God,
whom, taught by the Holy Spirit,
we dare to call our Father,
bring, we pray, to perfection in our hearts
the spirit of adoption as your sons and daughters,
that we may merit to enter into the inheritance
which you have promised.
Through our Lord Jesus Christ, your Son,
who lives and reigns with you in the unity of the Holy Spirit,
one God, for ever and ever.

FIRST READING   1 Kgs 19:9.11-13

A reading from the first book of the Kings.
Stand on the mountain before the Lord.

When Elijah reached Horeb, the mountain of God, he went into the cave and spent the night in it. Then he was told, 'Go out and stand on the mountain before the Lord.' Then the Lord himself went by. There came a mighty wind, so strong it tore the mountains and shattered the rocks before the Lord. But the Lord was not in the wind. After the wind came an earthquake. But the Lord was not in the earthquake. After the earthquake came a fire. But the Lord was not in the fire. And after the fire there came the sound of a gentle breeze. And when Elijah heard this, he covered his face with his cloak and went out and stood at the entrance of the cave.

The word of the Lord.

RESPONSORIAL PSALM   Ps 84:9-14

℟ **Let us see, O Lord, your mercy
and give us your saving help.**

1. I will hear what the Lord God has to say,
   a voice that speaks of peace.
   His help is near for those who fear him
   and his glory will dwell in our land. ℟

2. Mercy and faithfulness have met;
   justice and peace have embraced.
   Faithfulness shall spring from the earth
   and justice look down from heaven.

3. The Lord will make us prosper
   and our earth shall yield its fruit.
   Justice shall march before him
   and peace shall follow his steps. ℟

SECOND READING   Rm 9:1-5

A reading from the letter of St Paul to the Romans.
I would willingly be condemned if it could help my brothers.

What I want to say is no pretence; I say it in union with Christ – it is the truth – my conscience in union with the Holy Spirit assures me of it too. What I want to say is this: my sorrow is so great, my mental anguish so endless, I would willingly be condemned and be cut off from Christ if it could help my brothers of Israel, my own flesh and blood. They were adopted as sons, they were given the glory and the covenants; the Law and the ritual were drawn up for them, and the promises were made to them. They are descended from the patriarchs and from their flesh and blood came Christ who is above all, God for ever blessed! Amen.

The word of the Lord.

GOSPEL ACCLAMATION   Lk 19:38
**Alleluia, alleluia!
Blessings on the King who comes,
in the name of the Lord!**

**Peace in heaven
and glory in the highest heavens!
Alleluia!**

   Or: Ps 129:5

**Alleluia, alleluia!
My soul is waiting for the Lord,
I count on his word.
Alleluia!**

GOSPEL   Mt 14:22-33

A reading from the holy Gospel according to Matthew.

Tell me to come to you across the water.

Jesus made the disciples get into the boat and go on ahead
to the other side while he would send the crowds away. After
sending the crowds away he went up into the hills by himself to
pray. When evening came, he was there alone, while the boat,
by now far out on the lake, was battling with a heavy sea, for
there was a head-wind. In the fourth watch of the night he went
towards them, walking on the lake, and when the disciples saw
him walking on the lake they were terrified. 'It is a ghost' they
said, and cried out in fear. But at once Jesus called out to them,
saying, 'Courage! It is I! Do not be afraid.' It was Peter who
answered. 'Lord', he said 'if it is you, tell me to come to you
across the water.' 'Come' said Jesus. Then Peter got out of the
boat and started walking towards Jesus across the water, but as
soon as he felt the force of the wind, he took fright and began
to sink. 'Lord! Save me!' he cried. Jesus put out his hand at once
and held him. 'Man of little faith,' he said 'why did you doubt?'
And as they got into the boat the wind dropped. The men in the
boat bowed down before him and said, 'Truly, you are the Son
of God.'

   The Gospel of the Lord.

Profession of Faith – pages 14-15.

Prayer over the Offerings

Be pleased, O Lord, to accept the offerings of your Church,
for in your mercy you have given them to be offered
and by your power you transform them
into the mystery of our salvation.
Through Christ our Lord.

Preface I-VIII of Sundays in Ordinary Time – pages 23-26.

Communion Antiphon   Ps 147:12.14

O Jerusalem, glorify the Lord,
who gives you your fill of finest wheat.

    Or: Cf. Jn 6:51

The bread that I will give, says the Lord,
is my flesh for the life of the world.

Prayer after Communion

May the communion in your Sacrament
that we have consumed, save us, O Lord,
and confirm us in the light of your truth.
Through Christ our Lord.

Solemn Blessing – pages 57-59.

──────── **15 AUGUST** ────────

THE ASSUMPTION
OF THE BLESSED VIRGIN MARY

──────── At the Vigil Mass ────────

'Happy the womb that bore you and the breasts you sucked!' This is
a blessing for Mary as a woman by another anonymous woman from
the crowd. Womanhood itself has become a blessing in Mary. We all
treasure the Word of God – his saving presence – in earthen vessels.

Entrance Antiphon

Glorious things are spoken of you, O Mary,
who today were exalted above the choirs of Angels
into eternal triumph with Christ.

Greeting, Penitential Rite, Gloria – pages 7-13.

Collect

O God, who, looking on the lowliness
    of the Blessed Virgin Mary,
raised her to this grace,
that your Only Begotten Son was born of her
    according to the flesh

and that she was crowned this day with surpassing glory,
grant through her prayers,
that, saved by the mystery of your redemption,
we may merit to be exalted by you on high.
Through our Lord Jesus Christ, your Son,
who lives and reigns with you in the unity of the Holy Spirit,
one God, for ever and ever.

FIRST READING   1 Ch 15:3-4.15-16; 16:1-2

A reading from the first book of Chronicles.

They brought in the ark of God and set it inside the tent which David had pitched for it.

David gathered all Israel together in Jerusalem to bring the ark of God up to the place he had prepared for it. David called together the sons of Aaron and the sons of Levi. And the Levites carried the ark of God with the shafts on their shoulders, as Moses had ordered in accordance with the word of the Lord.

David then told the heads of the Levites to assign duties for their kinsmen as cantors, with their various instruments of music, harps and lyres and cymbals, to play joyful tunes. They brought the ark of God in and put it inside the tent that David had pitched for it; and they offered holocausts before God, and communion sacrifices. And when David had finished offering holocausts and communion sacrifices, he blessed the people in the name of the Lord.

The word of the Lord.

RESPONSORIAL PSALM   Ps 131:6-7.9-10.13-14

℟ **Go up, Lord, to the place of your rest,
    you and the ark of your strength.**

1. At Ephrata we heard of the ark;
    we found it in the plains of Yearim.
    'Let us go to the place of his dwelling;
    let us go to kneel at his footstool.' ℟

2. Your priests shall be clothed with holiness:
    your faithful shall ring out their joy.
    For the sake of David your servant
    do not reject your anointed. ℟

3. For the Lord has chosen Zion;
    he has desired it for his dwelling:

'This is my resting-place for ever,
here have I chosen to live.'

SECOND READING   1 Cor 15:54-57

A reading from the first letter of St Paul to the Corinthians.

He gave us victory through our Lord Jesus Christ.

When this perishable nature has put on imperishability, and
when this mortal nature has put on immortality, then the words
of scripture will come true: Death is swallowed up in victory.
Death, where is your victory? Death, where is your sting? Now
the sting of death is sin, and sin gets its power from the Law. So
let us thank God for giving us the victory through our Lord Jesus
Christ.

The word of the Lord.

GOSPEL ACCLAMATION   Lk 11:28

Alleluia, alleluia!
Happy are those who hear the word of God, and keep it.
Alleluia!

GOSPEL   Lk 11:27-28

A reading from the holy Gospel according to Luke.

Happy the womb that bore you!

As Jesus was speaking, a woman in the crowd raised her voice
and said, 'Happy the womb that bore you and the breasts you
sucked!' But he replied, 'Still happier those who hear the word
of God and keep it!'

The Gospel of the Lord.

Profession of Faith – pages 14-15.

Prayer over the Offerings

Receive, we pray, O Lord,
the sacrifice of conciliation and praise,
which we celebrate on the Assumption of
    the holy Mother of God,
that it may lead us to your pardon
and confirm us in perpetual thanksgiving.
Through Christ our Lord.

Preface – page 330.

Communion Antiphon   Cf. Lk 11:27

**Blessed is the womb of the Virgin Mary,
which bore the Son of the eternal Father.**

Prayer after Communion

Having partaken of this heavenly table,
we beseech your mercy, Lord our God,
that we, who honour the Assumption of the Mother of God,
may be freed from every threat of harm.
Through Christ our Lord.

Solemn Blessing – page 331.

——————— AT THE MASS DURING THE DAY ———————

*While we are used to thinking of Mary as enjoying exceptional
privileges as a human being, on this day what happened to her, being
in God's presence as a whole human being, prefigures our future
as well. So this is a feast which looks backwards to the grace Mary
enjoyed, but also forward to our own future in God's presence. There
we too, we believe, will stand before God with all the saints, fully
present to God. Even if we cannot really picture such a future, we
believe nevertheless in a God who loves all that we are: our bodies, our
relationships, our history, our engagement in the real world.*

Entrance Antiphon   Cf. Rv 12:1

**A great sign appeared in heaven:
a woman clothed with the sun, the moon beneath her feet,
and on her head a crown of twelve stars.**

   Or:

**Let us all rejoice in the Lord,
as we celebrate the feast day in honour of the Virgin Mary,
at whose Assumption the Angels rejoice
and praise the Son of God.**

Greeting, Penitential Rite, Gloria – pages 7-13.

Collect

Almighty ever-living God,
who assumed the Immaculate Virgin Mary,
     the Mother of your Son,
body and soul into heavenly glory,
grant, we pray,

that, always attentive to the things that are above,
we may merit to be sharers of her glory.
Through our Lord Jesus Christ, your Son,
who lives and reigns with you in the unity of the Holy Spirit,
one God, for ever and ever.

FIRST READING   Apoc 11:19; 12:1-6.10

A reading from the book of the Apocalypse.

A woman adorned with the sun, standing on the moon.

The sanctuary of God in heaven opened, and the ark of the
covenant could be seen inside it.

Now a great sign appeared in heaven: a woman, adorned
with the sun, standing on the moon, and with the twelve stars
on her head for a crown. She was pregnant, and in labour, crying
aloud in the pangs of childbirth. Then a second sign appeared
in the sky, a huge red dragon which had seven heads and ten
horns, and each of the seven heads crowned with a coronet. Its
tail dragged a third of the stars from the sky and dropped them
to the earth, and the dragon stopped in front of the woman as
she was having the child, so that he could eat it as soon as it was
born from its mother. The woman brought a male child into
the world, the son who was to rule all the nations with an iron
sceptre, and the child was taken straight up to God and to his
throne, while the woman escaped into the desert, where God
had made a place of safety ready. Then I heard a voice shout
from heaven, 'Victory and power and empire for ever have been
won by our God, and all authority for his Christ.'

The word of the Lord.

RESPONSORIAL PSALM   Ps 44:10-12.16

℞ **On your right stands the queen,
in garments of gold.**

1. The daughters of kings are among your loved ones.
    On your right stands the queen in gold of Ophir.
    Listen, O daughter, give ear to my words:
    forget your own people and your father's house. ℞

2. So will the king desire your beauty:
    he is your lord, pay homage to him.
    They are escorted amid gladness and joy;
    they pass within the palace of the king. ℞

SECOND READING
1 Cor 15:20-26

A reading from the first letter of St Paul to the Corinthians.

Christ as the first-fruits and then those who belong to him.

Christ has been raised from the dead, the first-fruits of all who have fallen asleep. Death came through one man and in the same way the resurrection of the dead has come through one man. Just as all die in Adam, so all will be brought to life in Christ; but all of them in their proper order: Christ as the first-fruits and then, after the coming of Christ, those who belong to him. After that will come the end, when he hands over the kingdom to God the Father, having done away with every sovereignty, authority and power. For he must be king until he has put all his enemies under his feet and the last of the enemies to be destroyed is death, for everything is to be put under his feet.

The word of the Lord.

GOSPEL ACCLAMATION

Alleluia, alleluia!
Mary has been taken up into heaven;
all the choirs of angels are rejoicing.
Alleluia!

GOSPEL
Lk 1:39-56

A reading from the holy Gospel according to Luke.

The Almighty has done great things for me, he has exalted the lowly.

Mary set out and went as quickly as she could to a town in the hill country of Judah. She went into Zechariah's house and greeted Elizabeth. Now as soon as Elizabeth heard Mary's greeting, the child leapt in her womb and Elizabeth was filled with the Holy Spirit. She gave a loud cry and said, 'Of all women you are the most blessed, and blessed is the fruit of your womb. Why should I be honoured with a visit from the mother of my Lord? From the moment your greeting reached my ears, the child in my womb leapt for joy. Yes, blessed is she who believed that the promise made her by the Lord would be fulfilled.'

And Mary said:

'My soul proclaims the greatness of the Lord
and my spirit exults in God my saviour;
because he has looked upon his lowly handmaid.

Yes, from this day forward all generations will call me
        blessed,
for the Almighty has done great things for me.
Holy is his name,
and his mercy reaches from age to age for those who fear
        him.
He has shown the power of his arm,
he has routed the proud of heart.
He has pulled down princes from their thrones and exalted
        the lowly.
The hungry he has filled with good things, the rich sent
        empty away.
He has come to the help of Israel his servant, mindful of his
        mercy
– according to the promise he made to our ancestors –
of his mercy to Abraham and to his descendants for ever.'
Mary stayed with Elizabeth about three months and then went
back home.

The Gospel of the Lord.

Profession of Faith – pages 14-15.

Prayer over the Offerings
May this oblation, our tribute of homage,
rise up to you, O Lord,
and, through the intercession of the most Blessed Virgin Mary,
whom you assumed into heaven,
may our hearts, aflame with the fire of love,
constantly long for you.
Through Christ our Lord.

Preface: The Glory of Mary Assumed into Heaven
The Lord be with you.
And with your spirit.

Lift up your hearts.
We lift them up to the Lord.

Let us give thanks to the Lord our God.
It is right and just.

It is truly right and just, our duty and our salvation,
always and everywhere to give you thanks,

Lord, holy Father, almighty and eternal God,
through Christ our Lord.

For today the Virgin Mother of God
was assumed into heaven
as the beginning and image
of your Church's coming to perfection
and a sign of sure hope and comfort to your pilgrim people;
rightly you would not allow her
to see the corruption of the tomb,
since from her own body she marvellously brought forth
your incarnate Son, the Author of all life.

And so, in company with the choirs of Angels,
we praise you, and with joy we proclaim:

Holy, Holy, Holy Lord God of hosts …

Communion Antiphon   Lk 1:48-49

**All generations will call me blessed,
for he who is mighty has done great things for me.**

Prayer after Communion

Having received the Sacrament of salvation,
we ask you to grant, O Lord,
that, through the intercession of the Blessed Virgin Mary,
whom you assumed into heaven,
we may be brought to the glory of the resurrection.
Through Christ our Lord.

Solemn Blessing

The Priest invites people to bow down for the blessing.

May God, who through the childbearing of the Blessed
    Virgin Mary
willed in his great kindness to redeem the human race,
be pleased to enrich you with his blessing.
Amen.

May you know always and everywhere the protection of her,
through whom you have been found worthy to receive the
    author of life.
Amen.

May you, who have devoutly gathered on this day,
carry away with you the gifts of spiritual joys and
    heavenly rewards.
Amen.

And may the blessing of almighty God,
the Father, and the Son, ✠ and the Holy Spirit,
come down on you and remain with you for ever.
Amen.

========= 20 AUGUST =========

TWENTIETH SUNDAY IN ORDINARY TIME

*In today's Gospel, Jesus changes his mind! How is that possible? Twice
in Matthew's Gospel, Jesus limits his ministry to the "lost sheep of the
house of Israel" (Mt 10:6; 15:24). In today's story, however, a very
feisty woman, clearly not a daughter of Abraham, with her urgency
and her witty retort, brings Jesus to recognise the needs of those
beyond the ethnic confines of the Jewish people. They are ordinary
human beings too, just as much in need of the Good News of the
Kingdom as anyone else.*

Entrance Antiphon   Ps 83:10-11

**Turn your eyes, O God, our shield;
and look on the face of your anointed one;
one day within your courts
is better than a thousand elsewhere.**

Greeting, Penitential Rite, Gloria – pages 7-13.

Collect

O God, who have prepared for those who love you
good things which no eye can see,
fill our hearts, we pray, with the warmth of your love,
so that, loving you in all things and above all things,
we may attain your promises,
which surpass every human desire.
Through our Lord Jesus Christ, your Son,
who lives and reigns with you in the unity of the Holy Spirit,
one God, for ever and ever.

FIRST READING   Is 56:1.6-7

A reading from the prophet Isaiah.

I will bring foreigners to my holy mountain.

Thus says the Lord: Have a care for justice, act with integrity, for soon my salvation will come and my integrity be manifest.

Foreigners who have attached themselves to the Lord to serve him and to love his name and be his servants – all who observe the sabbath, not profaning it, and cling to my covenant – these I will bring to my holy mountain. I will make them joyful in my house of prayer. Their holocausts and their sacrifices will be accepted on my altar, for my house will be called a house of prayer for all the peoples.

The word of the Lord.

RESPONSORIAL PSALM   Ps 66:2-3.5-6.8

℟ **Let the peoples praise you, O God;**
    let all the peoples praise you.

1. O God, be gracious and bless us
    and let your face shed its light upon us.
    So will your ways be known upon earth
    and all nations learn your saving help. ℟

2. Let the nations be glad and exult
    for you rule the world with justice.
    With fairness you rule the peoples,
    you guide the nations on earth. ℟

3. Let the peoples praise you, O God;
    let all the peoples praise you.
    May God still give us his blessing
    till the ends of the earth revere him.

SECOND READING   Rm 11:13-15.29-32

A reading from the letter of St Paul to the Romans.

With Israel, God never takes back his gifts or revokes his choice.

Let me tell you pagans this: I have been sent to the pagans as their apostle, and I am proud of being sent, but the purpose of it is to make my own people envious of you, and in this way save some of them. Since their rejection meant the reconciliation of the world, do you know what their admission will mean? Nothing less than a resurrection from the dead! God never takes back his gifts or revokes his choice.

Just as you changed from being disobedient to God, and now enjoy mercy because of their disobedience, so those who are disobedient now – and only because of the mercy shown to you – will also enjoy mercy eventually. God has imprisoned all men in their own disobedience only to show mercy to all mankind.

The word of the Lord.

GOSPEL ACCLAMATION   Jn 10:27

Alleluia, alleluia!
The sheep that belong to me listen to my voice,
says the Lord,
I know them and they follow me. Alleluia!

Or: Mt 4:23

Alleluia, alleluia!
Jesus proclaimed the Good News of the kingdom,
and cured all kinds of sickness among the people. Alleluia!

GOSPEL   Mt 15:21-28

A reading from the holy Gospel according to Matthew.

Woman, you have great faith.

Jesus left Gennesaret and withdrew to the region of Tyre and Sidon. Then out came a Canaanite woman from that district and started shouting, 'Sir, Son of David, take pity on me. My daughter is tormented by a devil.' But he answered her not a word. And his disciples went and pleaded with him. 'Give her what she wants,' they said 'because she is shouting after us.' He said in reply. 'I was sent only to the lost sheep of the House of Israel.' But the woman had come up and was kneeling at his feet. 'Lord,' she said 'help me.' He replied, 'It is not fair to take the children's food and throw it to the house-dogs.' She retorted, 'Ah yes, sir; but even house-dogs can eat the scraps that fall from their master's table.' Then Jesus answered her, 'Woman, you have great faith. Let your wish be granted.' And from that moment her daughter was well again.

The Gospel of the Lord.

Profession of Faith – pages 14-15.

Prayer over the Offerings

Receive our oblation, O Lord,
by which is brought about a glorious exchange,

that, by offering what you have given,
we may merit to receive your very self.
Through Christ our Lord.

Preface I-VIII of Sundays in Ordinary Time – pages 23-26.

Communion Antiphon   Ps 129:7

**With the Lord there is mercy;
in him is plentiful redemption.**

    Or: Jn 6:51-52

**I am the living bread that came down from heaven,
   says the Lord.
Whoever eats of this bread will live for ever.**

Prayer after Communion

Made partakers of Christ through these Sacraments,
we humbly implore your mercy, Lord,
that, conformed to his image on earth,
we may merit also to be his coheirs in heaven.
Who lives and reigns for ever and ever.

Solemn Blessing – pages 57-59.

---

27 AUGUST

TWENTY-FIRST SUNDAY IN ORDINARY TIME

*When Jesus presses the question, who do you say I am?, we feel him
speaking to us. Naturally, we think of our faith now in the light of
our own journey of life and pilgrimage of faith. How did I start out?
What was my image of Jesus then and how did I relate to him? Have
there been a major turning point for me and can I name one or two?
How have I deepened my familiarity with Jesus and who is he for me
now? If I were to choose an image or a metaphor what would come to
mind? If I were to explain to someone what my faith in Jesus is, what
words would I use?*

Entrance Antiphon   Cf. Ps 85:1-3

**Turn your ear, O Lord, and answer me;
save the servant who trusts in you, my God.
Have mercy on me, O Lord, for I cry to you all the day long.**

Greeting, Penitential Rite, Gloria – pages 7-13.

Collect

O God, who cause the minds of the faithful
to unite in a single purpose,
grant your people to love what you command
and to desire what you promise,
that, amid the uncertainties of this world,
our hearts may be fixed on that place
where true gladness is found.
Through our Lord Jesus Christ, your Son,
who lives and reigns with you in the unity of the Holy Spirit,
one God, for ever and ever.

FIRST READING   Is 22:19-23

A reading from the prophet Isaiah.

I place the key of the House of David upon his shoulder.

Thus says the Lord of hosts to Shebna, the master of the palace:

> I dismiss you from your office,
> I remove you from your post,
> and the same day I call on my servant
> Eliakim son of Hilkiah.
> I invest him with your robe,
> gird him with your sash,
> entrust him with your authority;
> and he shall be a father
> to the inhabitants of Jerusalem
> and to the House of Judah.
> I place the key of the House of David
> on his shoulder;
> should he open, no one shall close,
> should he close, no one shall open.
> I drive him like a peg
> into a firm place;
> he will become a throne of glory
> for his father's house.

> The word of the Lord.

RESPONSORIAL PSALM   Ps 137:1-3.6.8

℟ **Your love, O Lord, is eternal,
discard not the work of your hands.**

1. I thank you, Lord, with all my heart,
   you have heard the words of my mouth.
   Before the angels I will bless you.
   I will adore before your holy temple. ℟

2. I thank you for your faithfulness and love
   which excel all we ever knew of you.
   On the day I called, you answered;
   you increased the strength of my soul. ℟

3. The Lord is high yet he looks on the lowly
   and the haughty he knows from afar.
   Your love, O Lord, is eternal,
   discard not the work of your hands. ℟

SECOND READING   Rm 11:33-36

A reading from the letter of St Paul to the Romans.

All that exists comes from him; all is by him and for him.

How rich are the depths of God – how deep his wisdom and
knowledge – and how impossible to penetrate his motives or
understand his methods! Who could ever know the mind of the
Lord? Who could ever be his counsellor? Who could ever give
him anything or lend him anything? All that exists comes from
him; all is by him and for him. To him be glory for ever! Amen.

  The word of the Lord.

GOSPEL ACCLAMATION   2 Cor 5:19

Alleluia, alleluia!
God in Christ was reconciling the world to himself,
and he has entrusted to us the news that they are reconciled.
Alleluia!

  Or: Mt 16:18

Alleluia, alleluia!
You are Peter and on this rock I will build my Church.
And the gates of the underworld can never hold out against it.
Alleluia!

GOSPEL   Mt 16:13-20

A reading from the holy Gospel according to Matthew.

You are Peter, and I will give you the keys of the kingdom of heaven.

When Jesus came to the region of Caesarea Philippi he put this
question to his disciples, 'Who do people say the Son of Man
is?' And they said, 'Some say he is John the Baptist, some Elijah,

and others Jeremiah or one of the prophets.' 'But you,' he said, 'who do you say I am?' Then Simon Peter spoke up, 'You are the Christ,' he said, 'the Son of the living God.' Jesus replied, 'Simon son of Jonah, you are a happy man! Because it was not flesh and blood that revealed this to you but my Father in heaven. So I now say to you: You are Peter and on this rock I will build my Church. And the gates of the underworld can never hold out against it. I will give you the keys of the kingdom of heaven; whatever you bind on earth shall be considered bound in heaven; whatever you loose on earth shall be considered loosed in heaven.' Then he gave the disciples strict orders not to tell anyone that he was the Christ.

The Gospel of the Lord.

Profession of Faith – pages 14-15.

Prayer over the Offerings
O Lord, who gained for yourself a people by adoption
through the one sacrifice offered once for all,
bestow graciously on us, we pray,
the gifts of unity and peace in your Church.
Through Christ our Lord.

Preface I-VIII of Sundays in Ordinary Time – pages 23-26.

Communion Antiphon   Cf. Ps 103:13-15
The earth is replete with the fruits of your work, O Lord;
you bring forth bread from the earth
and wine to cheer the heart.

     Or: Cf. Jn 6:54
Whoever eats my flesh and drinks my blood
has eternal life, says the Lord,
and I will raise him up on the last day.

Prayer after Communion
Complete within us, O Lord, we pray,
the healing work of your mercy
and graciously perfect and sustain us,
so that in all things we may please you.
Through Christ our Lord.

Solemn Blessing – pages 57-59.

3 SEPTEMBER
TWENTY-SECOND SUNDAY IN ORDINARY TIME

Jesus had the gift of saying things directly and plainly, with a power to penetrate all our defences and lead us to a new awareness. Today's message puts before us the paradox of the Gospel: we gain life by letting go of it. If I put my happiness, my being loved, at the centre of my life, then I will surely fail, even though to be loved and to be happy are really important. If on the other hand, I put the happiness of others first and love them unconditionally, then I too will know unselfish love and deep happiness. This is the very insight and wisdom that Jesus puts before us as the key not just to love but to life and within that, the key to authentic discipleship precisely as a way of life.

Entrance Antiphon   Cf. Ps 85:3.5

**Have mercy on me, O Lord, for I cry to you all the day long.
O Lord, you are good and forgiving,
full of mercy to all who call to you.**

Greeting, Penitential Rite, Gloria – pages 7-13.

Collect
God of might, giver of every good gift,
put into our hearts the love of your name,
so that, by deepening our sense of reverence,
you may nurture in us what is good
and, by your watchful care,
keep safe what you have nurtured.
Through our Lord Jesus Christ, your Son,
who lives and reigns with you in the unity of the Holy Spirit,
one God, for ever and ever.

FIRST READING   Jr 20:7-9

A reading from the prophet Jeremiah.
The word of the Lord has meant insult for me.

You have seduced me, Lord, and I have let myself be seduced;
you have overpowered me: you were the stronger.
I am a daily laughing-stock,
everybody's butt.
Each time I speak the word, I have to howl
and proclaim: 'Violence and ruin!'
The word of the Lord has meant for me

insult, derision, all day long.
I used to say, 'I will not think about him,
I will not speak in his name any more.'
Then there seemed to be a fire burning in my heart,
imprisoned in my bones.
The effort to restrain it wearied me,
I could not bear it.

The word of the Lord.

RESPONSORIAL PSALM   Ps 62:2-6.8-9

℟ **For you my soul is thirsting, O Lord my God.**

1. O God, you are my God, for you I long;
   for you my soul is thirsting.
   My body pines for you
   like a dry, weary land without water. ℟

2. So I gaze on you in the sanctuary
   to see your strength and your glory.
   For your love is better than life,
   my lips will speak your praise. ℟

3. So I will bless you all my life,
   in your name I will lift up my hands.
   My soul shall be filled as with a banquet,
   my mouth shall praise you with joy. ℟

4. For you have been my help;
   in the shadow of your wings I rejoice.
   My soul clings to you;
   your right hand holds me fast. ℟

SECOND READING   Rom 12:1-2

A reading from the letter of St Paul to the Romans.

Offer your bodies as a living sacrifice.

Think of God's mercy, my brothers, and worship him, I beg
you, in a way that is worthy of thinking beings, by offering your
living bodies as a holy sacrifice, truly pleasing to God. Do not
model yourselves on the behaviour of the world around you,
but let your behaviour change, modelled by your new mind.
This is the only way to discover the will of God and know what
is good, what it is that God wants, what is the perfect thing to
do.

The word of the Lord.

GOSPEL ACCLAMATION   Cf. Ep 1:17.18

Alleluia, alleluia!
May the Father of our Lord Jesus Christ
enlighten the eyes of our mind,
so that we can see
what hope his call holds for us. Alleluia!

GOSPEL   Mt 16:21-27

A reading from the holy Gospel according to Matthew.

If anyone wants to be a follower of mine, let him renounce himself.

Jesus began to make it clear to his disciples that he was destined to go to Jerusalem and suffer grievously at the hands of the elders and chief priests and scribes, to be put to death and to be raised up on the third day. Then, taking him aside, Peter started to remonstrate with him. 'Heaven preserve you, Lord,' he said. 'This must not happen to you.' But he turned and said to Peter, 'Get behind me, Satan! You are an obstacle in my path, because the way you think is not God's way but man's.'

Then Jesus said to his disciples, 'If anyone wants to be a follower of mine, let him renounce himself and take up his cross and follow me. For anyone who wants to save his life will lose it; but anyone who loses his life for my sake will find it. What, then, will a man gain if he wins the whole world and ruins his life? Or what has a man to offer in exchange for his life?

'For the Son of Man is going to come in the glory of his Father with his angels, and, when he does, he will reward each one according to his behaviour.'

The Gospel of the Lord.

Profession of Faith – pages 14-15.

Prayer over the Offerings

May this sacred offering, O Lord,
confer on us always the blessing of salvation,
that what it celebrates in mystery
it may accomplish in power.
Through Christ our Lord.

Preface I-VIII of Sundays in Ordinary Time – pages 23-26.

Communion Antiphon   Ps 30:20

How great is the goodness, Lord,
that you keep for those who fear you.

Or: Mt 5:9-10

Blessed are the peacemakers,
for they shall be called children of God.
Blessed are they who are persecuted for the sake of
**   righteousness,**
for theirs is the Kingdom of Heaven.

Prayer after Communion
Renewed by this bread from the heavenly table,
we beseech you, Lord,
that, being the food of charity,
it may confirm our hearts
and stir us to serve you in our neighbour.
Through Christ our Lord.

Solemn Blessing – pages 57-59.

━━━━━━━━━ 10 SEPTEMBER ━━━━━━━━━

TWENTY-THIRD SUNDAY IN ORDINARY TIME

Our Gospel reading today has some harsh dimensions and most
likely it reflects not the teaching of Jesus directly but the practices in
the Church for which Matthew was writing. As often in Matthew,
however, there is a surprise. People who refuse to acknowledge their
failures are to be treated as pagans and tax collectors! But just how
are pagans and tax collectors treated by Jesus and in the Gospel of
Matthew? Remember the call of Matthew (Mt 9:9)! Recall the story
of the Canaanite woman (Mt 15:21-28)! They are welcomed and
forgiven! Any permanent exclusion is to be resisted on the example
and teaching of Jesus himself.

Entrance Antiphon   Ps 118:137.124
You are just, O Lord, and your judgement is right;
treat your servant in accord with your merciful love.

Greeting, Penitential Rite, Gloria – pages 7-13.

Collect
O God, by whom we are redeemed and receive adoption,
look graciously upon your beloved sons and daughters,
that those who believe in Christ

may receive true freedom
and an everlasting inheritance.
Through our Lord Jesus Christ, your Son,
who lives and reigns with you in the unity of the Holy Spirit,
one God, for ever and ever.

FIRST READING   Ezk 33:7-9

A reading from the prophet Ezekiel.

If you do not speak to the wicked man, I will hold you responsible for his death.

The word of the Lord was addressed to me as follows, 'Son of man, I have appointed you as sentry to the House of Israel. When you hear a word from my mouth, warn them in my name. If I say to a wicked man: Wicked wretch, you are to die, and you do not speak to warn the wicked man to renounce his ways, then he shall die for his sin, but I will hold you responsible for his death. If, however, you do warn a wicked man to renounce his ways and repent, and he does not repent, then he shall die for his sin, but you yourself will have saved your life.'

The word of the Lord.

RESPONSORIAL PSALM   Ps 94:1-2.6-9

℟ **O that today you would listen to his voice!
Harden not your hearts.**

1. Come, ring out our joy to the Lord;
    hail the rock who saves us.
    Let us come before him, giving thanks,
    with songs let us hail the Lord. ℟

2. Come in; let us bow and bend low;
    let us kneel before the God who made us
    for he is our God and we
    the people who belong to his pasture,
    the flock that is led by his hand. ℟

3. O that today you would listen to his voice!
    'Harden not your hearts as at Meribah,
    as on that day at Massah in the desert
    when your fathers put me to the test;
    when they tried me, though they saw my work.' ℟

SECOND READING   Rom 13:8-10

A reading from the letter of St Paul to the Romans.

Love is the answer to every one of the commandments.

Avoid getting into debt, except the debt of mutual love. If you love your fellow men you have carried out your obligations. All the commandments: You shall not commit adultery, you shall not kill, you shall not steal, you shall not covet, and so on, are summed up in this single command: You must love your neighbour as yourself. Love is the one thing that cannot hurt your neighbour; that is why it is the answer to every one of the commandments.

  The word of the Lord.

GOSPEL ACCLAMATION   Cf. Jn 17:17

Alleluia, alleluia!
Your word is truth, O Lord,
consecrate us in the truth.
Alleluia!

  Or: 2 Cor 5:19

Alleluia, alleluia!
God in Christ was reconciling the world to himself,
and he has entrusted to us the news that they are reconciled.
Alleluia!

GOSPEL   Mt 18:15-20

A reading from the holy Gospel according to Matthew.

If he listens to you, you have won back your brother.

Jesus said to his disciples: 'If your brother does something wrong, go and have it out with him alone, between your two selves. If he listens to you, you have won back your brother. If he does not listen, take one or two others along with you: the evidence of two or three witnesses is required to sustain any charge. But if he refuses to listen to these, report it to the community; and if he refuses to listen to the community, treat him like a pagan or a tax collector.

  'I tell you solemnly, whatever you bind on earth shall be considered bound in heaven; whatever you loose on earth shall be considered loosed in heaven.

  'I tell you solemnly once again, if two of you on earth agree to ask anything at all, it will be granted to you by my Father

in heaven. For where two or three meet in my name, I shall be
there with them.'

The Gospel of the Lord.

Profession of Faith – pages 14-15.

Prayer over the Offerings

O God, who give us the gift of true prayer and of peace,
graciously grant that, through this offering,
we may do fitting homage to your divine majesty
and, by partaking of the sacred mystery,
we may be faithfully united in mind and heart.
Through Christ our Lord.

Preface I-VIII of Sundays in Ordinary Time – pages 23-26.

Communion Antiphon   Cf. Ps 41:2-3

**Like the deer that yearns for running streams,
so my soul is yearning for you, my God;
my soul is thirsting for God, the living God.**

    Or: Jn 8:12

**I am the light of the world, says the Lord;
whoever follows me will not walk in darkness,
but will have the light of life.**

Prayer after Communion

Grant that your faithful, O Lord,
whom you nourish and endow with life
through the food of your Word and heavenly Sacrament,
may so benefit from your beloved Son's great gifts
that we may merit an eternal share in his life.
Who lives and reigns for ever and ever.

Solemn Blessing – pages 57-59.

17 SEPTEMBER
TWENTY-FOURTH SUNDAY IN ORDINARY TIME

*The Christian assembly is an assembly of disciples of Jesus. A disciple
is literally one who is learning. Learning requires openness of mind
and heart. The scripture readings and the prayers of today's liturgy are
a powerful force for teaching and learning about the way of Jesus.*

Entrance Antiphon   Sir 36:18

Give peace, O Lord, to those who wait for you,
that your prophets be found true.
Hear the prayers of your servant,
and of your people Israel.

Greeting, Penitential Rite, Gloria – pages 7-14

Collect

Look upon us, O God,
Creator and ruler of all things,
and, that we may feel the working of your mercy,
grant that we may serve you with all our heart.
Through our Lord Jesus Christ, your Son,
who lives and reigns with you in the unity of the Holy Spirit,
one God, for ever and ever.

FIRST READING   Sir 27:30-28:7

A reading from the book of Ecclesiasticus.

*Forgive your neighbour the hurt he does you, and when you pray, your sins will
be forgiven.*

Resentment and anger, these are foul things,
and both are found with the sinner.
He who exacts vengeance will experience the vengeance of
    the Lord,
who keeps strict account of sin.
Forgive your neighbour the hurt he does you,
and when you pray, your sins will be forgiven.
If a man nurses anger against another,
can he then demand compassion from the Lord?
Showing no pity for a man like himself,
can he then plead for his own sins?
Mere creature of flesh, he cherishes resentment;
who will forgive him his sins?

Remember the last things, and stop hating,
remember dissolution and death, and live by the
     commandments.
Remember the commandments, and do not bear your
     neighbour ill-will;
remember the covenant of the Most High,
and overlook the offence.

     The word of the Lord.

RESPONSORIAL PSALM   Ps 102:1-4.9-12

℟ **The Lord is compassion and love,
     slow to anger and rich in mercy.**

1. My soul, give thanks to the Lord,
    all my being, bless his holy name.
    My soul, give thanks to the Lord
    and never forget all his blessings. ℟

2. It is he who forgives all your guilt,
    who heals everyone of your ills,
    who redeems your life from the grave,
    who crowns you with love and compassion. ℟

3. His wrath will come to an end;
    he will not be angry for ever.
    He does not treat us according to our sins
    nor repay us according to our faults. ℟

4. For as the heavens are high above the earth
    so strong is his love for those who fear him.
    As far as the east is from the west
    so far does he remove our sins. ℟

SECOND READING   Rom 14:7-9

A reading from the letter of St Paul to the Romans.

Alive or dead we belong to the Lord.

The life and death of each of us has its influence on others; if
we live, we live for the Lord; and if we die, we die for the Lord,
so that alive or dead we belong to the Lord. This explains why
Christ both died and came to life, it was so that he might be the
Lord both of the dead and of the living.

     The word of the Lord.

GOSPEL ACCLAMATION   1 Sam 3:9; Jn 6:68
Alleluia, alleluia!
Speak, Lord, your servant is listening:
you have the message of eternal life.
Alleluia!

     Or   Jn 13:34

Alleluia, alleluia!
I give you a new commandment:
love one another, just as I have loved you,
says the Lord.
Alleluia!

GOSPEL   Mt 18:21-35

A reading from the holy Gospel according to Matthew.
I do not tell you to forgive seven times, but seventy-seven times.

Peter went up to Jesus and said, 'Lord, how often must I forgive my brother if he wrongs me? As often as seven times?' Jesus answered, 'Not seven, I tell you, but seventy-seven times.

'And so the kingdom of heaven may be compared to a king who decided to settle his accounts with his servants. When the reckoning began, they brought him a man who owed ten thousand talents; but he had no means of paying, so his master gave orders that he should be sold, together with his wife and children and all his possessions, to meet the debt. At this, the servant threw himself down at his master's feet. "Give me time," he said, "and I will pay the whole sum." And the servant's master felt so sorry for him that he let him go and cancelled the debt. Now as this servant went out, he happened to meet a fellow servant who owed him one hundred denarii; and he seized him by the throat and began to throttle him. "Pay what you owe me," he said. His fellow servant fell at his feet and implored him, saying, "Give me time and I will pay you." But the other would not agree; on the contrary, he had him thrown into prison till he should pay the debt. His fellow servants were deeply distressed when they saw what had happened, and they went to their master and reported the whole affair to him. Then the master sent for him. "You wicked servant," he said, "I cancelled all that debt of yours when you appealed to me. Were you not bound, then, to have pity on your fellow servant just as I had pity on you?" And in his anger the master handed him

over to the torturers till he should pay all his debt. And that
is how my heavenly Father will deal with you unless you each
forgive your brother from your heart.'

The Gospel of the Lord.

Profession of Faith – pages 14-15

Prayer over the Offerings
Look with favour on our supplications, O Lord,
and in your kindness accept these, your servants' offerings,
that what each has offered to the honour of your name
may serve the salvation of all.
Through Christ our Lord.

Preface of Sundays in Ordinary Time – pages 23-26

Communion Antiphon   Cf. Ps 35:8
How precious is your mercy, O God!
The children of men seek shelter in the shadow of your wings.

    Or: Cf. 1 Cor 10:16
The chalice of blessing that we bless
is a communion in the Blood of Christ;
and the bread that we break
is a sharing in the Body of the Lord.

Prayer after Communion
May the working of this heavenly gift, O Lord, we pray,
take possession of our minds and bodies,
so that its effects, and not our own desires,
may always prevail in us.
Through Christ our Lord.

Solemn Blessing – pages 57-59

24 SEPTEMBER
TWENTY-FIFTH SUNDAY IN ORDINARY TIME

The forty-two parables in the Gospels are designed to take us up short and make us think again. Today's parable is a good example. The actions of the employer and the treatment of the workers simply would not work today as a labour relations strategy and would also not have worked in the time of Jesus. And what is the point? Really that it doesn't matter when we come to the Gospel, early, middle or late, by routes direct or circuitous, in full stride or falteringly: all that matters is that we come to the Gospel. Achievement counts for nothing; grace is everything, thanks be to God!

Entrance Antiphon
I am the salvation of the people, says the Lord.
Should they cry to me in any distress,
I will hear them, and I will be their Lord for ever.

Greeting, Penitential Rite, Gloria – pages 7-13.

Collect
O God, who founded all the commands of your sacred Law
upon love of you and of our neighbour,
grant that, by keeping your precepts,
we may merit to attain eternal life.
Through our Lord Jesus Christ, your Son,
who lives and reigns with you in the unity of the Holy Spirit,
one God, for ever and ever.

FIRST READING   Is 55:6-9
A reading from the prophet Isaiah.
My thoughts are not your thoughts.
Seek the Lord while he is still to be found,
call to him while he is still near.
Let the wicked man abandon his way,
the evil man his thoughts.
Let him turn back to the Lord who will take pity on him,
to our God who is rich in forgiving;
for my thoughts are not your thoughts,
my ways not your ways – it is the Lord who speaks.
Yes, the heavens are as high above earth

as my ways are above your ways,
my thoughts above your thoughts.

The word of the Lord.

RESPONSORIAL PSALM Ps 144:2-3.8-9.17-18

℟ **The Lord is close to all who call him.**

1. I will bless you day after day
   and praise your name for ever.
   The Lord is great, highly to be praised,
   his greatness cannot be measured. ℟

2. The Lord is kind and full of compassion,
   slow to anger, abounding in love.
   How good is the Lord to all,
   compassionate to all his creatures. ℟

3. The Lord is just in all his ways
   and loving in all his deeds.
   He is close to all who call him,
   who call on him from their hearts. ℟

SECOND READING Ph 1:20-24.27

A reading from the letter of St Paul to the Philippians.

Life to me is Christ.

Christ will be glorified in my body, whether by my life or by
my death. Life to me, of course, is Christ, but then death would
bring me something more; but then again, if living in this body
means doing work which is having good results – I do not know
what I should choose. I am caught in this dilemma: I want to be
gone and be with Christ, which would be very much the better,
but for me to stay alive in this body is a more urgent need for
your sake.

Avoid anything in your everyday lives that would be
unworthy of the gospel of Christ.

The word of the Lord.

GOSPEL ACCLAMATION Lk 19:38;2:14

Alleluia, alleluia!
Blessings on the King who comes,
in the name of the Lord!
Peace in heaven
and glory in the highest heavens!
Alleluia!

Or: Cf. Ac 16:14

Alleluia, alleluia!
Open our hearts, O Lord,
to accept the words of your Son.
Alleluia!

GOSPEL   Mt 20:1-16

A reading from the holy Gospel according to Matthew.

Why be envious because I am generous?

Jesus said to his disciples: 'The kingdom of heaven is like a landowner going out at daybreak to hire workers for his vineyard. He made an agreement with the workers for one denarius a day, and sent them to his vineyard. Going out at about the third hour he saw others standing idle in the market place and said to them, "You go to my vineyard too and I will give you a fair wage." So they went. At about the sixth hour and again at about the ninth hour, he went out and did the same. Then at about the eleventh hour he went out and found more men standing round, and he said to them, "Why have you been standing here idle all day?" "Because no one has hired us" they answered. He said to them, "You go into my vineyard too." In the evening, the owner of the vineyard said to his bailiff, "Call the workers and pay them their wages, starting with the last arrivals and ending with the first." So those who were hired at about the eleventh hour came forward and received one denarius each. When the first came, they expected to get more, but they too received one denarius each. They took it, but grumbled at the landowner. "The men who came last" they said "have done only one hour, and you have treated them the same as us, though we have done a heavy day's work in all the heat." He answered one of them and said, "My friend, I am not being unjust to you; did we not agree on one denarius? Take your earnings and go. I choose to pay the last-comer as much as I pay you. Have I no right to do what I like with my own? Why be envious because I am generous?" Thus the last will be first, and the first, last.'

The Gospel of the Lord.

Profession of Faith – pages 14-15.

Prayer over the Offerings

Receive with favour, O Lord, we pray,
the offerings of your people,
that what they profess with devotion and faith
may be theirs through these heavenly mysteries.
Through Christ our Lord.

Preface I-VIII of Sundays in Ordinary Time – pages 23-26.

Communion Antiphon   Ps 118:4-5

You have laid down your precepts to be carefully kept;
may my ways be firm in keeping your statutes.

      Or: Jn 10:14

I am the Good Shepherd, says the Lord;
I know my sheep, and mine know me.

Prayer after Communion

Graciously raise up, O Lord,
those you renew with this Sacrament,
that we may come to possess your redemption
both in mystery and in the manner of our life.
Through Christ our Lord.

Solemn Blessing – pages 57-59.

1 OCTOBER
TWENTY-SIXTH SUNDAY IN ORDINARY TIME

In today's parable, the offence is to be found in the blindingly obvious answer to the question Jesus sets. The application is then very sharp: those who seemingly never have experienced sin and conversion (who are they?) are quick to judge others who come to God through failure and fracture. It is like the ninety-nine who have no need of conversion – we may doubt that they ever really existed! A certain complacency can mark any settled religious group and if we add to that self-righteousness, then the mix is explosive and we are far from the Gospel as preached by Jesus.

Entrance Antiphon   Dn 3:31.29.30.43.42

**All that you have done to us, O Lord,
you have done with true judgement,
for we have sinned against you
and not obeyed your commandments.
But give glory to your name
and deal with us according to the bounty of your mercy.**

Greeting, Penitential Rite, Gloria – pages 7-13.

Collect
O God, who manifest your almighty power
above all by pardoning and showing mercy,
bestow, we pray, your grace abundantly upon us
and make those hastening to attain your promises
heirs to the treasures of heaven.
Through our Lord Jesus Christ, your Son,
who lives and reigns with you in the unity of the Holy Spirit,
one God, for ever and ever.

FIRST READING   Ezk 18:25-28
A reading from the prophet Ezekiel.
When the sinner renounces sin, he shall certainly live.

The word of the Lord was addressed to me as follows: 'You object, "What the Lord does is unjust." Listen, you House of Israel: is what I do unjust? Is it not what you do that is unjust? When the upright man renounces his integrity to commit sin and dies because of this, he dies because of the evil that he himself has committed. When the sinner renounces sin to become law-abiding and honest, he deserves to live. He has chosen to renounce all his previous sins; he shall certainly live; he shall not die.'

The word of the Lord.

RESPONSORIAL PSALM   Ps 24:4-9

℞ **Remember your mercy, Lord.**

1. Lord, make me know your ways.
   Lord, teach me your paths.
   Make me walk in your truth, and teach me:
   for you are God my saviour. ℞

2. Remember your mercy, Lord,
   and the love you have shown from of old.
   Do not remember the sins of my youth.
   In your love remember me,
   because of your goodness, O Lord. ℞

3. The Lord is good and upright.
   He shows the path to those who stray,
   he guides the humble in the right path
   he teaches his way to the poor. ℞

SECOND READING   Ph 2:1-11

(For Shorter Form, read between ♦ ♦).

A reading from the letter of St Paul to the Philippians.

In your minds you must be the same as Christ Jesus.

♦If our life in Christ means anything to you, if love can persuade at all, or the Spirit that we have in common, or any tenderness and sympathy, then be united in your convictions and united in your love, with a common purpose and a common mind. That is the one thing which would make me completely happy. There must be no competition among you, no conceit; but everybody is to be self-effacing. Always consider the other person to be better than yourself, so that nobody thinks of his own interests first but everybody thinks of other people's interests instead. In your minds you must be the same as Christ Jesus:♦

His state was divine,
yet he did not cling
to his equality with God
but emptied himself
to assume the condition of a slave,

and became as men are;
and being as all men are,
he was humbler yet,
even to accepting death,
death on a cross.
But God raised him high
and gave him the name
which is above all other names
so that all beings
in the heavens, on earth and in the underworld,
should bend the knee at the name of Jesus
and that every tongue should acclaim
Jesus Christ as Lord,
to the glory of God the Father.

The word of the Lord.

GOSPEL ACCLAMATION   Jn 14:23

Alleluia, alleluia!
If anyone loves me he will keep my word,
and my Father will love him,
and we shall come to him.
Alleluia!

  Or: Jn 10:27

Alleluia, alleluia!
The sheep that belong to me listen to my voice,
says the Lord,
I know them and they follow me.
Alleluia!

GOSPEL   Mt 21:28-32

A reading from the holy Gospel according to Matthew.

He thought better of it and went. Tax collectors and prostitutes are making
their way into the kingdom of God before you.

Jesus said to the chief priests and the elders of the people, 'What
is your opinion? A man had two sons. He went and said to
the first, "My boy, you go and work in the vineyard today." He
answered, "I will not go", but afterwards thought better of it and
went. The man then went and said the same thing to the second
who answered, "Certainly, sir", but did not go. Which of the two
did the father's will?' 'The first' they said. Jesus said to them, 'I

tell you solemnly, tax collectors and prostitutes are making their way into the kingdom of God before you. For John came to you, a pattern of true righteousness, but you did not believe him, and yet the tax collectors and prostitutes did. Even after seeing that, you refused to think better of it and believe in him.'

The Gospel of the Lord.

Profession of Faith – pages 14-15.

Prayer over the Offerings

Grant us, O merciful God,
that this our offering may find acceptance with you
and that through it the wellspring of all blessing
may be laid open before us.
Through Christ our Lord.

Preface I-VIII of Sundays in Ordinary Time – pages 23-26.

Communion Antiphon   Cf. Ps 118:49-50

Remember your word to your servant, O Lord,
by which you have given me hope.
This is my comfort when I am brought low.

Or: 1 Jn 3:16

By this we came to know the love of God:
that Christ laid down his life for us;
so we ought to lay down our lives for one another.

Prayer after Communion

May this heavenly mystery, O Lord,
restore us in mind and body,
that we may be coheirs in glory with Christ,
to whose suffering we are united
whenever we proclaim his Death.
Who lives and reigns for ever and ever.

Solemn Blessing – pages 57-59.

8 OCTOBER
TWENTY-SEVENTH SUNDAY
IN ORDINARY TIME

The risk for Christians today is that we read the parable complacently,
because it clearly refers to Jews and Christians in the first century.
But it is not only in the past that the leadership of God's project has
changed hands, so to speak. Down through history, more committed
groups have challenged the established Church – they can attract by
more exciting worship and by a closer living of the Gospel. The hard
words of St Paul to the Gentile Christians in Rome may help to shake
us up: for if God did not spare the natural branches, perhaps he will
not spare you (Rm 11:21).

Entrance Antiphon   Cf. Est 4:17

Within your will, O Lord, all things are established,
and there is none that can resist your will.
For you have made all things, the heaven and the earth,
and all that is held within the circle of heaven;
you are the Lord of all.

Greeting, Penitential Rite, Gloria – pages 7-13.

Collect

Almighty ever-living God,
who in the abundance of your kindness
surpass the merits and the desires of those who entreat you,
pour out your mercy upon us
to pardon what conscience dreads
and to give what prayer does not dare to ask.
Through our Lord Jesus Christ, your Son,
who lives and reigns with you in the unity of the Holy Spirit,
one God, for ever and ever.

FIRST READING   Is 5:1-7

A reading from the prophet Isaiah.
The vineyard of the Lord of hosts is the House of Israel.

Let me sing to my friend
the song of his love for his vineyard.
My friend had a vineyard
on a fertile hillside.
He dug the soil, cleared it of stones,

and planted choice vines in it.
In the middle he built a tower,
he dug a press there too.
He expected it to yield grapes,
but sour grapes were all that it gave.

And now, inhabitants of Jerusalem
and men of Judah,
I ask you to judge
between my vineyard and me.
What could I have done for my vineyard
that I have not done?
I expected it to yield grapes.
Why did it yield sour grapes instead?

Very well, I will tell you
what I am going to do to my vineyard:
I will take away its hedge for it to be grazed on,
and knock down its wall for it to be trampled on.
I will lay it waste, unpruned, undug;
overgrown by the briar and the thorn.
I will command the clouds
to rain no rain on it.
Yes, the vineyard of the Lord of hosts
is the House of Israel,
and the men of Judah
that chosen plant.
He expected justice, but found bloodshed,
integrity, but only a cry of distress.

The word of the Lord.

RESPONSORIAL PSALM   Ps 79:9.12-16.19-20

℟ **The vineyard of the Lord is the House of Israel.**

1. You brought a vine out of Egypt;
    to plant it you drove out the nations.
    It stretched out its branches to the sea,
    to the Great River it stretched out its shoots. ℟

2. Then why have you broken down its walls?
    It is plucked by all who pass by.
    It is ravaged by the boar of the forest,
    devoured by the beasts of the field. ℟

3. God of hosts, turn again, we implore,
    look down from heaven and see.
    Visit this vine and protect it,
    the vine your right hand has planted.

4. And we shall never forsake you again:
    give us life that we may call upon your name.
    God of hosts, bring us back;
    let your face shine on us and we shall be saved. ℟

SECOND READING   Ph 4:6-9

A reading from the letter of St Paul to the Philippians.

The God of peace will be with you.

There is no need to worry; but if there is anything you need, pray
for it, asking God for it with prayer and thanksgiving, and that
peace of God, which is so much greater than we can understand,
will guard your hearts and your thoughts, in Christ Jesus. Finally,
brothers, fill your minds with everything that is true, everything
that is noble, everything that is good and pure, everything
that we love and honour, and everything that can be thought
virtuous or worthy of praise. Keep doing all the things that you
learnt from me and have been taught by me and have heard or
seen that I do. Then the God of peace will be with you.

The word of the Lord.

GOSPEL ACCLAMATION   Jn 15:15

Alleluia, alleluia!
I call you friends, says the Lord,
because I have made known to you
everything I have learnt from my Father.
Alleluia!

Or: Cf. Jn 15:16

Alleluia, alleluia!
I chose you from the world
to go out and bear fruit,
fruit that will last,
says the Lord.
Alleluia!

GOSPEL   Mt 21:33-43

A reading from the holy Gospel according to Matthew.

He will lease the vineyard to other tenants.

Jesus said to the chief priests and the elders of the people, 'Listen to another parable. There was a man, a landowner, who planted a vineyard; he fenced it round, dug a winepress in it and built a tower; then he leased it to tenants and went abroad. When vintage time drew near he sent his servants to the tenants to collect his produce. But the tenants seized his servants, thrashed one, killed another and stoned a third. Next he sent some more servants, this time a larger number, and they dealt with them in the same way. Finally he sent his son to them. "They will respect my son" he said. But when the tenants saw the son, they said to each other, "This is the heir. Come on, let us kill him and take over his inheritance." So they seized him and threw him out of the vineyard and killed him. Now when the owner of the vineyard comes, what will he do to those tenants?' They answered, 'He will bring those wretches to a wretched end and lease the vineyard to other tenants who will deliver the produce to him when the season arrives.' Jesus said to them, 'Have you never read in the scriptures:

It was the stone rejected by the builders
that became the keystone.
This was the Lord's doing
and it is wonderful to see?

'I tell you, then, that the kingdom of God will be taken from you and given to a people who will produce its fruit.'

The Gospel of the Lord.

Profession of Faith – pages 14-15.

Prayer over the Offerings
Accept, O Lord, we pray,
the sacrifices instituted by your commands
and, through the sacred mysteries,
which we celebrate with dutiful service,
graciously complete the sanctifying work
by which you are pleased to redeem us.
Through Christ our Lord.

Preface I-VIII of Sundays in Ordinary Time – pages 23-26.

Communion Antiphon   Lm 3:25
**The Lord is good to those who hope in him,
to the soul that seeks him.**

Or: Cf. 1 Cor 10:17

Though many, we are one bread, one body,
for we all partake of the one Bread and one Chalice.

Prayer after Communion
Grant us, almighty God,
that we may be refreshed and nourished
by the Sacrament which we have received,
so as to be transformed into what we consume.
Through Christ our Lord.

Solemn Blessing – pages 57-59.

━━━━━━━━━━ 15 OCTOBER ━━━━━━━━━━

TWENTY-EIGHTH SUNDAY IN ORDINARY TIME

*The wedding feast is a picture of God's desire to invite his people
to the joy of his kingdom, on the condition that they obey his will.
But the Israelites disobey God by doing evil and practising idolatry.
God sends prophets to denounce the people's faithlessness and acts of
injustice and then to invite them to repentance. In time, with God's
coming, God's invitation is opened also to those who are not 'God's
people' The Pagans, rejoice that they are invited and they accept Jesus
and his message. But it is not enough to accept the invitation. One
should prove oneself worthy of the banquet by being properly attired,
by putting in the goodwill and effort to live the message of Jesus.*

Entrance Antiphon   Ps 129:3-4
If you, O Lord, should mark iniquities,
Lord, who could stand?
But with you is found forgiveness,
O God of Israel.

Greeting, Penitential Rite, Gloria – pages 7-13.

Collect
May your grace, O Lord, we pray,
at all times go before us and follow after
and make us always determined
to carry out good works.
Through our Lord Jesus Christ, your Son,

who lives and reigns with you in the unity of the Holy Spirit,
one God, for ever and ever.

FIRST READING   Is 25:6-10

A reading from the prophet Isaiah.

The Lord will prepare a banquet, and will wipe away tears from every cheek.

On this mountain,
the Lord of hosts will prepare for all peoples
a banquet of rich food, a banquet of fine wines,
of food rich and juicy, of fine strained wines.
On this mountain he will remove
the mourning veil covering all peoples,
and the shroud enwrapping all nations,
he will destroy Death for ever.
The Lord will wipe away
the tears from every cheek;
he will take away his people's shame
everywhere on earth,
for the Lord has said so.
That day, it will be said: See, this is our God
in whom we hoped for salvation;
the Lord is the one in whom we hoped.
We exult and we rejoice
that he has saved us;
for the hand of the Lord
rests on this mountain.

    The word of the Lord.

RESPONSORIAL PSALM   Ps 22

℟ **In the Lord's own house shall I dwell
    for ever and ever.**

1. The Lord is my shepherd;
    there is nothing I shall want.
    Fresh and green are the pastures
    where he gives me repose.
    Near restful waters he leads me,
    to revive my drooping spirit. ℟

2. He guides me along the right path;
    he is true to his name.
    If I should walk in the valley of darkness
    no evil would I fear.

You are there with your crook and your staff;
with these you give me comfort. ℟

3. You have prepared a banquet for me
in the sight of my foes.
My head you have anointed with oil;
my cup is overflowing. ℟

4. Surely goodness and kindness shall follow me
all the days of my life.
In the Lord's own house shall I dwell
for ever and ever. ℟

SECOND READING   Ph 4:12-14.19-20
A reading from the letter of St Paul to the Philippians.

There is nothing I cannot master with the help of the One who gives me strength.

I know how to be poor and I know how to be rich too. I have been through my initiation and now I am ready for anything anywhere: full stomach or empty stomach, poverty or plenty. There is nothing I cannot master with the help of the One who gives me strength. All the same, it was good of you to share with me in my hardships. In return my God will fulfil all your needs, in Christ Jesus, as lavishly as only God can. Glory to God, our Father, for ever and ever. Amen.

The word of the Lord.

GOSPEL ACCLAMATION   Jn 1:12:14
Alleluia, alleluia!
The Word was made flesh and lived among us;
to all who did accept him
he gave power to become children of God.
Alleluia!

Or: Cf. Ep 1:17-18
Alleluia, alleluia!
May the Father of our Lord Jesus Christ
enlighten the eyes of our mind,
so that we can see what hope his call holds for us.
Alleluia!

GOSPEL   Mt 22:1-14

(For Shorter Form, read between ♦ ♦).

A reading from the holy Gospel according to Matthew.

Invite everyone you can find to the wedding.

♦Jesus said to the chief priests and the elders of the people: 'The kingdom of heaven may be compared to a king who gave a feast for his son's wedding. He sent his servants to call those who had been invited, but they would not come. Next he sent some more servants. "Tell those who have been invited" he said "that I have my banquet all prepared, my oxen and fattened cattle have been slaughtered, everything is ready. Come to the wedding." But they were not interested: one went off to his farm, another to his business, and the rest seized his servants, maltreated them and killed them. The king was furious. He despatched his troops, destroyed those murderers and burnt their town. Then he said to his servants. "The wedding is ready; but as those who were invited proved to be unworthy, go to the crossroads in the town and invite everyone you can find to the wedding." So these servants went out on to the roads and collected together everyone they could find, bad and good alike; and the wedding hall was filled with guests.♦ When the king came in to look at the guests he noticed one man who was not wearing a wedding garment, and said to him, "How did you get in here, my friend, without a wedding garment?" And the man was silent. Then the king said to the attendants, "Bind him hand and foot and throw him out into the dark, where there will be weeping and grinding of teeth." For many are called, but few are chosen.'

The Gospel of the Lord.

Profession of Faith – pages 14-15.

Prayer over the Offerings
Accept, O Lord, the prayers of your faithful
with the sacrificial offerings,
that, through these acts of devotedness,
we may pass over to the glory of heaven.
Through Christ our Lord.

Preface I-VIII of Sundays in Ordinary Time – pages 23-26.

Communion Antiphon   Cf. Ps 33:11

The rich suffer want and go hungry,
but those who seek the Lord lack no blessing.

    Or: 1 Jn 3:2

When the Lord appears, we shall be like him,
for we shall see him as he is.

Prayer after Communion

We entreat your majesty most humbly, O Lord,
that, as you feed us with the nourishment
which comes from the most holy Body and Blood
    of your Son,
so you may make us sharers of his divine nature.
Who lives and reigns for ever and ever.

Solemn Blessing – pages 57-59.

<hr>

=== 22 OCTOBER ===

TWENTY-NINTH SUNDAY IN ORDINARY TIME
(Mission Sunday)

The relationship between religious faith and public life is perplexing.
In some societies, even today, there is virtually no difference between
the two. In other more secular societies, any expression of religious
conviction is unacceptable in public. It is true of course that there is
an appropriate distinction and even separation to be made, as indeed
Jesus does make today in the Gospel. But on at least two issues, there
is bound to be some crossover. Religious faith informs our values
and in society today policies and laws must be grounded, not in a
particular faith certainly, but in values nevertheless.

Entrance Antiphon   Cf. Ps 16:6.8

To you I call; for you will surely heed me, O God;
turn your ear to me; hear my words.
Guard me as the apple of your eye;
in the shadow of your wings protect me.

Greeting, Penitential Rite, Gloria – pages 7-13.

Collect

Almighty ever-living God,
grant that we may always conform our will to yours
and serve your majesty in sincerity of heart.
Through our Lord Jesus Christ, your Son,
who lives and reigns with you in the unity of the Holy Spirit,
one God, for ever and ever.

FIRST READING   Is 45:1.4-6

A reading from the prophet Isaiah.

I have taken Cyrus by his right hand to subdue nations before him.

Thus says the Lord to his anointed, to Cyrus,
whom he has taken by his right hand
to subdue nations before him
and strip the loins of kings,
to force gateways before him
that their gates be closed no more:

It is for the sake of my servant Jacob,
of Israel my chosen one,
that I have called you by your name,
conferring a title though you do not know me.
I am the Lord, unrivalled;
there is no other God besides me.
Though you do not know me, I arm you
that men may know from the rising to the setting of the sun
that, apart from me, all is nothing.
The word of the Lord.

RESPONSORIAL PSALM   Ps 95:1.3-5.7-10

℟ **Give the Lord glory and power.**

1. O sing a new song to the Lord,
    sing to the Lord all the earth.
    Tell among the nations his glory
    and his wonders among all the peoples. ℟

2. The Lord is great and worthy of praise,
    to be feared above all gods;
    the gods of the heathens are naught.
    It was the Lord who made the heavens. ℟

3. Give the Lord, you families of peoples,
    give the Lord glory and power,

give the Lord the glory of his name.
Bring an offering and enter his courts. ℟

4. Worship the Lord in his temple.
    O earth, tremble before him.
    Proclaim to the nations: 'God is king.'
    He will judge the peoples in fairness. ℟

SECOND READING   1 Th 1:1-5

A reading from the first letter of St Paul to the Thessalonians.
We constantly remember your faith, your love and your hope.

From Paul, Silvanus and Timothy, to the Church in Thessalonika
which is in God the Father and the Lord Jesus Christ; wishing
you grace and peace from God the Father and the Lord Jesus
Christ.

  We always mention you in our prayers and thank God for
you all, and constantly remember before God our Father how
you have shown your faith in action, worked for love and
persevered through hope, in our Lord Jesus Christ.

  We know, brothers, that God loves you and that you have
been chosen, because when we brought the Good News to you,
it came to you not only as words, but as power and as the Holy
Spirit and as utter conviction.

  The word of the Lord.

GOSPEL ACCLAMATION   Cf. Jn 17:17

Alleluia, alleluia!
Your word is truth, O Lord,
consecrate us in the truth.
Alleluia!

    Or: Ph 2:15-16

Alleluia, alleluia!
You will shine in the world like bright stars
because you are offering it the word of life.
Alleluia!

GOSPEL   Mt 22:15-21

A reading from the holy Gospel according to Matthew.
*Give back to Caesar what belongs to Caesar – and to God what belongs to
God.*

The Pharisees went away to work out between them how
to trap Jesus in what he said. And they sent their disciples to

him, together with the Herodians, to say, 'Master, we know
that you are an honest man and teach the way of God in an
honest way, and that you are not afraid of anyone, because a
man's rank means nothing to you. Tell us your opinion, then. Is
it permissible to pay taxes to Caesar or not?' But Jesus was aware
of their malice and replied, 'You hypocrites! Why do you set this
trap for me? Let me see the money you pay the tax with.' They
handed him a denarius and he said, 'Whose head is this? Whose
name?' 'Caesar's' they replied. He then said to them, 'Very well,
give back to Caesar what belongs to Caesar – and to God what
belongs to God.'

The Gospel of the Lord.

Profession of Faith – pages 14-15.

Prayer over the Offerings

Grant us, Lord, we pray,
a sincere respect for your gifts,
that, through the purifying action of your grace,
we may be cleansed by the very mysteries we serve.
Through Christ our Lord.

Preface I-VIII of Sundays in Ordinary Time – pages 23-26.

Communion Antiphon   Cf. Ps 32:18-19

**Behold, the eyes of the Lord
are on those who fear him,
who hope in his merciful love,
to rescue their souls from death,
to keep them alive in famine.**

    Or: Mk 10:45

**The Son of Man has come
to give his life as a ransom for many.**

Prayer after Communion

Grant, O Lord, we pray,
that, benefiting from participation in heavenly things,
we may be helped by what you give in this present age
and prepared for the gifts that are eternal.
Through Christ our Lord.

Solemn Blessing – pages 57-59.

29 OCTOBER
THIRTIETH SUNDAY IN ORDINARY TIME

Jesus does not pluck his summary teaching from the air – he quotes from the Shema Yisrael, the great prayer of Judaism found in Deuteronomy 6. The second part about the love of neighbour is taken from Leviticus 18. This mission statement stands as a resounding appeal to us today. We are asked not just to believe that there is a God, but to love God. We are asked not just to respect our neighbour, but to love our neighbour. Love is not only the truth about human beings but also the truth about God, who is love itself.

Entrance Antiphon   Cf. Ps 104:3-4

**Let the hearts that seek the Lord rejoice;
turn to the Lord and his strength;
constantly seek his face.**

Greeting, Penitential Rite, Gloria – pages 7-13.

Collect
Almighty ever-living God,
increase our faith, hope and charity,
and make us love what you command,
so that we may merit what you promise.
Through our Lord Jesus Christ, your Son,
who lives and reigns with you in the unity of the Holy Spirit,
one God, for ever and ever.

FIRST READING   Ex 22:20-26
A reading from the book of Exodus.
If you are harsh with the widow, the orphan, my anger will flare against you.
The Lord said to Moses, 'Tell the sons of Israel this, "You must not molest the stranger or oppress him, for you lived as strangers in the land of Egypt. You must not be harsh with the widow, or with the orphan; if you are harsh with them, they will surely cry out to me, and be sure I shall hear their cry; my anger will flare and I shall kill you with the sword, your own wives will be widows, your own children orphans.

"If you lend money to any of my people, to any poor man among you, you must not play the usurer with him: you must not demand interest from him.

"If you take another's cloak as a pledge, you must give it back to him before sunset. It is all the covering he has; it is the cloak he wraps his body in; what else would he sleep in? If he cries to me, I will listen, for I am full of pity." '

The word of the Lord.

RESPONSORIAL PSALM   Ps 17:2-4.47.51

℟ **I love you, Lord, my strength.**

1. I love you, Lord, my strength,
   my rock, my fortress, my saviour.
   My God is the rock where I take refuge;
   my shield, my mighty help, my stronghold.
   The Lord is worthy of all praise:
   when I call I am saved from my foes. ℟

2. Long life to the Lord, my rock!
   Praised be the God who saves me.
   He has given great victories to his king
   and shown his love for his anointed. ℟

SECOND READING   1 Th 1:5-10

A reading from the first letter of St Paul to the Thessalonians.

You broke with idolatry and became servants of God; you are now waiting for his Son.

You observed the sort of life we lived when we were with you, which was for your instruction, and you were led to become imitators of us, and of the Lord; and it was with the joy of the Holy Spirit that you took to the gospel, in spite of the great opposition all round you. This has made you the great example to all believers in Macedonia and Achaia since it was from you that the word of the Lord started to spread – and not only throughout Macedonia and Achaia, for the news of your faith in God has spread everywhere. We do not need to tell other people about it: other people tell us how we started the work among you, how you broke with idolatry when you were converted to God and became servants of the real, living God; and how you are now waiting for Jesus, his Son, whom he raised from the dead, to come from heaven to save us from the retribution which is coming.

The word of the Lord.

GOSPEL ACCLAMATION   Cf. Ac 16:14
Alleluia, alleluia!
Open our hearts, O Lord,
to accept the words of your Son.
Alleluia!

  Or: Jn 14:23
Alleluia, alleluia!
If anyone loves me he will keep my word,
and my Father will love him,
and we shall come to him.
Alleluia!

GOSPEL   Mt 22:34-40
A reading from the holy Gospel according to Matthew.
You must love the Lord your God and your neighbour as yourself.

When the Pharisees heard that Jesus had silenced the Sadducees
they got together and, to disconcert him, one of them put a
question, 'Master, which is the greatest commandment of the
Law?' Jesus said, 'You must love the Lord your God with all
your heart, with all your soul, and with all your mind. This is
the greatest and the first commandment. The second resembles
it: you must love your neighbour as yourself. On these two
commandments hang the whole Law, and the Prophets also.'

    The Gospel of the Lord.

Profession of Faith – pages 14-15.

Prayer over the Offerings
Look, we pray, O Lord,
on the offerings we make to your majesty,
that whatever is done by us in your service
may be directed above all to your glory.
Through Christ our Lord.

Preface I-VIII of Sundays in Ordinary Time – pages 23-26.

Communion Antiphon   Cf. Ps 19:6
We will ring out our joy at your saving help
and exult in the name of our God.

  Or: Ep 5:2
Christ loved us and gave himself up for us,
as a fragrant offering to God.

Prayer after Communion

May your Sacraments, O Lord, we pray,
perfect in us what lies within them,
that what we now celebrate in signs
we may one day possess in truth.
Through Christ our Lord.

Solemn Blessing – pages 57-59.

========= 1 NOVEMBER =========
ALL SAINTS

*Today we celebrate the community of faith, being in communion with
all the saints, a day of both thanksgiving and vision. Thanksgiving
because of the example and inspiration of the saints, who have come
to maturity, to the measure of the full stature of Christ (Ep 4:13).
Vision because our Gospel today describes the path we must take to
make the same journey home to God. If we wish to join the saints both
now and in eternity, we must make our own the "mission statement"
of Jesus, which is the Sermon on the Mount and especially the opening
invitation to true happiness.*

Entrance Antiphon

**Let us all rejoice in the Lord,
as we celebrate the feast day in honour of all the Saints,
at whose festival the Angels rejoice
and praise the Son of God.**

Greeting, Penitential Rite, Gloria – pages 7-13.

Collect

Almighty ever-living God,
by whose gift we venerate in one celebration
the merits of all the Saints,
bestow on us, we pray,
through the prayers of so many intercessors,
an abundance of the reconciliation with you
for which we earnestly long.
Through our Lord Jesus Christ, your Son,
who lives and reigns with you in the unity of the Holy Spirit,
one God, for ever and ever.

FIRST READING   Apoc 7:2-4.9-14

A reading from the book of the Apocalypse.

I saw a huge number, impossible to count, of people from every nation, race, tribe and language.

I, John, saw another angel rising where the sun rises, carrying the seal of the living God; he called in a powerful voice to the four angels whose duty was to devastate land and sea, 'Wait before you do any damage on land or at sea or to the trees, until we have put the seal on the foreheads of the servants of our God.' Then I heard how many were sealed: a hundred and forty-four thousand, out of all the tribes of Israel.

After that I saw a huge number, impossible to count, of people from every nation, race, tribe and language; they were standing in front of the throne and in front of the Lamb, dressed in white robes and holding palms in their hands. They shouted aloud, 'Victory to our God, who sits on the throne, and to the Lamb!' And all the angels who were standing in a circle round the throne, surrounding the elders and the four animals, prostrated themselves before the throne, and touched the grounds with their foreheads, worshipping God with these words: 'Amen. Praise and glory and wisdom and thanksgiving and honour and power and strength to our God for ever and ever. Amen.'

One of the elders then spoke, and asked me, 'Do you know who these people are, dressed in white robes, and where they have come from?' I answered him, 'You can tell me, my Lord.' Then he said, 'These are the people who have been through the great persecution, and they have washed their robes white again in the blood of the Lamb.'

The word of the Lord.

RESPONSORIAL PSALM   Ps 23:1-6

℟ **Such are the men who seek your face, O Lord.**

1. The Lord's is the earth and its fullness,
    the world and all its peoples.
    It is he who set it on the seas;
    on the waters he made it firm. ℟

2. Who shall climb the mountain of the Lord?
    Who shall stand in his holy place?

The man with clean hands and pure heart,
who desires not worthless things. ℟

3. He shall receive blessings from the Lord
and reward from the God who saves him.
Such are the men who seek him,
seek the face of the God of Jacob. ℟

SECOND READING   1 Jn 3:1-3

A reading from the first letter of St John.
We shall see God as he really is.

Think of the love that the Father has lavished on us,
by letting us be called God's children;
and that is what we are.
Because the world refused to acknowledge him,
therefore it does not acknowledge us.
My dear people, we are already the children of God
but what we are to be in the future has not yet been revealed;
all we know is, that when it is revealed
we shall be like him
because we shall see him as he really is.
Surely everyone who entertains this hope
must purify himself, must try to be as pure as Christ.

The word of the Lord.

GOSPEL ACCLAMATION   Mt 11:28

Alleluia, alleluia!
Come to me, all you who labour and are overburdened,
and I will give you rest, says the Lord. Alleluia!

GOSPEL   Mt 5:1-12

A reading from the holy Gospel according to Matthew.
Rejoice and be glad, for your reward will be great in heaven.

Seeing the crowds, Jesus went up the hill. There he sat down and
was joined by his disciples. Then he began to speak. This is what
he taught them:

'How happy are the poor in spirit;
theirs is the kingdom of heaven.
Happy the gentle:
they shall have the earth for their heritage.
Happy those who mourn:
they shall be comforted.

Happy those who hunger and thirst for what is right:
they shall be satisfied.
Happy the merciful:
they shall have mercy shown them.
Happy the pure in heart:
they shall see God.
Happy the peacemakers:
they shall be called sons of God.
Happy those who are persecuted in the cause of right:
theirs is the kingdom of heaven.

'Happy are you when people abuse you and persecute you and speak all kinds of calumny against you on my account. Rejoice and be glad, for your reward will be great in heaven.'

The Gospel of the Lord.

Profession of Faith – pages 14-15.

Prayer over the Offerings
May these offerings we bring in honour of all the Saints
be pleasing to you, O Lord,
and grant that, just as we believe the Saints
to be already assured of immortality,
so we may experience their concern for our salvation.
Through Christ our Lord.

Preface: The Glory of Jerusalem, Our Mother
The Lord be with you.
And with your spirit.

Lift up your hearts.
We lift them up to the Lord.

Let us give thanks to the Lord our God.
It is right and just.

It is truly right and just, our duty and our salvation,
always and everywhere to give you thanks,
Lord, holy Father, almighty and eternal God.

For today by your gift we celebrate the festival of your city,
the heavenly Jerusalem, our mother,
where the great array of our brothers and sisters
already gives you eternal praise.

Towards her, we eagerly hasten as pilgrims advancing by faith,
rejoicing in the glory bestowed upon those exalted
members of the Church
through whom you give us, in our frailty,
both strength and good example.

And so, we glorify you with the multitude of Saints and Angels,
as with one voice of praise we acclaim:

Holy, Holy, Holy Lord God of hosts …

Communion Antiphon   Mt 5:8-10

**Blessed are the clean of heart, for they shall see God.
Blessed are the peacemakers,
for they shall be called children of God.
Blessed are they who are persecuted for the sake
of righteousness,
for theirs is the Kingdom of Heaven.**

Prayer after Communion

As we adore you, O God, who alone are holy
and wonderful in all your Saints,
we implore your grace,
so that, coming to perfect holiness in the fullness of your love,
we may pass from this pilgrim table
to the banquet of our heavenly homeland.
Through Christ our Lord.

Solemn Blessing

The Priest invites people to bow down for the blessing.

May God, the glory and joy of the Saints,
who has caused you to be strengthened
by means of their outstanding prayers,
bless you with unending blessings.
Amen.

Freed through their intercession from present ills
and formed by the example of their holy way of life,
may you be ever devoted
to serving God and your neighbour.
Amen.

So that, together with all,
you may possess the joys of the homeland,

where Holy Church rejoices
that her children are admitted in perpetual peace
to the company of the citizens of heaven.
Amen.

And may the blessing of almighty God,
the Father, and the Son, ✠ and the Holy Spirit,
come down on you and remain with you for ever.
Amen.

---

2 NOVEMBER

THE COMMEMORATION
OF ALL THE FAITHFUL DEPARTED

*To remember our beloved dead in the presence of God is wholesome
and it is natural to remember them in love and thanksgiving. We
thank God for the gifts bestowed on us through them – signs of his
grace and presence. We entrust our beloved to the love and mercy
of God because, even though we do not grieve as those who have
no hope (1 Th 4:13), remembering the dead is holy and devout
(2 Mac 12:45). All they have meant for us is not lost forever, for God
– the God of the living – is their life now and always.*

Entrance Antiphon　　　　　　　　　　Cf. 1 Th 4:14; 1 Cor 15:22
Just as Jesus died and has risen again,
so through Jesus God will bring with him
those who have fallen asleep;
and as in Adam all die,
so also in Christ will all be brought to life.

Greeting, Penitential Rite, Gloria – pages 7-13.

Collect
Listen kindly to our prayers, O Lord,
and as our faith in your Son,
raised from the dead, is deepened,
so may our hope of resurrection for your departed servants
also find new strength.
Through our Lord Jesus Christ, your Son,
who lives and reigns with you in the unity of the Holy Spirit,
one God, for ever and ever.

FIRST READING
Is 25:6-9

A reading from the prophet Isaiah.

The Lord will destroy Death for ever.

On this mountain,
the Lord of hosts will prepare for all peoples
a banquet of rich food.
On this mountain he will remove
the mourning veil covering all peoples,
and the shroud enwrapping all nations,
he will destroy Death for ever.
The Lord will wipe away
the tears from every cheek;
he will take away his people's shame
everywhere on earth,
for the Lord has said so.
That day, it will be said: See, this is our God
in whom we hoped for salvation;
the Lord is the one in whom we hoped.
We exult and we rejoice
that he has saved us.

    The word of the Lord.

RESPONSORIAL PSALM
Ps 26:1-4.7-9.13-14

℞ **The Lord is my light and my help.**

    Or:

    **I am sure I shall see the Lord's goodness
in the land of the living.**

1. The Lord is my light and my help;
   whom shall I fear?
   The Lord is the stronghold of my life;
   before whom shall I shrink? ℞

2. There is one thing I ask of the Lord,
   for this I long,
   to live in the house of the Lord,
   all the days of my life,
   to savour the sweetness of the Lord,
   to behold his temple. ℞

3. O Lord, hear my voice when I call;
   have mercy and answer.

It is your face, O Lord, that I seek;
hide not your face. ℟

4. I am sure I shall see the Lord' goodness
    in the land of the living.
    Hope in him, hold firm and take heart.
    Hope in the Lord! ℟

SECOND READING   Rm 5:5-11

A reading from the second letter of St Paul to the Romans.

Having died to make us righteous, is it likely that he would now fail to save us from God's anger?

Hope is not deceptive, because the love of God has been poured into our hearts by the Holy Spirit which has been given us. We were still helpless when at his appointed moment Christ died for sinful men. It is not easy to die even for a good man – though of course for someone really worthy, a man might be prepared to die – but what proves that God loves us is that Christ died for us while we were still sinners. Having died to make us righteous, is it likely that he would now fail to save us from God's anger? When we were reconciled to God by the death of his Son, we were still enemies; now that we have been reconciled, surely we may count on being saved by the life of his Son? Not merely because we have been reconciled but because we are filled with joyful trust in God, through our Lord Jesus Christ, through whom we have already gained our reconciliation.

The word of the Lord.

GOSPEL ACCLAMATION   Jn 6:39

Alleluia, alleluia!
It is my Father's will, says the Lord,
that I should lose nothing of all that he has given to me,
and that I should raise it up on the last day.
Alleluia!

GOSPEL   Mt 11:25-30

A reading from the holy Gospel according to Matthew.

I am gentle and humble in heart.

Jesus exclaimed, 'I bless you, Father, Lord of heaven and of earth, for hiding these things from the learned and the clever and revealing them to mere children. Yes, Father, for that is what it pleased you to do. Everything has been entrusted to me by my Father; and no one knows the Son except the Father, just as no one knows the Father except the Son and those to whom the Son chooses to reveal him.

'Come to me, all you who labour and are overburdened, and I will give you rest. Shoulder my yoke and learn from me, for I am gentle and humble in heart, and you will find rest for your souls. Yes, my yoke is easy and my burden light.'

The Gospel of the Lord.

Profession of Faith – pages 14-15.

Prayer over the Offerings
Look favourably on our offerings, O Lord,
so that your departed servants
may be taken up into glory with your Son,
in whose great mystery of love we are all united.
Who lives and reigns for ever and ever.

Preface III For The Dead: Christ, the salvation and the life
The Lord be with you.
And with your spirit.

Lift up your hearts.
We lift them up to the Lord.

Let us give thanks to the Lord our God.
It is right and just.

It is truly right and just, our duty and our salvation,
always and everywhere to give you thanks,
Lord, holy Father, almighty and eternal God,
through Christ our Lord.

For he is the salvation of the world,
the life of the human race,
the resurrection of the dead.

Through him the host of Angels adores your majesty
and rejoices in your presence for ever.
May our voices, we pray, join with theirs
in one chorus of exultant praise, as we acclaim:
Holy, Holy, Holy Lord God of hosts …

Communion Antiphon   Cf. Jn 11:25-26

**I am the Resurrection and the Life, says the Lord.
Whoever believes in me, even though he dies, will live,
and everyone who lives and believes in me
will not die for ever.**

Prayer after Communion

Grant we pray, O Lord, that your departed servants,
for whom we have celebrated this paschal Sacrament,
may pass over to a dwelling place of light and peace.
Through Christ our Lord.

Solemn Blessing

The Priest invites people to bow down for the blessing.

May the God of all consolation bless you,
for in his unfathomable goodness he created the human race,
and in the Resurrection of his Only Begotten Son
he has given believers the hope of rising again.
Amen.

To us who are alive, may God grant pardon for our sins,
and to all the dead, a place of light and peace.
Amen.

So may we all live happily for ever with Christ,
whom we believe truly rose from the dead.
Amen.

And may the blessing of almighty God,
the Father, and the Son, ✠ and the Holy Spirit,
come down on you and remain with you for ever.
Amen.

5 NOVEMBER
THIRTY-FIRST SUNDAY IN ORDINARY TIME

*One of the intentions behind the reforms of the liturgy which the
Second Vatican Council (1962-1965) undertook was to present
the mysteries of the Lord Jesus throughout the yearly cycle. Of these
the most fundamental is that victory which God the Father gave
to Jesus by raising him to a new life and which is variously termed
resurrection, exaltation, vindication glorification etc. Every Sunday is
primarily the day on which this mystery is celebrated.*

Entrance Antiphon   Cf. Ps 37:22-23

**Forsake me not, O Lord, my God;
be not far from me!
Make haste and come to my help,
O Lord, my strong salvation!**

Greeting, Penitential Rite, Gloria – pages 7-13

Collect

Almighty and merciful God,
by whose gift your faithful offer you
right and praiseworthy service,
grant, we pray,
that we may hasten without stumbling
to receive the things you have promised.
Through our Lord Jesus Christ, your Son,
who lives and reigns with you in the unity of the Holy Spirit,
one God, for ever and ever.

FIRST READING   (Ml 1:14-2:2.8-10)

A reading from the prophet Malachi.

*You have strayed from the way; you have caused many to stumble by your
teaching.*

I am a great king, says the Lord of hosts, and my name is feared
throughout the nations. And now, priests, this warning is for
you. If you do not listen, if you do not find it in your heart to
glorify my name, says the Lord of host, I will send the curse on
you and curse your very blessing. You have strayed from the way;
you have caused many to stumble by your teaching. You have
destroyed the covenant of Levi, says the Lord of hosts. And so I
in my turn have made you contemptible and vile in the eyes of

the whole people in repayment for the way you have not kept to my paths but have shown partiality in your administration.

Have we not all one Father? Did not one God create us? Why, then, do we break faith with one another, profaning the covenant of our ancestors?

The word of the Lord.

RESPONSORIAL PSALM   (Ps 130)

℟ **Keep my soul in peace before you, O Lord.**

1. O Lord, my heart is not proud
    nor haughty my eyes.
    I have not gone after things too great
    nor marvels beyond me. ℟

2. Truly I have set my soul
    in silence and peace.
    A weaned child on its mother's breast,
    even so is my soul. ℟

3. O Israel, hope in the Lord
    both now and for ever. ℟

SECOND READING   (1 Thess 2:7-9.13)
A reading from the first letter of St Paul to the Thessalonians.
We were eager to hand over to you not only the Good News but our lives as well.

Like a mother feeding and looking after her own children, we felt so devoted and protective towards you, and had come to love you so much, that we were eager to hand over to you not only the Good News but our whole lives as well. Let me remind you, brothers, how hard we used to work, slaving night and day so as not to be a burden on any one of you while we were proclaiming God's Good News to you.

Another reason why we constantly thank God for you is that as soon as you heard the message that we brought you as God's message, you accepted it for what it really is, God's message and not some human thinking; and it is still a living power among you who believe it.

The word of the Lord.

GOSPEL ACCLAMATION   (1 Sam 3:9; Jn 6:68)
Alleluia, alleluia!
Speak, Lord, your servant is listening:

you have the message of eternal life.
Alleluia!

    Or   (Mt 23:9.10)

Alleluia, alleluia!
You have only one Father, and he is in heaven;
you have only one Teacher, the Christ!
Alleluia!

GOSPEL   (Mt 23:1-12)

A reading from the holy Gospel according to Matthew.

They do not practise what they preach.

Addressing the people and his disciples Jesus said, 'The scribes and the Pharisees occupy the chair of Moses. You must therefore do what they tell you and listen to what they say; but do not be guided by what they do: since they do not practise what they preach. They tie up heavy burdens and lay them on men's shoulders, but will they lift a finger to move them? Not they! Everything they do is done to attract attention, like wearing broader phylacteries and longer tassels, like wanting to take the place of honour at banquets and the front seats in the synagogues, being greeted obsequiously in the market squares and having people call them Rabbi.

'You, however, must not allow yourselves to be called Rabbi, since you have only one Master, and you are all brothers. You must call no one on earth your father, since you have only one Father, and he is in heaven. Nor must you allow yourselves to be called teachers, for you have only one Teacher, the Christ. The greatest among you must be your servant. Anyone who exalts himself will be humbled, and anyone who humbles himself will be exalted.'

The Gospel of the Lord.

Profession of Faith – pages 14-15

Prayer over the Offerings
May these sacrificial offerings, O Lord,
become for you a pure oblation,
and for us a holy outpouring of your mercy.
Through Christ our Lord.

Preface of Sundays in Ordinary Time – pages 23-26

Communion Antiphon   (Ps 15:11)

**Lord, you will show me the path of life
and fill me with joy in your presence.**

    Or: (Jn 6:58)

**As the living Father sent me, and I live because of the Father,
so he who eats my flesh and drinks my blood
will live because of me.**

Prayer after Communion

May the working of your power, O Lord,
increase in us, we pray,
so that, renewed by these heavenly Sacraments,
we may be prepared by your gift
for receiving what they promise.
Through Christ our Lord.

Solemn Blessing – pages 57-58

───────────── 12 NOVEMBER ─────────────

THIRTY-SECOND SUNDAY IN ORDINARY TIME

*As we approach the end of the Church's liturgical year, the readings
are mostly from those sections of scripture called apocalyptic. This
is a very symbolic style of writing. Numbers and colours all have a
symbolic meaning. It is frequently full of cosmic images including sun,
moon and stars. It is a very vivid style of writing which is geared to
evoke a response in those who read it.*

Entrance Antiphon   Ps 87:3

**Let my prayer come into your presence.
Incline your ear to my cry for help, O Lord.**

Greeting, Penitential Rite, Gloria – pages 7-13

Collect

Almighty and merciful God,
graciously keep from us all adversity,
so that, unhindered in mind and body alike,
we may pursue in freedom of heart
the things that are yours.
Through our Lord Jesus Christ, your Son,

who lives and reigns with you in the unity of the Holy Spirit,
one God, for ever and ever..

FIRST READING   Wis 6:12-16

A reading from the book of Wisdom.

Wisdom is found by those who look for her.

Wisdom is bright, and does not grow dim.
By those who love her she is readily seen,
and found by those who look for her.
Quick to anticipate those who desire her, she makes herself
    known to them.
Watch for her early and you will have no trouble;
you will find her sitting at your gates.
Even to think about her is understanding fully grown;
be on the alert for her and anxiety will quickly leave you.
She herself walks about looking for those who are worthy of her
and graciously shows herself to them as they go,
in every thought of theirs coming to meet them.

    The word of the Lord.

RESPONSORIAL PSALM   Ps 62:2-8

℟ **For you my soul is thirsting, O God, my God.**

1. O God, you are my God, for you I long;
   for you my soul is thirsting.
   My body pines for you
   like a dry, weary land without water. ℟

2. So I gaze on you in the sanctuary
   to see your strength and your glory.
   For your love is better than life,
   my lips will speak your praise. ℟

3. So I will bless you all my life,
   in your name I will lift up my hands.
   My soul shall be filled as with a banquet,
   my mouth shall praise you with joy. ℟

4. On my bed I remember you.
   On you I muse through the night
   for you have been my help;
   in the shadow of your wings I rejoice. ℟

SECOND READING   1 Thess 4:13-18

(For Shorter Form, read between ◗ ◖).

A reading from the first letter of St Paul to the Thessalonians.

God will bring with him those who have died in Jesus.

◗ We want you to be quite certain, brothers, about those who have died, to make sure that you do not grieve about them, like the other people who have no hope. We believe that Jesus died and rose again, and that it will be the same for those who have died in Jesus: God will bring them with him. ◖ We can tell you this from the Lord's own teaching, that any of us who are left alive until the Lord's coming will not have any advantage over those who have died. At the trumpet of God, the voice of the archangel will call out the command and the Lord himself will come down from heaven; those who have died in Christ will be the first to rise, and then those of us who are still alive will be taken up in the clouds, together with them, to meet the Lord in the air. So we shall stay with the Lord for ever. With such thoughts as these you should comfort one another.

    The word of the Lord.

GOSPEL ACCLAMATION   Mt 24:42.44

Alleluia, alleluia!
Stay awake and stand ready,
because you do not know the hour
when the Son of Man is coming.
Alleluia!

GOSPEL   Mt 25:1-13

A reading from the holy Gospel according to Matthew.

The bridegroom is here! Go out and meet him.

Jesus told this parable to his disciples: 'The kingdom of heaven will be like this: Ten bridesmaids took their lamps and went to meet the bridegroom. Five of them were foolish and five were sensible: the foolish ones did take their lamps, but they brought no oil, whereas the sensible ones took flasks of oil as well as their lamps. The bridegroom was late, and they all grew drowsy and fell asleep. But at midnight there was a cry, "The bridegroom is here! Go out and meet him." At this, all those bridesmaids woke up and trimmed their lamps, and the foolish ones said to the sensible ones, "Give us some of your oil: our lamps are going out." But they replied, "There may not be enough for us and for you; you had better go to those who sell it and buy some for yourselves." They had gone off to buy it when the bridegroom arrived. Those who were ready went in with him to the wedding hall and the door was closed. The other bridesmaids arrived later. "Lord, Lord," they said "open the door for us." But he replied, "I tell you solemnly, I do not know you." So stay awake, because you do not know either the day or the hour.'

The Gospel of the Lord.

Profession of Faith – pages 14-15

Prayer over the Offerings
Look with favour, we pray, O Lord,
upon the sacrificial gifts offered here,
that, celebrating in mystery the Passion of your Son,
we may honour it with loving devotion.
Through Christ our Lord.

Preface of Sundays in Ordinary Time – pages 23-26

Communion Antiphon   Cf. Ps 22:1-2
The Lord is my shepherd; there is nothing I shall want.
Fresh and green are the pastures where he gives me repose,
near restful waters he leads me.

            Or: Cf. Lk 24:35

The disciples recognized the Lord Jesus in the breaking
    of bread.

Prayer after Communion
Nourished by this sacred gift, O Lord,
we give you thanks and beseech your mercy,
that, by the pouring forth of your Spirit,
the grace of integrity may endure
in those your heavenly power has entered.
Through Christ our Lord.

Solemn Blessing – pages 57-59

19 NOVEMBER
THIRTY-THIRD SUNDAY IN ORDINARY TIME

What does God desire of us? This simple question is perhaps not asked frequently enough! It can be made quite personal: what does God want of me, from me? In the end, the answer has to be – in the words of the song – "all that I am" precisely because God loves all that I am. This will mean allowing ourselves to be loved. It will also mean responding with my whole self, including all the gifts of body, mind and soul that God has bestowed upon me. In the end, God does hope that we may be and become our true selves. Nothing less is adequate to God's own love of us.

Entrance Antiphon   Jr 29:11.12.14

**The Lord said: I think thoughts of peace and not of affliction.
You will call upon me, and I will answer you,
and I will lead back your captives from every place.**

Greeting, Penitential Rite, Gloria – pages 7-13.

Collect

Grant us, we pray, O Lord our God,
the constant gladness of being devoted to you,
for it is full and lasting happiness
to serve with constancy
the author of all that is good.
Through our Lord Jesus Christ, your Son,
who lives and reigns with you in the unity of the Holy Spirit,
one God, for ever and ever.

FIRST READING   Prov 31:10-13.19-20.30-31

A reading from the book of Proverbs.

A perfect wife – who can find her?

A perfect wife – who can find her?
She is far beyond the price of pearls.
Her husband's heart has confidence in her,
from her he will derive no little profit.
Advantage and not hurt she brings him
all the days of her life.
She is always busy with wool and with flax,
she does her work with eager hands.

She sets her hands to the distaff,
her fingers grasp the spindle.
She holds out her hand to the poor,
she opens her arms to the needy.
Charm is deceitful, and beauty empty;
the woman who is wise is the one to praise.
Give her a share in what her hands have worked for,
and let her works tell her praises at the city gates.

The word of the Lord.

RESPONSORIAL PSALM   Ps 127:1-5

℟ **O blessed are those who fear the Lord.**

1. O blessed are those who fear the Lord
    and walk in his ways!
    By the labour of your hands you shall eat.
    You will be happy and prosper. ℟

2. Your wife like a fruitful vine
    in the heart of your house;
    your children like shoots of the olive,
    around your table. ℟

3. Indeed thus shall be blessed
    the man who fears the Lord.
    May the Lord bless you from Zion
    in a happy Jerusalem
    all the days of your life. ℟

SECOND READING   1 Th 5:1-6

A reading from the first letter of St Paul to the Thessalonians.
Let not the Day of the Lord overtake you like a thief.

You will not be expecting us to write anything to you, brothers,
about 'times and seasons', since you know very well that the
Day of the Lord is going to come like a thief in the night. It is
when people are saying, 'How quiet and peaceful it is' that the
worst suddenly happens, as suddenly as labour pains come on
a pregnant woman; and there will be no way for anybody to
evade it.

But it is not as if you live in the dark, my brothers, for that
Day to overtake you like a thief. No, you are all sons of light and
sons of the day: we do not belong to the night or to darkness,

so we should not go on sleeping, as everyone else does, but stay wide awake and sober.

The word of the Lord.

GOSPEL ACCLAMATION   Rv 2:10
Alleluia, alleluia!
Even if you have to die, says the Lord,
keep faithful, and I will give you
the crown of life.
Alleluia!

      Or: Jn 15:4.5
Alleluia, alleluia!
Make your home in me, as I make mine in you,
says the Lord.
Whoever remains in me bears fruit in plenty.
Alleluia!

GOSPEL   Mt 25:14-30
(For Shorter Form, read between ◆ ◆).

A reading from the holy Gospel according to Matthew.

You have been faithful in small things; come and join in your master's happiness.

◆Jesus spoke this parable to his disciples: 'The kingdom of heaven is like a man on his way abroad who summoned his servants and entrusted his property to them. To one he gave five talents, to another two, to a third one; each in proportion to his ability. Then he set out.◆

The man who had received the five talents promptly went and traded with them and made five more. The man who had received two made two more in the same way. But the man who had received one went off and dug a hole in the ground and hid his master's money.

◆Now a long time after, the master of those servants came back and went through his accounts with them. The man who had received the five talents came forward bringing five more. "Sir," he said "you entrusted me with five talents; here are five more that I have made."

His master said to him, "Well done, good and faithful servant; you have shown you can be faithful in small things, I will trust you with greater; come and join in your master's happiness."◆ Next the man with the two talents came forward.

"Sir," he said "you entrusted me with two talents; here are two more that I have made." His master said to him, "Well done, good and faithful servant; you have shown you can be faithful in small things, I will trust you with greater; come and join in your master's happiness." Last came forward the man who had the one talent. "Sir," said he "I had heard you were a hard man, reaping where you have not sown and gathering where you have not scattered; so I was afraid, and I went off and hid your talent in the ground. Here it is; it was yours, you have it back." But his master answered him, "You wicked and lazy servant! So you knew that I reap where I have not sown and gather where I have not scattered? Well then, you should have deposited my money with the bankers, and on my return I would have recovered my capital with interest. So now, take the talent from him and give it to the man who has the five talents. For to everyone who has will be given more, and he will have more than enough; but from the man who has not, even what he has will be taken away. As for this good-for-nothing servant, throw him out into the dark, where there will be weeping and grinding of teeth." '

The Gospel of the Lord.

Profession of Faith – pages 14-15.

Prayer over the Offerings
Grant, O Lord, we pray,
that what we offer in the sight of your majesty
may obtain for us the grace of being devoted to you
and gain us the prize of everlasting happiness.
Through Christ our Lord.

Preface I-VIII of Sundays in Ordinary Time – pages 23-26.

Communion Antiphon   Ps 72:28
To be near God is my happiness,
to place my hope in God the Lord.

    Or: Mk 11:23-24
Amen, I say to you: Whatever you ask in prayer,
believe that you will receive,
and it shall be given to you, says the Lord.

Prayer after Communion
We have partaken of the gifts of this sacred mystery,
humbly imploring, O Lord,

that what your Son commanded us to do
in memory of him
may bring us growth in charity.
Through Christ our Lord.

Solemn Blessing – pages 57-59.

26 NOVEMBER

OUR LORD JESUS CHRIST,
KING OF THE UNIVERSE

"King" is a foundational metaphor in the Bible, which in ordinary usage suggests power and glory. But even in the ancient biblical tradition, there are two great modifications. According to Old Testament understanding, a king is meant to be a shepherd to his people, a true shepherd who cares for and who knows and even loves his sheep. According to New Testament, Jesus our king rules paradoxically through loving service, humility and the gift of himself. This example and teaching of Jesus has lost none of its power today.

Entrance Antiphon   Rv 5:12; 1:6

**How worthy is the Lamb who was slain,
to receive power and divinity,
and wisdom and strength and honour.
To him belong glory and power for ever and ever.**

Greeting, Penitential Rite, Gloria – pages 7-13.

Collect
Almighty ever-living God,
whose will is to restore all things
in your beloved Son, the King of the universe,
grant, we pray,
that the whole creation, set free from slavery,
may render your majesty service
and ceaselessly proclaim your praise.
Through our Lord Jesus Christ, your Son,
who lives and reigns with you in the unity of the Holy Spirit,
one God, for ever and ever.

FIRST READING   Ezk 34:11-12.15-17

A reading from the prophet Ezekiel.

As for you, my sheep, I will judge between sheep and sheep.

The Lord says this: I am going to look after my flock myself and keep all of it in view. As a shepherd keeps all his flock in view when he stands up in the middle of his scattered sheep, so shall I keep my sheep in view. I shall rescue them from wherever they have been scattered during the mist and darkness. I myself will pasture my sheep, I myself will show them where to rest – it is the Lord who speaks. I shall look for the lost one, bring back the stray, bandage the wounded and make the weak strong. I shall watch over the fat and healthy. I shall be a true shepherd to them.

As for you, my sheep, the Lord says this: I will judge between sheep and sheep, between rams and he-goats.

The word of the Lord.

RESPONSORIAL PSALM   Ps 22:1-3.5-6

℟ **The Lord is my shepherd;**
   there is nothing I shall want.

1. The Lord is my shepherd;
   there is nothing I shall want.
   Fresh and green are the pastures
   where he gives me repose. ℟

2. Near restful waters he leads me,
   to revive my drooping spirit.
   He guides me along the right path;
   he is true to his name. ℟

3. You have prepared a banquet for me
   in the sight of my foes.
   My head you have anointed with oil;
   my cup is overflowing. ℟

4. Surely goodness and kindness shall follow me
   all the days of my life.
   In the Lord's own house shall I dwell
   for ever and ever. ℟

SECOND READING   1 Cor 15:20-26.28

A reading from the first letter of St Paul to the Corinthians.

He will hand over the kingdom to God the Father, so that God may be all in all.

Christ has been raised from the dead, the first-fruits of all who have fallen asleep. Death came through one man and in the same way the resurrection of the dead has come through one man. Just as all men die in Adam, so all men will be brought to life in Christ; but all of them in their proper order: Christ as the first-fruits and then, after the coming of Christ, those who belong to him. After that will come the end, when he hands over the kingdom to God the Father, having done away with every sovereignty, authority and power. For he must be king until he has put all his enemies under his feet and the last of the enemies to be destroyed is death. And when everything is subjected to him, then the Son himself will be subjected in his turn to the One who subjected all things to him, so that God may be all in all.

The word of the Lord.

GOSPEL ACCLAMATION   Mk 11:9.10

Alleluia, alleluia!
Blessings on him who comes in the name of the Lord!
Blessings on the coming kingdom of our father David!
Alleluia!

GOSPEL   Mt 25:31-46

A reading from the holy Gospel according to Matthew.

He will take his seat on his throne of glory, and he will separate men one from another.

Jesus said to his disciples: 'When the Son of Man comes in his glory, escorted by all the angels, then he will take his seat on his throne of glory. All the nations will be assembled before him and he will separate men one from another as the shepherd separates sheep from goats. He will place the sheep on his right hand and the goats on his left. Then the King will say to those on his right hand, "Come, you whom my Father has blessed, take for your heritage the kingdom prepared for you since the foundation of the world. For I was hungry and you gave me food; I was thirsty and you gave me drink; I was a stranger and you made me welcome; naked and you clothed me, sick and you visited me, in prison and you came to see me." Then the virtuous will say to him in reply, "Lord, when did we see you hungry and feed you; or thirsty and give you drink? When did we see you a stranger and make you welcome; naked and clothe you; sick or in prison and go to see you?" And the King will answer, "I tell you solemnly, in so far as you did this to one of the least of these brothers of mine, you did it to me." Next he will say to those on his left hand, "Go away from me, with your curse upon you, to the eternal fire prepared for the devil and his angels. For I was hungry and you never gave me food; I was thirsty and you never gave me anything to drink; I was a stranger and you never made me welcome, naked and you never clothed me, sick and in prison and you never visited me." Then it will be their turn to ask, "Lord, when did we see you hungry or thirsty, a stranger or naked, sick or in prison, and did not come to your help?" Then he will answer, "I tell you solemnly, in so far as you neglected to do this to one of the least of these, you neglected to do it to me." And they will go away to eternal punishment, and the virtuous to eternal life.'

The Gospel of the Lord.

Profession of Faith – pages 14-15.

Prayer over the Offerings

As we offer you, O Lord, the sacrifice
by which the human race is reconciled to you,
we humbly pray
that your Son himself may bestow on all nations
the gifts of unity and peace.
Through Christ our Lord.

Preface: Christ, King of the Universe

The Lord be with you.
And with your spirit.

Lift up your hearts.
We lift them up to the Lord.

Let us give thanks to the Lord our God.
It is right and just.

It is truly right and just, our duty and our salvation,
always and everywhere to give you thanks,
Lord, holy Father, almighty and eternal God.

For you anointed your Only Begotten Son,
our Lord Jesus Christ, with the oil of gladness
as eternal Priest and King of all creation,
so that, by offering himself on the altar of the Cross
as a spotless sacrifice to bring us peace,
he might accomplish the mysteries of human redemption
and, making all created things subject to his rule,
he might present to the immensity of your majesty
an eternal and universal kingdom,
a kingdom of truth and life,
a kingdom of holiness and grace,
a kingdom of justice, love and peace.

And so, with Angels and Archangels,
with Thrones and Dominions,
and with all the hosts and Powers of heaven,
we sing the hymn of your glory,
as without end we acclaim:

Holy, Holy, Holy Lord God of hosts …

Communion Antiphon   Ps 28:10-11
The Lord sits as King for ever.
The Lord will bless his people with peace.

Prayer after Communion
Having received the food of immortality,
we ask, O Lord,
that, glorying in obedience
to the commands of Christ, the King of the universe,
we may live with him eternally in his heavenly Kingdom.
Who lives and reigns for ever and ever.

30 NOVEMBER
SAINT ANDREW, APOSTLE
Patron of Scotland

Andrew is the patron saint of Scotland, Russia and Greece. He was the brother of Simon Peter the fisherman from Bethsaida and even though not one of the inner circle of three, several incidents concerning him are recorded in the gospels. There is a tradition about Saint Andrew's cross, shaped like the letter X but this cannot be traced back beyond the thirteenth century. The tradition also has it that he was a martyr.

Entrance Antiphon   Cf. Mt 4:18-19

**Beside the Sea of Galilee,
the Lord saw two brothers, Peter and Andrew,
and he said to them:
Come after me and I will make you fishers of men.**

Greeting, Penitential Rite, Gloria – pages 7-13.

Collect

We humbly implore your majesty, O Lord,
that, just as the blessed Apostle Andrew
was for your Church a preacher and pastor,
so he may be for us a constant intercessor before you.
Through our Lord Jesus Christ, your Son,
who lives and reigns with you in the unity of the Holy Spirit,
one God, for ever and ever.

FIRST READING   Wis 3:1-9

A reading from the book of Wisdom.

He accepted them as a holocaust.

The souls of the virtuous are in the hands of God,
no torment shall ever touch them.
In the eyes of the unwise, they did appear to die,
their going looked like a disaster,
their leaving us, like annihilation;
but they are in peace.
If they experienced punishment as men see it,
their hope was rich with immortality;
slight was their affliction, great will their blessings be.

God has put them to the test
and proved them worthy to be with him;
he has tested them like gold in a furnace,
and accepted them as a holocaust.
When the time comes for his visitation they will shine out;
as sparks run through the stubble, so will they.
They shall judge nations, rule over peoples,
and the Lord will be their king for ever.
They who trust in him will understand the truth,
those who are faithful will live with him in love;
for grace and mercy await those he has chosen.

　　The word of the Lord.

RESPONSORIAL PSALM   Ps 30:3-4.6.8.17.21

℟ **Into your hands, O Lord,**
　 I commend my spirit.

1.　Be a rock of refuge for me,
　　a mighty stronghold to save me,
　　for you are my rock, my stronghold.
　　For your name's sake, lead me and guide me. ℟

2.　Into your hands I commend my spirit.
　　It is you who will redeem me, Lord.
　　As for me, I trust in the Lord;
　　let me be glad and rejoice in your love. ℟

3.　Let your face shine on your servant.
　　Save me in your love.
　　You hide them in the shelter of your presence
　　from the plotting of men. ℟

SECOND READING   Rm 10:9-18

A reading from the letter of St Paul to the Romans.

Faith comes from what is preached, and what is preached comes from the word of Christ.

If your lips confess that Jesus is Lord and if you believe in your heart that God raised him from the dead, then you will be saved. By believing from the heart you are made righteous; by confessing with your lips you are saved. When scripture says: those who believe in him will have no cause for shame, it makes no distinction between Jew and Greek: all belong to the same Lord who is rich enough, however many ask his help, for everyone who calls on the name of the Lord will be saved.

But they will not ask his help unless they believe in him, and they will not believe in him unless they have heard of him, and they will not hear of him unless they get a preacher, and they will never have a preacher unless one is sent, but as scripture says: The footsteps of those who bring good news are a welcome sound. Not everyone, of course, listens to the Good News. As Isaiah says: Lord, how many believed what we proclaimed? So faith comes from what is preached, and what is preached comes from the word of Christ.

Let me put the question: is it possible that they did not hear? Indeed they did; in the words of the psalm, their voice has gone out through all the earth, and their message to the ends of the world.

The word of the Lord.

GOSPEL ACCLAMATION   Mt 4:19
Alleluia, alleluia!
Follow me, says the Lord,
and I will make you into fishers of men.
Alleluia!

GOSPEL   Mt 4:18-22
A reading from the holy Gospel according to Matthew.
And they left their nets at once and followed him.

As Jesus was walking by the Sea of Galilee he saw two brothers, Simon, who was called Peter, and his brother Andrew; they were making a cast in the lake with their net, for they were fishermen. And he said to them, 'Follow me and I will make you fishers of men.' And they left their nets at once and followed him.

Going on from there he saw another pair of brothers, James son of Zebedee and his brother John; they were in their boat with their father Zebedee, mending their nets, and he called them. At once, leaving the boat and their father, they followed him.

The Gospel of the Lord.

Profession of Faith – pages 14-15.

Prayer over the Offerings

Grant us, almighty God, that through these offerings,
which we bring on the feast day of Saint Andrew,
we may please you by what we have brought
and be given life by what you have accepted.
Through Christ our Lord.

Preface I of the Apostles

The Lord be with you.
And with your spirit.

Lift up your hearts.
We lift them up to the Lord.

Let us give thanks to the Lord our God.
It is right and just.

It is truly right and just, our duty and our salvation,
always and everywhere to give you thanks,
Lord, holy Father, almighty and eternal God.

For you, eternal Shepherd, do not desert your flock,
but through the blessed Apostles
watch over it and protect it always,
so that it may be governed
by those you have appointed shepherds
to lead it in the name of your Son.

And so, with Angels and Archangels,
with Thrones and Dominions,
and with all the hosts and Powers of heaven,
we sing the hymn of your glory,
as without end we acclaim:

Holy, Holy, Holy Lord God of hosts …

Communion Antiphon   Cf. Jn 1:41-42

Andrew told his brother Simon:
We have found the Messiah, the Christ,
and he brought him to Jesus.

Prayer after Communion

May communion in your Sacrament strengthen us, O Lord,
so that by the example of the blessed Apostle Andrew

we, who carry in our body the Death of Christ,
may merit to live with him in glory.
Who lives and reigns for ever and ever.

Solemn Blessing

The Priest invites people to bow down for the blessing.

May God, who has granted you
to stand firm on apostolic foundations,
graciously bless you through the glorious merits
of the holy Apostle Andrew.
Amen.

And may he, who endowed you
with the teaching and example of the Apostles,
make you, under their protection,
witnesses to the truth before all.
Amen.

So that through the intercession of the Apostles,
you may inherit the eternal homeland,
for by their teaching you possess firmness of faith.
Amen.

And may the blessing of almighty God,
the Father, and the Son, ✠ and the Holy Spirit,
come down on you and remain with you for ever.
Amen.

3 DECEMBER
FIRST SUNDAY OF ADVENT (Cycle B)

First Sunday of Advent invites us to reflect on my daily life – for what do I ask forgiveness? For what do I give thanks? We also look forward to a new beginning and a chance to start again on the way of discipleship. Both thanksgiving and renewal are to be found in today's readings. The Gospel is an invitation to wake up, to keep watch, to live fully the present moment under God, in whom we live and move and have our being.

Entrance Antiphon   Cf. Ps 24:1-3

To you, I lift up my soul, O my God.
In you, I have trusted; let me not be put to shame.
Nor let my enemies exult over me;
and let none who hope in you be put to shame.

Greeting, Penitential Rite – pages 7-12.

The Gloria is not said.

Collect

Grant your faithful, we pray, almighty God,
the resolve to run forth to meet your Christ
with righteous deeds at his coming,
so that, gathered at his right hand,
they may be worthy to possess the heavenly Kingdom.
Through our Lord Jesus Christ, your Son,
who lives and reigns with you in the unity of the Holy Spirit,
one God, for ever and ever.

FIRST READING   Is 63:16-17; 64:1.3-8

A reading from the prophet Isaiah.

Oh, that you would tear the heavens open and come down.

You, Lord, yourself are our Father,
Our Redeemer is your ancient name.
Why, Lord, leave us to stray from your ways
and harden our hearts against fearing you?
Return, for the sake of your servants,
the tribes of your inheritance.
Oh, that you would tear the heavens open and come down
– at your Presence the mountains would melt.

No ear has heard,
no eye has seen
any god but you act like this
for those who trust him.
You guide those who act with integrity
and keep your ways in mind.
You were angry when we were sinners;
we had long been rebels against you.
We were all like men unclean,
all that integrity of ours like filthy clothing.
We have all withered like leaves
and our sins blew us away like the wind.
No one invoked your name
or roused himself to catch hold of you.
For you hid your face from us
and gave us up to the power of our sins.
And yet, Lord, you are our Father;
we the clay, you the potter,
we are all the work of your hand.

> The word of the Lord.

RESPONSORIAL PSALM   Ps 79:2-3.15-16.18-19

℟ **God of hosts, bring us back;**
   let your face shine on us and we shall be saved.

1. O shepherd of Israel, hear us,
    shine forth from your cherubim throne.
    O Lord, rouse up your might,
    O Lord, come to our help. ℟

2. God of hosts, turn again, we implore,
    look down from heaven and see.
    Visit this vine and protect it,
    the vine your right hand has planted.

3. May your hand be on the man you have chosen,
    the man you have given your strength.
    And we shall never forsake you again:
    give us life that we may call upon your name. ℟

SECOND READING   1 Cor 1:3-9

A reading from the first letter of St Paul to the Corinthians.

We are waiting for our Lord Jesus Christ to be revealed.

May God our Father and the Lord Jesus Christ send you grace and peace.

I never stop thanking God for all the graces you have received through Jesus Christ. I thank him that you have been enriched in so many ways, especially in your teachers and preachers; the witness to Christ has indeed been strong among you so that you will not be without any of the gifts of the Spirit while you are waiting for our Lord Jesus Christ to be revealed; and he will keep you steady and without blame until the last day, the day of our Lord Jesus Christ, because God by calling you has joined you to his Son, Jesus Christ; and God is faithful.

The word of the Lord.

GOSPEL ACCLAMATION   Ps 84:8

Alleluia, alleluia!
Let us see, O Lord, your mercy
and give us your saving help.
Alleluia!

GOSPEL   Mk 13:33-37

A reading from the holy Gospel according to Mark.

Stay awake, because you do not know when the master of the house is coming.

Jesus said to his disciples: 'Be on your guard, stay awake, because you never know when the time will come. It is like a man travelling abroad: he has gone from home, and left his servants in charge, each with his own task; and he has told the doorkeeper to stay awake. So stay awake, because you do not know when the master of the house is coming, evening, midnight, cockcrow, dawn; if he comes unexpectedly, he must not find you asleep. And what I say to you I say to all: Stay awake!'

The Gospel of the Lord.

Profession of Faith – pages 14-15.

Prayer over the Offerings

Accept, we pray, O Lord, these offerings we make,
gathered from among your gifts to us,
and may what you grant us to celebrate devoutly here below,

gain for us the prize of eternal redemption.
Through Christ our Lord.

Preface I of Advent – page 17.

Communion Antiphon   Ps 84:13

**The Lord will bestow his bounty,
and our earth shall yield its increase.**

Prayer after Communion

May these mysteries, O Lord,
in which we have participated,
profit us, we pray,
for even now, as we walk amid passing things,
you teach us by them to love the things of heaven
and hold fast to what endures.
Through Christ our Lord.

Solemn Blessing – page 56.

======= 8 DECEMBER =======

THE IMMACULATE CONCEPTION
OF THE BLESSED VIRGIN MARY

*Falling in Advent, the feast of the Immaculate Conception celebrates
the preparation of the Blessed Virgin for the nativity of the Saviour.
Listen carefully to what is said of Jesus: 'He will be great and will be
called Son of the Most High. The Lord God will give him the throne
of his ancestor David; he will rule over the House of Jacob for ever
and his reign will have no end.' These names and roles are all marks
of the faithfulness of God, grounded in the past, yet full of surprises.
As Mary was open to God's grace, let us open ourselves to the God of
surprises, to whom nothing is impossible.*

Entrance Antiphon   Is 61:10

**I rejoice heartily in the Lord,
in my God is the joy of my soul;
for he has clothed me with a robe of salvation,
and wrapped me in a mantle of justice,
like a bride adorned with her jewels.**

Greeting, Penitential Rite, Gloria – pages 7-13.

Collect

O God, who by the Immaculate Conception of the Blessed
    Virgin
prepared a worthy dwelling for your Son,
grant, we pray,
that, as you preserved her from every stain
by virtue of the Death of your Son, which you foresaw,
so, through her intercession,
we, too, may be cleansed and admitted to your presence.
Through our Lord Jesus Christ, your Son,
who lives and reigns with you in the unity of the Holy Spirit,
one God, for ever and ever.

FIRST READING   Gn 3:9-15.20

A reading from the book of Genesis.

I will make you enemies of each other; your offspring and her offspring.

After Adam had eaten of the tree, the Lord God called to him.
'Where are you?' he asked. 'I heard the sound of you in the
garden', he replied. 'I was afraid because I was naked, so I hid.'
'Who told you that you were naked?' he asked. 'Have you been
eating of the tree I forbade you to eat?' The man replied, 'It was
the woman you put with me; she gave me the fruit, and I ate it.'
Then the Lord God asked the woman, 'What is this you have
done?' The woman replied, 'The serpent tempted me and I ate.'

Then the Lord God said to the serpent, 'Because you have
done this,

'Be accursed beyond all cattle,
all wild beasts.
You shall crawl on your belly and eat dust
every day of your life.
I will make you enemies of each other:
you and the woman,
your offspring and her offspring.
It will crush your head
and you will strike its heel.'

The man named his wife 'Eve' because she was the mother of all
those who live.

The word of the Lord.

RESPONSORIAL PSALM   Ps 97:1-4

℟ **Sing a new song to the Lord
for he has worked wonders.**

1. Sing a new song to the Lord
    for he has worked wonders.
    His right hand and his holy arm
    have brought salvation. ℟

2. The Lord has made known his salvation;
    has shown his justice to the nations.
    He has remembered his truth and love
    for the house of Israel. ℟

3. All the ends of the earth have seen
    the salvation of our God.
    Shout to the Lord all the earth,
    ring out your joy. ℟

SECOND READING   Ep 1:3-6.11-12

A reading from the letter of St Paul to the Ephesians.

Before the world was made, God chose us in Christ.

Blessed be God the Father of our Lord Jesus Christ,
who has blessed us with all the spiritual blessings of heaven in
        Christ.
Before the world was made, he chose us, chose us in Christ,
to be holy and spotless, and to live through love in his presence,
determining that we should become his adopted sons, through
        Jesus Christ
for his own kind purposes,
to make us praise the glory of his grace,
his free gift to us in the Beloved.
And it is in him that we were claimed as God's own,
chosen from the beginning,
under the predetermined plan of the one who guides all things
as he decides by his own will;
chosen to be,
for his greater glory,
the people who would put their hopes in Christ before he came.
        The word of the Lord.

GOSPEL ACCLAMATION   Lk 1:28

Alleluia, alleluia!
Hail, Mary, full of grace; the Lord is with thee!
Blessed art thou among women.
Alleluia!

GOSPEL   Lk 1:26-38

A reading from the holy Gospel according to Luke.

You are to conceive and bear a Son.

The angel Gabriel was sent by God to a town in Galilee called Nazareth, to a virgin betrothed to a man named Joseph, of the House of David; and the virgin's name was Mary. He went in and said to her, 'Rejoice, so highly favoured! The Lord is with you.' She was deeply disturbed by these words and asked herself what this greeting could mean, but the angel said to her, 'Mary, do not be afraid; you have won God's favour. Listen! You are to conceive and bear a son, and you must name him Jesus. He will be great and will be called Son of the Most High. The Lord God will give him the throne of his ancestor David; he will rule over the House of Jacob for ever and his reign will have no end.' Mary said to the angel, 'But how can this come about, since I am a virgin?' 'The Holy Spirit will come upon you' the angel answered, 'and the power of the Most High will cover you with its shadow. And so the child will be holy and will be called Son of God. Know this too: your kinswoman Elizabeth has, in her old age, herself conceived a son, and she whom people called barren is now in her sixth month, for nothing is impossible to God.' 'I am the handmaid of the Lord', said Mary, 'let what you have said be done to me.' And the angel left her.

The Gospel of the Lord.

Profession of Faith – pages 14-15.

Prayer over the Offerings

Graciously accept the saving sacrifice
which we offer you, O Lord,
on the Solemnity of the Immaculate Conception
of the Blessed Virgin Mary,
and grant that, as we profess her,
on account of your prevenient grace,
to be untouched by any stain of sin,
so, through her intercession,

we may be delivered from all our faults.
Through Christ our Lord.

Preface: The Mystery of Mary and the Church

The Lord be with you.
And with your spirit.

Lift up your hearts.
We lift them up to the Lord.

Let us give thanks to the Lord our God.
It is right and just.

It is truly right and just, our duty and our salvation,
always and everywhere to give you thanks,
Lord, holy Father, almighty and eternal God.

For you preserved the most Blessed Virgin Mary
from all stain of original sin,
so that in her, endowed with the rich fullness of your grace,
you might prepare a worthy Mother for your Son
and signify the beginning of the Church,
his beautiful Bride without spot or wrinkle.

She, the most pure Virgin, was to bring forth a Son,
the innocent Lamb who would wipe away our offences;
you placed her above all others
to be for your people an advocate of grace
and a model of holiness.

And so, in company with the choirs of Angels,
we praise you, and with joy we proclaim:

Holy, Holy, Holy Lord God of hosts …

Communion Antiphon

**Glorious things are spoken of you, O Mary,
for from you arose the sun of justice,
Christ our God.**

Prayer after Communion

May the Sacrament we have received,
O Lord our God,
heal in us the wounds of that fault
from which in a singular way
you preserved Blessed Mary in her Immaculate Conception.
Through Christ our Lord.

Solemn Blessing

The Priest invites people to bow down for the blessing.

May God, who through the childbearing of the Blessed
    Virgin Mary
willed in his great kindness to redeem the human race,
be pleased to enrich you with his blessing.
Amen.

May you know always and everywhere the protection of her,
through whom you have been found worthy to receive the
    author of life.
Amen.

May you, who have devoutly gathered on this day,
carry away with you the gifts of spiritual joys and
    heavenly rewards.
Amen.

And may the blessing of almighty God,
the Father, and the Son, ✠ and the Holy Spirit,
come down on you and remain with you for ever.
Amen.

═══ 10 DECEMBER ═══
SECOND SUNDAY OF ADVENT

*As Christmas approaches, we could ask ourselves: how can we prepare
to celebrate the birthday of our Saviour? The proclamation of John
the Baptist points to the preparation that really counts: conversion
of heart and life. The deeper meaning of metanoia is a change of
vision, a radically new outlook, in the light of the Gospel. God is our
compassionate Father, our Abba, who desires nothing less than our
hearts, our whole selves. We are accepted and loved by him, while
we are still sinners (Rm 5:8). Receiving his forgiving-love means a
revolution in values, beliefs and direction in life.*

Entrance Antiphon   Cf. Is 30:19.30

O People of Sion, behold,
the Lord will come to save the nations,
and the Lord will make the glory of his voice heard
in the joy of your heart.

Greeting, Penitential Rite – pages 7-12.

The **Gloria** is not said.

Collect

Almighty and merciful God,
may no earthly undertaking hinder those
who set out in haste to meet your Son,
but may our learning of heavenly wisdom
gain us admittance to his company.
Who lives and reigns with you in the unity of the Holy Spirit,
one God, for ever and ever.

FIRST READING   Is 40:1-5.9-11

A reading from the prophet Isaiah.

Prepare a way for the Lord.

'Console my people, console them'
says your God.
'Speak to the heart of Jerusalem
and call to her
that her time of service is ended,
that her sin is atoned for,
that she has received from the hand of the Lord
double punishment for her crimes.'

A voice cries, 'Prepare in the wilderness
a way for the Lord.
Make a straight highway for our God
across the desert.
Let every valley be filled in,
every mountain and hill be laid low,
let every cliff become a plain,
and the ridges a valley;
then the glory of the Lord shall be revealed
and all mankind shall see it;
for the mouth of the Lord has spoken.'

Go up on a high mountain,
joyful messenger to Zion.
Shout with a loud voice,
joyful messenger to Jerusalem.
Shout without fear,
say to the towns of Judah,
'Here is your God.'

Here is the Lord coming with power,
his arm subduing all things to him.
The prize of his victory is with him,
his trophies all go before him.
He is like a shepherd feeding his flock,
gathering lambs in his arms,
holding them against his breast
and leading to their rest the mother ewes.

   The word of the Lord.

RESPONSORIAL PSALM   Ps 84:9-14

℟ **Let us see, O Lord, your mercy
   and give us your saving help.**

1. I will hear what the Lord God has to say,
   a voice that speaks of peace,
   peace for his people.
   His help is near for those who fear him
   and his glory will dwell in our land. ℟

2. Mercy and faithfulness have met;
   justice and peace have embraced.
   Faithfulness shall spring from the earth
   and justice look down from heaven. ℟

3. The Lord will make us prosper
   and our earth shall yield its fruit.
   Justice shall march before him
   and peace shall follow his steps. ℟

SECOND READING   2 Pt 3:8-14

A reading from the second letter of St Peter.

We are waiting for the new heavens and new earth.

There is one thing, my friends, that you must never forget:
that with the Lord, 'a day' can mean a thousand years, and a
thousand years is like a day. The Lord is not being slow to carry
out his promises, as anybody else might be called slow; but he
is being patient with you all, wanting nobody to be lost and
everybody to be brought to change his ways. The Day of the
Lord will come like a thief, and then with a roar the sky will
vanish, the elements will catch fire and fall apart, the earth and
all that it contains will be burnt up.

Since everything is coming to an end like this, you should be living holy and saintly lives while you wait and long for the Day of God to come, when the sky will dissolve in flames and the elements melt in the heat. What we are waiting for is what he promised; the new heavens and new earth, the place where righteousness will be at home. So then, my friends, while you are waiting, do your best to live lives without spot or stain so that he will find you at peace.

The word of the Lord.

GOSPEL ACCLAMATION   Lk 3:4.6

Alleluia, alleluia!
Prepare a way for the Lord,
make his paths straight,
and all humankind shall see the salvation of God.
Alleluia!

GOSPEL   Mk 1:1-8

A reading from the holy Gospel according to Mark.

Make his paths straight.

The beginning of the Good News about Jesus Christ, the Son of God. It is written in the book of the prophet Isaiah:

Look, I am going to send my messenger before you;
he will prepare your way.
A voice cries in the wilderness:
Prepare a way for the Lord,
make his paths straight,

and so it was that John the Baptist appeared in the wilderness, proclaiming a baptism of repentance for the forgiveness of sins. All Judaea and all the people of Jerusalem made their way to him, and as they were baptised by him in the river Jordan they confessed their sins. John wore a garment of camel-skin, and he lived on locusts and wild honey. In the course of his preaching he said, 'Someone is following me, someone who is more powerful than I am, and I am not fit to kneel down and undo the strap of his sandals. I have baptised you with water, but he will baptise you with the Holy Spirit.'

The Gospel of the Lord.

Profession of Faith – pages 14-15.

Prayer over the Offerings

Be pleased, O Lord, with our humble prayers and offerings,
and, since we have no merits to plead our cause,
come, we pray, to our rescue
with the protection of your mercy.
Through Christ our Lord.

Preface I of Advent – page 17.

Communion Antiphon　　　　　　　　　　　　　Ba 5:5; 4:36

**Jerusalem, arise and stand upon the heights,
and behold the joy which comes to you from God.**

Prayer after Communion

Replenished by the food of spiritual nourishment,
we humbly beseech you, O Lord,
that, through our partaking in this mystery,
you may teach us to judge wisely the things of earth
and hold firm to the things of heaven.
Through Christ our Lord.

Solemn Blessing – page 57.

──────── 17 DECEMBER ────────

THIRD SUNDAY OF ADVENT

*In the words of John's Gospel, John the Baptist came as a witness, to
speak for the light, the true light who was coming into the world. In
this season of Advent, he points us towards the coming one and he
invites us to reflect on our need of the light of Jesus in the darkness of
our lives. Darkness means many things: a sense of being lost, a lack
of direction, helplessness, sin or indeed lack of faith. This Christmas,
may the God who said: "Let light shine out of darkness," shine in our
hearts to give the light of the knowledge of the glory of God in the face
of Jesus Christ (2 Cor 4:6).*

Entrance Antiphon　　　　　　　　　　　　　　Ph 4:4-5

**Rejoice in the Lord always; again I say, rejoice.
Indeed, the Lord is near.**

Greeting, Penitential Rite – pages 7-12.

The **Gloria** is not said.

Collect

O God, who see how your people
faithfully await the feast of the Lord's Nativity,
enable us, we pray,
to attain the joys of so great a salvation
and to celebrate them always
with solemn worship and glad rejoicing.
Through our Lord Jesus Christ, your Son,
who lives and reigns with you in the unity of the Holy Spirit,
one God, for ever and ever.

FIRST READING   Is 61:1-2.10-11

A reading from the prophet Isaiah.

I exult for joy in the Lord.

The spirit of the Lord has been given to me,
for the Lord has anointed me.
He has sent me to bring good news to the poor,
to bind up hearts that are broken;

to proclaim liberty to captives,
freedom to those in prison;
to proclaim a year of favour from the Lord.

'I exult for joy in the Lord,
my soul rejoices in my God,
for he has clothed me in the garments of salvation,
he has wrapped me in the cloak of integrity,
like a bridegroom wearing his wreath,
like a bride adorned in her jewels.

'For as the earth makes fresh things grow,
as a garden makes seeds spring up,
so will the Lord make both integrity and praise
spring up in the sight of nations.'

    The word of the Lord.

RESPONSORIAL PSALM   Lk 1:46-50.53-54

℟ **My soul rejoices in my God.**

1. My soul glorifies the Lord,
    my spirit rejoices in God, my Saviour.
    He looks on his servant in her nothingness;
    henceforth all ages will call me blessed. ℟

2. The Almighty works marvels for me.
   Holy his name!
   His mercy is from age to age,
   on those who fear him.

3. He fills the starving with good things,
   sends the rich away empty.
   He protects Israel, his servant,
   remembering his mercy. ℞

SECOND READING   1 Th 5:16-24

A reading from the first letter of St Paul to the Thessalonians.

May you all be kept safe, spirit, soul and body, for the coming of the Lord.

Be happy at all times; pray constantly; and for all things give thanks to God, because this is what God expects you to do in Christ Jesus.

Never try to suppress the Spirit or treat the gift of prophecy with contempt; think before you do anything – hold on to what is good and avoid every form of evil.

May the God of peace make you perfect and holy; and may you all be kept safe and blameless, spirit, soul and body, for the coming of our Lord Jesus Christ. God has called you and he will not fail you.

The word of the Lord.

GOSPEL ACCLAMATION   Is 61:1; Lk 4:18

Alleluia, alleluia!
The Spirit of the Lord has been given to me.
He has sent me to bring good news to the poor.
Alleluia!

GOSPEL   Jn 1:6-8.19-28

A reading from the holy Gospel according to John.

There stands among you, unknown to you, the one who is coming after me.

A man came, sent by God.
His name was John.
He came as a witness,
as a witness to speak for the light,
so that everyone might believe through him.
He was not the light,
only a witness to speak for the light.

   This is how John appeared as a witness. When the Jews sent

priests and Levites from Jerusalem to ask him, 'Who are you?' he
not only declared, but he declared quite openly, 'I am not the
Christ.' 'Well then,' they asked 'are you Elijah?' 'I am not' he said.
'Are you the Prophet?' He answered, 'No.' So they said to him,
'Who are you? We must take back an answer to those who sent
us. What have you to say about yourself?' So John said, 'I am, as
Isaiah prophesied:

> a voice that cries in the wilderness:
> Make a straight way for the Lord.'

Now these men had been sent by the Pharisees, and they put
this further question to him, 'Why are you baptising if you
are not the Christ, and not Elijah, and not the prophet?' John
replied, 'I baptise with water; but there stands among you –
unknown to you – the one who is coming after me; and I am
not fit to undo his sandal-strap.' This happened at Bethany, on
the far side of the Jordan, where John was baptising.

The Gospel of the Lord.

Profession of Faith – pages 14-15.

Prayer over the Offerings
May the sacrifice of our worship, Lord, we pray,
be offered to you unceasingly,
to complete what was begun in sacred mystery
and powerfully accomplish for us your saving work.
Through Christ our Lord.

Preface I or II of Advent – pages 17-18.

Communion Antiphon   Cf. Is 35:4
Say to the faint of heart: Be strong and do not fear.
Behold, our God will come, and he will save us.

Prayer after Communion
We implore your mercy, Lord,
that this divine sustenance may cleanse us of our faults
and prepare us for the coming feasts.
Through Christ our Lord.

Solemn Blessing – page 56.

24 DECEMBER
FOURTH SUNDAY OF ADVENT

*The season of preparation is drawing to a close. Like Mary, my getting
ready involves deep listening to what God is asking of me now and
an interior willingness to say: "Let what you have said be done to
me." What is God asking of me now, as a person, in the family, at
work, and indeed within the faith community of the Church? Have
I noticed a pattern of "nudges" from God calling me to a deeper,
perhaps different engagement as a disciple? Are my gifts – tokens of
God's grace – fully at the service of my neighbour?*

Entrance Antiphon   Cf. Is 45:8

**Drop down dew from above, you heavens,
and let the clouds rain down the Just One;
let the earth be opened and bring forth a Saviour.**

Greeting, Penitential Rite – pages 7-12.

The **Gloria** is not said.

Collect

Pour forth, we beseech you, O Lord,
your grace into our hearts,
that we, to whom the Incarnation of Christ your Son
was made known by the message of an Angel,
may by his Passion and Cross
be brought to the glory of his Resurrection.
Who lives and reigns with you in the unity of the Holy Spirit,
one God, for ever and ever.

FIRST READING   2 Sm 7:1-5.8-12.14.16

A reading from the second book of Samuel.

The kingdom of David will always stand secure before the Lord.

Once David had settled into his house and the Lord had given
him rest from all the enemies surrounding him, the king said to
the prophet Nathan, 'Look, I am living in a house of cedar while
the ark of God dwells in a tent.' Nathan said to the king, 'Go and
do all that is in your mind, for the Lord is with you.'

But that very night the word of the Lord came to Nathan:

'Go and tell my servant David, "Thus the Lord speaks:
Are you the man to build me a house to dwell in? I took you

from the pasture, from following the sheep, to be leader of my people Israel; I have been with you on all your expeditions; I have cut off all your enemies before you. I will give you fame as great as the fame of the greatest on earth. I will provide a place for my people Israel; I will plant them there and they shall dwell in that place and never be disturbed again; nor shall the wicked continue to oppress them as they did, in the days when I appointed judges over my people Israel; I will give them rest from all their enemies. The Lord will make you great; the Lord will make you a House. And when your days are ended and you are laid to rest with your ancestors, I will preserve the offspring of your body after you and make his sovereignty secure. I will be a father to him and he a son to me. Your House and your sovereignty will always stand secure before me and your throne be established for ever." '

The word of the Lord.

RESPONSORIAL PSALM   Ps 88:2-5.27.29

℟ **I will sing for ever of your love, O Lord.**

1. I will sing for ever of your love, O Lord;
    through all ages my mouth will proclaim your truth.
    Of this I am sure, that your love lasts for ever,
    that your truth is firmly established as the heavens. ℟

2. 'I have made a covenant with my chosen one;
    I have sworn to David my servant:
    I will establish your dynasty for ever
    and set up your throne through all ages.' ℟

3. He will say to me: 'You are my father,
    my God, the rock who saves me.'
    I will keep my love for him always;
    for him my covenant shall endure.

SECOND READING   Rom 16:25-27

A reading from the letter of St Paul to the Romans.

The mystery, which was kept secret for endless ages, is now made clear.

Glory to him who is able to give you the strength to live according to the Good News I preach, and in which I proclaim Jesus Christ, the revelation of a mystery kept secret for endless ages, but now so clear that it must be broadcast to pagans everywhere to bring them to the obedience of faith. This is only what scripture has predicted, and it is all part of the way the eternal God wants things to be. He alone is wisdom; give glory therefore to him through Jesus Christ for ever and ever. Amen.

The word of the Lord.

GOSPEL ACCLAMATION   Lk 1:38
Alleluia, alleluia!
I am the handmaid of the Lord:
let what you have said be done to me.
Alleluia!

GOSPEL   Lk 1:26-38
A reading from the holy Gospel according to Luke.
Listen! You are to conceive and bear a son.

The angel Gabriel was sent by God to a town in Galilee called Nazareth, to a virgin betrothed to a man named Joseph, of the House of David; and the virgin's name was Mary. He went in and said to her, 'Rejoice, so highly favoured! The Lord is with you.' She was deeply disturbed by these words and asked herself what this greeting could mean, but the angel said to her, 'Mary, do not be afraid; you have won God's favour. Listen! You are to conceive and bear a son, and you must name him Jesus. He will be great and will be called Son of the Most High. The Lord God will give him the throne of his ancestor David; he will rule over the House of Jacob for ever and his reign will have no end.' Mary said to the angel, 'But how can this come about, since I am a virgin?' 'The Holy Spirit will come upon you' the angel answered 'and the power of the Most High will cover you with its shadow. And so the child will be holy and will be called Son of God. Know this too: your kinswoman Elizabeth has, in her old age, herself conceived a son, and she whom people called barren is now in her sixth month, for nothing is impossible to God.' 'I am the handmaid of the Lord,' said Mary, 'let what you have said be done to me.' And the angel left her.

The Gospel of the Lord.

Profession of Faith – pages 14-15.

Prayer over the Offerings
May the Holy Spirit, O Lord,
sanctify these gifts laid upon your altar,
just as he filled with his power
    the womb of the Blessed Virgin Mary.
Through Christ our Lord.

Preface II of Advent – page 18.

Communion Antiphon   Is 7:14
Behold, a Virgin shall conceive and bear a son;
and his name will be called Emmanuel.

Prayer after Communion
Having received this pledge of eternal redemption,
we pray, almighty God,
that, as the feast day of our salvation draws ever nearer,
so we may press forward all the more eagerly
to the worthy celebration of the mystery of your Son's Nativity.
Who lives and reigns for ever and ever.

Solemn Blessing – page 56.

25 DECEMBER
THE NATIVITY OF THE LORD

─────────── AT THE VIGIL MASS ───────────

*Mary 'will give birth to a son and you – Joseph – must name him
Jesus.' Tonight we will realise that this prophecy by a messenger from
heaven is fulfilled. God is born of a woman. Jesus is one of us for ever.
We can trace his ancestry in the history of Israel. From now on no
human being should be named 'Forsaken' or 'Abandoned'. You shall be
called 'My Delight' by God.*

Entrance Antiphon   Cf. Ex 16:6-7

**Today you will know that the Lord will come,
    and he will save us,
and in the morning you will see his glory.**

Greeting, Penitential Rite, Gloria – pages 7-13.

Collect

O God, who gladden us year by year
as we wait in hope for our redemption,
grant that, just as we joyfully welcome
your Only Begotten Son as our Redeemer,
we may also merit to face him confidently
when he comes again as our Judge.
Who lives and reigns with you in the unity of the Holy Spirit,
one God, for ever and ever.

FIRST READING   Is 62:1-5

A reading from the prophet Isaiah.
The Lord takes delight in you.

About Zion I will not be silent,
about Jerusalem I will not grow weary,
until her integrity shines out like the dawn
and her salvation flames like a torch.

The nations then will see your integrity,
all the kings your glory,
and you will be called by a new name,
one which the mouth of the Lord will confer.
You are to be a crown of splendour in the hand of the Lord,

a princely diadem in the hand of your God;
no longer are you to be named 'Forsaken',
nor your land 'Abandoned',
but you shall be called 'My Delight'
and your land 'The Wedded';
for the Lord takes delight in you
and your land will have its wedding.
Like a young man marrying a virgin,
so will the one who built you wed you,
and as the bridegroom rejoices in his bride,
so will your God rejoice in you.

The word of the Lord.

RESPONSORIAL PSALM   Ps 88:4-5.16-17.27.29

℞ **I will sing for ever of your love, O Lord.**

1. 'I have made a covenant with my chosen one;
    I have sworn to David my servant:
    I will establish your dynasty for ever
    and set up your throne through all ages.' ℞

2. Happy the people who acclaim such a king,
    who walk, O Lord, in the light of your face,
    who find their joy every day in your name,
    who make your justice the source of their bliss. ℞

3. 'He will say to me: "You are my father,
    my God, the rock who saves me."
    I will keep my love for him always;
    for him my covenant shall endure.' ℞

SECOND READING   Acts 13:16-17.22-25

A reading from the Acts of the Apostles.
Paul's witness to Christ, the son of David.

When Paul reached Antioch in Pisidia, he stood up in the
synagogue, held up a hand for silence and began to speak:

'Men of Israel, and fearers of God, listen! The God of our
nation Israel chose our ancestors, and made our people great
when they were living as foreigners in Egypt; then by divine
power he led them out.

'Then he made David their king, of whom he approved in
these words, "I have selected David son of Jesse, a man after
my own heart, who will carry out my whole purpose." To

keep his promise, God has raised up for Israel one of David's descendants, Jesus, as Saviour, whose coming was heralded by John when he proclaimed a baptism of repentance for the whole people of Israel. Before John ended his career he said, "I am not the one you imagine me to be; that one is coming after me and I am not fit to undo his sandal.'"

The word of the Lord.

GOSPEL ACCLAMATION

Alleluia, alleluia!
Tomorrow there will be an end to the sin of the world
and the saviour of the world will be our king.
Alleluia!

GOSPEL (SHORTER FORM)   Mt 1:18-25

A reading from the holy Gospel according to Matthew.

Mary will give birth to a son and will name him Jesus.

This is how Jesus Christ came to be born. His mother Mary was betrothed to Joseph; but before they came to live together she was found to be with child through the Holy Spirit. Her husband Joseph, being a man of honour and wanting to spare her publicity, decided to divorce her informally. He had made up his mind to do this when the angel of the Lord appeared to him in a dream and said, 'Joseph son of David, do not be afraid to take Mary home as your wife, because she has conceived what is in her by the Holy Spirit. She will give birth to a son and you must name him Jesus, because he is the one who is to save his people from their sins.' Now all this took place to fulfil the words spoken by the Lord through the prophet:

The Virgin will conceive and give birth to a son
and they will call him Emmanuel,

a name which means 'God-is-with-us'. When Joseph woke up he did what the angel of the Lord told him to do: he took his wife to his home and, though he had not had intercourse with her, she gave birth to a son; and he named him Jesus.

The Gospel of the Lord.

Profession of Faith – pages 14-15.

All kneel at the words *and by the Holy Spirit was incarnate.*

Prayer over the Offerings

As we look forward, O Lord,
to the coming festivities,
may we serve you all the more eagerly
for knowing that in them
you make manifest the beginnings of our redemption.
Through Christ our Lord.

Preface I, II or III of the Nativity of the Lord – pages 18-19.

Communion Antiphon Cf. Is 40:5

**The glory of the Lord will be revealed,
and all flesh will see the salvation of our God.**

Prayer after Communion

Grant, O Lord, we pray,
that we may draw new vigour
from celebrating the Nativity of your Only Begotten Son,
by whose heavenly mystery we receive both food and drink.
Who lives and reigns for ever and ever.

Solemn Blessing – page 431.

—————— AT THE MASS DURING THE NIGHT ——————

'I bring you news of great joy: Today a Saviour has been born to you.'
The real motive of our joy and celebration is Jesus. He is one of us, in
darkness and poverty, and in our hardships and discomforts.

Entrance Antiphon Ps 2:7

**The Lord said to me: You are my Son.
It is I who have begotten you this day.**

Or:

**Let us all rejoice in the Lord,
for our Saviour has been born in the world.
Today true peace has come down to us from heaven.**

Greeting, Penitential Rite, Gloria – pages 7-13.

Collect

O God, who have made this most sacred night
radiant with the splendour of the true light,
grant, we pray, that we, who have known the mysteries of his
    light on earth,

may also delight in his gladness in heaven.
Who lives and reigns with you in the unity of the Holy Spirit,
one God, for ever and ever.

FIRST READING   Is 9:1-7

A reading from the prophet Isaiah.

A Son is given to us.

The people that walked in darkness
has seen a great light;
on those who live in a land of deep shadow
a light has shone.
You have made their gladness greater,
you have made their joy increase;
they rejoice in your presence
as men rejoice at harvest time,
as men are happy when they are dividing the spoils.
For the yoke that was weighing on him,
the bar across his shoulders,
the rod of his oppressor,
these you break as on the day of Midian.
For all the footgear of battle,
every cloak rolled in blood,
is burnt, and consumed by fire.
For there is a child born for us,
a son given to us
and dominion is laid on his shoulders;
and this is the name they give him:
Wonder-Counsellor, Mighty-God,
Eternal-Father, Prince-of-Peace.
Wide is his dominion
in a peace that has no end,
for the throne of David
and for his royal power,
which he establishes and makes secure
in justice and integrity.
From this time onwards and for ever,
the jealous love of the Lord of hosts will do this.

The word of the Lord.

RESPONSORIAL PSALM   Ps 95:1-3.11-13

℞ **Today a saviour has been born to us;**
    he is Christ the Lord.

1. O sing a new song to the Lord,
   sing to the Lord all the earth.
   O sing to the Lord, bless his name. ℞

2. Proclaim his help day by day,
   tell among the nations his glory
   and his wonders among all the peoples. ℞

3. Let the heavens rejoice and earth be glad,
   let the sea and all within it thunder praise,
   let the land and all it bears rejoice,
   all the trees of the wood shout for joy
   at the presence of the Lord for he comes,
   he comes to rule the earth. ℞

4. With justice he will rule the world,
   he will judge the peoples with his truth. ℞

SECOND READING   Tt 2:11-14

A reading from the letter of St Paul to Titus.

God's grace has been revealed to the whole human race.

God's grace has been revealed, and it has made salvation possible for the whole human race and taught us that what we have to do is to give up everything that does not lead to God, and all our worldly ambitions; we must be self-restrained and live good and religious lives here in this present world, while we are waiting in hope for the blessing which will come with the Appearing of the glory of our great God and saviour Christ Jesus. He sacrificed himself for us in order to set us free from all wickedness and to purify a people so that it could be his very own and would have no ambition except to do good.

The word of the Lord.

GOSPEL ACCLAMATION   Lk 2:10-11

Alleluia, alleluia!
I bring you news of great joy:
today a saviour has been born to us, Christ the Lord.
Alleluia!

GOSPEL   Lk 2:1-14

A reading from the holy Gospel according to Luke.

Today a saviour has been born to you.

Caesar Augustus issued a decree for a census of the whole world to be taken. This census – the first – took place while Quirinius was governor of Syria, and everyone went to his own town to be registered. So Joseph set out from the town of Nazareth in Galilee and travelled up to Judaea, to the town of David called Bethlehem, since he was of David's House and line, in order to be registered together with Mary, his betrothed, who was with child. While they were there the time came for her to have her child, and she gave birth to a son, her first-born. She wrapped him in swaddling clothes, and laid him in a manger because there was no room for them at the inn. In the countryside close by there were shepherds who lived in the fields and took it in turns to watch their flocks during the night. The angel of the Lord appeared to them and the glory of the Lord shone round them. They were terrified, but the angel said, 'Do not be afraid. Listen, I bring you news of great joy, a joy to be shared by the whole people. Today in the town of David a saviour has been born to you; he is Christ the Lord. And here is a sign for you: you will find a baby wrapped in swaddling clothes and lying in a manger.' And suddenly with the angel there was a great throng of the heavenly host, praising God and singing:

'Glory to God in the highest heaven,
and peace to men who enjoy his favour.'

The Gospel of the Lord.

Profession of Faith – pages 14-15.

All kneel at the words **and by the Holy Spirit was incarnate.**

Prayer over the Offerings

May the oblation of this day's feast
be pleasing to you, O Lord, we pray,
that through this most holy exchange
we may be found in the likeness of Christ,
in whom our nature is united to you.
Who lives and reigns for ever and ever.

Preface I, II or III of the Nativity of the Lord – pages 18-19.

Communion Antiphon   Jn 1:14

The Word became flesh, and we have seen his glory.

Prayer after Communion

Grant us, we pray, O Lord our God,
that we, who are gladdened by participation
in the feast of our Redeemer's Nativity,
may through an honourable way of life become worthy of union
    with him.
Who lives and reigns for ever and ever.

Solemn Blessing

The Priest invites people to bow down for the blessing.

May the God of infinite goodness,
who by the Incarnation of his Son has driven darkness
    from the world
and by that glorious Birth has illumined this most holy
    night (day),
drive far from you the darkness of vice
and illumine your hearts with the light of virtue.
Amen.

May God, who willed that the great joy
of his Son's saving Birth
be announced to shepherds by the Angel,
fill your minds with the gladness he gives
and make you heralds of his Gospel.
Amen.

And may God, who by the Incarnation
brought together the earthly and heavenly realm,
fill you with the gift of his peace and favour
and make you sharers with the Church in heaven.
Amen.

And may the blessing of almighty God,
the Father, and the Son, ✠ and the Holy Spirit,
come down on you and remain with you for ever.
Amen.

──────── AT THE MASS AT DAWN ────────

'They hurried away and found Mary and Joseph, and the baby lying in the manger.' The shepherds found the Baby Jesus at the centre of his family. He will live with his parents for thirty years before his identity will be known to all.

Entrance Antiphon   Cf. Is 9:1.5; Lk 1:33

**Today a light will shine upon us, for the Lord is born for us;
and he will be called Wondrous God,
Prince of peace, Father of future ages:
and his reign will be without end.**

Greeting, Penitential Rite, Gloria – pages 7-13.

Collect

Grant, we pray, almighty God,
that, as we are bathed in the new radiance of your incarnate
    Word,
the light of faith, which illumines our minds,
may also shine through in our deeds.
Through our Lord Jesus Christ, your Son,
who lives and reigns with you in the unity of the Holy Spirit,
one God, for ever and ever.

FIRST READING   Is 62:11-12

A reading from the prophet Isaiah.
Look, your Saviour comes.

This the Lord proclaims to the ends of the earth:

    Say to the daughter of Zion, 'Look,
    your saviour comes,
    the prize of his victory with him,
    his trophies before him'.
    They shall be called 'The Holy People',
    'The Lord's Redeemed'.
    And you shall be called 'The-sought-after',
    'City-not-forsaken'.

    The word of the Lord.

RESPONSORIAL PSALM   Ps 96:1.6.11-12

℟ **This day new light will shine upon the earth:
    the Lord is born for us.**

1. The Lord is king, let earth rejoice,
   the many coastlands be glad.
   The skies proclaim his justice;
   all peoples see his glory. ℞

2. Light shines forth for the just
   and joy for the upright of heart
   Rejoice, you just, in the Lord;
   give glory to his holy name. ℞

SECOND READING   Tt 3:4-7

A reading from the letter of St Paul to Titus.

It was for no reason except his own compassion that he saved us.

When the kindness and love of God our saviour for mankind
were revealed, it was not because he was concerned with any
righteous actions we might have done ourselves; it was for no
reason except his own compassion that he saved us, by means of
the cleansing water of rebirth and by renewing us with the Holy
Spirit which he has so generously poured over us through Jesus
Christ our Saviour. He did this so that we should be justified by
his grace, to become heirs looking forward to inheriting eternal
life.

   The word of the Lord.

GOSPEL ACCLAMATION   Lk 2:14

Alleluia, alleluia!
Glory to God in the highest heaven,
and peace to men who enjoy his favour.
Alleluia!

GOSPEL   Lk 2:15-20

A reading from the holy Gospel according to Luke.

The shepherds found Mary and Joseph and the baby.

Now when the angels had gone from them into heaven, the
shepherds said to one another, 'Let us go to Bethlehem and see
this thing that has happened which the Lord has made known
to us.' So they hurried away and found Mary and Joseph, and the
baby lying in the manger. When they saw the child they repeated
what they had been told about him, and everyone who heard it
was astonished at what the shepherds had to say. As for Mary,
she treasured all these things and pondered them in her heart.

And the shepherds went back glorifying and praising God for all they had heard and seen; it was exactly as they had been told.

The Gospel of the Lord.

Profession of Faith – pages 14-15.

All kneel at the words and by the Holy Spirit was incarnate.

Prayer over the Offerings

May our offerings be worthy, we pray, O Lord,
of the mysteries of the Nativity this day,
that, just as Christ was born a man
    and also shone forth as God,
so these earthly gifts may confer on us what is divine.
Through Christ our Lord.

Preface I, II or III of the Nativity of the Lord – pages 18-19.

Communion Antiphon Cf. Zc 9:9

**Rejoice, O Daughter Sion; lift up praise, Daughter Jerusalem:
Behold, your King will come,
the Holy One and Saviour of the world.**

Prayer after Communion

Grant us, Lord, as we honour with joyful devotion
the Nativity of your Son,
that we may come to know with fullness of faith
the hidden depths of this mystery
and to love them ever more and more.
Through Christ our Lord.

Solemn Blessing – page 431.

——————— AT THE MASS DURING THE DAY ———————

The birth of any child is always a source of wonder when we feel nearer the mystery of life and closer to God. In the birth of Jesus, we see our God made visible and so are caught up in love of the God we cannot see. The thrilling reality of the Word made flesh is both gift and call. In the words of the first letter of John: Beloved, since God loved us so much, we also ought to love one another (1 Jn 4:11). We are challenged to love the God we cannot see in the neighbour we can see. There can be no separation of these two realities: to love God is to love our neighbour and to love our neighbour is to love God.

Entrance Antiphon   Cf. Is 9:5

A child is born for us, and a son is given to us;
his sceptre of power rests upon his shoulder,
and his name will be called Messenger of great counsel.

Greeting, Penitential Rite, Gloria – pages 7-13.

Collect

O God, who wonderfully created the dignity of human nature
and still more wonderfully restored it,
grant, we pray,
that we may share in the divinity of Christ,
who humbled himself to share in our humanity.
Who lives and reigns with you in the unity of the Holy Spirit,
one God, for ever and ever.

FIRST READING   Is 52:7-10

A reading from the prophet Isaiah.
All the ends of the earth shall see the salvation of our God.

How beautiful on the mountains,
are the feet of one who brings good news,
who heralds peace, brings happiness,
proclaims salvation,
and tells Zion,
'Your God is king!'
Listen! Your watchmen raise their voices,
they shout for joy together,
for they see the Lord face to face,
as he returns to Zion.
Break into shouts of joy together,
you ruins of Jerusalem;
for the Lord is consoling his people,
redeeming Jerusalem.
The Lord bares his holy arm
in the sight of all the nations,
and all the ends of the earth shall see
the salvation of our God.

    The word of the Lord.

RESPONSORIAL PSALM

Ps 97:1-6

℟ **All the ends of the earth have seen
the salvation of our God.**

1. Sing a new song to the Lord
   for he has worked wonders.
   His right hand and his holy arm
   have brought salvation. ℟

2. The Lord has made known his salvation;
   has shown his justice to the nations.
   He has remembered his truth and love
   for the house of Israel. ℟

3. All the ends of the earth have seen
   the salvation of our God.
   Shout to the Lord all the earth,
   ring out your joy. ℟

4. Sing psalms to the Lord with the harp,
   with the sound of music.
   With trumpets and the sound of the horn
   acclaim the King, the Lord. ℟

SECOND READING

Heb 1:1-6

A reading from the letter to the Hebrews.

God has spoken to us through his Son.

At various times in the past and in various different ways, God spoke to our ancestors through the prophets; but in our own time, the last days, he has spoken to us through his Son, the Son that he has appointed to inherit everything and through whom he made everything there is. He is the radiant light of God's glory and the perfect copy of his nature, sustaining the universe by his powerful command; and now that he has destroyed the defilement of sin, he has gone to take his place in heaven at the right hand of divine Majesty. So he is now as far above the angels as the title which he has inherited is higher than their own name.

God has never said to any angel: You are my Son, today I have become your father, or: I will be a father to him and he a son to me. Again, when he brings the First-born into the world, he says: Let all the angels of God worship him.

The word of the Lord.

GOSPEL ACCLAMATION

Alleluia, alleluia
A hallowed day has dawned upon us.
Come, you nations, worship the Lord,
for today a great light has shone down upon the earth.
Alleluia!

GOSPEL   Jn 1:1-18

(For Shorter Form, read between ♦ ♦).

A reading from the holy Gospel according to John.

The Word was made flesh, and lived among us.

♦In the beginning was the Word:
the Word was with God
and the Word was God.
He was with God in the beginning.
Through him all things came to be,
not one thing had its being but through him.
All that came to be had life in him
and that life was the light of men,
a light that shines in the dark,
a light that darkness could not overpower.♦

A man came, sent by God.
His name was John.
He came as a witness,
as a witness to speak for the light,
so that everyone might believe through him.
He was not the light,
only a witness to speak for the light.

♦The Word was the true light
that enlightens all men;
and he was coming into the world.
He was in the world
that had its being through him,
and the world did not know him.
He came to his own domain
and his own people did not accept him.
But to all who did accept him
he gave power to become children of God,
to all who believe in the name of him
who was born not out of human stock

or urge of the flesh
or will of man
but of God himself.
The Word was made flesh,
he lived among us,
and we saw his glory,
the glory that is his as the only Son of the Father,
full of grace and truth. ◆

John appears as his witness. He proclaims:
'This is the one of whom I said:
He who comes after me
ranks before me
because he existed before me.'

Indeed, from his fullness we have, all of us, received –
yes, grace in return for grace,
since, though the Law was given through Moses,
grace and truth have come through Jesus Christ.
No one has ever seen God;
it is the only Son, who is nearest to the Father's heart,
who has made him known.

    The Gospel of the Lord.

Profession of Faith – pages 14-15.

All kneel at the words and by the Holy Spirit was incarnate.

Prayer over the Offerings
Make acceptable, O Lord, our oblation on this solemn day,
when you manifested the reconciliation
that makes us wholly pleasing in your sight
and inaugurated for us the fullness of divine worship.
Through Christ our Lord.

Preface I, II or III of the Nativity of the Lord – pages 18-19.

Communion Antiphon   Cf. Ps 97:3
All the ends of the earth have seen the salvation of our God.

Prayer after Communion
Grant, O merciful God,
that, just as the Saviour of the world, born this day,
is the author of divine generation for us,
so he may be the giver even of immortality.

Who lives and reigns for ever and ever.

Solemn Blessing

The Priest invites people to bow down for the blessing.

May the God of infinite goodness,
who by the Incarnation of his Son has driven darkness
    from the world
and by that glorious Birth has illumined this most holy
    night (day),
drive far from you the darkness of vice
and illumine your hearts with the light of virtue.
Amen.

May God, who willed that the great joy
of his Son's saving Birth
be announced to shepherds by the Angel,
fill your minds with the gladness he gives
and make you heralds of his Gospel.
Amen.

And may God, who by the Incarnation
brought together the earthly and heavenly realm,
fill you with the gift of his peace and favour
and make you sharers with the Church in heaven.
Amen.

And may the blessing of almighty God,
the Father, and the Son, ✠ and the Holy Spirit,
come down on you and remain with you for ever.
Amen.

31 DECEMBER
THE HOLY FAMILY OF JESUS, MARY AND JOSEPH

This feast comes at Christmas, a time when families are thrown together more than usual. A sense of humour can help, as we are reminded of family resemblances, both physical and personal! A sense of gratitude too is not out of place – gratefulness especially to parents who always love us. A sense of service, when we make the extra effort to be helpful and kind, would be a real Christmas gift to all the family. A sense of belonging can help us experience the love and joy of being part of this particular family.

Entrance Antiphon   Lk 2:16

**The shepherds went in haste,
and found Mary and Joseph and the Infant lying in a manger.**

Greeting, Penitential Rite, Gloria – pages 7-13.

Collect

O God, who were pleased to give us
the shining example of the Holy Family,
graciously grant that we may imitate them
in practising the virtues of family life
    and in the bonds of charity,
and so, in the joy of your house,
delight one day in eternal rewards.
Through our Lord Jesus Christ, your Son,
who lives and reigns with you in the unity of the Holy Spirit,
one God, for ever and ever.

FIRST READING   Gn 15:1-6;21:1-3

A reading from the book of Genesis.

Your heir shall be your own flesh and blood.

The word of the Lord was spoken to Abram in a vision, 'Have no fear, Abram, I am your shield; your reward will be very great'.

'My Lord,' Abram replied 'what do you intend to give me? I go childless…' Then Abram said, 'See, you have given me no descendants; some man of my household will be my heir'. And then this word of the Lord was spoken to him, 'He shall not be your heir; your heir shall be one of your own flesh and blood'. Then taking him outside he said, 'Look up to heaven and count the stars if you can. Such will be your descendants' he told him. Abram put his faith in the Lord, who counted this as making him justified.

The Lord dealt kindly with Sarah as he had said, and did what he had promised her. So Sarah conceived and bore a son to Abraham in his old age, at the time God had promised. Abraham named the son born to him Isaac, the son to whom Sarah had given birth.

The word of the Lord.

RESPONSORIAL PSALM   Ps 104:1-6.8-9

℟ **He, the Lord, is our God.**
   He remembers his covenant for ever.

1. Give thanks to the Lord, tell his name,
   make known his deeds among the peoples.
   O sing to him, sing his praise;
   tell all his wonderful works! ℟

2. Be proud of his holy name,
   let the hearts that seek the Lord rejoice.
   Consider the Lord and his strength;
   constantly seek his face. ℟

3. Remember the wonders he has done,
   his miracles, the judgements he spoke.
   O children of Abraham, his servant,
   O sons of the Jacob he chose. ℟

4. He remembers his covenant for ever,
   his promise for a thousand generations,
   the covenant he made with Abraham,
   the oath he swore to Isaac. ℟

SECOND READING   Heb 11:8.11-12.17-19

A reading from the letter to the Hebrews.
The faith of Abraham, Sarah, and Isaac.

It was by faith that Abraham obeyed the call to set out for a country that was the inheritance given to him and his descendants, and that he set out without knowing where he was going.

It was equally by faith that Sarah, in spite of being past the age, was made able to conceive, because she believed that he who had made the promise would be faithful to it. Because of this, there came from one man, and one who was already as good as dead himself, more descendants than could be counted, as many as the stars of heaven or the grains of sand on the seashore.

It was by faith that Abraham, when put to the test, offered up Isaac. He offered to sacrifice his only son even though the promises had been made to him and he had been told: It is through Isaac that your name will be carried on. He was confident that God had the power even to raise the dead; and so, figuratively speaking, he was given back Isaac from the dead.

The word of the Lord.

GOSPEL ACCLAMATION   Heb 1:1-2
Alleluia, alleluia!
At various times in the past
and in various different ways,
God spoke to our ancestors through the prophets;
but in our own time, the last days,
he has spoken to us through his Son.
Alleluia!

GOSPEL   Lk 2:22-40

(For Shorter Form, read between ◆ ◆).

A reading from the holy Gospel according to Luke.

The child grew, filled with wisdom.

◆When the day came for them to be purified as laid down by the Law of Moses, the parents of Jesus took him up to Jerusalem to present him to the Lord◆ – observing what stands written in the law of the Lord: Every first-born male must be consecrated to the Lord – and also to offer in sacrifice, in accordance with what is said in the Law of the Lord, a pair of turtledoves or two young pigeons. Now in Jerusalem there was a man named Simeon. He was an upright and devout man; he looked forward to Israel's comforting and the Holy Spirit rested on him. It had been revealed to him by the Holy Spirit that he would not see death until he had set eyes on the Christ of the Lord. Prompted by the Spirit he came to the Temple; and when the parents brought in the child Jesus to do for him what the Law required, he took him into his arms and blessed God; and he said:

'Now, Master,
you can let your servant go in peace,
just as you promised;
because my eyes have seen the salvation
which you have prepared for all the nations to see,
a light to enlighten the pagans
and the glory of your people Israel.'

As the child's father and mother stood there wondering at the things that were being said about him, Simeon blessed them and said to Mary his mother, 'You see this child: he is destined for the fall and for the rising of many in Israel, destined to be a sign that is rejected – and a sword will pierce your own soul too – so that the secret thoughts of many may be laid bare.'

There was a prophetess also, Anna, the daughter of Phanuel, of the tribe of Asher. She was well on in years. Her days of girlhood over, she had been married for seven years before becoming a widow. She was now eighty-four years old and never left the Temple, serving God night and day with fasting and prayer. She came by just at that moment and began to praise God; and she spoke of the child to all who looked forward to the deliverance of Jerusalem.

♦When they had done everything the Law of the Lord required, they went back to Galilee, to their own town of Nazareth. Meanwhile the child grew to maturity, and he was filled with wisdom; and God's favour was with him.♦

The Gospel of the Lord.

Profession of Faith – pages 14-15.

Prayer over the Offerings
We offer you, Lord, the sacrifice of conciliation,
humbly asking that,
through the intercession of the Virgin Mother of God
    and Saint Joseph,
you may establish our families firmly in your grace
    and your peace.
Through Christ our Lord.

Preface I, II or III of the Nativity of the Lord – pages 18-19.

Communion Antiphon   Bar 3:38

Our God has appeared on the earth, and lived among us.

Prayer after Communion

Bring those you refresh with this heavenly Sacrament,
most merciful Father,
to imitate constantly the example of the Holy Family,
so that, after the trials of this world,
we may share their company for ever.
Through Christ our Lord.

Solemn Blessing – page 439.

DEVOTIONAL PRAYERS

Common Prayers

Thanksgiving after Communion

Adoration. I adore you present in me, Incarnate Word, only-begotten Son and splendour of the Father, born of Mary. I thank you, sole Master and Truth, for your supreme condescension in coming to me, ignorant and sinful as I am. With Mary I offer you to the Father: through you, with you, in you, may there be eternal praise, thanksgiving and supplication for peace to humankind. Enlighten my mind; make me a docile disciple of the Church; grant that I may live of faith; give me an understanding of the Scriptures. Make me your ardent apostle. Let the light of your Gospel, O Divine Master, shine to the farthest bounds of the world.

Resolution. O Jesus, you are the Way which I must follow; the perfect model which I must imitate. In presenting myself at the judgement I want to be found similar to you.

O divine model of humility and obedience, make me similar to you.

O perfect example of mortification and purity, make me similar to you.

O Jesus, poor and patient, make me similar to you.

O exemplar of charity and ardent zeal, make me similar to you.

Petition. O Jesus, my Life, my joy and source of all good, I love you. Above all, I ask of you that I may love you more and more and the souls redeemed by your Blood.

You are the vine and I am the branch: I want to stay united to you always so as to bring forth many fruits.

You are the source: pour out an ever greater abundance of grace to sanctify my soul.

You are my head; I, your member: communicate to me your Holy Spirit with all his gifts.

May your kingdom come through Mary.

Console and save those dear to me. Free the souls in purgatory.

Prayer of Saint Thomas Aquinas

I give you thanks,
Lord, holy Father, almighty and eternal God,
who have been pleased to nourish me,
a sinner and your unworthy servant,
with the precious Body and Blood
of your Son, our Lord Jesus Christ:
this through no merits of mine,
but due solely to the graciousness of your mercy.

And I pray that this Holy Communion
may not be for me an offence to be punished,
but a saving plea for forgiveness.
May it be for me the armour of faith,
and the shield of good will.
May it cancel my faults,
destroy concupiscence and carnal passion,
increase charity and patience, humility and obedience
and all the virtues,
may it be a firm defence against the snares of all my enemies,
both visible and invisible,
the complete calming of my impulses,
both of the flesh and of the spirit,
a firm adherence to you, the one true God,
and the joyful completion of my life's course.

And I beseech you to lead me, a sinner,
to that banquet beyond all telling,
where, with your Son and the Holy Spirit
you are the true light of your Saints,
fullness of satisfied desire, eternal gladness,
consummate delight and perfect happiness.
Through Christ our Lord.
Amen.

Spiritual Communion

My Jesus, I believe that you are truly present in the Blessed Sacrament. I love you above all things and I desire you in my soul. As I cannot now receive you sacramentally, come at least spiritually into my heart. I embrace you and unite myself entirely to you. Do not let me leave you ever.

To Jesus, the Divine Master

Jesus, Divine Master, I adore you as the Word Incarnate sent by the Father to instruct humankind in life-giving truths. You are uncreated Truth, the only Master. You alone have words of eternal life. I thank you for having ignited in me the light of reason and the light of faith, and for having called me to the light of glory. I believe, submitting my whole mind to you and to the Church, and I condemn all that the Church condemns. Master, show me the treasures of your wisdom, let me know the Father, make me your true disciple. Increase my faith so that I may attain to the eternal vision in heaven.

Prayer of St Francis

Lord, make me an instrument of your peace!
where there is hatred, let me sow love,
where there is injury, pardon,
where there is doubt, faith,
where there is despair, hope,
where there is darkness, light,
where there is sadness, joy.

O Divine Master, grant that I may
not try to be comforted but to comfort,
not try to be understood but to understand,
not try to be loved but to love.

Because it is in giving that we receive,
it is in forgiving that we are forgiven,
and it is in dying that we are born to eternal life.

The Divine Praises

Blessed be God.
Blessed be His holy Name.
Blessed be Jesus Christ, true God and true man.
Blessed be the Name of Jesus.
Blessed be His most Sacred Heart.
Blessed be His most precious Blood.
Blessed be Jesus in the most holy Sacrament of the Altar.
Blessed be the Holy Spirit, the Paraclete.
Blessed be the great Mother of God, Mary most holy.
Blessed be her holy and immaculate Conception.
Blessed be her glorious Assumption.

Blessed be the name of Mary, Virgin and Mother.
Blessed be St Joseph, her most chaste spouse.
Blessed be God in His angels and in His saints.

Soul of Christ

Soul of Christ, sanctify me,
Body of Christ, save me.
Blood of Christ, inebriate me.
Water from the side of Christ, wash me.
Passion of Christ, strengthen me.
O good Jesus, hear me.
Within your wounds hide me.
Permit me not to be separated from you.
From the malignant enemy defend me.
In the hour of my death call me
And bid me come to you,
That with your saints I may praise you
For ever and ever. Amen.

Consecration to the Most Holy Trinity

O divine Trinity, Father, Son and Holy Spirit, present and active
in the Church and the depths of my soul, I adore you, I thank
you, I love you! And through the hands of Mary most holy, my
Mother, I offer, give, and consecrate myself entirely to You for
life and for eternity.

To You, heavenly Father, I offer, give and consecrate myself as
Your child.

To You, Jesus Master, I offer, give and consecrate myself as
Your brother (sister) and disciple.

To You, Holy Spirit, I offer, give and consecrate myself as "a
living temple" to be consecrated and sanctified.

O Mary, Mother of the Church and my Mother, teach me
to live, through the liturgy and the sacraments, in ever more
intimate union with the three Divine Persons, so that my whole
life may be a "glory be to the Father, to the Son and to the Holy
Spirit." Amen.

Prayer to the Holy Spirit

O divine Holy Spirit, eternal Love of the Father and of the Son, I adore you, I thank you, I love you, and I ask you pardon for all the times I have grieved you in myself and in my neighbour.

Descend with many graces during the holy ordination of bishops and priests, during the consecration of men and women religious, during the reception of Confirmation by all the faithful; be light, sanctity and zeal.

To you, O Spirit of Truth, I consecrate my mind, imagination and memory; enlighten me. May I know Jesus Christ our Master and understand his Gospel and the teaching of holy Church. Increase in me the gifts of wisdom, knowledge, understanding and right judgement.

To you, O sanctifying Spirit, I consecrate my will. Guide me in your will, sustain me in the observance of the commandments, in the fulfilment of my duties. Grant me the gifts of courage and reverence.

To you, O life-giving Spirit, I consecrate my heart. Guard and increase the divine life in me. Grant me the gift of filial love. Amen.

Act of Submission to the Will of God

My God, I do not know what will happen to me today. I only know that nothing will happen to me that was not foreseen by you and directed to my greater good from all eternity. This is enough for me.

I adore your holy, eternal and unfathomable designs. I submit to them with all my heart for love of you. I make a sacrifice of my whole being to you and join my sacrifice to that of Jesus, my divine Saviour.

In his name and by his infinite merits, I ask you to give me patience in my sufferings and perfect submission, so that everything you want or permit to happen will result in your greater glory and my sanctification. Amen.

Invocations to the Divine Master

Jesus Master, sanctify my mind and increase my faith.

Jesus, teaching in the Church, draw everyone to your school.

Jesus Master, deliver me from error, from vain thoughts, and from eternal darkness.

O Jesus, Way between the Father and us, I offer you everything and look to you for everything.

O Jesus, Way of sanctity, make me your faithful imitator.

O Jesus Way, render me perfect as the Father who is in heaven.

O Jesus Life, live in me, so that I may live in you.

O Jesus Life, do not permit me to separate myself from you.

O Jesus Life, grant that I may live eternally in the joy of your love.

O Jesus Truth, may I be light for the world.

O Jesus Way, may I be an example and model for others.

O Jesus Life, may my presence bring grace and consolation everywhere.

To Recall God's Presence

I believe, my God, that I am in your presence, that you are looking at me and listening to my prayers.

You are so great and so holy: I adore you.

You have given me all: I thank you.

You have been so offended by me: I ask your pardon with all my heart.

You are so merciful: and I ask of you all the graces which you know are beneficial to me.

Act of Faith

O my God, I firmly believe that you are one God in three Divine Persons; Father, Son, and Holy Spirit; I believe that your divine Son became man and died for our sins, and that he will come to judge the living and the dead. I believe these and all truths which the holy catholic Church teaches, because you have revealed them who can neither deceive nor be deceived.

Act of Hope

O my God, relying on your infinite goodness and promises, I hope to obtain pardon of my sins, the help of your grace, and life everlasting, through the merits of Jesus Christ, my Lord and Redeemer.

Act of Love

O my God, I love you above all things, with my whole heart and soul, because you are all good and worthy of all love. I love my neighbour as myself for the love of you. I forgive all who have injured me and I ask pardon of all whom I have injured.

Act of Contrition

My God, I am heartily sorry for having offended you, and I detest all my sins, because of your just punishment, but most of all because they offend you, my God, who are all good and deserving of all my love. I firmly resolve, with the help of your grace, to sin no more and to avoid the near occasions of sin.

PRAYERS TO OUR LADY

The Angelus

The angel of the Lord declared unto Mary.
And she conceived of the holy Spirit.
Hail Mary....

Behold the handmaid of the Lord.
Be it done unto me according to thy word.
Hail Mary...

And the Word was made flesh,
And dwelt among us.
Hail Mary...

Pray for us, O Holy Mother of God.
That we may be made worthy of the promises of Christ.

Let us pray.
Pour forth, we beseech thee, O Lord, thy grace into our hearts, that we, to whom the incarnation of Christ, thy Son, was made known by the message of an angel, may by his passion and cross be brought to the glory of his resurrection. Through the same Christ our Lord.
Amen.

Regina Coeli

This prayer is said instead of the **Angelus** from the Easter Vigil until the evening of Pentecost Sunday.

O Queen of heaven, rejoice, **alleluia!**
For he whom thou didst merit to bear, **alleluia!**
Has risen, as he said, **alleluia!**
Pray for us to God, **alleluia!**
Rejoice and be glad, O Virgin Mary, **alleluia!**
For the Lord has risen indeed, **alleluia!**

Let us pray.
O God, who gavest joy to the world through the resurrection of thy Son our Lord Jesus Christ; grant that we may obtain, through his Virgin Mother, Mary, the joys of everlasting Life. Through the same Christ our Lord. Amen.

The Rosary

Joyful Mysteries

1. The Annunciation
2. The Visitation
3. The Nativity
4. The Presentation in the Temple
5. The Finding of the Child Jesus in the Temple

Luminous Mysteries

1. Jesus' Baptism in the Jordan
2. Jesus' Self-manifestation at the Wedding Feast of Cana
3. Jesus' Proclamation of the Kingdom of God, with His Call to Conversion
4. The Transfiguration
5. The Institution of the Holy Eucharist

Sorrowful Mysteries

1. The Agony in the Garden
2. The Scourging at the Pillar
3. The Crowning with Thorns
4. Jesus Carries His Cross
5. Jesus Dies on the Cross

Glorious Mysteries

1. The Resurrection
2. The Ascension
3. The Coming of the Holy Spirit
4. The Assumption of Our Lady into Heaven
5. The Coronation of Our Lady and the Glory of All the Saints

Salve Regina

Hail, holy Queen, mother of mercy, hail, our life, our sweetness, and our hope. To you do we cry, poor banished children of Eve. To you do we send up our sighs, mourning and weeping in this vale of tears. Turn then, most gracious advocate, your eyes of mercy towards us, and after this our exile show to us the blessed fruit of your womb, Jesus. O Clement, O loving, O sweet Virgin Mary.

St Bernard's Prayer

Remember, O most gracious Virgin Mary, that never was it known that anyone who fled to your protection, implored your help or sought your intercession, was left unaided. Inspired with this confidence, I fly to you, O Virgin of virgins, my Mother. To you I come, before you I stand, sinful and sorrowful. O Mother of the Word Incarnate! Despise not my petitions, but in your mercy hear and answer me. Amen.

Song of Mary (The Magnificat)

My soul proclaims the greatness of the Lord,
my spirit rejoices in God, my Saviour;
for he has looked with favour on his lowly servant,
and from this day all generations will call me blessed.
The Almighty has done great things for me:
holy is his Name.
He has mercy on those who fear him in every generation.
He has shown the strength of his arm,
he has scattered the proud in their conceit.
He has cast down the mighty from their thrones,
and has lifted up the lowly.
He has filled the hungry with good things,
and has sent the rich away empty.
He has come to the help of his servant Israel
for he has remembered his promise of mercy,
the promise he made to our fathers,
to Abraham and his children for ever.

(ICET translation)

THE WAY OF THE CROSS

Holy and merciful Father,
grant that we may follow the way of the cross
in faith and love, so that we may share
in Christ's passion and together with him
reach the glory of your Kingdom.
We ask you this through your Son Jesus Christ.

First Station

JESUS IS CONDEMNED TO DEATH

℣ We adore you, O Christ, and we bless you.
℞ Because by your holy cross you have redeemed the world.

So Pilate, wishing to satisfy the crowd, released for them Barabbas; and having scourged Jesus, he delivered him to be crucified (Mk 15:15).

"He came to his own home, and his own people received him not." The whole world – a world made up of Christians, Jews and non-believers – judges its own Creator and Redeemer. It was a judgement passed on Jesus by a small group among those who had followed him: by Judas who, not finding this Messiah up to his expectations, betrayed him to those who were seeking political power and liberation. Peter denied Jesus, while the other disciples fled.

Lord our God, have mercy on us all who have condemned you to death. Your mercy is already manifest in the sublime freedom with which you have borne our ingratitude and rejection.

All:

Our Father...

At the cross her station keeping
Stood the mournful Mother weeping,
Close to Jesus to the last.

Second Station

Jesus Takes up his Cross

℣ We adore you, O Christ, and we bless you.

℟ Because by your holy cross you have redeemed the world.

... Jesus went out, bearing his cross, to the place called 'Place of the Skull', which is called in Hebrew Golgotha (Jn 19:17).

Lord, you accept from humankind the same cross of which from all eternity you told your heavenly Father you were ready to bear in freedom and in love. It was not the human race who placed their sins on your shoulders, making of you a scapegoat, but it was you who had freely taken upon yourself our sins: everything you suffered would have otherwise been in vain.

To impose the burden of one's guilt on another is to disclaim any sort of personal culpability. It was not your Father who placed the burden on your shoulders, but the whole Trinity decreed that you should redeem the world lost in sin. You offered yourself to the Father in the Holy Spirit, in order to bring to completion on the cross the work of creation, and the Father – moved by the same Spirit – accepted your sacrifice.

Welcome, beloved Cross! You are the means by which we can finally and effectively show the world the immensity of God's love.

All:

Our Father...

Through her heart, his sorrow sharing,
All his bitter anguish bearing,
Now at length the sword had passed.

Third Station

Jesus Falls for the First Time

℣ We adore you, O Christ, and we bless you.
℟ Because by your holy cross you have redeemed the world.

Unless a grain of wheat falls into the earth and dies, it remains alone; but if it dies it bears much fruit (Jn 12:24).

The Bible mentions neither this fall nor the others. But we must remember that Jesus had undergone the appalling Roman scourging, the pain and exhaustion enough to kill anyone.

With repeated blows of the cudgel, the crown of thorns was driven into his sacred head. It is astonishing how our Lord did not lose consciousness when the heavy weight of the cross was placed on his shoulders. His resources were not totally drained.

People of goodwill can surely help the Redeemer as he carries his cross. There are those who wish to do so, and we shall encounter them as we go along.

Let us now ask our Lord to forgive us, for we too have placed unnecessary burdens on his shoulders.

All:

Our Father...

Oh, how sad and sore distressed
Was that Mother highly blest
Of the sole-begotten one!

Fourth Station

Jesus Meets his Mother

℣   We adore you, O Christ, and we bless you.
℟   Because by your holy cross you have redeemed the world.

Simeon said to Mary, "This child is set for the fall and rising of many in Israel, and for a sign that is spoken against and a sword will pierce through your own soul also" (Lk 2:34-35).

As Mary, the mother, played an essential role in Jesus' conception and birth, likewise she played an essential part in his passion by sharing in his suffering and death. No one is without a companion or a friend, yet on the cross the two criminals crucified with Jesus were of no comfort to him; he needed the presence of the sinless woman, Mary, the ever-Virgin Mother, whom he would make the mother of his mystical body, the Church.

Jesus entrusts to his sorrowful Mother his beloved disciple, John, who would be spiritually united with Peter, the representative of ecclesial unity. Thus, Mary the Immaculate becomes the Mother of the Petrine Church where – on behalf of all believers – she pleads the Holy Spirit by whom she was overshadowed at Nazareth.

All:

Our Father...

Christ above in torment hangs,
She beneath beholds the pangs
of her dying glorious Son.

Fifth Station

SIMON OF CYRENE HELPS JESUS CARRY HIS CROSS

℣   We adore you, O Christ, and we bless you.
℟   Because by your holy cross you have redeemed the world.

And they compelled a passer-by, Simon of Cyrene, who was coming in from the country, the father of Alexander and Rufus, to carry his cross (Mk 15:21).

Mary, in the most profound sorrow, accompanies her son on his way to Calvary. Simon, an ordinary man, is not prepared for anything unusual. He is on his way home from work. The evangelists underline the fact that he had to be forced to carry the cross that is too heavy for Jesus.

Even our most feeble "yes" to suffering – despite our resistance and our being unaware of it – becomes a transforming grace, provided that we accept it from the hands of God. Job, a patient man, uttered bitter words for his undeserved fate and great suffering, nevertheless was able to accept everything as coming from God: "The Lord has given and the Lord has taken away. The Lord's name be praised," – this earned him God's justification.

All:

Our Father...

Is there anyone who would not weep,
Whelmed in miseries so deep,
Christ's dear Mother to behold?

Sixth Station

Veronica Wipes the Face of Jesus

℣ We adore you, O Christ, and we bless you.
℟ Because by your holy cross you have redeemed the world.

He had no form or comeliness that we should look at him, and no beauty to attract us. He was despised and rejected by men as one from whom men hide their faces (Is 53:2-3).

Veronica is not mentioned in the Bible, but several women were present along the way to Calvary: women who wished by their presence, not only to profess their faith in the Lord but also to help him unreservedly.

Women in the Gospel are marked by Christ's preferential love of which John, the beloved disciple, was privileged. The Church, the bride of Christ, is therefore graced by the presence of women. In so far as the Church professes her faith and fidelity in loving humility to the Lord, as Veronica did in a gesture of love, Jesus leaves the imprint of his features on all those who are ready to accept it as a peace-token of his love.

Veronica's linen cloth, bearing the features of Jesus, is a sign and a promise to all believers that he will help them who call upon him.

Lord God, imprint in my spirit the sufferings of your Son Jesus.

All:

Our Father...

Can the human heart refrain
From partaking in her pain,
In that Mother's pain untold?

Seventh Station

JESUS FALLS FOR THE SECOND TIME

℣   We adore you, O Christ, and we bless you.
℞   Because by your holy cross you have redeemed the world.

Jesus said to them, 'My soul is very sorrowful, even to death....' And going a little farther, he fell on the ground and prayed that, if it were possible, this hour might pass from him (Mk 14:34-35).

To know that the Son of God's strength should fail him is indeed terrifying, yet it reminds us of what John (3:16) says of him: "God so loved the world that he gave his only Son..." to take upon himself the weight of man's sins and, as man, succumb under it. Humanly speaking, what would the Father have felt upon seeing his Son's sufferings, who in fulfilment of his Father's will gave himself up to death?

We always want to know why God allows so much suffering in the world. There is no easy answer to this. God can only offer a gesture of fatherly love: he loves the world so much that "he gave his only Son" to fall and be crushed under its massive weight.

We should not dwell so much on our own suffering which is nothing compared to what the Son of God suffered for us. Whenever we are able to share in a small way in Christ's suffering, it is indeed a grace.

All:

Our Father...

Bruised, derided, cursed, defiled
She beheld her tender Child
All with bloody scourges rent.

Eighth Station

Jesus Comforts the Women of Jerusalem

℣ We adore you, O Christ, and we bless you.
℟ Because by your holy cross you have redeemed the world.

And there followed him a great multitude of the people, and of women who bewailed and lamented him. But Jesus turning to them said, 'Daughters of Jerusalem, do not weep for me, but weep for yourselves and for your children' (Lk 23:27-28).

In this station we are faced with a gnawing question about the role played by the people of Israel in the Passion of Jesus.

We cannot ignore the fact that Israel not only disowned its long-awaited Messiah, but also condemned him to death; we should nonetheless bear in mind that both pagans and Christians are also guilty of his death. Jesus however would not let himself be comforted by the women of Jerusalem: "…weep not for me but for yourselves and for your children."

He foresees the imminent catastrophe which is to befall Jerusalem, and indeed the whole of Israel. The people of Israel could not give solace to the Son of God while he is being condemned.

All:

Our Father...

Let me share with you his pain
who for all my sins was slain
who for me in torment died.

Ninth Station

Jesus Falls for the Third Time

℣ We adore you, O Christ, and we bless you.
℟ Because by your holy cross you have redeemed the world.

Come to me, all who labour and are heavy-laden, and I will give you rest. Take my yoke upon you, and learn from me; for I am gentle and lowly in heart, and you will find rest for your souls. For my yoke is easy, and my burden is light (Mt 11:28-30).

It would not be inappropriate to think that this third fall of Jesus came about to the advantage of the people of Israel. Jesus' greatest pain was possibly the rejection by his own people who condemned him to the most atrocious death. We should not forget that his first mission was to gather together the scattered sheep of Israel. Not having been recognized as the Messiah was the most poignant defeat and the greatest humiliation he had to undergo.

This last burden, surely, must redound to Israel's advantage: how could it be otherwise? The tears of the daughters of Jerusalem could undoubtedly mingle with the tears of Jesus over that city whose destruction was imminent (cf. Lk 19:41).

All:

Our Father...

O my Mother, fount of love,
Touch my spirit from above;
Make my heart with yours accord.

Tenth Station

Jesus Is Stripped of his Garments

℣   We adore you, O Christ, and we bless you.
℟   Because by your holy cross you have redeemed the world.

They divided his garments among them, casting lots for them, to decide what each should take (Mk 15:24).

What do clothes matter to a human body which is about to be crucified? Jesus is stripped of his garments to enable the soldiers to work without being hampered.

Since that time in the Garden of Eden, fallen man has been covering himself with all sorts of clothing: from fig leaves and animal skins to the latest fashion of today. On Calvary everything is cast away: the new Adam stands before the Father as he is, having freely taken upon himself the sins and shame of the old Adam.

On the cross man fully manifests himself, and God restores to him his lost dignity – his most precious gift to mankind. In every eucharistic celebration down the centuries he gives to humanity this unadorned body. "The body of Christ" – says the priest as he gives communion – "who takes away the sins of the world": the body which bears your sins and the wounds inflicted on it.

All:

Our Father...

Make me feel as you have felt,
Make my soul to glow and melt
with the love of Christ my Lord.

Eleventh Station

Jesus Is Nailed to the Cross

℣ We adore you, O Christ, and we bless you.

℟ Because by your holy cross you have redeemed the world.

It was the third hour, when they crucified him. And the inscription of the charge against him read, 'The King of the Jews.' And with him they crucified two robbers, one on his right and one on his left (Mk 15:25-27).

"They know not what they do" (Lk 23:34). They nailed him to the cross in order to get rid of him, but in so doing, bonded him the more firmly to the earth. They nailed him down so that he could no longer go away but remain with us forever: neither the Resurrection nor the Ascension could alter this.

No one binds Jesus to sinful humanity; he remains with us, of his own accord, to the very end. And when he returns on judgement day the cross, "the sign of the Son of Man, will appear in heaven" (Mt 24:30).

"All things were created through him and for him" (Col 1:16-17), that is, for the Son whom the Father allows to be nailed to the cross of the world.

Overwhelmed by this unfathomable mystery we can only kneel in grateful adoration.

All:

Our Father...

Holy Mother, pierce me through;
In my heart each wound renew
Of my Saviour crucified.

Twelfth Station

Jesus Dies on the Cross

℣ We adore you, O Christ, and we bless you.
℟ Because by your holy cross you have redeemed the world.

And when the sixth hour had come, there was darkness over the whole land until the ninth hour. And at the ninth hour Jesus cried with a loud voice, 'Eloi, Eloi, lama sabachtani?' which means, 'My God, my God, why hast thou forsaken me?' … And one ran and, filling a sponge full of vinegar, put it on a reed and gave it to him to drink… And Jesus uttered a loud cry, and breathed his last…. And when the centurion, who stood facing him, saw that he thus breathed his last, he said, 'Truly this man was the Son of God' (Mk 15:33-39).

Jesus is suspended between heaven and earth, repudiated by men and forsaken by his Father, thus restoring the unity between them. Extending his arms he reaches out to both the sinner who goes back to him and to the one who turns away from him and yet could not hinder Christ to reach out to him. The vertical beam of the cross bridges the gap between God and man, while the horizontal one embraces the ends of the earth.

Bending his head, Jesus gives up the spirit, the same spirit whom he will breathe on the Church on the day of his Resurrection, and in this way all is truly accomplished.

All:

Our Father...

For the sins of his own nation
She saw him hang in desolation
Till his spirit forth he sent.

Thirteenth Station

JESUS IS TAKEN DOWN FROM THE CROSS

℣ We adore you, O Christ, and we bless you.

℞ Because by your holy cross you have redeemed the world.

Standing by the cross of Jesus were his mother and his mother's sister, Mary the wife of Clopas, and Mary Magdalene… The soldiers came to Jesus and when they saw that he was already dead, they did not break his legs. But one of the soldiers pierced his side with a spear, and at once there came out blood and water. After this Joseph of Arimathea… asked Pilate that he might take away the body of Jesus (Jn 19:25.32-34.38).

Jesus is taken down from the cross and his mother accepting the pain that his Son bore for the sake of the world – is there to receive him in her bosom. Each of the seven swords which transfixed the heart of the mother was Mary's renewed assent to her Son's sufferings. It is beyond human comprehension that a person should say "yes" to everything, even to the most harrowing pain.

In her unconditional "yes" Mary becomes the "redeemed earth", capable of receiving on her lap the dead body of the Redeemer. This scene wrapped in silence reveals that Christ's Passion was not suffered in vain: Mary in this moment of weariness and infinite sorrow, represents humanity who accepts with gratitude heaven's blessings.

All:

Our Father...

Let me mingle tears with you
Mourning him who mourned for me,
All the days that I may live.

Fourteenth Station

Jesus Is Laid in the Tomb

℣   We adore you, O Christ, and we bless you.
℟   Because by your holy cross you have redeemed the world.

When Pilate learned from the centurion that Jesus was dead, he granted the body to Joseph. And he bought a linen shroud, and taking him down, wrapped him in the linen shroud, and laid him in a tomb which had been hewn out of the rock; and he rolled a stone against the entrance of the tomb. Mary Magdalene and Mary the mother of Joses saw where he was laid (Mk 15:45-47).

The fact that Jesus' body – wrapped in a linen shroud lay in the tomb for three days, rules out any possibility of apparent death. He died as all people die. A large stone indicates definitiveness: everything that had been lived until then is now decisively in the past.

Nevertheless Jesus' death – a death which is absolutely real – was different from any other. For this unique death was the ultimate expression of God's infinite love, and love is the only living reality that cannot die.

Love is nothing else but perfect self-oblation and abnegation, in order to give oneself completely to the loved one. Is this not a form of death? And when one loves in a Christian way, placing his life completely at the service of his neighbour, is this not a "dying to self"?

All:

Our Father...

While my body here decays,
May my soul your goodness praise,
Safe in paradise with you. Amen.

> "He descended into hell;
> on the third day he rose again from the dead;
> he ascended into heaven,
> and is seated at the right hand of God the Father almighty;
> from there he will come to judge the living and the dead."
>
> – *Apostles' Creed*

HYMNS

Abide with Me

1. Abide with me, fast falls the eventide;
   the darkness deepens, Lord, with me abide!
   When other helpers fail, and comforts flee,
   help of the helpless, O abide with me.

2. Swift to its close ebbs our life's little day;
   earth's joys grow dim, its glories pass away;
   change and decay in all around I see;
   O thou who changest not, abide with me.

3. I need thy presence every passing hour;
   what but thy grace can foil the tempter's power?
   Who like thyself my guide and stay can be?
   Through cloud and sunshine, O abide with me.

4. I fear no foe with thee at hand to bless;
   ills have no weight, and tears no bitterness.
   Where is death's sting? Where, grave, thy victory?
   I triumph still if thou abide with me.

5. Hold thou thy Cross before my closing eyes;
   shine through the gloom, and point me to the skies;
   heaven's morning breaks, and earth's vain shadows flee;
   in life, in death, O Lord, abide with me!

– H.F. Lyte

Amazing Grace

1. Amazing grace! How sweet the sound
   that saved a wretch like me.
   I once was lost, but now I'm found,
   was blind, but now I see.

2. 'Twas grace that taught my heart to fear,
   and grace my fears relieved.
   How precious did that grace appear
   the hour I first believed.

3. Through many dangers, toils and snares
   I have already come.
   'Tis grace hath brought me safe thus far,
   and grace will lead me home.

4. The Lord has promised good to me;
    his word my hope secures.
    He will my shield and portion be
    as long as life endures.

– John Newton

Christ Be beside Me

1. Christ be beside me, Christ be before me,
    Christ be behind me, King of my heart.
    Christ be within me, Christ be below me,
    Christ be above me, Never to part.

2. Christ on my right hand, Christ on my left hand.
    Christ all around me, Shield in the strife.
    Christ in my sleeping, Christ in my sitting,
    Christ in my rising, Light of my life.

3. Christ be in all hearts Thinking about me,
    Christ be on all tongues Telling of me.
    Christ be the vision In eyes that see me,
    In ears that hear me, Christ ever be.

– St Patrick's Breastplate – J. Quinn

Praise to the Holiest in the Height

1. Praise to the Holiest in the height,
    And in the depth be praise,
    In all his words most wonderful,
    most sure in all his ways.

2. O loving wisdom of our God!
    When all was sin and shame,
    a second Adam to the fight,
    and to the rescue came.

3. O wisest love! That flesh and blood
    which did in Adam fail,
    should strive afresh against the foe,
    should strive and should prevail.

4. And that a higher gift than grace
    should flesh and blood refine,
    God's presence and his very self,
    and essence all divine.

5. O generous love! that he who smote
    in man for man the foe,

the double agony in man
for man should undergo.

6. And in the garden secretly,
and on the cross on high,
should teach his brethren, and inspire,
to suffer and to die.

7. Praise to the Holiest in the height,
and in the depth be praise,
in all his words most wonderful,
most sure in all his ways.

– John Henry Newman

Praise to the Lord, the Almighty

1. Praise to the Lord, the Almighty, the King of creation!
O my soul, praise him, for he is your health and salvation.
All you who hear, now to his altar draw near,
join in profound adoration.

2. Praise to the Lord, let us offer our gifts at his altar;
let not our sins and transgressions, now cause us to falter.
Christ, the High Priest, bids us all join in his feast;
victims with him on the altar.

3. Praise to the Lord, oh let all that is in us adore him!
All that has life and breath, come now in praises before him.
Let the Amen sound from his people again,
now as we worship before him.

– J. Neander – C. Winkworth

The Lord's My Shepherd

1. The Lord's my shepherd, I'll not want.
He makes me down to lie
in pastures green. He leadeth me
the quiet waters by.

2. My soul he doth restore again,
and me to walk doth make
within the paths of righteousness,
e'en for his own name's sake.

3. Yea, though I walk in death's dark vale,
yet will I fear no ill.
For thou art with me, and thy rod
and staff me comfort still.

4. My table thou hast furnished
    in presence of my foes,
    my head thou dost with oil anoint,
    and my cup overflows.

5. Goodness and mercy all my life
    shall surely follow me.
    And in God's house for evermore
    my dwelling place shall be.

– Ps 22, Scottish Psalter

When I Behold the Wondrous Cross

1. When I behold the wondrous cross,
    On which the prince of glory died,
    My richest gain I count but loss,
    And pour contempt on all my pride.

2. Forbid it, Lord, that I should boast,
    Save in the death of Christ, my God;
    The vain things that attract me most,
    I sacrifice them to his blood.

3. See, from his dead, his hands, his feet,
    What grief and love flow mingled down;
    Did e'er such love and sorrow meet,
    Or thorns compose so rich a crown?

4. Were all the realm of nature mine,
    It would be offering far too small;
    Love so amazing, so divine,
    Demands my soul, my life, my all.

– I. Watts

Praise, My Soul, the King of Heaven

1. Praise, my soul, the king of heaven!
    To his feet your tribute bring.
    Ransomed, healed, restored, forgiven,
    who am I his praise to sing?

    Praise him! Praise him! (2x)
    Praise the everlasting king!

2. Praise him for his grace and favour
    to our fathers in distress;
    praise him still the same for ever,
    slow to chide and swift to bless.

3. Fatherlike, he tends and spares us;
    well our feeble frame he knows:
    in his hands he gently bears us,
    rescues us from all our foes.

4. Angels, help us to adore him;
    you behold him face to face;
    sun and moon bow down before him,
    ev'rything in time and space.

– H.F. Lyte

Soul of My Saviour

1. Soul of my Saviour, sanctify my breast;
    Body of Christ, be thou my saving guest;
    Blood of my Saviour, bathe me in thy tide,
    wash me ye waters, streaming from thy side.

2. Strength and protection may thy passion be;
    O Blessed Jesus, hear and answer me;
    deep in thy wounds, Lord, hide and shelter me;
    so shall I never, never part from thee.

3. Guard and defend me from the foe malign;
    in death's dread moments make me only thine;
    call me, and bid me come to thee on high,
    where I may praise thee with thy saints for aye.

– Pope John XXII

Sweet Heart of Jesus

1. Sweet Heart of Jesus, fount of love and mercy,
    today we come, thy blessing to implore;
    O touch our hearts, so cold and so ungrateful,
    and make them, Lord, thine own for evermore.

    Sweet Heart of Jesus, we implore,
    O make us love thee more and more.

2. Sweet Heart of Jesus, make us know and love thee,
    unfold to us the treasures of thy grace;
    that so our hearts, from things of earth uplifted,
    may long alone to gaze upon thy face.

3. Sweet Heart of Jesus, make us pure and gentle,
    and teach us how to do thy blessed will;
    to follow close the print of thy dear footsteps,
    and when we fall – Sweet Heart, oh, love us still.

4.   Sweet Heart of Jesus, bless all hearts that love thee,
      and may thine own Heart ever blessed be;
      bless us, dear Lord, and bless the friends we cherish,
      and keep us true to Mary and to thee.

                                                      – *Author Unknown*

Lord, Accept the Gifts We Offer

1.   Lord, accept the gifts we offer
      At this Eucharistic feast.
      Bread and wine to be transformed now,
      Through the action of thy priest.
      Take us too Lord, and transform us,
      Be thy grace in us increased.

2.   May our souls be pure and spotless
      As this host of wheat so fine,
      May all stain of sin be crushed out,
      Like the grape that forms the wine,
      As we, too, become partakers
      In this sacrifice divine.

3.   Take our gifts, almighty Father,
      Living God, eternal, true,
      Which we give, through Christ our Saviour,
      Pleading here for us anew.
      Grant salvation to all present
      And our faith and love renew.

                                                       – *Sr M. Teresine*

Hail! Redeemer, King Divine!

1.   Hail! Redeemer, King divine!
      Priest and lamb, the throne is thine,
      King whose reign shall never cease,
      Prince of everlasting peace.

           Angels, saints and nations sing:
           Praised be Jesus Christ, our King:
           Lord of life, earth, sky and sea,
           King of love on Calvary.

2.   Eucharistic King, what love
      Draws thee daily from above,
      Clad in signs of bread and wine,
      Feed us, lead us, keep us thine.

3.   King whose name creation thrills,
      Rule our minds, our hearts, our wills,
      Till in peace each nation rings,
      With thy praises, King of kings.

– P. Brennan

Jesus Christ Is Risen Today

1.   Jesus Christ is ris'n today, alleluia.
      Our triumphant holy day, alleluia.
      Who did once upon the cross, alleluia.
      Suffer to redeem our loss, alleluia.

2.   Hymns of praise then let us sing, alleluia.
      Unto Christ, our heavenly king, alleluia.
      Who endured the cross and grave, alleluia.
      Sinners to redeem and save, alleluia.

3.   But the pain which he endured, alleluia.
      Our salvation has procured, alleluia.
      Now above he reigns as king, alleluia.
      Where the angels ever sing, alleluia.

– J. Arnold

O Come, Emmanuel

1.   O come, O come, Emmanuel,
      To free your captive Israel,
      That mourns in lonely exile here,
      Until the Son of God appear.

      Rejoice, rejoice, O Israel,
      To you shall come Emmanuel.

2.   O royal branch of Jesse's tree,
      Redeem us all from tyranny;
      From pain of hell your people free,
      And over death win victory.

3.   O come, great daystar, radiance bright,
      And heal us with your glorious light.
      Disperse the gloomy clouds of night,
      And death's dark shadows put to flight.

4.   O key of David's city, come
      And open wide our heav'nly home:
      Make safe the way that leads above,
      Protect us ever by your love.

5. O come, O come, great Lord of might,
    Who once appeared on Sinai's height,
    And gave your faithful people law,
    In all the splendour we adore.

                                                    – J.M.Neale

Hark, the Herald Angels Sing

1. Hark, the herald angels sing,
    glory to the new-born king;
    peace on earth and mercy mild,
    God and sinners reconciled:
    joyful all ye nations rise,
    join the triumph of the skies,
    with the angelic host proclaim,
    Christ is born in Bethlehem.

            Hark, the herald angels sing,
            Glory to the new-born King.

2. Christ, by highest heaven adored,
    Christ, the everlasting Lord,
    late in time behold him come,
    offspring of a Virgin's womb!
    Veiled in flesh the Godhead see,
    hail the Incarnate Deity!
    Pleased as man with man to dwell,
    Jesus, our Emmanuel.

3. Hail the heaven-born Prince of peace!
    Hail the Son of righteousness!
    Light and life to all he brings,
    risen with healing in his wings;
    mild he lays his glory by,
    born that man no more may die,
    born to raise the sons of earth,
    born to give them second birth.

                                                    – C. Wesley

O Come, All Ye Faithful

1. O come, all ye faithful, joyful and triumphant,
    O come ye, O come ye to Bethlehem;
    Come and behold him, born the king of angels:

            O come, let us adore him (3x)
            Christ the Lord.

2. Born of the Father, light from light eternal,
    Son of the gentle maid our flesh and blood;
    Honour and praise him with the hosts of angels.

3. Sing, choirs of angels, sing in exultation,
    Sing, all ye citizens of heaven above,
    Glory to God in the highest.

4. Now, Lord, we greet you, born this happy morning,
    Jesus to you be glory given, Word of the Father,
    Now in flesh appearing.

– John Wade, tr F. Oakley

Silent Night

1. Silent night, holy night,
    all is calm, all is bright,
    round yon virgin mother and child;
    holy infant so tender and mild:
    sleep in heavenly peace,
    sleep in heavenly peace.

2. Silent night, holy night.
    Shepherds quake at the sight,
    glories stream from heaven afar,
    heavenly hosts sing alleluia:
    Christ the Saviour is born,
    Christ the Saviour is born.

3. Silent night, holy night.
    Son of God, love's pure light,
    radiant beams from thy holy face,
    with the dawn of redeeming grace:
    Jesus, Lord, at thy birth, Jesus,
    Lord, at thy birth.

– Joseph Mohr, tr J. Young

Hail, Queen of Heav'n

1. Hail, Queen of heav'n, the ocean star,
    guide of the wand'rer here below;
    thrown on life's surge, we claim thy care;
    save us from peril and from woe.
    Mother of Christ, star of the sea,
    pray for the wanderer, pray for me.

2. O gentle, chaste and spotless maid,
    we sinners make our prayers through thee;

remind thy Son that he has paid
the price of our iniquity.
Virgin most pure, star of the sea,
pray for the sinner, pray for me.

3.　Sojourners in this vale of tears,
to thee, blest advocate, we cry;
pity our sorrows, calm our fears,
and soothe with hope our misery.
Refuge in grief, star of the sea,
pray for the mourner, pray for me.

4.　And while to him who reigns above,
in Godhead One, in Persons Three,
the source of life, of grace, of love,
homage we pay on bended knee,
do thou, bright Queen, star of the sea,
pray for thy children, pray for me.

– John Lingard

I'll Sing a Hymn to Mary

1.　I'll sing a hymn to Mary, the Mother of my God,
the Virgin of all virgins, of David's royal blood.
O teach me, holy Mary, a loving song to frame,
when wicked men blaspheme thee, to love and bless
　　thy name.

2.　O noble Tower of David, of gold and ivory,
the Ark of God's own promise, the gate of heav'n to me,
to live and not to love thee would fill my soul with shame;
when wicked men blaspheme thee, I'll love and bless
　　thy name.

3.　The saints are high in glory, with golden crowns so bright;
but brighter far is Mary, upon her throne of light.
O that which God did give thee, let mortal ne'er disclaim;
when wicked men blaspheme thee I'll love and bless
　　thy name.

4.　But in the crown of Mary, there lies a wondrous gem,
as Queen of all the angels, which Mary shares with them:
no sin hath e'er defiled thee, so doth our faith proclaim;
when wicked men blaspheme thee I'll love and bless
　　thy name.

– John Wyse

Hail Glorious Saint Patrick

1. Hail glorious Saint Patrick, dear saint of our isle,
   On us thy poor children bestow a sweet smile,
   And now thou art high in the mansions above,
   On Erin's green valleys look down in thy love.

2. Ever bless and defend the dear land of our birth,
   Where shamrock still blooms as when thou wert on earth,
   Our hearts shall still burn wheresoever we roam,
   For God and Saint Patrick, and our native home.

   – Sr Agnes